Meaning in Henry James

Meaning in Henry James

· Millicent Bell ·

HARVARD UNIVERSITY PRESS

CAMBRIDGE, MASSACHUSETTS
LONDON, ENGLAND
1991

This book is printed on acid-free paper, and its binding materials have
been chosen for strength and durability.

Library of Congress Cataloging-in-Publication Data
Bell, Millicent.
    Meaning in Henry James / Millicent Bell.
        p.   cm.
    Includes index.
    ISBN 0-674-55762-X (acid-free paper)
        1. James, Henry, 1843–1916—Criticism and interpretation.
    I. Title.
PS2124.B43   1991   91-8164
813'.4—dc20   CIP

For Gene above all

Contents

Preface

My title may seem to assert that *the* meaning of all or any one of Henry James's works has at last been isolated from the complex figuration of his carpet. But this is not what I have intended or could have achieved. Rather, I have been interested in the process by which meanings, fleeting or lasting, emerge for the reader of James's stories or novels—the *how* of this process as much as the finality of significance the reader thinks he remembers when he shuts the book. So, I have wanted to take *my* reader with me in a recapitulation of my own exploration, without necessarily coming to rest upon a simple summary either of the message of any one of James's works or the total intent of his effort as a writer. I have thought it would be interesting to recall what the experience of reading such novels or stories is like (though it is generally forgotten); how the portent of word and episode dances before one over the print and how our sense of larger, organizing meaning grows and changes but does not arrive at a condition that altogether blots out earlier appearances if we still remember what happened to us as we read. I have tried to arrive at final statements about what such experiences have added up to, but I have also wanted to show that the journey has been as important and wonderful—the way global travel is promised to be—as any arrival.

Such a way of taking James responds, I think, to the way he constructs his fictions, for he makes us read with a constant sense of different directions glimpsed alongside the forward path. His forward path itself is seldom so well marked as we expect. And his fictional design is, ultimately, a reflection of the way he sees life—as just such a "garden of forking paths" (to use Borges's phrase)—and also of the way his works came into being. One may gather this from remarks scattered in the eighteen prefaces he wrote to the volumes of the famous New York Edition of his works, published in 1907–1909 as a capstone to his lifelong labors. These ruminative rereadings of his tales and novels look back upon their original composition. They say again and again that James's fiction grew out of a process by which "developments" proposed themselves to him at every step because "really, universally, relations stop nowhere." He had to struggle against the emergence of possibilities that expanded—"exploded," he even said—out of the form he intended. The struggle to subdue and control was one he called "dire"—both necessary and dreadful, in a way. It was a struggle, he seems ready to acknowledge, always only partly won. Because he believed that human life was itself a path picked out, like a tapestry design, upon a canvas of innumerable sacrificed possibilities, he could perceive the shadow of paths not chosen in the most clearly determined life-story. It was because he could not subdue the imaginative responses life aroused in him, violating preconceptions and intentions at every turn, that his art remained full of a sense of alternatives. As the reader of his own works he is aware of their rich progression of possibilities—and we experience this progression in reading him in our turn. It is why, in this most formally self-conscious of writers, we retain the sensation of "life" never quite contained by art.

It is this rich awareness of possibility, and a positive valuation of possibility in all human circumstance and choice, that made James, I think, suspicious of conventional plot-schemes, formulas of explanation, and characterology, of all ideas of typicality with which literary tradition—and ultimately the general culture of which he was a part—was so plentifully provided. He was bound to accept such schemes and to use them, and yet to resent them, to be aware of their origins in a restrictive, even repressive system of social destiny. It was not only human minds, lamentably, that were banal, after all. Fate was banal. He was to show tenderness for those efforts of his characters which look like negativity in their resistance to such constriction. And yet he understood that no life can be lived except by submission to some recognized prescription of outcome for what one is, a socially recognized story, an ordering interpretation of one's history which the world can identify.

I seem to have said that form is theme, in James, and that the *way* of meaning in his fictions expresses his deepest convictions about human potentiality as a sacred fount of unending possibility which must be channeled into a flow that brings its waters, somehow, to the sea. This assertion itself is more telic than I would have liked, for

James is always busy about many matters at once. I have tried to take account of some of these matters, but my readings have been unable, after all, to avoid the critic's inveterate tendency toward selective emphasis. As this book developed, I strove constantly, as James's narrative seems to urge, to recognize what comes up *as* it comes up, to restrain the critical habit of asking what it means ultimately. But this proved an impossible discipline—and I catch myself, repeatedly, violating the suspension of interpretation I advocate, and yielding to the desire to leap to an end, to isolate certain ideas and pursue them. I will be asserting final meanings, after all. Such a contest in my own process duplicates, I suppose, the very experience that was the writer's own, in writing his fictions—and is the reader's own, in reading him.

Reading James in this way reflects not only upon such rich journeys as he takes one on but upon the exploratory adventure made possible by other writers, with more or less rich results, as the case may be. In the first chapter of this book, I have not only offered an overview of the chapters to follow, but suggested that all literary meaning is an experience as well as a goal. I have tried to make, tentatively, some addition to the "theory" of fiction, if there can be said to be any such coherent set of ideas today. Like most who try to say something on this matter, I have benefited from the lessons of various contending viewpoints—the sense of the value of close study of exact design and language, inherited from the New Critics and earlier Formalists; the illuminations of structuralism, particularly the idea of "intertextuality"; the corrective relativity of psychological and historical interpretation; the poststructuralist unpinning of earlier confidence in the stability of literary artifacts. In the end, however, it has seemed most obvious that fiction of any complexity can be shown to express a centrifugal-centripetal contest between meaning and unmeaning, unity and disunity, the urge toward cohesion and the acknowledgment of the rebellious disorder of our perceptions. But it is James, in particular, who has helped to bring this conviction about. He was aware of the contention I describe and his fiction is an expression of that awareness.

But he does not seem to have found it distressing to discover either that human lives are seldom to be described by a clear and singular story—or that some sort of story, some enactment, dictated by the real world, must be acknowledged as inevitable and even necessary. Without fear or the sense of "modernist" angst, he embraced the idea of the many possibilities that the individual human spirit aspires to, or is, even deplorably, capable of—and the acknowledgment that we do live after all only one life, largely framed by particular circumstances and social expectations. The fullness of his sympathy with others enabled him to imagine experience as justifying all our hopes and all our fears at the same time. This was the reason for his stress upon the imaginations with which his characters were endowed—and his skepticism when it came to prepared and inflexible definitions of selfhood. Life was an "adventure," he would insist. It was most an adventure when imagination—the power to respond to others as possible expressions of what one might have been oneself, to remain alert to *all* the possibilities of living—was most active. His fictions exhibit his best characters' adventures of perception. And these same fictions, because of the way we are made to experience them, make for such adventures for the perceiving reader as well. Thus, James's fictions can even be said to suggest how each reader's own adventure of living may become greater.

The development of this book as a continuous argument has been itself, for me, an adventure of discovery into James's meanings, an adventure during which insight into each of his fictions was augmented, as my writing proceeded, by what had emerged in my study of his other stories or novels. The different parts of my discussion, I hope it will appear, represent this cumulative experience, though the first chapter can be seen either as start or conclusion. At a few points, I found myself catching up some earlier ideas I had had about James's various works, and I found that these ideas were modified or much developed if they won any place at all in the new context. Some of the thoughts elaborated in the first chapter were first broached in rudimentary form in "Henry James, Meaning and Unmeaning," *Raritan* 4, no. 2 (1984), 29–46. Some fragments of my essay on *Washington Square*, "Style as Subject: *Washington Square*," *The Sewanee Review* 83, no. 2 (1975), 19–38, persist in the new treatment of that work in the second half of chapter 2. An earlier treatment of some of the discussion of "The Aspern Papers" offered in chapter 6 appears in " 'The Aspern Papers': The Unvisitable Past," *Henry James Review* 10, no. 2 (1989), 120–127. And a portion of my discussion of "The Turn of the Screw" offered in chapter 8 is based on my earlier essay, " 'The Return of the Screw' and the *Recherche de l'Absolu*," in *Henry James: Fiction as History*, ed. Ian F. A. Bell (London, Vision and Barnes and Noble, 1984), pp. 65–81.

There was always the difficulty—I have in the course of these so numerous preliminary observations repeatedly referred to it, but the point is so interesting that it can scarce be made too often—that the simplest truth about a human entity, a situation, a relation, an aspect of life, however small, on behalf of which the claim to charmed attention is made, strains ever, under one's hand, more intensely, *most* intensely, to justify that claim; strains ever, as it were, towards the uttermost end or aim of one's meaning or of its own numerous connexions; struggles at each step, and in defiance of one's raised admonitory finger, fully and completely to express itself. Any real art of representation is, I make out, a controlled and guarded acceptance, in fact a perfect economic mastery, of that conflict: the general sense of the expansive, the explosive principle in one's material thoroughly noted, adroitly allowed to flush and colour and animate the disputed value, but with its other appetites and treacheries, its characteristic space-hunger and space-cunning kept down.

The Novels and Tales of Henry James: The New York Edition (1909), preface to volume XVIII.

· I ·

Henry James
and Narrative Meaning

THE READING of a story or novel which holds us by its power is full of mysterious joys and frustrations. There is a sense of carnal delight, feelings awakened by a tale that enchants us we hardly know why, an "illusion of reality" of scene or person so intense that we feel we are voyaging at once into some hitherto inaccessible otherness and into the most intimate and secret caves of ourselves. In a way difficult to explain this carnal delight is mingled with spiritual expectation, the desire for "meaning"—but as we read we do not question the intermittence of our illumination, the large measure of the unmeaningful. We find ourselves in a landscape bathed in the equal light of its sky, under which all things vibrate with their own presence, and nothing is so unreal as to "mean."

If a less visionary mood succeeds this, one may still discover that literature resists interpretation, that even the most explicated work may contain elements of the inexplicable. Sometimes this intractability is seen as "difficulty," but obscure words or references can be explained, historical and cultural contexts which the ignorant reader lacks can be supplied, and even a writer's private references may sometimes be recovered. Sometimes a complexity of possible meanings coexist, enriching one another. But not all difficulties can be solved; not all possible meanings can be combined into a significant ambiguity.[1] In longer works, especially—in the novel more than in the short poem—there are things which are simply there for themselves. As Erich Auerbach pointed out, in the Homeric epics we never forget the real world that exists for itself and means nothing but itself—the hunts, banquets, palaces, shepherds' cots, athletic contests, and washing days of the ordinary life that must be imagined as enveloping the heroic action.[2] This situation can be contrasted with the severe economy of biblical story, in which there

I

is no feature that cannot be made, and has not been made by a long tradition of exegesis, to *mean,* since it is nothing less than the Divine Word adapted to human language. Frank Kermode has suggested that this biblical mode of textual pregnancy is a source of our expectations of all narratives, our sense that they may contain meanings in every part, even if these are not accessible.[3] The kind of interpretation which produced the literature of biblical commentary also applied itself, in past ages, to other writing, even to those very Homeric narratives that Auerbach contrasted with the narratives of the Bible. But there has never been any doubt that these classical poems cannot altogether yield all their detail and complexity to the interpretive assault. There must be some stuff that does not boil down.

Criticism will probably always be reluctant to surrender the desire to see great art as so integrated by a single idea that, as the novelist Vereker says in Henry James's "The Figure in the Carpet," "the order, the form, the texture [should] constitute for the initiated a complete representation of it."[4] We tend, now, to be too dismissive of the New Criticism, which produced so many brilliant readings. Yet the expectation that it would anatomize the masterpieces of fiction so exhaustively that nothing in them would be left unrelated to the rest—as might sometimes seem possible in the case of a short poem—was not realized, coming up particularly against the tradition of the realist novel with its large residue of "irrelevant" detail. We are more ready today to accept the idea that a literary work is rife with forces that threaten to disrupt it, that this is a feature even of works in which everything seems to "count" towards a single end. James's story of a critic in search of a meaning discloses itself to us, more sharply than to earlier readers, as a cautionary tale. It seems to suggest that no totalizing figure such as Vereker spoke of could be found even in the most perfect work.[5]

To say that form is a fiction is to assert that it is a lie, for the root of the word "fiction" meant "to feign" and always, one supposes, carried a certain moral taint. Yet the making of form seems to be the attribute of humans that links them with divinity. Almost all creation myths judge chaos to have been a condition of primitive evil into which deity enters as a shaping, dividing, and ordering principle. It is true that the sense seems to linger that undifferentiated disorder is the natural condition to which, entropically, all things strive to return. The suspicion of latent universal *un*meaning may be as ancient as the conviction of universal meaningfulness. And perhaps, in any case, as has been recently said, we can only know reality or deal with it in shapes that our shape-loving minds create, structures or codes, cultural epistemes or communities of meaning. That form is a fiction is also a redundant statement, for the word "fiction" derives from the Latin for "to form," to give shape, to stroke into an object of use or beauty as the potter strokes his lump of clay. The "rage for order," to use Wallace Stevens's famous phrase, seems to have profound and ineradicable sources in our natures and to be the basis of all our mechanisms of mind, not merely of the artistic impulse—or the critical.

Yet the storyteller will allow for "ragged ends," as E. M. Forster called them—turns that lead nowhere like the character of Miss Grizzle in *The Antiquary*. Scott, Forster wrote, did not need to "hammer away all the time at cause and effect. He keeps just as well within the simple boundaries of his art if he says things that have no bearing on the development. The audience thinks they will develop, but the audience is shock-headed and tired and easily forgets."[6] Or as Walter Benjamin observed in his essay, "The Storyteller," "To write a novel means to carry the incommensurable to extremes in the representation of human life. In the midst of life's fullness, and through the representation of this fullness, the novel gives evidence of the profound perplexity of the living."[7] The novel, it seems, inherits the traditions of the epic and often seems to celebrate the plenitude of life as found, making even that deliberate gesture toward irrelevance in its details which Roland Barthes called "l'effet du réel."[8]

And *at the same time,* I would say, the novel also continues to suggest, like biblical story, that a totality of hidden meaning might be found beneath its surface. Even the nineteenth-century realist novel strives to suffuse its density with a unitary sociological vision which makes every detail a metonymy for the vast unreproducible social whole of which it is a sample. The details of the domestic interior of Madame Aubain's house in Flaubert's "Un coeur simple," from among which Barthes selects an example, are really of the same illustrative kind as Balzac's, though without Balzac's insistent reminder to the reader that "this is what you would be likely to find in such a place." Balzac's imagination strove to subdue the mere thingness of things by stressing not their accidental features but their typicality, and this despite the element of the melodramatic or grotesque mingled in with his realism. Whether Flaubert always did the same with *his* particularities has been questioned by Jonathan Culler.[9] Culler insists that Flaubert's irrelevancies of description were a nosethumbing at all meaningfulness, a deliberate reminder of indeterminacy. The effect of the real in this case would seem to be the endorsing of the sense that the real is unknowable and any interpretation of it is vain.

But the paradox that such an antisemantic gesture should have been made by Flaubert is obvious, I think, to all but the most dogmatic indeterminist. No novelist before Flaubert had striven so strenuously to achieve the cohesiveness of effect that makes for the feeling of total significance. Flaubert may have declared that it was his intention to write a novel about nothing, but *Madame Bovary* remains *the* novel in which the elements of structure and style are so minutely organized that our sense of subject is never lost for an instant. As I shall be showing in this book, a similar double movement *toward* as well as away from a confidence in meaning can be traced in fictions by Flaubert's great near-contemporary, James, who in his own way worked to bring the novel to the highest possible point of formal centering. It would seem that both masters, if they were precursors of a modern skepticism in sometimes doubting the validity of interpretation, also brought to unprecedented heights the art of fiction that strives to make everything luminous with sense.

James's novels may be said to participate in the general tendency of impressionism—a movement in the arts which attempts to dispense with formal traditions of conceptualization and invites the painter or writer to appear to record reality as it impinges on unprepared perception. I say "appear to," for the preference for the anonymous subject, the painting surface which suggests spontaneity and the rendering which gives an effect of things seen before they can be identified, the canvas margin which appears to cut off a figure arbitrarily, as of no more importance than anything else—all these denials of preconception invite other kinds of meaning and unity. The works of the Impressionist painters may assert formal significance and retain reference to the real world just as *To the Lighthouse*, which seems to neglect ordinary continuities and explanations, to court the accidental and the fragmentary, is articulated toward its own semantic and formal discoveries. Monet, the greatest of the Impressionists, is actually denied the title by the critic François

Fosca because he so often deliberately planned his works, and painted from sketches and memory rather than directly from what he saw before him;[10] but it is not so much *how* they worked, whether in *plein air* or the studio, as the *effect* of unstudied apprehension that really distinguishes the Impressionists.

In Impressionist art the undeclared subject becomes, more often than not, the artist or viewer. Like the brushwork which reminds one of the artist's role, the frame that cuts the scene off so arbitrarily introduces the presence of an observer who is limited by his position, unlike paintings that make the edge less important than the center. In a similar way, James's development of a restricted "point of view" becomes a discovery of the subjective interest which gives its own outline to what is "accidentally" perceived. The novelist's emphasis upon vision, upon the immediate, "scenic" effect, has often been noticed—James declared in his autobiography that the only terms in which life had treated him to experience were "in the vivid image and the very scene";[11] his was, said F. O. Matthiessen, always an "intensely visual imagination."[12] So, impressionistically, in his novels, the "look" of things is the major way of knowing, and interpretation only follows as the inference of the witness. Yet the tension between appearance and meaning is precisely what must be felt in Monet or in James. It may be that it is the expression of the oscillation of the modern consciousness between the idea of order and the experience of disorder.[13]

James's impressionism is an attitude toward experience and a principle of composition that can be felt throughout his work. It reaches fullest expression in *The Ambassadors,* and in *The Princess Casamassima,* I believe, James opposes impressionism to the view of the naturalists, often assumed to be the Impressionists' aesthetic siblings because they were their personal friends and defenders. It is true that James didn't like the new painting when he first say it.[14] Ten years later he resisted the common view that his friend John Sargent was a recruit to the Impressionist camp, but he was ready to agree that some form of impressionism might be acceptable: "It will depend upon what, I won't say the object, but the impression may have been."[15] At last, early in the new century, he wrote in "An Autumn Impression" about an "array of 'impressionistic' pictures, mainly French," he was shown—"wondrous examples of Manet, of Degas, of Claude Monet, of Whistler, of other rare recent hands [which] treated us to the momentary effect of a large slippery sweet inserted, without a warning, between the compressed lips of half-conscious inanition . . . no proof of the power of art could have been, for the moment, sharper . . . it made everything else shrivel and fade: it was like the sudden trill of a nightingale, lord of the hushed evening."[16]

But he had all along participated in that general cultural shift which promotes the idea that meaning is not to be imposed upon experience but, problematically, discovered in it—an idea emerging well in advance of the Impressionists. He had absorbed this from what we may think of as the cultural "air"—from, perhaps, Pater, perhaps Maupassant, perhaps no easily definable source. The viewpoint of the preface to *Pierre et Jean* is anticipated in James's statement in *The Art of Fiction,* that the novel is "a personal, a direct impression of life" whose value varies with the "intensity of the impression" (1:50).[17] But in 1884, when his essay was written, James was just back from Paris, where he had talked with the members of the *cénacle* to which Maupassant belonged. And like everyone of his intellectual generation, James had felt, long before, the impact of Pater's famous conclusion to *The Renaissance* (1868–1873), which declared that "each mind keeps as a solitary prisoner its own dream of a world," knowing directly only "the passage and dissolution of impressions, images, sensations."[18] Such a tradition of "impressionism" can be related, obviously, to a literary attitude which privileges the faithful representation of immediate states of mind over traditional conceptions of linear story or unitary meaning.

Joseph Conrad, in what is often held to be a manifesto of literary impressionism, the preface to *The Nigger of the "Narcissus,"* insisted that impressions should ultimately disclose "the truth, manifold and one, underlying . . . every aspect" of the universe.[19] Such an expectation is not realized in his own fiction, however—and it is not even hoped for in James's. But the privileging of impressions in James's fictions does not deny that narrative interpretation is constantly provoked by them. James realized, I think, that no mind, including his own, could ever be so free of preconception as to constitute a true *tabula rasa;* inevitably one is prepared with shaping concepts by which impressions are given one meaning or another. Even Pater concedes that "each mind keeps as a solitary prisoner its own dream of the world," for impressionism has a way of turning around toward symbolism, its opposite. Both, as Ian Watt has observed, "are anti-traditional assertions of the private individual vision; and they both took their full shape during the epistemological crisis of the late nineteenth century, a crisis most familiar to literary history under the twin rubrics of the death of God and the disappearance of the omniscient author."[20] James's fiction dramatizes the encounter of impressions and the mind's play of symbolic interpretation, but acknowledges the ever-provisional nature of the latter.

Perhaps more acutely than most novelists before him, James was also aware that his reader, receiving a succession of impressions from a reading, has an interpretive compulsion. The reader's final view of what has been read is a spatialization of what is really never seen all at once. Fiction, modern or premodern, is not, after all, "spatial."[21] Reading is temporal, a process that transpires in time as one turns the pages. As we read we both remember and forget. Forgetting is as essential as memory in our grasp of experience itself, and so is essential to our grasp of stories. If we were blessed or cursed, like Borges's Funes the Memorious, with total recall, we could not "make sense" of anything. Only forgetting enables us to construct a final view of plot and character and theme; we need to forget things encountered along the way that do not fit these conceptions; we forget also any previous, "incorrect" notions of the evolving structure in which they seemed to find place. We come to the end and look back and select our bits and pieces and compose them in our minds. We may even, by a process that resembles the midrash of Hebraic commentators on sacred text,[22] supply what is not in the text at all but which we now imagine to have been there, in order to make a particular pattern. We have, perhaps, been too prone to condemn the naive way in which a fictional character acquires, in our minds, a history outside the text, as though he were a person only a part of whose life has been shown. Every presented element implies others unpresented. There is some midrash in every reading.

But the danger of seeing the text from a fixed point, our state of mind after reading it through, is that it falsifies our adventure as readers. That adventure has consisted of disappointments and unanticipated pleasures. We have experienced a succession of states of mind, each different, linked though they are by recollection and prediction. Criticism has tended to emphasize something different in finding in James and other writers what is called "ambiguity" or even "undecidability," a condition of possibilities of interpretation among which it is impossible to make a *final* choice. But in any extended fiction, things happen one at a time—despite all devices to give the effect of simultaneity—because they have an order in the telling. At any particular moment of importance choice *is* possible. Like music, literature cannot really be "summarized" but must be replayed; its meaning is nothing less and nothing more than the reading of it. I will argue that James is a writer who deliberately promotes impressionism in the *reader,* encourages the *reader's* passive acceptance of the immediate, the temporary, and the suspension of the *reader's* drive toward a conclusion.

Even James's readers must strive to put together an emergent form out of formulas their cultural experiences have provided—types of character, conventions of story—ideas not at all exclusively literary, though encoded in the traditions of literature both popular and elegant; readers imitate by recognition the planting of such clues by the writer, who has invoked these same cultural formulae in composing his work. We as readers strive to make the text "vraisemblable"[23] by attaching it to a model with which we are familiar. We are made aware "intertextually" and sometimes unconsciously of some paradigmatic form or even a specific model, a precursor, a source which guides our expectations. To interpret at all requires that we anticipate, that we have presuppositions, some form of *vor-sich* or foreseeing, as Heidegger calls it.[24]

Sometimes, our expectations are justified in the end. The character has conformed to type; the story has displayed a structure of a kind immediately predictable. But these expectations may also be frustrated; the work we are reading "disappoints" us by its deviation, by not after all conforming to its model or paradigm or by leaving out some necessary part. The story as we have understood it so far seems to require something denied us. The things we felt we needed may never have arrived, and no amount of midrash on our part will supply them. Contradictions, inconsistencies, obstructive irrelevancies lie across our path, and "deconstruct" the story we thought we understood. Plot and character may remain stubbornly "open" to remind us, as in many modernist works, that our efforts are not going to succeed.

Such disappointment itself demonstrates the fact that our *desire* to comprehend, to make a *gestalt,* has been at work. Our effort to mend the gaps and eliminate the irrelevancies by seeing them as part of a new whole makes reading a jostling progression through provisional interpretations of what has been accumulated and what is anticipated. And we may, after all, succeed in reconstructing new continuities out of the fragments of the discarded ones. Our ideas of the plot or the characters may reform themselves so that no gap or irrelevancy remains. But whether we succeed or not in constructing a formal coherence among our impressions, *re*construction (a process stimulated by our mind's hunger for form and meaning) is always at work among the ruins. At times we need to surrender our desire rather than accept a banal or factitious reconcilement of difficulties, but the effort of "deconstructive" criticism to repudiate our constructive compulsion may be futile, for our minds are machines for making *con*structs.

Roland Barthes urged the superiority of the reading of a book which follows upon a previous reading; it is *re*reading, he wrote in *S/Z*, that gives us fully the plurality of the text.[25] But the first reading of a literary work gives us most sharply the sense of the intertextual by arousing in us one recognition and anticipation after another. As we embrace and reject these, it is the first reading that most stimulates surprise and turnabout. On a second reading we know when to rebuff a false hint of the future, and when to anticipate true revelation. Some stories lure us into themselves with what we discover to be flagrant deceptiveness. James's narrator in "The Aspern Papers" describes himself misleadingly at the start of his tale. His claims of noble motive are, when we first encounter them, uninfected with irony. Then, as the pages turn, we erase and rewrite our interpretation. After we have finished the story and gone back to look at the opening we may suspect the narrator of hypocrisy—but not before; only rereading makes possible the irony of foreknowledge which works against naive surprise and strengthens the linearity of the story, reducing the struggle involved when we are forced to surrender early theories.

Yet no tale is so linear that we have consumed it, once known, as a single meaning. To know the end in advance is, of course, the case with early literature; folk tale, epic, classical drama—all made use of stories already perfectly known. In Christian times, the rereading of Bible narrative was the essence of religious practice; the gospels themselves tell the same story four times, with slight differences. The lives of the saints are written as imitations of the life of Christ, and even establish their authenticity by conventional anaphoric features. Yet the art of telling refreshes the sense of alternatives that makes this literature rereadable. And the first reading need not exhaust modern fictions, though once having been told they cannot repeat the promise of a story never told before. Even the first reading of these is far from innocent, for there are always old stories and familiar persons the reader expects to find in any narrative, master tales he has already heard. These engage themselves in contest as the story is read and make it, if one attends, full of those discords of possibility that recover interest again on subsequent readings. A story may be "solved" by the addition of a missing piece. But delay has enabled us to entertain alternative possibilities by which the other pieces assemble themselves. Even a rereading may not erase all the traces of this experience of discarded forms. We need not lose altogether the propositional value of the first, "misleading" impression made by the narrator of "The Aspern Papers."

The process I have been describing has been studied—as a process—surprisingly little. Phenomenological or "reader reception" criticism—associated with the ideas of Roman Ingarden, Wolfgang Iser, Stanley Fish, Norman Holland,[26] and others—has given a theoretic importance, in recent years, to the reader's role in the "creation" of a text; but what I am trying to uncover in the case of certain works by James is the history of such reading, a complex movement, dictated by the author's language, which—like all language—brings not only immediate meanings to mind but expectations of future, more comprehensive frames of significance. In prose fiction, it is not only language itself in word-by-word and sentence-by-sentence sequence that must be observed as the source of successive effects, but also the larger units of effect that precipitate in our minds as narrative events. While it is nearly a platitude to say, now, that texts invoke a multitude of "codes," there have been few attempts to show the shifts and replacements that make for the wars of reading. My review of a number of James's fictions in the following chapters is an experiment which revives the practice of "close" or, rather, "slow" reading in order to display how a story or novel of James's arouses expectations in us, stimulates us to hypotheses of its further course, and seems to propose and cancel meanings at successive moments.

Barthes, in undertaking to apply his own kind of slow reading to Balzac's "Sarrasine," advised, "If we want to remain attentive to the plural of a text (however limited it may be), we must renounce structuring this text in large masses, as was done by classical rhetoric and by secondary school explication: no *construction* of the text; everything signifies ceaselessly and several times, but without being delegated to a great final ensemble, to an ultimate structure. Whence the idea, and so to speak the necessity, of a gradual analysis of a single text."[27] But in renouncing the final synoptic structures reared by memory Barthes chooses not to note the fact that the structuring impulse is part of the process of moment-to-moment reading and, indeed, is essential to it. Reading is a constant anticipation of "the way it will come out," in terms not only of the unfolding of plot but of all possible subtleties of thematic meaning growing out of the accumulation of suggestions which may reinforce or alter or erase what we have previously supposed. What I propose is to see how the structuring nature of reading surges against the "deconstructive" cancellations or revisions of our hypotheses.

Will it be objected that such a way of reading James goes counter to the view of him as the exponent of an art of supremely organized unity? If James, as I shall be saying, created works that are full of alterity and resist summary and closure, if James permitted *un*meaning to play a part in his fictions, allowing us to participate in the process by which they offer the reader designs which live and die along the way of reading, what is the meaning of his stated devotion to expressive economy and stability? Reviewing Victor Hugo's *Quatrevingt-treize* in 1874, he confessed to "a conservative taste in literary matters—to a relish for brevity, for conciseness, for elegance, for perfection of form" (2:455). And thirty years later he still was able to deprecate such insufficiently "composed" novels as *The Newcomes, the Three Musketeers,* or *War and Peace* with the impertinent question, "What do such large loose baggy monsters, with their queer elements of the accidental and the arbitrary, artistically *mean*?" (2:1107). James spoke more than once of the "waste" of life being "all confusion and inclusion and art being all discrimination and selection," and declared, "I delight in a deep breathing and an organic form" (2:1108). He said that he believed that the finished work of art should be constructed by such an "exquisite chemistry" that there will be at the end, "not a drop of one's liquor left nor a hair's breath of one's glass to spare" (2:1110).

H. G. Wells anticipated the view that James, as the first of the moderns, aimed for a novel of perfectly organized "spatial" design, and Wells opposed to such an ideal an old-fashioned or, rather, "postmodernist" view that such a novel would be false to the contingency and formlessness of experience. James, Wells said,

> wants a novel to be simply and completely *done*. He wants it to have a unity, he demands homogeneity . . . Why *should* a book have that? For a picture it's reasonable, because you have to see it all at once. But there's no need to see a book all at once. It's like wanting to have a whole country done in one style and one period of architecture. It's like insisting that a walking tour must stick to one valley . . . But James *begins* by taking it for granted that a novel is a work of art that must be judged by its oneness. Judged first by its oneness . . . His "Notes on Novelists." It's one sustained demand for the picture effect. Which is the denial of the sweet complexity of life, of the pointing this way and that . . . If the novel is to follow life it must be various and discursive. Life is diversity and entertainment, not completeness and satisfaction. All actions are half-hearted, shot delightfully with wandering thoughts—about something else. All true stories are a felt of irrelevances. But James sets out to make his novels with the presupposition that they can be made continuously relevant . . . He talks of "selection" and of making a novel deal definitely *about* a theme. He objects to a "saturation" that isn't oriented.[28]

Wells's summary of James's theory of art is not altogether unfair, as the statements I have just quoted show. Yet there was another side to James's critical creed that Wells—and most critics since—have tended to miss. It is often overlooked that "The Art of Fiction" of 1884 is not only a plea for a more aesthetic view of the novel; it is also a plea for freedom in the face of schoolmasterly prescriptions like those of Walter Besant, the third-rate writer whose essay had provoked James's riposte. James wrote of the need to resist form, to respond to life's own disorder, in a declaration that curiously resembles Wells's own:

> As people feel life, so they will feel the art that is most closely related to it. This closeness of relation is what we should never forget in talking of the effort of the novel. Many people speak of it as a factitious, artificial form, a product of ingenuity, the business of which is to alter and arrange the things that surround us, to translate them into conventional, traditional moulds. This, however, is a view of the matter which carries us but a very short way, condemns the art to an eternal repetition

of a few familiar *clichés,* cuts short its development, and leads us straight up to a dead wall. Catching the very note and trick, the strange irregular rhythm of life, that is the attempt whose strenuous force keeps Fiction upon her feet. In proportion as in what she offers we see life *without* rearrangement do we feel that we are touching the truth; in proportion as we see it *with* rearrangement do we feel that we are being put off with a substitute, a compromise, a convention.   (1:58)

The later prefaces to the New York Edition, though they are a continual testimony to James's struggle to assert dominion over his own writing, include admissions that an "explosive principle" had to be acknowledged, even embraced. He insisted: "Any real art of representation is, I make out, a controlled and guarded acceptance, in fact a perfect economic mastery, of that conflict: the general sense of the expansive, the explosive principle in one's material thoroughly noted, adroitly allowed to flush and colour and animate the disputed value, but with its other appetites and treacheries, its characteristic space-hunger and space-cunning kept down" (2:1278). He gives striking humorous expression to the idea that these rebel forces might not always be successfully subdued: "The memory of my own work preserves for me no theme that, at some moment or other of its development . . . hasn't signally refused to remain humble . . . Once 'out' like a housedog of a temper above confinement, it defies the mere whistle, it roams, it hunts, it seeks out and 'sees' life; it can be brought back but by hand and then only to take its futile thrashing" (2:1159–1160). In the preface to *The Portrait of a Lady,* which conceives of the "building" of a novel in architectural terms in the well-known metaphor of the "house of fiction," James says, nonetheless, that the novel has the power "positively to appear more true to its character in proportion as it strains, or tends to burst, with a latent extravagance, its mould" (2:1075).

But it is James's fiction itself which shows how incomplete was his confidence in the power of art to "keep down" the "explosive principle." Or rather, it illustrates a conception of the formal impulse as engaged against "waste" within the work, always struggling *there* to find a way to put the elements of fiction together into a scheme of meaning. If life is a "felt of irrelevancies," in Wells's phrase, fiction exists by constantly wrestling to subdue these, but also surrendering by turns, so that we have not one final victory but a series of battles waged by the highest formal effort.

The very devices that promise to subdue contradiction become the way it is let in after all, though the war continues. The chief of these is the centralizing consciousness, a mirror drawing all the elements of narration together into the focus of a single perception, which James liked to think had been his chief source of success from his earliest to his latest efforts.[29] He was not entirely justified in believing in his own consistency. Few of his works, not even *The Ambassadors,* which he thought had done the thing best, fail to show deviations from such concentration. But the use of the restricted point of view, is, in any case, no barrier to waste of another kind than the irrelevancies it excludes. If it eliminates the dispersion of interest—functioning like the unities of classical drama to intensify our sense of a single subject—it is also a bar to verifiability. It confines us to the subjectivity of a single observer who can never know everything, and who must be acknowledged to have no final vision. James distrusted the ominiscient narrator who acted as an intrusive authorial presence; the puppeteer's careless exposure of his hand, he complained, destroyed illusion in writers like Thackeray or Trollope (1:46). But in the place of theatrical suspension of disbelief the older style of narrative had offered its readers a world securely validated because confidently subscribed to. It is in modern times that the reader finds himself unable to trust that validation. A modernist illusion of reality is more likely to be based on the feeling that life is *not* a determined-upon narrative in the head of an author-God. *Our* sense of reality includes the recognition of randomness and irrelevance. James removed the oppressive interpreter whose account we have learned to distrust but made the reader dependent upon a source that he understood also to be fallible.

Reducing the authority of the narrator, James still gave his perceptive source in the novel, the perceiving *character,* more than common powers of observation and understanding, making him a "*lucid* reflector." His observer is someone on whom "nothing is lost"—whether a member of the educated upper classes like Isabel, Fleda, Milly, Kate, Strether, Maggie, and others, or naturally keen, like Hyacinth Robinson, or even the butler Brooksmith or the telegraphist of "In the Cage," and, if only a child, a child of acute sensibility, like Maisie. But this endowment must not go so far as to make the perceiving witness identical with the banished omniscient narrator. Pondering the example of Hyacinth, James observed, "It seems possible that if we were never to be bewildered there would never be a story to tell about us; we should partake of the superior nature of the all-knowing immortals whose annals are dreadfully dull so long as flurried humans are not, for the positive relief of bored Olympians, mixed up with them. Therefore it is that the wary reader for the most part warns the novelist against making his characters too interpretive of the muddle of fate, or in other words too divinely, too priggishly clever" (2:1090). The very source of interest for the restricted narrative had to be, he saw, its surrender to the condition of bewilderment.

As already noted, James only occasionally left the bewildered observer totally unaided and unshielded—as he is in a first-person narrative, which openly exposes its source to be fallible human intelligence and suspect motive. His occasional sorties into the first-person mode are open demonstrations that absolute truth is inaccessible to the reader. In longer works, as he says in the preface to *The Ambassadors,* he preferred to avoid the "terrible fluidity of self-revelation" (2:1316) by enclosing the bewilderment of the observer in another discourse. But this discourse is only delusively privileged. He has not escaped the doubt attending the viewpoint from which the narrative originates. The problematic, the subjective, though it is someone else's, is all the narrator's matter, and he is now twice rather than only once removed from "outer" reality. He is even, more often than James's own theory of artistic distancing allows for, likely himself to confess to his limited "autobiographic" existence and to confess to ignorance or doubt as he now and then lets himself be felt as an authorial "I." The voice of Jamesian authority disputes its own forward motion towards certainty.

More often than we sometimes realize, too, the blanks must stay open for the full richness of the work to continue to operate. *What Maisie Knew* seems to be about the gradual invasion of a child's mind by exact knowledge about her elders' relations with one another—relations that are never directly exhibited in the text. One may say, of course, that these blanks are only there to be confidently filled by the reader, who is of the company of Maisie's elders. Sexuality, in this case, is what we know all about, even if Maisie does not. Sexuality, indeed, is repeatedly the missing term we can supply, we are apt to think, as we read much of James's fiction, and we may feel that James is censoring the sexual reality out of his own text, suppressing, out of prudery, what was not "mentionable" in polite conversation in his day, while covertly hinting at it to stimulate our prurience. Isn't it the adulterous sexuality of Chad and Madame de Vionnet that the astonishingly naive Strether fails to suspect? There may not be anything really so "indeterminate" about the offenses at school of little Miles or the nature of the relations that had existed between Miss Jessel and Quint—we may guess both to have been sexual, though the governess seems unable to rest until she has forced a name for them from the children.

But to take a less Freudian view of the relation of suppression to meaning, we may note that in literary texts the suppression of terms may allow for a variety of other meanings to enter, as James suggested in the case of the unspecified "evil" of the governess's ghosts. "Only make the reader's general vision of evil intense enough . . . and his own experience, his own imagination, his own sympathy . . . and horror . . . will supply him quite sufficiently with all the particulars," he claimed to have calculated in writing that story (2:1188). The reticence of *The Scarlet Letter* provides a precedent of linguistic as well as presentational ellipsis which invites the "writing in" what has been left out. The sin which is never named becomes, by a filling-in performed both by the community of Hester's fellow townspeople and by the reader, a variety of alternates. The same sin, adultery, is only named late in *What Maisie Knew,* and the absence of this name allows Maisie to give her own silence a value, to transform the meaning of the unnamed. The silence of narrative omission which she compels upon the story is also a literal silence which, like Catherine Sloper's in *Washington Square,* contrasts with the vociferous play of language resorted to by those older persons who surround her. But James does not make Maisie's blanks altogether negative; he permits us to value her noumenal perceptions, her intuitions of others "embalmed in her wonder." We momentarily can conceive, through her, of qualities and possibilities in persons and conditions we "know" to be hopelessly irredeemable. Her perceptions, which surrender to silence, escape the prison house of conventional ideas. It is just such an escape, as I shall suggest, that we are forced to experience with Lambert Strether, even though, from an early point, we see so much farther and so much less imaginatively than he does.

Of course, no prose testifies more than James's to the value of language; his writing is a performance that celebrates itself, that seems by its rhetorical exuberance to declare completest commitment to the interpretive act. Yet a doubt lingers behind his confident volubility, a suspicion of statement. James's fiction is a fiction of talking; his narrative voice and the voices of many of his characters strive for expressiveness—yet there are moments when a blank of some sort suggests the inadequacy of words and stories. In his late fiction, particularly, the often-parodied syntactical structures that seem to delay the revelation of precise reference, the elliptical dialogue in which speakers move among implications and allusion without specification—these are stylistic features in which some important fact may remain unuttered while alternatives of finality enter our minds.

Reading *The Ambassadors*, we suspect long before Strether does that Madame de Vionnet and Chad are lovers, yet confirmation does not come until it comes to him, and we cannot be sure until he is of what we suspect. Before that, we share his narrative hypotheses—drawn from that "text" of his culture which is expressed so well in James's own phrase, "the crabbed page of life" (2:1089). We also share with him their cancellations. But the scrupulous narrator does not step far outside of Strether's own insight, and we have to engage, with the hero, in the temporary imagining of fictions other than the one that emerges as final, and these have a status in our imagination for so long that they cannot be altogether expunged. When revelation comes it cannot have the significance it might once have had. Strether cannot now—nor can we—consider Madame de Vionnet to be the postulated bad woman he imagined before he met her. At the same time, the relationship between his friends remains in darkness. Strether will never quite penetrate the unknowable nature of the liaison he has already twice misunderstood, first in believing it to be depraved, and then in believing it to be "innocent."

Preserving "bewilderment" in the reader as well as in the character, the Jamesian narrative does not progress toward an ultimate and irreversible clarification. It also tends to dispense with the linkages of normal plot. It is a succession of conditions that do not look back to causes in what has preceded, nor look forward to anticipated consequences. The idea of consciousness as a "stream" rather than a "state" of mind was his own brother's conception—and it is often loosely supposed that James's novels anticipate the modern novels that have been taken to to illustrate this idea. But William James's image implies a flow which goes always forward, rather than a constant mingling of immediate sensation with memory and reverie.

And it is surprising how little there is in his brother's novels not only of the unconscious and of the world of night- and daydreams, but of memory. There are a few exceptions—as when Isabel Archer does look back upon her married life in the famous chapter 42—but this retrospect, as we shall see, is curiously abstract, an undramatic summary, though James claims for it a new kind of mental drama. True retrospect is rare in James's fiction. As Georges Poulet observed, "the Jamesian novel," unlike a novel by Proust, "will frequently be divested of the past. Its characters find themselves in relationships which more often than not are the effect of present junctures. They take new positions because of events which are themselves just as new."[30] This has the effect of suggesting that the fictional person has had no previous history; character as the continuity of certain features is severed from time. James himself thought of character as synchronic, and our interest in its successive appearances as more important than a final view, when he wrote that "a character is interesting as it comes out, and by the process and duration of that emergence; just as a procession is effective by the way it unrolls, turning to a mere mob if all of it passes at once" (2:1145). The fictional person is not only allowed to be inconsistent, he is also disengaged from the chain of determining events which make plot predictable. He is free to defy conventional plot structures. He is free to figure as the subject of a new story, of more than one story.

James's "open" endings have often been noted,[31] though much of this discussion begs the question of what an ending is—whether it is a "tying-up" of narrative loose ends, a final distribution of rewards and punishments, a disposition of the characters that leaves us no longer curious about their further lives, or rather some kind of end of the subject whose exploration has now been concluded. James's own reply to those who might say that he had left Isabel Archer *en l'air* at the end of *The Portrait of a Lady* was a profound one: "The *whole* of anything is never told; you can only take what groups together."[32] Even a more decisive disposition of his heroine would not have eliminated the sense he had that "the whole" was untellable, and that he had merely exposed the arbitrariness of the usual pretense that it was. Endings were an example of the artist's contrivance to make the process of narrative choices appear to stop, though "really, universally, relations stop nowhere." Yet the "sense of an ending" is deeply ingrained in our narrative expectations, despite the impulse, in fiction, to recognize the disorder and term-lessness of human experience.[33] My discussion of James's "literary openness" doesn't concentrate on the final pages of his fiction and what happens or fails to happen there, so much as it regards James's endings as a latest moment in the play of continuities and potential conclusion which has been at work all along.

What has been less remarked is that his beginnings are also, in a sense, "open"—they do not restrict what comes after them by any but the most perfunctory provision of determining *pre*-history. It is an unnoted effect of James's famous "international situation" that it introduces an American lately landed in Europe whose home condi-tions lie behind, not ever to be revisited, even by memory. Such characters bring with them to the new scene no trailing encum-brance of relationships, or if they are followed by some representa-tive of the old life, like Isabel's Casper Goodwood, that representa-tive proves inessential to the history now entered upon. All they bring with them is their own quality—which may, of course, be the quintessential representation of their native culture—to be tested in the new medium. It is because such characters lack priority that they are so peculiarly possessed of experience's antonymic quality, innocence. Quite aside from the degree of their presumed previous acquaintance with good and evil is the fact that they *seem* to have little memory of past experience, and whether through the revela-tions of their own minds or the minds of others, this past seldom breeches the barriers of the narrative. James rarely resorts to the "flashback," an old as well as a modern way of recovering the past of one's personages; he never begins in the middle so that he must loop back again to recover the origins of his story, but takes one only forward.

James was anticipated in this emphasis upon present states, this general indifference to the past of his characters, by the daring experiment of Hawthorne in *The Scarlet Letter*, as I have already suggested. James could have studied that striking elision of prelimi-naries, the omission of Hester Prynne's adultery. Never named, only evidenced by its consequential signs, the child and the letter, her "sin" is never recalled into presented vision, and proves unrepeatable (when the attempt is made in the forest scenes in which she again meets her lover it is inconceivable there, as it is fictionally). Hester, like James's transplanted characters, is also acting out her story in another place than its actual beginning, but the England of her past life, like the America of James's Americans in Europe, has ceased to count in this new world. On this foreign shore she will acquire a special identity, wearing, one might even say, her "A" as much for America as for anything that once happened elsewhere. It is for this reason that her story must really end as it begins, here, in the New World.

Only in the earliest version of his international situation, *Roderick Hudson,* did James try to explain his transported character by direct presentation of native, initiating conditions—Roderick's home life in Northampton, Mass. And this, he decided later, had been a mistake. He had thought he was writing another kind of novel than the sort really congenial to him, and tried to write one that "nestled, technically . . . in the great shadow of Balzac" (2:1044). *Washington Square,* which begins and ends in the same patch of America, might gesture towards the Balzacian model of a character rooted in her world, but Christopher Newman's fortune building in a vague American West is a void out of which his pristine character emerges in *The American* with no sign of rough usage. Even Daisy Miller's Schenectady is represented only by the comic—and not at all explanatory—accompaniment of her mother and brother upon the strange European ground. So, as we shall see, it is no accident that Isabel Archer and Milly Theale are orphans—Milly with no living relative at all—and that we briefly glance back only once at Isabel's Albany, while Milly's New York, though Merton Densher had met her there, never presents itself to our vision. And though Maggie Verver's American father and American friend are to be a part of her present drama, her earlier American City is a remote, undenoted place toward which neither she nor the reader gives a retrospective glance; it is only the European and the Europeanized, the Prince and Charlotte, who have a past—a European past—that persists into the present. All three of these American heroines appear as characters whose potentiality has not been reduced by their pasts. As for Lambert Strether, it is crucially important to his free exploration of possibility that his originating Woolett should never become visible to us and that we do not follow him there on his return.

That these characters, then, are, *narratively,* peculiarly free, may be expressive of the American ideal of personal freedom of choice and the myth of American history as a new start upon a blank page. They represent the spirit of people who have sometimes liked to believe themselves a race which has severed all connections with the past of human history. Reversing the journey of their ancestors from an Old to a New World, James's American voyagers nevertheless arrive upon the scene of their adventure in the same spirit of completest expectation of a condition where nothing is determined by what may already have happened to them. Displaced from their native background and past in both the scenic and the historic sense, they seem newborn.

This quality, not only in James's characters but in other figures in classic American literature, led some years ago to the idea of an "American Adam" who was, as R. W. B. Lewis wrote, "the hero of a new adventure, an individual emancipated from history, happily bereft of ancestry, untouched and undefiled by the usual inheritances of family and race"[34]—which seems to suggest that our great writers thought it was really possible to escape social reality and its compulsions and restrictions. But recent over-correction may have set too completely aside the mythic importance of such a conception in fictions that also recognized its inadequacy. Our great nineteenth-century writers—especially Melville, Hawthorne, and Twain, as well as James—were not unaware of the ironic truth that there was really nowhere, no "elsewhere" for this (hardly "happy"!) hero to go. Yet the gesture, the dream, the withholding of commitment to social forms that reduced the soul's best potential, this *is* a vision that takes account—by rejection—of a reducing reality, though the vision of freedom which imbues an Isabel Archer is proven to be an illusion, and her defeat seems a reflection on the American dream of such impossible disconnection.

So, honoring his freedom-seeking characters and their potentiality, testing their very attachment to essence in the face of the novel's compulsion to enactment, James obscures for the reader not only their origination, but the sense of inescapable destiny implied in all plot. His restricted focalization assists this obscuring. The narrator who disclaims omniscience is chary of those gestures of anticipation and reflection—forward-pointing and backward-glancing—which string the parts of traditional third-person narrative together, but James also eschewed the opposite of omniscience, the first-person narrative in its usual form, in which the backward-looking teller will repress the tendency of his story to suggest alternatives to itself. It is not surprising that James's experiments in the first person avoid the cohesion of the traditional story or novel of education by the use of a narrator who *fails* to progress from illusion to knowledge, who never appears to understand how his beginnings have made for his endings—as in "The Aspern Papers," "The Turn of the Screw," or "The Sacred Fount."

The principle of artistic unity which insists that the ending of a tale be implicit in its opening words—Poe's injunction for the short story in his review of Hawthorne's tales in 1847[35]—is clearly, as Poe conceded, inapplicable to the novel, and as he didn't see, may not be a true description of any but the simplest of short tales. "The idea of the tale, its thesis, has been presented unblemished, because undisturbed," Poe wrote of this ideal of artistic unity, but it is precisely disturbance that cannot be avoided; the very interest of all fiction may be the spectacle of control engaged with disturbance. The openings of even the briefest of James's fictions are "open" to a variety of exfoliations. But, as they proceed, James's plots tend to preserve the sense of alternate possibilities.

That his narratives have this synchronic quality makes them not so much "spatial" as richly potential at any chosen interval. The effect is dramatization—an immersion in a series of enacted present moments. "Dramatize, dramatize," James urged the writer of fiction. In one sense, this injunction is aimed at the correction of the atrophy of action in novels such as his own, which are concerned with what someone is thinking rather than doing. James redefined action to include the drama of feelings and ideas. He objected to after-the-fact "telling" of the events of this inner drama as much as he objected to the static summary of the visible action.

James's plots tend to resist the kind of summary that is such a convenience in discussions of fiction. We tend to think that everyone will agree about "the story" in a story. But while very simple stories may be reducible to a synopsis that looks the same to all readers, like the folk tale motifs collected by the formalist Vladimir Propp in *The Morphology of the Folk Tale*,[36] more complicated literature is not so easily simplified. And James, even more than most novelists, makes such a process dubious. The summarizing of plot as a single linear development is so often misleading in his case that even where we think we have a salient, not to say melodramatic, plot organizing the whole, we still find contrary descriptions possible. To try to write a synopsis of one of James's longer novels, especially, serves to remind one how plots are made up, in the reading process, by a collection of certain—and not other—possibilities which appear to be different at a succession of moments. One may easily compose a number of versions of "what happens"—each legitimate and an arbitrary schematization and immobilization of a text that from moment to moment is a different story.

In fact, Aristotelian conceptions of plot do not apply to such complex narratives as *The Ambassadors*. We may think we see a progressive outline which climaxes in anagnorisis and peripeteia in the final chapters, with revelation in chapter 30, when Strether sees how things really are between his friends on his encounter with them in the country, and then in the following chapter when he calls upon Madame de Vionnet and discovers that it is she—and not Chad— who needs his help. But the disclosure and turnabout have not been prepared for from the first; they are merely the latest in a series of such changes—and there is no guarantee that they are the last.

To see this veering of narrative direction in another way, one can note that, typically, James's fictions are dynamically intertextual; they propose to the reader not one stable antecedent, but a sequence of possible relationships with cultural models of human experience, of character types and paradigmatic life histories, of literary genres and archetypal narratives, and even of specific literary models. At one time or another, *Washington Square* invokes a reminiscence of Balzac or of Hawthorne; *The Portrait of a Lady* is meant to remind one of Jane Austen or George Eliot; *The Bostonians* is sometimes reminiscent of Hawthorne and sometimes of Daudet—and all of these bring into our consciousness the successful formulas of popular novels in the market of James's time,[37] or at other moments older patterns of folk and fairy tale. But it is important to notice that these effects are successive rather than simultaneous.

Even in such a limpid work as "Daisy Miller," everything depends on choices of narrative focus; if the story is Daisy's altogether we have a different story than if it is Winterbourne's and what "happens" to her is only important because it produces a succession of responses in him. Carol Ohmann has been alone among critics in noticing contrasts in tone between the "comedy of manners" in the early presentation of Daisy and the scenes of the second half of the story, which link her poetically with nature; but Ohmann concludes that James started out doing one thing and then altered his idea—to the detriment of his story's unity.[38] In fact, however, the comic and mythic tones exist in alternation from the beginning, and the reader is appropriately in the same condition as Winter-bourne in his bemused insistence on a choice.

Similarly, *The Bostonians* resists a unique recapitulation. Is it a love story? Is it an examination of the situation of women? Is it a critique of the New England reform tradition? Our description of the narrative will depend upon our interpretation. We are free to pick and choose among the matérials that fit one scheme or another. The question of psychic center remains unsettled; we cannot say unarguably that the story is Ransom's or Olive's or Verena's, and according to the way the choice is made, the story has a different shape. So, until recently, critical consensus made Ransom the hero and read the story as the romantic tale of maiden rescue in which Olive Chancellor figures as the good knight's evil opponent. By con-trast, she emerges as the novel's tragic heroine as Ransom's sexist brutality becomes more apparent to modern readers.[39]

Alfred Habegger has responded to *The Bostonians* very much as Ohmann to "Daisy Miller" by declaring the novel to be a failure of disunity.[40] But we may read this book in a more passive way, without suppressing the various contrary impulses of plot making it stirs in us. At different stages the characters seem entrained in one or another recognizable destiny, whether familiar from folk litera-ture, myth, or novelistic traditions—the nineteenth-century novel of marriage, the Balzacian novel of realism with its prototypical aspiring hero, the new formulas of naturalism, and others. The characters of *The Bostonians* seem at various moments both to be imprisoned in one of these destinies and to struggle to escape it, and the result risks incoherence. Yet, though James seems to have been unsure of the success of *The Bostonians*, feeling that it would need a great deal of rewriting if it were to be included in the New York Edition,[41] it is not certain that he would have altered this quality.

In this work, as in *The Princess Casamassima*, written at the same point in his career, James was challenged by the example of natu-ralism's extreme diachronicness, its insistence that human destiny is a progressive chain of events. In *The Princess Casamassima*, partic-ularly, he pays tribute to the determining sequences of environment and heredity. But he seizes upon naturalism's own invitation to the idea of experiment, and, by making his elements peculiar, produces something unlike the novel of inflexible common fate. His Hyacinth Robinson is no prototypical slum child, but a striking exception to the type of persons situated as he is; the "experiment" of imagining his fate is an invitation to extraordinary consequences. As Derek Brewer has pointed out, one real poor bookbinder's apprentice in the London of the 1880s miraculously managed to become the successful publisher J. M. Dent.[42] It is interesting to note, moreover, that Hyacinth's persistent potentiality for a fortunate rescue is a reminder, in an ironic way, of James's own exemption from the eventual history of his hero. James was not a poor and unconnected petitioner for entrance into London society when he first arrived there to make his home in 1875. But he was distinctly an outsider, an unknown American literary apprentice still with his way to make— a young man from the provinces, indeed, for America was the provinces just as England's other nation of the working class was of provincial origin. James would not have expected his reader to sense this identity, but as he explains in the New York Edition preface to the novel, he conceived of Hyacinth by recalling how his own sensibility had responded to the spectacle, from the outside, of London's privileged world—*except* for the fact that doors had opened to him which would remain shut to his hero.

The element of romance inherent in Hyacinth's story—that he is a kind of foundling with high antecedents, like the lost princelings of myth—will serve, almost to the end, to keep alive the expectation that he will be saved from destruction by being acknowledged by his father's family. In his wanderings from his lowly beginnings, his penetration into high places, he invokes Tom Jones, and the reader hopes that he will, in some sense, find his lost father. But, of course, nothing of the sort happens; the intertextual reference to myth and literary tradition and even autobiography lives only fitfully in the text and is finally thrust aside. And yet, having been aroused, the premonition of this closing does not altogether play us false, either, and survives in Hyacinth's recovery of his *cultural* patrimony, repeating the social conservatism of the foundling tale in his reconciliation with the paternal class.

In the later *The Ambassadors,* plot more conspicuously retains potentiality, keeps alternatives alive. "What might have been," a theme in this as in so many of James's fictions, is also a structural quality which makes the plot seem part of at least a pair of alternatives, one of which has been lost. The narrative will seem to have suffered a mutilation, to be incomplete, one possibility surviving but the other, like a severed leg or arm, still seeming to tingle though absent. Strether's is a sensibility that entertains this awareness to an exquisite degree. But hovering over "Daisy Miller," "The Beast in the Jungle," and also "The Aspern Papers," is the story that did not take place, the overlooked possibility that Winterbourne, Marcher, or the manuscript hunter might have embraced but failed to. Their refusal of these potentialities makes the story.

The illusions of these characters may also keep an alternative story alive. The narrator of "The Aspern Papers" is only dimly aware—though we are more so—of the story he might have lived if he had appreciated Tina's love. But his own self-exculpating viewpoint constitutes still another story hypothetically present to the reader. It is not altogether quenched in James's presentation, which allows us to give some credence to his plea that his aim was unselfish, his injury to the Bordereau ladies inadvertent. James's own aesthetic idealism, though vulnerable to our skepticism, is allowed to contradict the portrait of the "publishing scoundrel."

So, too, the very self-deceptions practiced by Merton Densher in his behavior toward Milly Theale in *The Wings of the Dove* have a positive function. Despite—or rather because of—them, he is not entirely contemptible. Densher convinces himself that he is acting honorably, and Sir Luke understands that he "had meant awfully well," while the actual blow that destroys Milly is delivered by Lord Mark. Though Densher suspects his damning identity with Lord Mark and any other exploiter of Milly's generosity—an alterity perilously present to our own suspicions—his delusion has a ghostly reality. It prevents us from despising him, so that, in the end, he can become worthy of Milly's love, after all. Potentiality, for James, is a part of being.

It is for this reason that James's fictions make so significant a use of the doubling of character and situation. In James, as in Conrad, the old theme of the double acquires a modern meaning as a way of representing the way personality and destiny lose their relation to immutable patterns of the past, and to fixed moral standards. Is Conrad's "secret sharer" in the famous story a more heroic or a more criminal self of the narrator? Does the casting off of this other self involve a rejection or an assimilation? James's "The Aspern Papers" narrator seems to enact a degraded version of the great Jeffrey Aspern's affair with Juliana Bordereau—and yet the elevation of aim which inspires the researcher's mimicry is as noble, in its way, as the poet's own—a true replication. Densher is haunted by the base versions of himself in Lord Mark and Eugenio, but his sense of distinction from them is also justified; his gestures of court-ship, very much like those of the "Aspern Papers's" man, *become* true, and he seems to absorb his own role into a new integrity.

And there is, in other works, a more subtle duplication, which stands for the alternative lives of hero or heroine. We will note how Isabel Archer shares with almost all of those who surround her some aspect of herself to which they have given enactment, illustrations of possibilities latent in herself. Strether more consciously sees the possibilities foregone in himself as he contemplates others. He is projected backward to a youthful moment of choice in the young Little Bilham, whom he urges to seize a different life from his own, or forward to the embodiment of Chad, who has so "wonderfully" flourished and developed (and in the end, he may even duplicate Chad's adventure—and (cad)ishness, too—in his own way).

"What is there in the idea of *Too late*—of some friendship or passion or bond—some affection long desired and waited for, that is formed too late?" James wrote in his notebook in 1895.[43] The result was one of his most suggestive ghost stories, "The Friends of the Friends," which relates the failure ever to meet of two perfectly matched persons—until one dies and becomes a ghost. Here, as in others of James's ghost stories, alterity is represented by the ghostly persistence of the might-have-been. James's ghosts are doubles who tempt or warn or represent a possibility no longer available to the living. The ghost of a dead military ancestor is confronted by Owen Wingrave, who has refused to repeat his ancestor's career. Sir Edmund Orme was jilted by the mother of the girl now wooed by the young man who sees his ghost until she has accepted him. In "The Turn of the Screw," the ghosts of Miss Jessel and Peter Quint are projections of the governess herself and of her imagination of the Master, suggesting a once-enacted story she might have relived if she had been seduced and abandoned by him—and we are tempted to believe this *has* happened to her. And the representation of possibility by such doubling is not confined to the ghosts but extends to the living children, Miles and Flora, as well.

But it is "The Jolly Corner" that makes the Jamesian ghost story a final representation of the presence at once of both the potential and the actual. The story may be compared, as a fable, to Borges's "The Garden of Forking Paths" in illustrating the rival reality of the unlived life. Or it may represent that reading of a text which discovers it to be, in Barthes's words (though perhaps not exactly in his sense), "a network with a thousand entrances."[44] That the actual must defeat the merely possible is, seemingly, James's moral in "The Jolly Corner." We can only be held accountable for what we have done. This, though it limits the self and may sometimes force us to surrender belief in an unrealized betterness, permits us to deny the unrealized worse of ourselves. But in other cases, a rich imagination sustains a possibility life has not fulfilled. In "The Story In It," the unrealized love of the "honnête femme" is a more passionate fact than the love affair of her rival. "The Special Type" tells of a woman who has agreed to act the role of corespondent in a divorce case but who falls in love with the man for whom she faked an affair, and "The Tone of Time" depicts a woman painter who, in response to an order for an ideal *belhomme,* paints a man who has abandoned her. Each of these women retains the treasure of her imagined fulfillment. The foregone possibility, the unlived life, is Strether's loss at the beginning of his adventure but his positive possession in the end, when his passionate witnessing gives him again his lost youth.

The renunciation of anything more—his final gesture, as it is the final gesture of other Jamesian characters, like Fleda Vetch of *The Spoils of Poynton,* has the effect of keeping his potentiality still active. Often pointed to as an implicitly religious theme in James, or else as a sign of crippled will in the characters or their author, renunciation is, structurally, a renunciation of plot. That James honored the gesture of renunciation seems more true when one realizes that it expresses his distrust of the materializations of selfhood available in modern society. James understood and resisted the obsession with accumulation and exchange in modern capitalism; these make an overt theme in such works as *The Spoils of Poynton* and *The Wings of the Dove.* But he also viewed more warily all social role and enactment, tainted as these were by a commodity society— and it is this moral or aesthetic abstention that is duplicated in the structures of his fiction.[45]

The specific renunciation which aborts the marriage ending is a primary way of keeping plot open in James's fiction, and reflects both James's view of marriage and his resistance to other available closures, both actual and formal. Whereas, as Forster remarked, "love, like death, is congenial to a novelist because it ends a book conveniently,"[46] James accepts the inconvenience of ending his stories with neither. Daisy Miller does die at the end of James's short novel, but one realizes that the story is not, after all, about her, but about a man who is unable to come to any final conclusion about her and who has failed, not by a conscious renunciation but by his own resistance to illumination, to achieve a marriage. But even James's nobler and more perceiving characters abort the marriage ending by deliberate renunciation. Fleda Vetch's sacrifice of the possibility of union with the man she loves is often felt to be either perverse or superbly moral—like Strether's "not, out of the whole affair to have got anything for myself."

Moreover, James sees such consummations as limiting the free play of imaginative possibility while being false to the continuity of experience upon which the human mind imposes its sense of starts and stops. James's endings are seldom without their coherence in some scheme of interpretive meaning; the absence of a finality which permits no forward projection is not quite the same thing as the phenomenon often identified in modernist literature—a frustration also of our ability to interpret, to see the offered fragment of life as making a whole meaning. Yet the complex progress of his fictions allows us to realize that there is no absolute inevitability to the plot which, now that we have come to the end, makes the end seem what has been in prospect all along. Such, philosophically, seems to have been Conrad's interpretation of James's "solution(s) by rejection," the commonest form of those open endings of which I have already spoken:

a solution by rejection must always present a certain apparent lack of finality, especially startling when contrasted with the usual methods of solution by rewards and punishments, by crowned love, by fortune, by a broken leg or a sudden death. Why the reading public which, as a body, has never laid upon a story-teller the command to be an artist, should demand from him this sham of Divine Omnipotence, is utterly incomprehensible. But so it is; and these solutions are legitimate, inasmuch as they satisfy the desire for finality, for which our hearts yearn, with a longing greater than the longing for the loaves and fishes of this earth. Perhaps the only true desire of mankind, coming thus to light in its hours of leisure, is to be set at rest. One is never set at rest by Henry James's novels. His books end as an episode in life ends. You remain with the sense of the life still going on; and even the subtle presence of the dead is felt in that silence that comes upon the artist-creation when the last word has been read. It is eminently satisfying, but it is not final. Mr. Henry James, great artist and faithful historian, never attempts the impossible.[47]

James's endings, as I have been suggesting, have only been reached by a process which has permitted us to entertain the possibilities of other stopping points. "End" takes on its added sense of "goal" only by a certain suppression of prior impressions. In the famous passage in the preface to *Roderick Hudson,* in which he says that "relations stop nowhere," though the artist must make them seem as though they do, James is referring to the fact that life does not provide the embroiderer's stopping places at any point—only the infinite perforations which his needle may enter or ignore. But even the work of art is, for the *reader,* a sort of perforated canvas upon which his gathering impressions make a design, and he, too, must arrive at final limits "by a difficult, dire process of selection and comparison, of surrender and sacrifice." (2:1041) "Sacrifice" is a word, here, whose connection with James's plots of renunciation is blatant.

The sense of alternatives lives in James's stories with a particular liveliness probably because James himself was conscious that the victory of his final artistic decisions was never complete. Repeatedly, in the prefaces, he finds himself looking back at his own notebooks to discover the possibilities of development that beckoned him at the outset of any undertaking. The notebooks which have survived themselves testify to the way his imagination winnowed away possibilities of one sort or another until the final design was chosen. But, illuminatingly, these "false starts" sometimes reveal their presence in the text. There is, for example, the case of the character of Sir Claude in *What Maisie Knew.* In one of the preliminary scenarios for the novel James described his young heroine's stepfather as a "simple, good, mild chap, bullied, hustled by his wife," and calls him "the captain." The Sir Claude we know is hardly described here—his goodness, mildness, even his fear of women are all to be in the finished portrait, but mingled with different qualities, with a subtlety and a sensuousness and deviousness combined with his good will; he is by no means simple. Yet it would appear that James wanted, still, to have such a presence as he originally conceived of to be felt in the novel, if only for a moment. He preserves it in the character of the anonymous "Captain" whom Maisie meets in Kensington Gardens, in the touching scene in which she hears—as never from Sir

Claude—that her mother is lovable. But part of the original conception remains attached to Sir Claude, despite this siphoning off; he is, *potentially,* his double, and the novel shows Maisie and Mrs. Wix laboring to the end to convert him into the more idealized self they adore in him.

Repeatedly, as James reviews the origins of his works, he continues not only to see what other shapes they might have taken but also to acknowledge that these alternatives were not always subdued in the end. So, he would write,

> There was always the difficulty . . . that the simplest truth about a human entity, a situation, a relation, an aspect of life, however small, on behalf of which the claim to charmed attention is made, strains ever, under one's hand, more intensely, *most* intensely, to justify that claim . . . struggles at each step, and in defiance of one's raised admonitory finger, fully and completely to express itself. Any real art of representation is, I make out, a controlled and guarded acceptance, in fact a perfect economic mastery, of that conflict: the general sense of the expansive, the explosive principle in one's material thoroughly noted, adroitly allowed to flush and colour and animate the disputed values, but with its other appetites and treacheries, its characteristic space-hunger and space-cunning, kept down.   (2:1278)

"Appetites and treacheries"—so James viewed the forces in his own stories that at every moment in the narrative thrust aside the clear appearance of undeviating progress and clear intention. These forces filled him with an acknowledged "fear" of a loss of control over his own work. Yet he recognized that in the end his achievement depended upon acceptance, albeit controlled and guarded, of the conflict by which the alternatives of life richly survive.

Yet one consequence of James's preservation of such alternatives is that his most important characters seem curiously deficient in that definition which character gains from its manifestation in choice. *The Portrait of a Lady* postulates in Isabel a vivid young woman who might have posed for one of Sargent's portraits. But the "portrait" of this heroine is never painted. The narrator, speaking for her, offers lists of her abstract expectations of herself and, in addition, we learn of the general hopes of those who meet her. She is the object of her own contemplation, too—this is the reason and effect of James's centering the story, to a large extent, in her consciousness. But she is no more able than others to write by her own choices a story which will fulfill her nature. She is no more able than those who would portray her to discover those lineaments life draws upon the canvas. To narrator, enemies, friends, herself—and the reader—she remains an expectation rather than a presence. She is James's most absolute heroine of potentiality, whose true destiny, as contrasted with plots proposed for her and imposed upon her, is expressed in the vaguest optative, as something she might do or might have done.

In *The Ambassadors* James places the object of interpretation outside the witnessing consciousness—or seems to. Strether has come to Europe to understand and do something about another man, to direct him away from his Paris digression to the resumption of the story he was born to live. It is soon evident that we are never to know much about Chad's inner self; his change of mind is accomplished, but not by any process we have witnessed or can closely understand. On the other hand, Strether accumulates before our eyes external impression after impression of Chad and of the Paris and the Parisian woman involved with Chad. The interest of the narrative is in Strether's speculations, his musing hypotheses and reconsiderations canceling those preceding, which never lead to the mind of the other man. It is this speculative play that governs the novel and creates the reader's experience of a series of possible plots.

James realized early that his method would invariably make for subjectivity as subject, making his "passive" observers the only actors, the true observed. He noted, in his preface to *Roderick Hudson,* "My subject, all blissfully, in the face of difficulties, had defined itself—and this in spite of the title of the book—as not directly, in the least, my young sculptor's adventure. This it had been but indirectly, being all the while in essence and in final effect another man's, his friend's and patron's, view and experience of him" (2:1049). What may have been the inadvertent thematic discovery resulting from choice of technique in this novel of 1875 became, by 1903 in *The Ambassadors,* a deliberate plan. The reader who knows both cannot help reading the early novel as an anticipation of the later—with its similar relation between a younger and an older man, New Englanders who visit Europe and there encounter a fascinating woman. But it is not plot so much as projective method that established a connection between the two novels. James, in the preface he wrote in 1907, marked the signal start of *Roderick Hudson* by calling it "my first attempt at a novel" (2:1040). As a matter of fact, he had written another previously, but this *was* the first to find its story in the ordeal of a witnessing consciousness. That witnessing *is* an ordeal is because of the uncertainty that attends its labors to get at the truth. Observing, deciphering appearances, it dramatizes the effort which is not only the character's but the author's and, as has been observed already, the reader's, to create a history. The labors of the Jamesian consciousness are narratological. They aim, often with only partial success, at a putting-together of events to make a story and at the discovery of meaning in this story.

A bemused, detached, central consciousness is the characteristic center of Jamesian fiction. The witness of the press and thrust of outer life who holds himself apart from the visible "doing" of others is a characteristically Jamesian figure; like Baudelaire's *flâneur*, the gatherer of "impressions," he is "assailli par une émeute de détails, qui tous demandent justice avec furie d'une foule amoureuse d'égalité absolue."[48] James's impressionistic emphasis upon transitory perceptions, above all impressions for the eye, the method that suggests that one view of a matter will be replaced by another, is, then, related to this choice of focus, with its renunciation of absolute knowledge of things, its unwillingness to penetrate and ascertain truth. James, the inveterate tourist, made his whole life an act of tourism by living chiefly in foreign places where the insider's view was not readily available to him. His early travel writings, written as journalistic "impressions" for American periodicals, have this special importance for the understanding of his fiction: they establish the narrative pose that will govern it, the viewpoint of the detached observer of appearances, the stroller making his solitary way among men and women.

As in other profoundly intertextual ways, Hawthorne had acted as a precedent. Early in his own career James described the narrator of *The Blithedale Romance* in terms that exactly apply to many of his own characters, and if it is true that Coverdale resembles Hawthorne, James identifies with these similar characters in his own fiction:

> In so far as we may measure this lightly indicated identity of his, it has a great deal in common with that of his creator. Coverdale is a

picture of the contemplative, observant, analytic nature, nursing its fancies, and yet, thanks to an element of strong good sense, not bringing them up to be spoiled children; having little at stake in life, at any given moment, and yet indulging, in imagination, in a good many adventures; a portrait of a man, in a word, whose passions are slender, whose imagination is active, and whose happiness lies, not in doing, but in perceiving—half a poet, half a critic, and all a spectator.   (1:419)

James's contemplators are, significantly, persons who prefer viewing to doing, and resemble Coverdale, moreover, in the way their posture is contrasted with that of those they contemplate. James observed that Hawthorne's narrator is "contrasted excellently with the figure of Hollingsworth, the heavily treading Reformer, whose attitude with regard to the world is that of the hammer to the anvil, and who has no patience with his friend's indifferences and neutralities." But Coverdale's political "neutrality," to which James refers, does not inhibit intense observation of others. Hawthorne's neutral observer, seated in his treetop balcony or glimpsing the figures of his friends from a window, is like a theatergoer as he follows the loves of Hollingsworth, Zenobia, and Priscilla with what Zenobia calls "insolent curiosity; a meddlesome temper; a cold-blooded criticism, founded on a shallow interpretation of half-perceptions; a monstrous scepticism in regard to any conscience or any wisdom, except one's own; a most irreverent propensity to thrust Providence aside, and substitute one's self in its awful place."[49]

James's witnessing characters are not always so harshly judged, but some suspicion of voyeurism and coldness clings to all of them. "You're a searcher of hearts—that frivolous thing, an observer!" says the actress Blanche Adney to the narrator of "The Private Life."[50] These observers do not always understand their own suppressed passions—Coverdale's belated discovery that he himself is in love with Priscilla is like Rowland Mallet's discovery that he loves Mary Garland. And such discovery may be only a further regress of self-deception in both cases, for each man is probably in love with the more powerful, dangerous female figure in the novel—Zenobia or Christina Light. It is perhaps an exaggeration on James's part to say that the subject of *Roderick Hudson,* as of *The Ambassadors,* is *only* the witness who attends another, more "active" figure. Those grand livers—Roderick and Chad—are the alterity of

Rowland and Strether, the lives they might have led, the plots they might have had. Rowland and Strether's half-envious love of these others, their urge to foster passionate development in them, is the phantom limb that vibrates with the illusion of present life. The twinship that binds each to his more active friend is the recognition that this other is an unlived selfhood.

To separate, in speaking this way, character and plot, or the person from the life he lives, is, no doubt, to court a danger that James himself warned against in his essay, "The Art of Fiction." "What is character," he challenged, "but the determination of incident? What is incident but the illustration of character? . . . It is an incident for a woman to stand with her hand resting on a table and look out at you in a certain way; or if it be not an incident I think it will be hard to say what it is. At the same time it is an expression of character" (1:55). James's argument was strictly defensive in this statement, published in the fall of 1884[51]—only three years after *The Portrait of a Lady,* which reviewers had criticized as deficient in action. Already, his conviction was established that "happening" was as much mental as external. The standing woman described in his example might have been Madame Merle as she appears in that scene when Isabel glimpses her silently erect beside the seated Gilbert Osmond. What "happens" is a mental event, Isabel's realization of the nature of the relationship between her husband and her friend, while Isabel herself may be said to be engaged in the act of "reading" action that is neither visible nor audible. James must have appreciated with mixed feelings the defense that he was creating a new sort of fiction in which action is unimportant, a defense which had been made on his behalf by his friend Howells shortly after the novel was published. James's essay is probably a reply to this supporter as much as to Walter Besant's recent lecture.[52] Howells had written,

> Evidently it is the character, not the fate of his people which occupies him; when he has fully developed their character, he leaves them to what destiny the reader pleases . . . Will the reader be content to accept a novel which is an analytic study rather than a story, which is apt to leave him arbiter of the destiny of the author's creations? . . . A novelist he is not, after the old fashion, or after any fashion but his own; yet since he has finally made his public in his own way of story-telling—or call it character-painting if you prefer,—it must be conceded that he has chosen best for

himself and his readers in choosing the form of fiction for what he has to say . . . In one way or another the stories were all told long ago; and now we want merely to know what the novelist thinks about persons and situations.[53]

The view that character and plot are functions of one another is a recent one. Aristotle gave the primacy to plot, probably because what happened, in classical drama, was what had been destined to happen, while character, tending to be consistent, did not have a "story." In the epic, the epithet irremovably attached to a name, repeated throughout the poem, reminds us that character is a simple and static endowment; what happens comes from some other source. In Shakespeare, on the other hand, the hero has a surplus of character, much of it irrelevant to his destiny. Judged only by their acts, how fatuous and cruel Othello is, how tawdry the ambitious Macbeth, how preposterous the self-deceiving Lear, how dilatory Hamlet! It is that very discrepancy that arouses our pity. But in the modern period we are likely to insist that a person is known by his deeds. Surrendering along with the general idea of essence the idea of character as an independent entity, we tend to accept the view expressed in Sartre's *Huis Clos* that we *are* only our acts. As Inès says to Garcin, "Tu n'es rien d'autre que ta vie."[54]

For James, neither view, in fact, was altogether acceptable. The contest between these alternatives in viewing character and destiny, played out as it is in the language and structure of his fiction, is ideological, one he shared with his moment of history. Like Conrad, he seems to have experienced the anguish of the rift between what someone like Lord Jim *is,* and what he does. The self that dreams of its own alterity was still an essence that rivaled existence, and, romantically, Jim was justified in his view that his reprehensible act had not been an expression of himself. Nor was that act valid as an expression of his class type. Jim was "one of us," a Conway boy. But Conrad, like James, suspected the collapse of this type—perhaps of social type generally—at a historical moment when the design of Empire and a once immutable class structure were going down.

James had been fascinated by the way his acquaintances in literary Paris were working out the naturalist idea that circumstances made character, even were character; he would make some attempt to test their notions in fictions of his own, particularly *The Bostonians* and *The Princess Casamassima.* But if the voices of late-nineteenth-century positivism were loud for James, the romantic view of selfhood was a music that still sounded on the air. In the American tradition there had been earlier versions of the persistent belief (in still earlier times a religious belief) that the soul was independent of the spectacle of human acts. The Puritans thought that only God knew the hidden nature of man or woman, and Emerson also believed that the independent spirit was accounted for in no way by "circumstances." "You think me a child of my circumstances: I make my circumstance," Emerson had written. He concluded the sixth chapter of *Nature:* "The Soul . . . is a watcher more than a doer, and a doer, only that it may the better watch."[55] If the new naturalism tended to swallow up the idea of essential character, this contrary tradition asserted that character had no need of plot.

I have mentioned the way *The Scarlet Letter* gave James a precedent for a protagonist who comes to us with her initiating circumstances, formulated on another continent, hidden in an irrecoverable past. Hawthorne's novel also anticipates James's fiction because it is so devoid of action in the old sense even within the course of its exhibited narrative. Chiefly, like *The Portrait of a Lady,* it is the history of a mind, Hester's, which, like Isabel Archer's, grows richer and richer while outer action stands still. The abortion of any active expression of Hester's feminist radicalism, is, perhaps an expression of Hawthorne's conservatism or, at least, his caution—which made him, in life, dislike female liberationist *doers* like Margaret Fuller. Perhaps James—for conservative or more probably simply pessimistic reasons—follows Hawthorne in the abortion of action with which his own novel about a developing female mind closes.

Emerson's preference for watching over doing must be related, after all, to the fact that doing had already, even in his time, begun to seem questionable. As the century advanced, the Victorian work ethic, the worship of *productive* energy, had produced an increasingly vulgar materialism, an arrogant imperialism, a brutal class war, and the mechanization of ordinary life. As I have already remarked, James's celebration of consciousness, his deprecation of action, the severance of his heroes or heroines from antecedents, along with the attenuation of realistic setting in his late fictions may be seen not as the marks of a turning away from the concerns of the social world but as a critique of that world. But, coming back to the critical debate over the "myth" of the American free spirit, it should also be pointed out that writers from Hawthorne to James understood, too, that romantic individualism was not only an idealist principle, but had its material expression in the rampant entrepreneurism that was taking over the American economic and political world. The free spirit was apt to discover its complicity with what it strove to reject. So, Isabel, a heroine of the abstaining consciousness, must ultimately discover her likeness to those opposites of herself, Osmond and Madame Merle. Her preference for delegating action to others—which explains her marriage—is a disablement and delegation no less fatal than the disease which requires that Ralph donate his own fortune, his potency, to her. It is also exploitive, a form of expropriation of the value created by the labor of others, a representation of capitalist exploitation itself. James will expose the penalty of such error as Isabel's in other stories. His condition-disclaiming, freedom-seeking characters are fatally constrained and conditioned, after all, or they exercise their freedom at the expense of the freedom of others. He will test these contrarieties in the freedom-seeking design of his narratives, which must, however much the process is resisted, go somewhere, stop sometime.

But it was not only the American transcendental heritage that conveyed this doubled message. For a Europeanized writer like James, there was also the influence of fin-de-siècle aestheticism which, in England, culminated by the end of his life in the pacifism and dandyism of Bloomsbury, its valuation of *states* of mind, and in repudiations of the parental generation such as Strachey's *Eminent Victorians,* published at the conclusion of the First World War. I have already spoken of the importance of impressionism as a source of James's own sensationalism, and mentioned the relationship between this movement and the aestheticism of Pater. In addition, one should note that aestheticism also gave a heightened value to the cultivation of Being while deprecating mere Doing. In his 1874 essay on Wordsworth, Pater had already written, "That the end of life is not action but contemplation—*being* as distinct from doing— a certain disposition of the mind, is, in some shape or other, the principle of all the higher morality."[56] It was in the light of such a redefinition of morality—a repudiation of Victorian do-gooding in the face of the corruption of doing in general—that he had probably intended the famous conclusion to *The Renaissance* of 1868 ("not the fruit of experience but experience itself is the end") and the dis-

covery of Marius the Epicurean that "revelation, vision, the discovery of a vision . . . he had always set that above the having or
even the doing, of anything."[57] Aesthetic essentialism was attractive
because practical life had become unacceptable. The reversal of
Victorian valuations of doing and being is, thus, the historic basis of
aestheticism; historicist-biographical explanation, with all its ambi-
guities, applies itself not only in the case of the English aesthetes but
of James.

For James, personally, the issue had probably been joined by his
choice of art in the place of the available modes of masculine
doing—the public worlds of politics, commerce, and even the
"doing" of a man in marriage. His upbringing had promoted this
choice. Like Ruskin, who described in *Praeterita* (1885) the way his
parents cultivated the habit of spectatorship in their children, James
would recall how the elder Henry James encouraged, by travel and
in other ways, a systematic displacement which would keep his off-
spring from forming fixed attachments to places or life roles. "What
we were to do instead was just to *be* something, something unconnected with specific doing, something free and uncommitted." As
for himself—"What does your father do?" the playmates of Henry
James, Sr.'s, children asked. And they were hard put to answer that
he was more than a well-to-do gentleman who liked to read and talk.
He advised them to tell their friends he was "A Seeker After
Truth."[58]

James's preference for open structures in his fiction may be a
mark of his own refusal to accept the available systems of closure in
life as well as literature. His own early life not only encouraged
valuing Being over Doing, but gave him an awareness of personal
alterity not as a trying-out of varied acts, but as unexpressed aspiration or hidden fear. The question of what he might have been, what
he should have been, or what he escaped being was always present.
Could he have been or should he have been a soldier in the War, as
so many of his friends had been in 1861–1865? Had he escaped a
more restricted artistic destiny by resolving to live abroad? Such
questions are implicit whenever he considers his own destiny, as in
Notes of a Son and Brother or certain of his letters and notebook
observations, or the biography he published in 1879 of his greatest
American predecessor, Hawthorne.

One refusal goes unmentioned but, one may speculate, must have
most often come to mind: Would he have been the man he was if he

had married? Marriage as an institution had come to seem not a conclusion to the quest for selfhood but a problematic, imprisoning "end to experience," as Ursula calls it on the first page of Lawrence's *Women in Love,* published in 1920.[59] The marriage-ending of the novel, its most traditional form of closure, was also becoming problematic. The late Victorian novel had already, before James, rejected the easy marriage-ending as it operated in the novels of Fanny Burney or Jane Austen or even the Gothic novels which portrayed a good marriage as the refuge which must finally enclose the heroine within its protective walls. Entering the domestic world of ordinary middle-class life, Thackeray, Meredith, George Eliot, and then Hardy and George Moore as well as James, developed plots of new tensions and danger besetting men and women after marriage. The bad marriage might then, of course, be terminated by the convenient death of a partner—like the marriage of Dorothea Brooke to Casaubon or David Copperfield to Dora—and the heroine or hero then could be free to make, after all, the ideal marriage which closes the last page upon silence. James had this later model available to him in describing Isabel Archer's bad marriage—yet he chooses not to find his drama in the story of her domestic unhappiness, omitting scenically this part of her history. And though he might have rounded out her story by the death of her husband and a second union, he doesn't. Nor does he allow her to leave her husband, an ending offered her in Goodwood's final appeal. Such an ending still seemed inconceivable to James. Divorce, and a new marriage following it, was a futurity he could not yet treat, and would treat later only in the corrosive satire of *What Maisie Knew.*

One may connect James's interest in a woman's defiance of the assumption that she must marry with his own embracing of bachelorhood. This was a decision he was making in the very same period when he produced *The Portrait of a Lady,*[60] when he might have echoed Isabel's "Why should I necessarily marry?" His precise psychic determinants may be beyond our reach. We will never know if he had by then confirmed without doubt his own disinclination for heterosexual intimacy; if he had also become aware of his fear of something restricting and compromising, some terribly purchased quality in the exchanges by which men and women bound themselves to one another (as he suggests in *The Bostonians* or *The Wings of the Dove*); or if he believed, as he expressed in "The Lesson of the Master," that the artist could not afford, economically or spiritually, to enter the cage of marriage and its obligations. His secret alterity may have been sexual, but whether he knew himself to be homosexual or not, the celibacy which his biographer, Leon Edel, claims for him was the most personal restriction to Being, renunciation of Doing.

James runs the danger of convicting Isabel Archer of some sexual inhibition—in this intensely "natural" person nothing seems less natural than her lack of sexual responsiveness. And yet, he subscribes to her fear of marriage, despite the greater difficulties of spinsterhood. In all his writing, in fact, he seems to have taken the grimmest view of marriage, from the point of view of either men or women. A happy marriage is almost never depicted in his writings because of his profound doubt of the capacity of marriage to liberate rather than confine human individuality. James's ambiguous response to marriage is like Isabel's upon the occasion of Osmond's proposal, when she is said to feel that a bolt has been slipped, "backward or forward, she couldn't have said which—freedom or prison?" (IV:18). It is not only women who resist the marriage-plot in James's fictions. Strether might, at the last, have "lived" in the active sense by embracing the most essential form of masculine doing in the sexuality of marriage. The narrator of "The Aspern Papers" and Marcher, in "The Beast in the Jungle," resist marriage. But most of the refusals are those of his female characters. Catherine Sloper never marries Townsend, though the possibility reappears for her at the end of *Washington Square*, and she does not marry anyone else, though other suitors offer themselves. Daisy Miller, who would not have married Giovanelli, might have married Winterbourne if he had understood her. Fleda Vetch loves and is even loved by Owen Gereth, but refuses to contrive to gain him. Claire Cintré retreats from Newman behind the walls of a convent. Kate refuses Densher's conditions for their marriage after Milly's death. In most of his longer works, and in one short story after another, marriages that might shut down the narrative fail to take place.

Marriage may seem only one among other social contracts that confirm the individual in his membership in society, but it is probably the most important, representing all those other choices and decisions by which one acquires a history in ways society recognizes. James's resistance to a marriage solution for his characters is thus the most conspicuous sign of his resistance to prescriptive form, an assumption of finalized being, an end to potentiality. And so it figures both as a concrete theme with a direct reference to society and history, and as a device by which the more total human issue may be explored. In the real world, of course, it is women who are most absolutely confined by the marriage-plot, though it prescribes male life as well; this is one reason why women—from Daisy Miller to Milly Theale and Kate Croy—are of such primary interest in James's fiction. But it is not merely that he empathized to a greater degree than most men with the woman of his time, with her problems and with her strengths and weaknesses. He identifies with the female condition simply because it is, more absolutely, the human condition as he sees it.

From such issues of personal and social life, which lie at the heart of James's fictions, I return again to the process of reading that brings them into being. James's reader, who is encouraged to constantly renew efforts to integrate and interpret James's narratives, just as the fictional characters themselves struggle for self-definition, is someone engaged in his own struggle to understand his life as he lives it. Art and the human mind have both this ultimately conservative compulsion to restore control—social or psychological or aesthetic—to the scene disordered by the unclassifiable character, the incoherent plot, or the plot which may once have served to produce life but can do so no longer. So, in the end, plot makes itself felt in the very teeth of denying itself, and human character establishes itself in our minds even when frustrated of performance. James, as already recalled, said the artist's problem was to "draw by a geometry of his own the circle within which" human relations may "appear" to be contained. Using the same image he wrote of the geometric "circle" (2:1041) which makes the endless continuities of life seem to end, a "sharp, black line" which artfully "isolates" it or, like a picture frame, "frames" the expansive reality in "a square . . . a charming oval" (2:1122).

That such geometry can be a kind of tyranny—analogous to, even when it does not directly represent, the tyrannies of social or sexual convention—James also realized. Those who would cruelly box others into their fictions abound in James—from Winterbourne to the narrator of *The Sacred Fount*. The figure of the geometer is, after all, used to characterize Dr. Sloper, who when his sister asks him whether he will change his view of his daughter and her lover, replies "Shall a geometrical proposition relent?" Catherine's father is only one of the many representatives of the oppressive and restrictive force of cultural expectation which, like the novel itself, confines and coerces the spirit that longs for an impossible freedom. The interpretive impulse betrays the total potentiality of its object even when it is benevolent. Isabel Archer is the victim not only of the schemes of others who desire to exploit her but of the dreams of her best friend, Ralph; her own generous designs of life make the scheming Gilbert Osmond himself *her* victim. Maggie Verver is victimized by the plots of others but discovers an imperial power of illusionary manipulation—and reduction—when she reconstitutes her marriage by force of will and imagination.

But still, the geometry of art, the form making of the human mind of both writer and reader, is the meaning-making power that, as James said, "makes life."[61] And in the social world it is the necessity to contain and coordinate individualities—to give them life histories of expectable form—that makes society. The *constructive* compulsion which is our way of coping with life was never more powerful in a writer than it was in James. His Isabel Archer affronts the social world which prescribes a confining rather than liberating outcome to her selfhood—and is given the writer's sympathy for doing so. Yet is there any alternative to her eventual acceptance of prescribed role, her subjection to *story*, James seems to ask? The contest between order and freedom, is, after all, a social struggle that James is representing with divided sympathy. In the process we duplicate in our progressive reading, the process that invites us to apply our conventionalized ideas of characters and plot to phenomena which disturb those expectations, to find them wanting, and to seek out new forms to contain our "impressions," we are only enacting again the struggles of the self that cannot find expression except through limitation and ordering.

But James's interest in the attempts of his characters to keep themselves ideally free, to evade the literary designs that bind them into the structures of convention, is not merely a mark of his subscription to indeterminacy in the philosophic sense. The art of fiction itself, he believed, must express the writer's freedom, his escape from the geometry of form, since "the tracing of a line to be followed, of a tone to be taken, of a form to be filled out, is a limitation of that freedom and a suppression of the very thing we are most curious about, "a personal, direct impression of life" (1:50). James encourages, by the richness of his narratives, the free development of his readers' responses. He joins hands with those benevolent presences in his novels, like Ralph Touchett, who want to give the freedom-loving character fullest opportunity to escape prescribed forms—though he knows he is bound, like Ralph, to write a story just the same, and not, in all likelihood, a new one, even perhaps a worse one than if he had not intervened. He wants the reader to sympathize with those characters who resist plot and established "type"; they are representatives of all forms of challenge to the offered forms of social life, though the resistance founders in the end. They express his sympathy with social as well as artistic indeterminacy. Altogether he seems to distrust an overready reading of life. He makes the very contest between interpretive limitation and freedom the essence of his most moving stories.

· 2 ·

"Daisy Miller"
and *Washington Square*

A T T H E S T A R T of his career in the seventies and eighties, James was acutely aware that the formulas of literature are dependent on the sense that life itself can be shaped according to concepts which, with a significant ambiguity, we use when talking about life or about art. He envied the European artist the way an idea of "character" or "story" came to hand out of a scene ordered by ideas of personal type and destiny. He thought that Balzac, whom he admired most among the French masters, had had the good luck to inherit a world which supplied such concepts in quantity. Some years later, he wrote that Balzac

> had indeed a striking good fortune, the only one he was to enjoy as an harrassed and exasperated worker: the great garden of life presented itself to him absolutely and exactly in the guise of the great garden of France, a subject vast and comprehensive enough, yet with definite edges and corners . . . What he did above all was to read the universe, as hard and as loud as he could, *into* the France of his time; his own eyes regarding his work as at once the drama of man and a mirror of the mass of social phenomena the most rounded and registered, most organized and administered, and thereby most exposed to systematic observation and portrayal, that the world had seen. There are happily other interesting societies, but these are for schemes of such an order comparatively loose and incoherent, with more extent and perhaps more variety, but with less of the great enclosed and exhibited quality, less neatness and sharpness of arrangement, fewer categories, subdivisions, juxtapositions. (2:92–93)

Such an ideological world of human formulations and a prepared and controlled practical world of defined social roles and institutions had been precisely what Hawthorne had lacked, James

45

had pityingly observed in his 1879 biographical study of his American predecessor. Too familiar to need quotation is his catalogue of the "items of high civilization"—the human types as well as the long established institutions—absent from American life (1:351–352). But his condescension is curiously qualified. It is generally overlooked that James goes on to insist that Hawthorne had in some way achieved the miracle of expressing his peculiar national inheritance without such support. Though Hawthorne had even missed such opportunities of recording the "social idiosyncrasies" of his countrymen as New England life presented, and his characters were "not portraits of actual types," there was something profoundly local to be felt in his writing. It is, he wrote, "redolent of the social system in which he had his being" (1:321). And having said this, James finds the situation of the American writer not altogether pitiable after all. In America, James explains, "the individual counts for more, as it were, and, thanks to the absence of a variety of social types and settled heads under which he may be easily and conveniently pigeon-holed, he is to a certain extent, a wonder and a mystery" (1:356–357). Thus, while he appreciated to the point of envy the Balzacian array of social classifications and personal history rooted in the expectations of an ancient culture, James also had an American relish for the unclassified, the new, the uncertain. The open American world Hawthorne had lived in seemed to invite a free development of personal forms; the artist even felt himself prompted to celebrate the idea of disengagement from Balzac's "categories, subdivisions, juxtapositions."

But James's analysis of Hawthorne's difficult achievement was a way of seeing his own problem, which was not, in fact, exclusively geographic or national. In the later stage of Western history, which we share with him rather than with Balzac or Hawthorne, the concepts which form the substructure of the novelist's reality may not be so securely anchored in social consensus. Not because he was an American, merely, but because he was a modern, James felt the disjunction that had opened between selfhood and social role. In his preface to the New York Edition volume that contains "Daisy Miller," he finally writes, "A human, a personal 'adventure' is no *a priori*, no positive and absolute and inelastic thing, but just a matter of relation and appreciation—a name we conveniently give, after the fact, to any passage, to any situation, that has added the sharp taste of uncertainty to a quickened sense of life" (2:1285).

James's early experiments in narrative design tested established ways of bounding experience and giving it design. There was his well-known "international theme"—really a way of treating typologically a popular subject (the difference between Americans and the older nations they had sprung from). Along with Howells and other observers, James had been struck by the idea of the emergence of new, native types. But he had a quite detached view of how such phenomena were not so much objective actualities as concepts he himself was in the process of creating as formulas of fiction. Once assimilated by a larger cultural consciousness than the novel reader's, they even became facts of experience. He did not, perhaps, regard the American Girl—who was held to be his own particular discovery[1]—so much as a part of nature or society-as-found as a mental structure made actual by life's imitation of the model. Much later, in *The American Scene*, he calls the Girl "a new human convenience, not unlike fifty of the others, of a slightly different order, the ingenious mechanical appliances, stoves, refrigerators, sewing-machines, type-writers, cash-registers, that have done so much in the house and the place of business for the American name."[2] Like so many statements in that remarkable cultural study, this one shows how well James understood not only what we now might call the "commodification" of persons, but also how our ways of looking at anything are "inventions" produced to serve a social need.

He must have understood that his types were peculiarly abstract in such a work as *The American*, which, with its generic title, is ostensibly about nothing so much as the question of being an American. No American was ever so American—that is, so "innocent"— as Christopher Newman, whose name itself is a giveaway of his mythic character. Despite the fact that he is an American millionaire who has built a fortune in America in the age of the "robber barons," he retains the exquisite conscience of a heroine of romance—and it is not surprising that James's next novel concerned a feminine explorer of the European dark forest, an "Americana," Isabel Archer, whose feminine inexperience would lend greater plausibility to her character. No Europeans, on the other hand, were so "experienced" as the Bellegarde family to whom Newman is opposed. James wrote the novel, he admitted afterward, in the spirit of romantic exaggeration, and he became painfully aware of the improbability of the Bellegardes, though he tried to believe that the figure of Newman was "more or less convincing" despite "an occasional extra inch or so [he] might smuggle into his measurements" (2:1069). The truth is, that even Newman is convincing only in a symbolic way.

Though James continued to be interested in the question of national definition—and in other categorical definitions beloved by the social realist—he would find such conceptions treacherous as much as useful. One might be, like Maria Gostrey in *The Ambassadors*, "mistress of a hundred cases or categories, receptacles of the mind, subdivisions for convenience, in which, from a full experience, she pigeon-holed her fellow mortals with a hand as free as that of a compositor scattering type" (XXI:11)—and yet be less equipped than Strether, his typesetter's hand empty of "type" (as James puns) to appreciate the complex paradoxes of life. It was part of James's own Americanism—but also of his modernism—to suspect that these "receptacles of the mind" were bound to betray life in some way, to deny its indeterminacy. Tradition, literary and social, was a great ragbag of definitions and categories, of conventions and styles, of epistemes, as Foucault would call them in our time. But the novelist knew that these were only confining conveniences.

"Daisy Miller" is generally seen as a comedy or tragicomedy of manners—which, of course, it is—and James's later dramatization of it suggests that he himself saw how his tale could be taken even farther in the direction of this dramatic genre. But the 1883 play, one of James's weakest in a literary form he never mastered, only vulgarizes the exaggeration of characterization and finally reduces the delicate and problematic qualities of the original story by providing a preposterous stage liveliness, complete with a villainous Eugenio and Giovanelli, and a Madame de Katkoff actively conniving on the scene in the place of Winterbourne's vague Geneva "attachment"; Winterbourne and Daisy become hero and heroine of melodrama, to be united finally in tender understanding.

The story's original 1878 title ("Daisy Miller: A Study") seems to bear out the idea that James had intended a work of scientific observation. Yet when he revised the story for the New York Edition in 1909, James decided, as he explained, "to suppress at all events here the appended qualification—in view of the simple truth, which ought from the first have been apparent to me, that my little exhibition is made to no degree whatever in critical, but, quite inordinately and extravagantly, in poetical terms" (2:1270). Some had

charged him with having dealt *too* critically with the real young
ladies to be found in such hotels as the Trois Couronnes in Vevey,
but he had also been reproached, he remembered, for having roman-
ticized the real Daisy Millers, vulgar rich American girls of fact
rather than fancy. He answered that in any case his "supposedly
typical little figure was of course pure poetry, and had never been
anything else; since this is what helpful imagination, in however
slight a dose, ever directly makes for" (2:1271).

James's denial of the "critical" motive of his story and the suppositious typicality of its heroine may be a bit disingenuous—meant to
disarm the offended. In fact, the heroine of James's *succès de scandale*
was one of James's early studies of "the American Girl." She was a
type he thought he had seen among his wealthy compatriots in
Europe, a type so recognizable to others that his literary definition,
which was only a schematic container for new kinds of behavior,
became a popular formula of description; readers saw Daisy Millers
wherever they went in their travels thereafter. But if "Daisy Miller"
was not literally about the way American girls abroad behaved—or
not exclusively so—what was it about? There is some profit in
reflecting upon what James meant by insisting on its "poetry." He
seems to have conceived of a romantic idealization that abstracted
certain mythic American qualities—while still preserving an illusion of ordinary portraiture. The naive rebel, Daisy, an embodiment
of willful freedom from conventional definition, might seem more
eccentric than real. Yet such a figure might represent a significant
resistant impulse at work in American life.

And it might signify, on the literary level, a resistance to the very
process by which realistic portraiture was established in the novel,
especially the fulfillment of familiar expectations of plot. The
assault upon such a character's "freedom" is the author's own as
well as that of those others within the fiction who would "type" the
innocent character or dictate its story. In "Daisy Miller," this is the
failed enterprise of that author-surrogate and anti-hero, Winterbourne—and of the reader too, who must be forced to remain in
some doubt while craving certainty. It is for this reason that the
progress of the narrative, which follows the seesaw mental swings
of Winterbourne, exhibits, already, that crab-wise narrative progress which will reach its full expression in *The Ambassadors.* The
question: "What sort of a woman is Daisy?" is not unlike, after all,
Strether's question, "What sort of a woman is Madame de

Vionnet?" It will produce, even in this brief tale, that sense of sustained narrative alternatives which predominates in his later fiction.

Washington Square seems to turn its back altogether on the device of international comparisons and, along with *The Bostonians* (also excluded from the New York Edition), resolutely concentrates on a corner of the unfurnished American scene. But it would seem to have been conceived in the beginning as an essay in the description of *moeurs de province* in the Balzacian mode. Although James based his tale on a real-life anecdote told him by an English friend,[3] its most obvious literary model is *Eugénie Grandet*. Balzac's work of 1833 had stirred James's admiration for years. As early as 1865, in a review of a now-forgotten novel by Harriet Elizabeth Prescott, the twenty-one-year-old James had recommended to Prescott the study of Balzac's tale.[4] Ten years later, when he wrote his first article about the French master, he tried, himself, to put the model to use—and discovered his mistake. In the opening chapters of *Roderick Hudson,* he wanted to "do" Northampton, Massachusetts, in a Balzacian way. "I . . . was not sufficiently on my guard to see how easily his high practice might be delusive for my case," he admitted later. "One nestled, technically, in those days, and with yearning, in the great shadow of Balzac; his august example, little as the secret might ever be guessed, towered for me over the scene; so that what was clearer than anything else was how, if it was a question of Saumur, of Limoges, of Guérande, he 'did' Saumur, did Limoges, did Guérande" (2:1044).

But only a couple of years after *Roderick Hudson,* he must have been thinking, again, of how Balzac had done Saumur in *Eugénie Grandet* as he remembered the Washington Square of his own childhood. If Balzac could show how the miserly paternal tyrant and his daughter were both products of *his* own home region, why could not James relate Dr. Sloper and his daughter to Old New York? There is significance in James's choice of a stage—his title referring not to a person but a place, the realist-naturalist context of his story. In the little square where the tide of upward-mounting wealth appeared to have paused for a moment in the red brick mansions with their white stone steps and delicate fanlights, "you had come into a world which appeared to offer a variety of sources of interest,"[5] the narrator declares. Here was a milieu with as much custom and form as America had to offer.

As in "Daisy Miller," he had tried to identify phenomena peculiar to the new environment, like a naturalist in a strange region who comes upon a plant or animal previously unclassified. Catherine Sloper is less "national" in speech or gesture than Daisy Miller—and less a comic drawing. She resembles her French prototype, though her simplicity has no religious dimension like the French girl's. It is her father who represents James's chief attempt at defining an American species. Dr. Austin Sloper is no European "gentleman of leisure" but a practical scientist with a mature understanding of human types arising from his professional habit of observation. His cultivation is combined with ability in appraising consequences, in deciding what things are good *for,* and in acting upon such decision.

But James's types in *Washington Square* were not really rooted in immemorial custom and place, like Old Grandet and his daughter. He described his story to his friend Howells as "poorish . . . a tale purely American, the writing of which made me acutely feel the want of paraphernalia"—Hawthorne's handicap, again—a diagnosis which he would consider refuted only, he said, by the appearance in America of a novelist "belonging in the company of Balzac or Thackeray."[6] And here it is that Hawthorne himself, who had been unable to utilize the "lesson of Balzac," (James gave this title to a lecture he delivered in America in 1905; 2:115) might have been of some help. Though this has hardly been noted, *Washington Square* may also be said to derive from "Rappaccini's Daughter." In the latter there are, again, three principals, a doctor-father of merciless intellectuality (who is much closer to Dr. Sloper than Balzac's primitive old cooper), a pure-souled daughter, and her handsome, treacherous lover. The resemblance is, of course, far and near, but it suggests that James's story vibrates, intertextually, between Balzac's and Hawthorne's examples. Hawthorne's romantic tale may be closer than Balzac's to James's ultimate intention. It may be read as a story about a female nature too presumptuously defined by male authorities—by father and lover alike. The mystery of Beatrice Rappaccini's character may also be an inner representation of the story's own resistance to interpretive reduction, by which it expresses such resistance to reality itself.

Another significant intertext may be one of James's own works, *The Europeans,* written just months earlier. The differences between these two short novels are conspicuous, and the resemblances have to be exposed by turning each work around in an unexpected way, but once this is done one can see how James passed from one to the other in 1878. Despite the title, the earlier story, too, is located in a thoroughly American scene—Boston and its suburbs—and the "Europeans" who visit their American cousins are actually Americans, though thoroughly steeped in the European dye. Townsend, Catherine's distant cousin, is also an American modified by a long European sojourn—if not a total upbringing in Europe, like that of Felix Young. Gertrude Wentworth is thought by her family to be, like Catherine Sloper, dull and even plain, though the quality that most distinguishes her from everyone else—as it does Catherine— is that she is "natural." But, of course, Felix is really in love with *his* heiress, however much it may be to his advantage to be so (very much as Dr. Sloper himself had once been when he had married "for love" a girl with $10,000 a year)—and this genial story has in the place of the forbidding Dr. Sloper the gentle old Puritan, Mr. Wentworth. The marriage-plot amiably completes itself in *The Europeans* for everyone except the too-designing Eugenia (whose theatrical personality oddly resembles Mrs. Penniman's). *Her* defeat is hardly tragic, though one might—if James had permitted it—have felt some pity for her and some distaste for the cool curiosity and dismissive logic of Robert Acton, the man who decides not to be beguiled.

James did not include either *The Europeans* or *Washington Square* in the New York Edition. The second work is richer; pathos is mingled with the comedy. Gertrude, the odd American girl who resists Mr. Bland but finds happiness in her beautiful young cousin, is replaced by Catherine, who loves another beautiful young man who this time deserves her father's bad opinion. Yet although Catherine seems powerless, victimized by both father and lover, she does in the end exercise choice, refusing a belated ringing down of the curtain on a marriage ceremony; she is left free to work out her own destiny, however limited.

One need not agree with James that *Washington Square* is a failure. It is a masterpiece. But it has turned its back on its author's original intention and accomplished something more interesting. By beginning and then betraying such a study as Dr. Sloper himself might have appreciated—a Balzacian study of types and local circumstances—James composed, in the end, a more severe critique of the categorical mind than "Daisy Miller." The story is the testing ground of its affinities, which offer other modes of interpretation besides the realistic, as well as challenging the conditions of objective social reality and its confining categories. In this skeptical fiction James examines by means of his story and its presentational devices literary modes and their analogous life attitudes, such as those of the ironist, the melodramatist, and the romantic fabulist, all of which had been resources of his previous writing along with those of the realist-historian. Releasing himself from the grip of one system of forms, he found that he wanted to try to escape from others, from all.

Thus, one may also find if one wishes the components of fairy tale in *Washington Square,* though they enter only to be proven inadequate. Do we not have the cold-hearted father (a widowed king), the orphaned ugly-duckling princess, the treacherous stepmother-aunt who has replaced her dead mother, and the handsome young prince? All these betray their fairy-tale roles, and the fairy-tale ending is repudiated. One may say the same about the story's character as melodrama. It is a melodrama which becomes a criticism of the melodramatic principle. The melodramatists it presents us with—the cruel, typecasting director-father, the limelight-stealing bad actress of an aunt, the falsely declamatory actor-lover—are forced to give over the script to the naive improvisations of the heroine, whose melodramatic final triumph is also the defeat of the style of her fellow actors.

Not only conventions of genre but varieties of "artificial" style make their appearance, only to be ultimately undermined in this artistically self-conscious, self-mocking work. All the chief characters save Catherine are engaged in the contest enacted not merely on the narrative but on the verbal level between what is held to be "sincere" and what is not only seen as literary but as personal and social pretense, or even between what is "natural" and what is sometimes called "civilized." Opposed to them James presents a heroine whose style is so mute and motionless as to be almost a surrender of style—a practical and intellectual "innocence" which derives from her inability to employ any rhetoric dictated by social or literary convention, almost an inability to speak or do at all. Out of her dilemma, an authenticity of silence emerges, a resistance to the betrayals of expression.

Catherine Sloper may still, like Daisy Miller, be seen to express certain "national" qualities of resistance to the impositions of custom and convention. However humble, Catherine is not pliant—

she asserts her independence. And though what she desires is only
so conventional a thing as marriage to a handsome suitor, her
attachment to her own rather than her father's choice is an American love of freedom. She meets experience by the unaided prompt-
ings of a virgin nature, the expression of a mythic national origin
uninstructed by the past. But her story is not a happy one and James,
in describing her and her fate, holds out no great promise of creative
future for the integrity—personal or national—she signifies.

"Daisy Miller"

Despite its compact shapeliness and the narrative tone which seems
to emanate from a fixed elevation of authorial detachment, this early
work nonetheless focuses on a central consciousness, whose
inability to arrive at certainty is the source of so much Jamesian
drama. It is Daisy Miller, and not the bemused and sluggish Winterbourne, whose name figures in James's title, but she is the subject of
Winterbourne's inquiry rather than ours. Whether we like it or not,
we are compelled to occupy ourselves with his unengaging personality rather than with Daisy's. This is again the result of a shift of
narrative focus—from observed to observer—similar to that made
in *Roderick Hudson,* published three years before. Despite that
novel's title, James later realized, the "centre of interest" hadn't so
much been Roderick as it had been the consciousness of his witnessing friend, Rowland Mallet.[7]

In "Daisy Miller," as in *Roderick Hudson,* James makes use of a
third-person narrator who depends upon the perceptions of a character whose interest is directed upon someone to whom we have no
other access. We can never arrive except by guesswork at the truth
about Daisy; she can only be seen from the outside through the lens
of Winterbourne's special viewpoint. We are never allowed to
know her unspoken thoughts but only the reflections about her
uttered to him by others, and only his surmises. Unlike the situation
in *Roderick Hudson,* in which Rowland Mallet maintains a claim to
some trust, skepticism must slowly emerge as we find ourselves
studying Winterbourne even more closely than we do Daisy, and, in
the end, we become convinced of the inadequacy of his insight in a
way that looks forward to the "autobiographic" form[8] of "The
Aspern Papers," in which the observer-narrator himself loses our
confidence.

Winterbourne, rather than Rowland Mallet, is the first of those

Jamesian witnesses whose efforts to truly know the Other, to understand the Other's story, are representations of the writer's—and the reader's—bemused efforts to solve the mystery of character and plot. His unease about his young countrywoman's propriety is quaint today; and we are unlikely to share the prejudices of the contemporary reader who was shocked by her as much as was Winterbourne himself. But if we jump to the conclusion that the story "dates" and so has only historical interest, we miss the truth that Winterbourne's *process* of observation and placement is not at all foreign to us. We are no less likely than the nineteenth-century reader to strive to place others in ready-made categories and to interpret their fates conventionally; only the categories and conventions have changed.

Among the categories and conventions still relevant are those that confine the female subject—and if "Daisy Miller" is not about Daisy exactly, it is certainly about recognizably *masculine* ways of looking at women. Winterbourne, the girl-watcher who idly sits on his hotel terrace waiting for a particularly arresting feminine figure to come into his purview, is prototypically poised for the encounter, equipped with preconceptions and, one may imagine, practiced ploys of approach. As soon as we realize that *he* is what *we* are watching, we can put aside the charge by some feminist readers that James is simply showing his own attachment to female stereotypes.[9]

James must have been aware of his complicity with Winterbourne, nonetheless. In writing this very story was he not himself assisting the development of a popular stereotype? If he aimed to expose the fallacies of stereotypical thinking, the further life of his Daisy Miller in the popular imagination must have afterward shown him that he, too, could be held responsible for creating a concept as limiting as any that had gone before. His intention to criticize such thinking was—and still is—seldom understood. Just the same, however, he was himself a young man, and could not have helped sharing Winterbourne's masculine perspective. In any case, as I observed at the start of this chapter, he was a young writer for whom the whole question of typological definition had a special importance; how else but by means of types could character be understood? The process of art itself is represented in Winterbourne's encounters with Daisy; Winterbourne's way of making her comprehensible to himself, his reduction of her to a "character" for whom he anticipates a certain story, is a literary effort.

It is interesting, therefore, to notice the signs of James's identification with this imaginary young American observer. To begin with, the narrative voice reveals a mind close to Winterbourne's, for Winterbourne is exactly the sort of sophisticated traveler who would understand the narrator's discriminations among the various hotels at Vevey and also be able to compare and contrast them with scenes at Saratoga, as the narrative persona, that of a traveled American, does. This anonymous personality may become personal and erupt into an "I" from time to time in self-conscious separation from his subject: "I hardly know whether it was the analogies or the differences that were uppermost in the mind of a young American, who two or three years ago, sat in the garden of the 'Trois Couronnes,' looking about him rather idly at some of the graceful objects I have mentioned" (XVIII:4). But the habit of mind we have just seen illustrated—of making cultural comparisons of scene and, personal type—is one which narrator and character share.

They also share this habit with the novelist and writer of charming travel essays for American magazines. But there is a further mark of Winterbourne's affiliation with Henry James. We are told that Winterbourne had gone "on trial" to the old "Academy on the steep and stony hillside" in Geneva. Winterbourne has an affection, consequently, for the "little capital of Calvinism" (XVIII:5) and some continuing friendships there—a prehistory drawn so precisely from James's own youthful experience as to seem the writer's sly reminder (perhaps only to himself) of this identity with his character. In 1860, the James family had been in Geneva, where the seventeen-year-old Henry was enrolled at the Academy as a special student.[10] The wording of the 1909 text increases this autobiographical element; his first version in the *Cornhill Magazine*[11] said simply that Winterbourne had "gone to College" in Geneva. But in his essay "Swiss Notes," published in *Transatlantic Sketches* three years before "Daisy Miller," James expressed a feeling of "old-time kindness for Geneva, to which I was introduced years ago, in my school-days, when I was as good an idler as the best."[12] He paraphrases this thought in "Daisy Miller" as "Winterbourne had an old attachment for the little capital of Calvinism; he had been put to school there as a boy" (XVIII:5).

The process of composing fictions about others is not limited to author, narrator, and Winterbourne. Everyone plays at the same game. To remind us of this, Winterbourne's friends speak of his

"studying" in Geneva; his enemies ("but after all he had no enemies," the narrator interjects when his own pointed style has
betrayed him into an antithesis) say that he spent time there
because "he was extremely devoted to a lady who lived there—a
foreign lady, a person older than himself" (XVIII:4–5). As though
anticipating the way James's tale will enforce upon us the realization of the unreliability of *any* narrative, no choice is made among
these theories; we will be returned at the end to the same alternatives by the gossip which reports that he is either studying hard in
Geneva or much interested in a very clever foreign lady. This return
to the beginning, announcing that for Winterbourne there has been
no significant change, should also have the function of reminding us
that Winterbourne has always had a sexual liaison with a European,
but that since he is a man of discretion and not, like Daisy, a rash
young woman, there can be no real "story in it" after all.

Winterbourne's own observations exhibit from start to finish the
categorical judgment which is the object of major scrutiny in "Daisy
Miller." Comically, he shares it first with Randolph, Daisy's small
brother, who already has the habit of cultural comparison when it
comes to candy, and says, "American candy's the best candy." To this,
Winterbourne responds, "Are American boys the best little boys?"
and is told, "American men are the best." So, Daisy is welcomed upon
the scene by Winterbourne with the same comparative tribute:
"American girls are the best girls" (XVIII:7). He still sees only a
category rather than an individual when he looks at her for the first
time and exclaims to himself, "How pretty they are!" (XVIII:8).

For a moment, Winterbourne finds himself a litle adrift from the
familiar boundaries which, particularly in sexual relations, stan-
dardize not only persons but behavior, and forecast expectable stories: "In Geneva, as he had been perfectly aware, a young man
wasn't at liberty to speak to a young unmarried lady save under
certain rarely-occurring conditions; but here at Vevey what conditions could be better than these?" (XVIII:8–9). But his generalizing
soon puts him at ease:

> She might be cold, she might be austere, she might even be
> prim; for that was apparently—he had already so generalized—
> what the most "distant" American girls did: they came and
> planted themselves straight in front of you to show how rigidly
> unapproachable they were. There hadn't been the slightest flush

in her fresh fairness however; so that she was clearly neither offended nor fluttered. Only she was composed—he had seen that before too—of charming little parts that didn't match and that made no *ensemble*; and if she looked another way when he spoke to her, and seemed not particularly to hear him, this was simply her habit, her manner, the result of her having no idea whatever of "form."   (XVIII:10–11)

As he listens to Daisy's chatter in this opening scene, Winterbourne is amused and perplexed, for his frames of reference—his collection of "cases" and "types"—don't satisfactorily collect her "little parts." They particularly fail to accommodate her stories of "gentlemen friends": "He had never yet heard a young girl express herself in just this fashion; never at least save in cases where to say such things was to have at the same time some rather complicated consciousness about them"—and he decides that he has "lost the right sense for the young American tone. Never indeed since he had grown old enough to appreciate things had he encountered a young compatriot of so 'strong' a type as this." He is at sea, unable to choose the appropriate formula for the "type" confronting him. "Were they all like that, the pretty girls who had had a good deal of gentlemen's society? Or was she also a designing, an audacious, in short an expert young person? . . . Some people had told him that after all American girls *were* exceedingly innocent, and others had told him that after all they weren't" (XVIII:16–17). Is she what the Europeans would call a coquette?

It is significant that Winterbourne resorts to a foreign concept, the "coquette," in his desperate need of a category for Daisy. This and other foreign terms he seizes upon suggest not merely his cosmopolitanism but his need to make imprisoning divisions which have no labels in English or can be more comfortably referred to by a foreign word than by an embarrassing native one. He will wonder if he can accuse her of all that is implied by " 'inconduite,' as they say in Geneva." He will try, unsuccessfully, to assert that Daisy belongs to the "meilleur monde," but also characterize her meeting with her Italian friend as a "rendezvous," which, in the English mouth, suggests a secret or even illicit romantic meeting; even her earlier "têtes-à-têtes" with Giovanelli sound more covert in French. Finally, when he is convinced of Daisy's depravity he speaks of her Italian friend as her "amoroso"—evading the explictness of the English "lover."

But nothing is more abhorrent to the classifying mind than doubt, and the dynamics of James's narrative consist exactly of Winterbourne's efforts to secure himself from uncertainty by means of a fixed system of generalities. The reader is compelled to share his anxious effort, to consider seriously whether or not each hypothesis will not eventually provide a closure to the inquiry upon which he is jointly launched with this man—to expect a further unfolding of plot which will make one conclusion absolute and kill off all alternatives glimpsed along the way. Winterbourne is relieved to "discover" at this point that there is a class, after all, to which Daisy can be assigned: "He must on the whole take Miss Daisy Miller for a flirt—a pretty American flirt. He had never as yet had relations with representatives of that class." And having established her membership in the class, he is at his ease. "Winterbourne was almost grateful for having found the formula that applied to Miss Daisy Miller. He leaned back in his seat . . . he wondered what were the regular conditions and limitations of one's intercourse with a pretty American flirt" (XVIII:17).

This is not the last time that we will observe the way the need for "formula" preys upon Winterbourne and the relief with which he arrives at one that appears to fit the instance. One may want to analyze this compulsion psychologically, and ask, as one would ask if he were a real person, what fear of Daisy's sexual attractiveness is at the root of his desire to reduce her to an intellectual concept. A feminist reading of the story can certainly assert confidently that Daisy's nature is being read by a masculine mind nervously in need of those imprisoning definitions which assure its dominance. However motivated, psychologically or sociologically, James's categorizer exhibits the desperation underlying the need of category generally. But if the writer wondered whether it was possible for fiction to dispense with such means for recognizing and identifying human personality—whether characters in fiction could be "natural" or "free"—the problem had an acute form when it came to female character. These words, we shall see, are to be associated very soon with Catherine Sloper and even more with James's greater American heroine, Isabel Archer, whose explicit desire it is to resist the traps of definition. But even the crude, inarticulate Daisy seems engaged in the defense of her own indeterminacy.

Winterbourne's aunt, Mrs. Costello, has a categorical dismissal ready for the whole Miller family—"They're the *sort* of Americans that one does one's duty by just ignoring" (XVIII:23, my emphasis). Confused by her calling Daisy "a horror," Winterbourne resorts to another trite conception in the place of his "pretty American flirt," and asks his aunt if Daisy is "the sort of young lady who expects a man sooner or later to—well, we'll call it carry her off?" (XVIII:25) The exchange between nephew and aunt is high comedy. Mrs. Costello has an unshakable attachment to her generalizing view of Daisy—she does not need to verify it by meeting her, and when she hears further news of the young woman she calls her simply "an abomination" (both this word and "horror" (XVIII:25) are additions in the New York Edition text of Mrs. Costello's remarks; she is less categorically dismissive in the 1878 text. Winterbourne, on the other hand, is driven to surrender first one and then another of his "sorts," each time replacing his idea by one as banal as the previous. His uneasy journey from one concept to another is the story's profoundest plot and at the same time a dramatization of our reading experience.

Of course, Winterbourne is charmed by Daisy—this is one of the sources of his difficulty while it gives zest to the inquiry. " 'Common' she might be, as Mrs. Costello had pronounced her; yet what provision was made by that epithet for her queer little native grace?" (XVIII:31). The epithet, the abstraction, may be inadequate to contain this specimen after all. At the conclusion of the discussion with her mother and the courier, Eugenio, about a jaunt to the Chateau de Chillon with Winterbourne, Daisy seems merely whimsical as she teases him with a demand for some judgment: "Good-night—I hope you're disappointed or disgusted or something!" But Winterbourne can only offer, "I'm puzzled, if you want to know!" (XVIII:38). Two days later he is off across the lake on the little steamer, his companion making "many characteristic remarks" while he ponders the "character" of which they give evidence: "If he had assented to the idea that she was 'common,' at any rate, *was* she proving so, after all, or was he simply getting used to her commonness?" (XVIII:39, 40).

Just as he watches Daisy for the "characteristic" behavior she exhibits to him, so for Winterbourne the occasion has distinctly a conventional character; it is something to be identified by that term for a certain commonplace narrative, an "adventure"—a word which has a suggestion of the unprincipled (as when we call someone a "mere" adventurer) or, at least, the improper. He is somewhat disappointed to notice that his companion does not seem to have his own sense of the delightfully illicit. When she challenges him familiarly about his reasons for returning the next day to Geneva, he can only conclude that she is "an extraordinary mixture of innocence and crudity" (XVIII:43).

In Rome, he hears more about the "dreadful" behavior of the Millers, and tries to reassure his aunt: "They're very ignorant— very innocent only, and utterly uncivilised. Depend on it they're not 'bad,' " the last word used with self-conscious quotation-marks. The slippery relativity of language is acknowledged by Mrs. Costello, who remarks, "Whether or no being hopelessly vulgar is being 'bad' is a question for the metaphysicians. They're bad enough to blush for, at any rate; and for this short life that's quite enough" (XVIII:46). For Winterbourne, however, mere vulgarity is not an adequate synonym for badness, and in the case of Daisy herself, it is clear that female "badness" has for him its traditional sense of sexual irregularity—and it is of this that he wants to exempt her. Then, to fill the gap of his doubt, he hears her announce, at the house of his American friend, Mrs. Walker, that she is going for an evening walk on the Pincio with a "Mr. Giovanelli." Winterbourne escorts her to this dubious rendezvous, and one glance is enough to convince him that "the beautiful Giovanelli" isn't "the right gentleman" for a nice young lady. His quick perception of "types" enables him to "take his measure" unhesitatingly: "He's anything but a gentleman . . . He's a music-master or a penny-a-liner or a third rate artist"—regretting that Miss Miller hasn't "instinctively discriminated against such a type" (XVIII:58). The word "type" is an addition of the New York Edition; in 1878 James had written, "Winterbourne felt a superior indignation at his own lovely fellow-countrywoman's not knowing the difference between a spurious gentleman and a real one" (27), but in revising he wanted, clearly, to stress Winterbourne's typological compulsion.

Not to understand types is a mark against one's own membership in the right type. "Would a nice girl—even allowing for her being a little American flirt—make a rendezvous with a presumably low-lived foreigner?" (XVIII:58). He swings to the conviction that she is not merely vulgar; she is not even "nice"—the word suggesting sexual laxness at the same time that it retains the sense of an inability to make discriminations. And, again, we notice that his devotion to the absolute category is so determined that it makes him impatient of discrepancy. He is positively annoyed that her assignation occurs in a crowded public place in broad daylight instead of some dark corner. He is "vexed that the girl, in joining her *amoroso* shouldn't appear impatient of his own company . . . It was impossible to regard her as a wholly unspotted flower—she lacked a certain indispensable fineness; and it would therefore much simplify the situation to be able to treat her as the subject of one of the visitations known to romancers as 'lawless passions' " (XVIII:59).

That James is parodying common ideas of virtue and vice as well as trite literature is obvious from the language which his free indirect style employs in representing Winterbourne's thinking. "Unspotted flower" is a sentimental cliché heightening the literary self-consciousness of the passage, and it should have the same quotation-marks about it as "lawless passions." (It is an addition of the New York Edition text. The 1878 text has in its place "a perfectly well-conducted young lady," 27.) The tale Winterbourne's imagination "writes" for Daisy is vulgar romance. James's reference to literary or sub-literary tradition is, of course, an explicit reflexiveness by the writer who understood the uses of such language in the popular literature of the day. "Daisy Miller" may have been suggested to James, in fact, not only by his own observation but by a forgotten novel by a Swiss writer, Victor Cherbuliez, whose *Paule Méré* (1864) James summarized as "a tale expressly to prove that frank nature is out of favor (in Geneva), and his heroine dies of a broken heart because her spontaneity passes for impropriety.[13] Translated into English, Cherbuliez's novel had attained the kind of popularity that James might have envied for himself, while his own ironic version of it distanced itself from the model and its sentimental typology.[14]

At Mrs. Walker's party Winterbourne tries to fit his concepts of "flirt" and "nice girl" to Daisy, who conflates them; "I'm a fearful frightful flirt! Did you ever hear of a nice girl that wasn't?" In the face of this cynicism he collapses into a more cynical gallantry, "You're a very nice girl, but I wish you'd flirt with me, and me only," only to be told, "You're the last man I should think of flirting with" (XVIII:71). Winterbourne decides that "she was nothing every way if not light" (XVIII:75), this word implying the sexual sense of a wanton, a "light woman" along with its overt meaning simply of "unserious."

His interest reaches a new stage of ease, quite free of tension despite the constant presence of the Italian admirer who turns out to be "a perfectly respectable little man" (XVIII:77), a *cavaliere avvocato*—not really, at all, the "type" Winterbourne had earlier identified. Daisy has quite ruined her reputation with the Anglo-American colony; Mrs. Walker has turned her back on her, and all the others close their doors. Winterbourne still insists that she is "du meilleur monde" (XVIII:79), and holds on, with forced gallantry, to the idea of her "innocence." He alternates between thinking her childishly oblivious of the effect she is producing and, insisting on a category, thinking her "a young person of the reckless class," whatever that is. The narrator, obtruding once more, remarks, "As I have already had occasion to relate, he was reduced without pleasure to this chopping of logic and vexed at his poor fallibility, his want of instinctive certitude as to how far her extravagance was generic and national and how far it was crudely personal" (XVIII:81).

Daisy, however, gives him little help. When he meets her one day with Giovanelli in the Palace of the Caesars, he tries to make her understand how people regard her and mentions that her mother thinks she is engaged. Her response is perversely teasing. She is— but if he really believes it—she isn't! And then, a week later, he finds her taking the night air with her companion in the Colosseum. His struggles of definition are over; his relief is total.

> Winterbourne felt himself pulled up with final horror now—and, it must be added, with final relief. It was as if a sudden clearance had taken place in the ambiguity of the poor girl's appearances and the whole riddle of her contradictions had grown easy to read. She was a young lady about the *shades* of whose perversity a foolish puzzled gentleman need no longer trouble his head or his heart. That once questionable quantity *had* no shades—it was a mere black little blot. He stood looking at her, looking at her companion too, and not reflecting that though he saw them vaguely he himself must have been more brightly presented. He felt angry at all his shiftings of view—he felt ashamed of all his tender little scruples and all his witless little mercies. He was about to advance again, and then again checked himself; not from the fear of doing her injustice, but from the sense of the danger of showing undue exhilaration for this disburdenment of cautious criticism.   (XVIII:86)

The passage is remarkable for its exposure of the meaning of Winterbourne's enterprise—the establishment of that certainty which Daisy has so far managed to resist. And it is he who is "more brightly presented" by the episode than is Daisy. She calls him "stiff," as she has already done several times before—"it had always been her great word." He *is* stiff as the sides of a pigeon-hole are stiff, stiff as the inflexible categories which govern his thinking. The third sentence of the passage just quoted, with its emphasis, again, upon Winterbourne's compulsion to define and classify, is the alteration of the New York Edition from the earlier, "She was a young lady whom a gentleman need no longer be at pains to respect" (37). Having placed her, all secondary questions are futile: it makes very little difference, he tells her, whether or not she is engaged. Dying, she will send him the message that she had never been engaged to Giovanelli "but as Winterbourne had originally judged, the truth on this question had small actual relevance" (XVIII:91).

At the Colosseum, he decides not to "cut her dead" but instead threatens her with literal death—the Roman fever which she imprudently risks. Daisy's response suggests either that she is a silly fool or that her romantic desire to "see the Colosseum by moonlight" (or as it is described in the famous passage from *Manfred* which Winterbourne had been murmuring to himself just a few moments earlier) is a better thing than his prudence. That she may feel for Winterbourne himself, despite his stiffness, a romantic emotion suitable to the context of the moonlight and Byron, one that he wounds by his own harshness, is suggested by the suicidal (or is it merely petulant?) quality of her last remark, "I don't care whether I have Roman fever or not!" (XVIII:89). If this is so, she is one of those feminine characters—who appear early and late in James—whose capacity for love is unperceived or unvalued by a colder (a "winter-born") man; she is, then, cousin to Tina Bordereau of "The Aspern Papers" and May Bartram of "The Beast in the Jungle." Her own death-defying extravagance is itself a romantic expression of the passion of a character who desires, at whatever cost, to preserve the potentiality of her own being, something denied by Winterbourne's compulsion to "read . . . the riddle of her contradictions."

That Daisy dies so romantically as to be a martyr to her own faith in an unconfined selfhood seems too large a claim—and James undermines our readiness to give her such grand proportions by making her literally the victim of imprudence, of a disease still not understood to be conveyed by a nocturnal insect but correctly associated with the dangerous air of summer nights in nineteenth-century Rome. Yet her posture in the arena where Christian martyrs had died before her is not entirely an ironic touch. Her individuality, such as it is, is doomed by Winterbourne's decision to "cut her dead" and the stiff box into which his categorical mind has thrust her is in effect a coffin.

But the interpretive contest that has seemingly come to rest at last is not really over. There is Giovanelli's declaration at Daisy's grave, "She was the most beautiful young lady I ever saw, and the most amiable . . . Also . . . the most innocent" (XVIII:92). So she lingers in Winterbourne's mind—if not in his heart: he "often thought of the most interesting member of that [Miller family] trio—of her mystifying manner and her queer adventure," and even confesses to his aunt that he may have done her an injustice—"she would have appreciated one's esteem." Mrs. Costello, taking the measure of his erotic regret, says that this means merely that "she would have reciprocated one's affection" (XVIII:93), but Winterbourne's view of Daisy may not be so simple any longer, and it is on no certain closure of conviction that the story ends. Few readers notice the slippage that has taken place in his final observation to his aunt, "You were right in that remark you made to me last summer. I was booked to make a mistake. I've lived too long in foreign parts" (XVIII:93). But the mistake she had predicted was quite the opposite of the one he may be admitting now. When, at the outset, she warned, "You've lived too long out of the country. You'll be sure to make some great mistake" (XVIII:25–26), it was because he seemed, then, to be inclined to think too well of Daisy rather than too ill. But James does not make this explicit, preferring the ambiguity of his close. He wrote a reviewer of "Daisy Miller", "Nothing is my *last* word about anything—I am interminably super-subtle and analytic."[15]

Washington Square

When Catherine Sloper is twelve years old, her father says to his sister Mrs. Penniman, "Try and make a clever woman of her, Lavinia," to which that lady rejoins, "My dear Austin, do you think it is better to be clever than to be good?" The doctor answers her, "Good for what? You are good for nothing unless you are clever" (8). In dismissing any but a utilitarian sense of "good," the doctor does no injury to Mrs. Penniman, for her reference to goodness as a higher value is, like nearly everything she says, affectation. From her brother's assertion, James writes, she "saw no reason to dissent; she possibly reflected that her own great use in the world was owing to her aptitude for many things" (9).

Indeed, good—and its opposite, evil—are not significant terms in *Washington Square.* "Clever," on the other hand, is a term of significance—suggesting abilities in the direction of conceptualization, analysis, and expression, which Catherine signally lacks. It carries with it also the connotation of artifice, and its opposite is "natural." "You are so natural," Catherine's lover says to her, making a true statement which associates her with the romantic idea of Nature— that which has not been reduced to human uses by man's cleverness; what is "natural" has not been made "good for" some utilitarian end but simply exists in its own being. After making his statement about Catherine, Townsend adds dishonestly, "I am natural myself" (33). But, actually, like Catherine's father, he is clever—that is, unnatural, unspontaneous, insincere, with a well-developed sense of the uses of things.

Catherine "grew up peacefully and prosperously; but at the age of eighteen Mrs. Penniman had not made a clever woman of her" (10). Does this mean that she is stupid, as many readers have supposed? Early in the story we suspect that both her father and her aunt misjudge her intelligence. Her father thinks that Catherine is incapable of seeing through Mrs. Penniman, but she "saw her all at once, as it were, and was not dazzled by the apparition" (11). Without any sort of style herself she is protected by her failure to appreciate her aunt's. In being natural rather than clever, she is also without the ability to compose fictions. She is described as being "addicted to speaking the truth" (10). Balzac's heroine unhesitatingly and expertly deceives her father without arousing any criticism in the reader, who knows that she is not only good, but pious, whereas her father is an irreligious miser. No odor of formal piety clings to Catherine, who is simply "incapable of elaborate artifice" (29); when her situation does lead her into some dissimulation, the narrator ironically notes the first and then the second time in her life that she makes "an indirect answer" (22).

Mrs. Penniman is all indirection, all airs and arts, none of them very high in quality; her speech and her behavior constantly blossom forth in dusty paper blooms of rhetoric, secondhand and second-rate histrionic gestures. She has "a taste for light literature"

(9) and is forever at work composing trite narrative. She is the widow of a poor clergyman with a "sickly constitution and a flowery style of eloquence . . . a certain vague aroma of which hovered about her own conversation" (7); perhaps she learned both futility and floridity from him. Her affectation is quite the poorest in quality among the styles of pretense surrounding her. Indeed, she has the effect of compelling her fellow stylists to cast aside their own mannerisms in their irritation at hers, adopting a temporary tone of savage plainness, as when she tells Townsend that Dr. Sloper is "impervious to pity"—employing language belonging to popular romance—and the young man harshly simplifies, "Do you mean that he won't come round?" (84).

About Morris Townsend the conventional question, of course, is, "Is he sincere?" In his two interviews with the young man and in his conversation with Townsend's sister, Mrs. Montgomery, Dr. Sloper establishes that the answer to this question is no; Morris is a fortune hunter. James has his jest, however, with the varied senses of sincere, an idea which might be thought to be equivalent to Catherine's naturalness. Says Mrs. Almond, Dr. Sloper's other, more sensible, sister, "I don't see why you should be incredulous. It seems to me that you have never done Catherine justice. You must remember that she has the prospect of thirty thousand a year." Mrs. Almond chooses to ignore the assumption that a suitor's sincerity means that he loves a girl for herself alone—Townsend is as interested as he appears to be, though for reasons other than Catherine's charms. The doctor comments on the clear fact that his daughter has been, till now, "absolutely unattractive" to young men—which makes him realize, he says, that the young men of New York are "very disinterested. They prefer pretty girls—lively girls—girls like your own." "If our young men appear disinterested," Mrs. Almond responds, "it is because they marry, as a general thing, so young, before twenty-five, at the age of innocence and sincerity, before the age of calculation (36-37). In Townsend, then, one has a man who has put such youthful "sincerity" behind him and is a finished example of the sincerity of calculation. As such he is a clever man, though unlike Dr. Sloper he will be a failure, neither making his fortune nor gaining his heiress. "I suppose you can't be too clever," Catherine humbly remarks to Townsend's cousin Arthur. And that alert young New Yorker replies, "I don't know. I know some people that call my cousin too clever" (27).

Dr. Sloper, of course, is "the cleverest of men" (10), as his daughter thinks him, cleverer than Morris Townsend. It is only ultimately that we realize that even he was too clever—or else that life can provide surprises beyond the calculation of the cleverest. Like all whose analyses of others' characters and probable fate is generally correct, he seemingly ran only one risk, that of boredom— things so often turned out as he anticipated; his narrative anticipations were too readily fullfilled. As a man one may imagine that he is particularly provoked by the paradox that he thinks he knows exactly how a woman, whatever her "type," will behave—and is wearied of the limited interest consequent upon such certainty. At the heart of sexist certainty lurks the ennui which provokes a certain longing for doubt. Confident that he understands perfectly his daughter's character by the time she is eighteen and knows that she is "incapable of giving surprises," he allows for a remotely possible diversion. "I expect nothing," he says, "so that if she gives me a surprise, it will be all clear gain" (12). The irony of the plot, which is outside his own ironic perspective (and refutes it), is that his daughter *will* surprise him by writing her own history—and he will not enjoy it. The mind that desired some teasing resistence—as in love-making—to its own conventional view of the female subject is really not able to accommodate a total refutation.

This dramatic outcome also expresses a literary view of life, which is given form and entertainment value by the element of surprise, particularly in the ending, which just barely escapes being a cheap and melodramatic surprise through the richness of James's handling. Dr. Sloper's taste for surprise is aesthetic; he expects that experience can be made to conform to his formal expectations, allowing for the unexpected in discreet amounts that do not threaten the genre, like a permitted element of the natural in a certain kind of classic garden plan or like a novel which conforms to a familiar plot despite some minor unpredictability. In the character of the doctor as a reader of stories we see the internalized representation of a conventional reader who, because of the revisionism of the plot, is in for "rude" surprises. Catherine's surprises seem to Dr. Sloper to be disruptive of the story he expects, without giving pleasure. Upon discovering the obstinacy of her attachment to Morris Townsend, he tells Mrs. Almond, "At first I had a good deal of . . . genial curiosity about it; I wanted to see if she really would stick. But, good Lord, one's curiosity is satisfied! I see she is capable of it, and now she can let go" (140). He has forgotten that life has surprised him before by his wife's early death and by the birth of his daughter when he had lost a son.

In his predictions of others, however, he is generally correct. Though he is "very curious to see whether Catherine might really be loved for her moral worth" (38), he is correct in anticipating that she will not be appreciated. He is correct in his analysis of Townsend's character and of how he will behave if his hopes are disappointed. He is even correct about his own death, which he describes exactly as it comes to pass, though instructing his daughter to nurse him "on the optimistic hypothesis" (177). His conclusions seem to him comparable to the discoveries of mathematics. "Shall you not relent?" Mrs. Almond asks him. "Shall a geometrical proposition relent? I am not so superficial" (109), he answers her. James had already, in *The Europeans*, described Robert Acton as fond of mathematics and inclined to find Eugenia Young's behavior "as interesting as the factors in an Algebraic problem,"[16] identifying in this observer a coldly analytic quality. As I have noted earlier, one may also suspect James's self-reflexiveness in this image, which echoes the passage in which he compares the art of the writer of fiction to a "geometry" by which the endless continuities or "relations" of life may be made to seem to have an ending within the circle of the literary work. If this suspicion is justified, one may conclude that James is willing to admit that art is arbitrary and sometimes cruel in its imposition of design. Sloper's very glance is expressive of his mind; we hear of his "clear eyes," his "cold quiet reasonable eye" (22, 59). Only when, in the terrifying scene with his daughter in the Alps, he is forced to declare, "Though I am very smooth externally, at bottom I am very passionate" (125), do we suspect the wild "nature" beneath his civilization.

Meanwhile, he exhibits an intellect which endows its possessor with such foresight that it naturally results in irony, the consequence always, as I have remarked, of narrative foreknowledge. But not only does he see life ironically, from the point of view of superior prescience, but his characteristic style of speech is that of a man accustomed to express his meaning by ironic indirection, even sarcasm—styles which imply a context which enables one to read a statement as part of a larger whole which negates it. In this, he represents the reader, who thinks, also, at this point, that he sees through everything and to the end of everything long before the bemused Catherine. When Catherine appears in her showy red dress at the party at which she meets Townsend, her father exclaims, "Is it possible that this magnificent person is my child?" Catherine's dress is a metaphor for a personal style which, as her father accurately recognizes, does not suit her. But his question is rhetorical in the worst sense. He has used the weapon of language against the defenseless girl, pointing out, justly enough, the ludicrousness of her attire awhile ignoring the message in her inept effort to please. "It is a literal fact," we are told at this point, "that he almost never addressed his daughter save in the ironical form" (22). It is irony, of course, that makes words change their meaning to their opposites—and the time may come when the reader will be surprised to discover a certain "magnificence" in Catherine. But Sloper is himself so invariable that we can think of him as destined to remain locked within his character as ironist.

As I have so far been indicating, *Washington Square* is all about language, and one could say that the principal players in its verbal drama are such *words* as "clever," "natural," or "sincere," which change their roles in the contest of rhetoric conducted by the characters. It is obvious that each of the characters in *Washington Square* is made known to us by his or her habitual mode of expression, and Catherine's plain style is constantly drawn into verbal and enacted contrast with varieties of "clever" speech and behavior. The passage just quoted continues in the metaphor of dressmaking as though the things that people do or say are made out of yard goods, since "style is the man": "Whenever he addressed her he gave her pleasure; but she had to cut her pleasure out of the piece, as it were. There were portions left over, light remnants and snippets of irony, which she never knew what to do with, which seemed too delicate for her own use" (22). In her humility, Catherine acknowledges her inability to wear the garmet of irony. Of her actual taste in dress, the narrator remarks earlier, "Her great indulgence of it was really the desire of a rather inarticulate nature to manifest itself; she sought to be eloquent in her garments, and to make up for her diffidence of speech by a fine frankness of costume. But if she expressed herself in her clothes, it is certain that people were not to blame for not thinking her a witty person" (13). To this misrepresenting "eloquence," this misplaced "wit"—and verbal rhetoric here is explicitly identified with behavior—her father responds with his superior ironic style, as we have seen. "You are sumptuous, opulent, expensive," he continues. "You look as if you had eighty thousand a year." To which Catherine "illogically" replies, "Well so long as I haven't—". Her father, correcting her, snaps, "So long as you haven't you shouldn't look as if you had" (22)—for that is not the pretension he values, though all style is, essentially, pretension.

Catherine's awkward show, a child's "dressing up," is harmless, unlike Dr. Sloper's. It is the latter that is chastised in *Washington Square,* an ironic account of the discomfiture of an ironist. The narrator tells us early: "He desired experience, and in the course of twenty years he got a great deal. It must be added that it came to him in some forms which, whatever might have been their intrinsic value, made it the reverse of welcome." The "irony of fate" and the narrative tone are at one in the revelation of the death of wife and son. "For a man whose trade was to keep people alive he had certainly done poorly in his own family." The world "pitied him too much to be ironical" (5), an indulgence he did not learn from. Later, he is given no quarter when Catherine refuses to tell him the truth about her rupture with her lover. "It was his punishment that he never knew," says the narrator, "his punishment, I mean, for the abuse of sarcasm in his relations with his daughter. There was a good deal of effective sarcasm in her keeping him in the dark, and the rest of the world conspired with her, in this sense, to be sarcastic" (169). Sarcasm, it should be noted, is here both rhetoric and behavior. To be sarcastic, significantly, Catherine does not have to speak at all; she has only to keep still.

In addition to the four characters I have discussed, there is a fifth who is of importance in this testing of styles. This is the narrator. Though the narrator is, of course, far from the developed central consciousness which James later preferred, he serves as a center, particularly because the chief character, Catherine, is incapable of that reflexive function herself. As he tells her story he has in some degree the experience of it, like some of James's more developed narrating consciousnesses. I have hesitated to call him James, but one may justifiably identify this anonymous voice with the writer, and not merely because of the frequent use of first-person voice and small turns of expression here and there, marking him as a personalized narrator with assumed authorial identity. An interpolation in the third chapter identifies this persona as Jamesian. "I know not whether it is owing to the tenderness of early associations, but this portion of New York appears to many persons the most delectable"—these words begin a description of the Washington Square of "forty years ago," the time of James's own infancy. The many persons soon become a particular one. "It was here that your grandmother lived . . . it was here that you took your first walks abroad." "You" remembers the odor of ailanthus trees and his first school kept by "a broad-bosomed, broad-based old lady with a ferule" (15–16). The "topographical parenthesis," for which the narrator apologizes, resurrects an image of James's New York childhood.[17]

This "parenthesis" functions much as do the Geneva associations of Winterbourne and, as will later be seen, Isabel Archer's Albany childhood, to insert an autobiographical element into the story. It suggests, as the other examples do, that the writer is himself involved in the tale, even though no effort is made at pseudo-realistic claims—such as that the narrator had known the Slopers or heard their story. As I have noted in the case of "Daisy Miller," such an identification with the author reinforces a thematic emphasis upon the artist's own role as the creater of "character" and "story" and "style"—at the same time that such activity is to be seen in the events of the story. Like his characters, the narrator is subject to the temptations of art—its violation of life's essential formlessness and mystery. He borrows method and language from the stylists he describes until, like someone learning from experience, he casts these aside.

His language takes little or no cue from the shabby artifice of Mrs. Penniman, except in a direct, mocking simulation of her thought, but it should be noted that her theatricality is underscored by the narrator's own references to the theater. It may be that the theatrical character of Mrs. Penniman was suggested to James by the fact that the anecdote on which he had based his story had been told to him by an actress, Fanny Kemble, whose brother was the real-life Townsend.[18] But in describing Catherine's manipulative aunt as setting scenes, assuming roles, and drawing curtains, she is made to represent not an actress but a theatrical director. She also resembles the novelist, who is the director of his created company, and the narrator, who is his surrogate. Novelist and narrator borrow her style in a nonverbal sense. Presenting a drama of melodramatic design with successive scenes that have a tableau quality, the act of narrative composition is parodied by the romantic melodramatist within the story.

But the narrator's tone is closer to Dr. Sloper's than to Mrs. Pen-

niman's. The doctor's categorizing instinct and sense of probabili-
ties are those of a novelist who admires Balzac. "You belong to the
wrong category," Sloper tells Townsend, who protests, "Your
daughter doesn't marry a category, she marries an individual." The
categorizer wins; Townsend's claim of individuality is a lie. "I turn
to our category again. Even with that solemn vow on your lips you
take your place in it" (63–64), says Sloper. The narrator possesses a
similar perception of the typical. He begins, as we have seen, by
locating Dr. Sloper in a world of conditions making for type, and
proceeds similarly with other characters in turn. The narrator imi-
tates Dr. Sloper's ironic wit, and uses it even against its own representative. Since the narrator is the doctor's double he comments not
only upon the doctor, therefore, but reflexively upon himself.

Eventually the narrator moves from these models, and his voice,
particularly when he speaks of Catherine, becomes more and more
sober, plain, unmocking. One object compels his respect, and that is
Catherine's love.

> The girl was very happy. She knew not as yet what would come of
> it; but the present had suddenly grown rich and solemn. If she had
> been told that she was in love, she would have been a good deal
> surprised; for she had an idea that love was an eager and exacting
> passion, and her own heart was filled in these days with the
> impulse of self-effacement and sacrifice. Whenever Morris
> Townsend had left the house, her imagination projected itself,
> with all its strength, into the idea of his soon coming back; but if
> she had been told at such a moment that he would not return for a
> year, or even that he would never return, she would not have
> complained nor rebelled, but would have humbly accepted the
> decree, and sought for consolation in thinking over the times she
> had already seen him, the words he had spoken, the sound of his
> voice, of his tread, the expression of his face. Love demands cer-
> tain things as a right; but Catherine had no sense of her rights; she
> had only a consciousness of immense and unexpected
> favors. (42)

Let us now look more sequentially at her history as it is given
form by these willful stylists until she takes it out of their hands. To
father, aunt, and lover the situation assumes at the outset the character of a play—sentimental melodrama to Mrs. Penniman, satiric
comedy to Dr. Sloper, and to Townsend something of each genre by
turns. The doctor "went so far as to promise himself some enter-

tainment from the little drama . . . of which Mrs. Penniman desired
to represent the ingenious Mr. Townsend as the hero. He had no
intention, as yet, of regulating the dénouement" (38). After their
first encounter at dinner Morris realizes, however, that Catherine's
father dislikes him. He reports this to her, but she fails to utter the
expected lines: "If my father doesn't think well of you, what does it
matter?"—lines from the play, one might put it, he is writing, a trite
plot he is urging upon the narrative. Mrs. Penniman, however,
promptly says them; she is a practiced lady of the theater. Catherine, who has no theatrical sense at all, only exclaims, aborting
such a story, "Ah, but it would matter" (40).

Dr. Sloper has made up his mind on the basis of "thirty years of
observation," and recognizes a familiar type. "He is a plausible cox-
comb" (41), he says, as though life were the Restoration stage, or as
though diagnosing a "case" of a kind familiar in his medical practice. Townsend's circumstances—he has already wasted his inheritance and is now without prospects—automatically condemn him.
Sloper "had passed his life in estimating people (it was part of the
medical trade), and in nineteen cases out of twenty he was right"
(68). Perhaps Townsend is the twentieth case, Mrs. Almond suggests, whereupon the doctor confirms his view by interrogating the
young man's sister.

Mrs. Penniman, meanwhile, proceeds to mount her own play,
for, as we know, she

> delighted of all things in a drama . . . Combining as she did the
> zeal of the prompter with the impatience of the spectator, she had
> long since done her utmost to pull up the curtain. She, too,
> expected to figure in the performance—to be the confidant, the
> Chorus, to speak the epilogue. It may even be said that there were
> times when she lost sight altogether of the modest heroine of the
> play, in the contemplation of certain great scenes which would
> naturally occur between the hero and herself.   (53-54)

She is impatient with Catherine, who is not even sulky ("a style of
behavior for which she had too little histrionic talent," 79), and,
"pervaded by an earnest desire that Catherine should do something
striking," she "wished the plot to thicken." She longed for the girl
to "make a secret marriage" to be performed in some "subterranean
chapel" and for the "guilty couple" to be lodged in the suburbs
where she could visit them "in a thick veil." Eventually she would

effect Dr. Sloper's relenting "in an artistic tableau, in which she herself should be somehow the central figure" (81–82).

Dr. Sloper has sharp words for her interference and ready scorn for her banal histrionic notions. Yet he, too, begins to exhibit behavior which may be deemed melodramatic, as though, by some Gresham's law, melodrama has driven out the better money of his irony. When he understands that Catherine does not intend to give Townsend up, he says, "You can wait till I die, if you like . . . Your engagement will have one delightful effect upon you; it will make you extremely impatient for that event." The tone of this remark involves both sarcastic and melodramatic distortion. It is logical and untrue. And Catherine, who has only her simplicity to oppose to it, is unable to reply. "It came to Catherine with the force—or rather with the vague impressiveness—of a logical axiom which it was not in her province to controvert; and yet, though it was a scientific truth, she felt wholly unable to accept it" (97). Her geometer-father then concludes with a declaration that is purely melodramatic: "If you see him, you will be an ungrateful, cruel child; you will have given your old father the greatest pain of his life" (99). After this she passes a night of weeping but, to her aunt's annoyance, descends to breakfast with undiminished bloom on her healthy cheeks. She has no sense of her role and shows no sign of having "lain quivering beneath a father's curse" (the narrator's free indirect style again parodies Mrs. Penniman's melodramatic clichés. She was "really too modest for consistent pathos" (102).

When Catherine wants time to convince her father of her lover's worth, Townsend, who is thinking of a runaway marriage (one of the hackneyed plots of which his head has a store), accuses *her*, "You are not sincere" (105). Of course, the *pose* of sincerity is in his own repertoire. And Mrs. Penniman claims sincerity when she offers him advice, the reverse of her former counsel, and he asks, "Will you come to me next week and recommend something different and equally sincere?" (111). So the situation in Washington Square stands still. Mrs. Penniman "elaborately reserved" (115) and silent—alert to the demands of literary form—has, of the little group, "most of the manner that belongs to a great crisis," while Catherine, going about her daily occupations, "was quietly quiet . . . her pathetic effects, which there was no one to notice, were entirely unstudied and unintended" (114).

Then Dr. Sloper takes his daughter to Europe for six months so that she may forget her lover—the standard treatment for infatuated girls, a history that should have a narrative consequence as certain as one of his medical prescriptions. And Townsend, in parting, suggests (proposing an alternate expectable story, appropriate to the romantic settings before which he sees her posed with her father) that she try "among beautiful scenes and noble monuments" to "be a little clever about it and touch the right chord," and bring Dr. Sloper around. But still Catherine commands no art: "The idea of being 'clever' in a gondola by moonlight appeared to her to involve elements of which her grasp was not active" (120).

Truth bursts from its disguises finally against a background more stern and majestic than a gondola by moonlight—a lonely alpine pass which the narrator describes with a grave sobriety. When Dr. Sloper discloses the cruelty and possessiveness behind his former coolness, Catherine even recedes a step from him in fear, almost ready to say to herself "that it might be part of his plan to fasten his hand—the neat fine supple hand of a distinguished physician—in her throat." James's language gives us an hallucinatory glimpse of the physician's hand—like the writer's writing hand the instrument of his accomplished mind—in the act of murder. "Should you like to be left in such a place as this, to starve?" he says next, and the girl is certain that he proposes to abandon her until he adds, "That's how he will leave you," referring to Townsend.

When the doctor admits, "I am not a very good man," the fairy-tale king is revealed as being wicked and not merely witty. But to his daughter even this confession proves only that he is too clever for her simplicity. "Such a saying as that was a part of his great subtlety—men so clever as he might say anything or mean anything." It is clear that she does not understand that her father has for once resorted to her own style and spoken without indirection. Catherine, who has been schooled to expect only deliberated rhetoric from others, wonders at his intention. When he says, truly, "I can be very hard," she replies, "I am sure you can be anything you please," as though insisting on regarding his behavior as a style which can be this or that, under the command of the will. There is an irony, unnoticed by either the ironist or his constant subject, in his statement, "You ought to know what I am" (125–126), for she has never been permitted to recognize his undissimulated core.

Yet the brutality of Dr. Sloper's cleverness and the mendaciousness of Mrs. Penniman's theatricality continue to expose themselves, and now violence erupts into the doctor's very language. "If she doesn't let go, she will be shaken off—sent tumbling into the dust" (140), he exclaims to Mrs. Almond. Mrs. Penniman, having spent the previous months entertaining Morris Townsend in Washington Square, reveals, despite the narrator's ironic circumspection, the sexual motive behind her roles of confidante and intercessor. We are permitted to give an erotic meaning to the discovery that her "romantic interest in this attractive and unfortunate young man" (141), however maternal, was such as to supplant her duty of maternal protection for Catherine. She is ready to betray her niece, and she agrees to take Catherine down, ease Townsend off, stipulating only, "Ah, but you must have your last parting!" (148), as she holds by the merest ribbon the nearly dropped garment of theatrical disguise.

When Catherine realizes her abandonment it is entirely private; she gives no sign, though Mrs. Penniman scents out melodrama and receives, for her intrusive comfort, her niece's challenge, "Is it you, then, that has changed him and made him so unnatural?" (162). Of course, Townsend has always been unnatural. It is only she who has ever been natural among these clever persons. It is appropriate that Townsend's parting attitude should be expressed in a letter which is an example of the deceits of rhetoric. It "was beautifully written, and Catherine, who kept it for many years after this, was able, when her sense of the bitterness of its meaning and the hollowness of its tone had grown less acute, to admire its grace of expression" (166).

Though she cannot herself utilize rhetoric she can be silent with the father who now desires, in vain, to know *her* truth. He had called her a "plain, inanimate girl" (47) in earlier days, and now she rewards him for regarding her as a mere stone by being as immovable as one and as voiceless. In the end he is reduced to supposing her to be a well of deception, the "vilest of hypocrites" (171)—the antirhetoric of her silence is incomprehensible to him, and he comes to believe his earlier histrionic outburst, which had invited her to wait for his death. He tries to get her to promise that she will not marry Townsend after his death—and she refuses. But he does not live to be surprised by the final scene of Townsend's return. The "most beautiful young man in the world," now fat and bald, a manifest failure, his very appearance proven only a passing rhetorical flourish, has returned. Aunt Lavinia is present to draw the curtain and prompt the actors. But Catherine, her simplicity having emerged as more profound than their cleverness, leaves them to interpret vainly the mystery of her refusal.

She also leaves that mystery to the contemplation of the invisible participant who records, "Catherine, meanwhile, in the parlor, picking up her morsel of fancy-work, had seated herself with it again—for life as it were" (189). In the end it is she who has given a form to her life, imposed style upon it in making her own ending. It is she who writes her own modest story, her "morsel of *fancy-work*," the work of her own plain nature which has refused the designs of others. But this last sentence may also express the restrictedness of the mere morsel of life on which she is permitted to work her own design; in James's favorite image of art as needle-work—that tapestry woven upon a canvas with infinite perforations for the needle—this creativity is the most insignificant of embroideries.

In so meager a triumph it is possible to see even less than James intended. That Catherine has preferred to embrace the destiny of an old maid, refusing not only Townsend but other quite plausible suitors—a widower of "a genial temperament," a clever young lawyer who "was seriously in love with her" and shrewd enough to appreciate her qualities—suitors who might have consoled her— her father explains by the suspicion that she is waiting for Townsend's return. It is hard for him to accept the fact that she has made singleness a positive choice: "Limited as her intelligence may be, she must understand perfectly well that she is made to do the usual thing," he grumbles. Her final refusal of Townsend ultimately may seem a conventional sentimental ending; Catherine's "broken heart" can never be mended, or as the narrator, invoking trite pathos by his parodic language, puts it, "From her own point of view the great facts of her career were that Morris Townsend had trifled with her affection, and that her father had broken its spring. Nothing could ever alter these facts; they were always there, like her name, her age, her plain face." The phrase "trifled with her affection" belongs to the context of sentimental pathos, which offers as a model the history of the wronged female martyr who must die unconsoled or live the living death of a lonely recluse ("there was something dead in her life"; 173). James's ending would seem to conform to the sentimental platitude that not to marry is the tragic aborting of female destiny.

But there are signs in the text that point another way. She

became, we are told, "an admirable old maid"—neither pitiable nor ridiculous—and though nothing could undo the pain both Townsend and her father had inflicted, she "had a great disapproval of brooding and moping." Her public history became one of mild social participations, much charity, and the role of "kindly maiden-aunt" to the young, who unfolded themselves to this gentle nature "as they never did to Mrs. Penniman" (173), that odious image of the man-less woman as perverted meddler. That she continued to live in her father's house after his death, "in spite of its being represented to her that a maiden lady of quiet habits might find a more convenient abode in one of the smaller dwellings, with brown stone fronts, which had at this time begun to adorn the transverse thoroughfares in the upper part of the town" (179–180), may seem to signify that she is still enclosed in her father's will;[19] but it can be taken to signify simply that she refuses to consider herself diminished by her single life—she likes the old house and the fact that its spaciousness protects her from "closer quarters with her aunt."

Her morsel of fancy-work thus has a greater dignity, after all, than Mrs. Penniman's preposterous embroidery of plot (again, James's metaphor for story-telling). Unlike Catherine, Mrs. Penniman has hardly known what to make of the leisure of the passing years, the blank spread of canvas: "The elder lady hardly knew what use to make of this larger margin of her life; she sat and looked at it very much as she had often sat, with her poised needle in her hand, before her tapestry-frame. She had a confident hope, however, that her rich impulses, her talent for embroidery, would still find their application" (179). This confidence seemed justified upon Morris' return, only to be refuted by Catherine's plain art.

· 3 ·

Isabel Archer
and the Affronting of Plot

IN JAMES'S succession of heroines Isabel Archer sums up and goes beyond Daisy Miller and Catherine Sloper as the one who most profoundly explores the policy of resistance to social and narrational expectations—the conventions of character which the culture would impose upon her, the role which life, as well as literature, seems to insist must be the outcome of her selfhood. James spoke of her in his 1908 preface as "affronting her destiny" (2:1076), and his peculiar choice of word has not been sufficiently remarked upon; he did not mean simply that she *con*fronted or faced up to her destiny but that she hostilely defied it, slapped it in the face. Yet she is a more interesting figure than Daisy or Catherine, whose silent, immobile tenacity of pure being is all they have. As they are victimized by—yet resist—the story-making of others, so is and does she; but she is, in addition, the victim of her own romantic expectation of some unforeseeable state when all that she feels herself to be might find adequate outcome. Fortified against a commonplace, foreseeable future, she still does not succeed in finding the enactment, the history that would bring this finer state about. This failure makes her more tragic than the earlier heroines, who suffer only at the hands—or minds—of others.

It is possible to think of her as a character in search of its plot. We can thus identify her in a primary way with the writer, who conceived her, he recalled, as a "detached character." His novel had not originated in a suggestion of events for which he imagined the actors.

> I see that it must have consisted not at all in any conceit of a "plot," nefarious name, in any flash, upon the fancy, of a set of relations, or in any one of those situations that, by a logic of their

80

own, immediately fall, for the fabulist, into movement, into a
march or a rush, a patter of quick steps; but altogether in the sense
of a single character, the character and aspect of a particular
engaging young woman, to which the usual elements of a "subject," certainly of a setting, were to be superadded. (2:1071)

That plot should be "nefarious" is as peculiar, perhaps, as the idea
that a character should "affront" its destiny. As he recalls the way
his novel grew from its "germ" of character, how he sought out its
plot, as the imagined person herself would do, James seems to think
of plot as threatening as well as promising fulfillment of that first
conception. Turgenev had told James that his own stories always
originated in

> the vision of some person or persons, who hovered before him,
> soliciting him, as the active or passive figure, interesting him and
> appealing to him just as they were and by what they were. He saw
> them, in that fashion, as *disponibles,* saw them subject to the
> chances, the complications of existence, and saw them vividly, but
> then had to find for them the right relations, those that would
> most bring them out; to imagine, to invent and select and piece
> together the situations most useful and favourable to the sense of
> the creatures themselves, the complications they would be most
> likely to produce and to feel. (2:1072)

The result of such an effort, Turgenev had admitted, was still that he
was "often accused of not having 'story' enough." Yet he protested,
James remembered, by saying,

> I seem to myself to have as much as I need—to show my people,
> to exhibit their relations with each other; for that is all my mea-
> sure. If I watch them long enough I see them come together, I see
> them *placed,* I see them engaged in this or that act and in this or
> that difficulty. How they look and move and speak and behave,
> always in the setting I have found for them, is my account of
> them—of which I dare say, alas, *que cela manque souvent
> d'architecture.* (2:1072)

James claims to take "higher warrant" from Turgenev for his own
habit of being, as he said, "so much more antecedently conscious of
my figures than of their setting . . . I might envy, though I couldn't
emulate, the imaginative writer so constituted as to see his fable first
and to make out its agents afterwards" (2:1073). One might suspect

some disingenuousness here. A good many of James's stories, as his notebooks show, started from an anecdote, a whisp of *plot,* for which he then had to imagine the actors. But the idea of a discrepancy between character and story—a technical problem on the one hand—is profoundly thematic also. It is related to the way James conceives the experience of his heroine, but also to the way in which he finds himself forced to look at all human attempts to bring into relation the claim of personal essence and a design of life which validates it to itself and to the world. From one point of view the result of the author's search for a story that will fully express such a heroine is only in part successful, as her search for role is also frustrated, and even self-frustrated. At the same time, the negativity that marks her career, her profound distrust of offered roles, is both an acceptance of personal defeat and the writer's renunciation of story in its traditional sense.

James does not acknowledge, however, any renunciation of the "architecture" of narrative, though others might say his stories lacked it, as was said of Turgenev's. In "The Art of Fiction," his only extended statement of general principles,[1] James declared the equality and inseperability of "incident" and character. "What is character but the determination of incident? What is incident but the illustration of character?" he wrote in 1884 (1:55). *The Portrait of a Lady* had been published only three years earlier, and James's essay was in part an answer to those detractors who had claimed that "nothing happened" in that book. To those who missed "adventure" in "certain tales in which 'Boston nymphs' appear to have rejected English dukes for psychological reasons" (1:60), he had responded, "What *is* adventure, when it comes to that . . . ? It is an adventure—an immense one, for me to write this little article [and] a psychological reason is, to my imagination, an object adorably pictorial" (1:61). A quarter of a century later, revising this novel for the New York Edition, he still felt the need to defend his novel for depending so largely on mental events.

James's recourse, as I have noted, is a matter of "plot" redefined to make "being" a mode of "doing," as in Isabel's "motionless seeing" during her famous reverie in Chapter 42. The preface urges the novel reader to regard this occasion, when Isabel simply sits by a dying fire and thinks, as dramatic and "exciting": "It throws the action further forward than twenty 'incidents' might have done" (2:1084). Peter Brooks has spoken of the "melodrama of consciousness" which replaces external melodrama in James's fiction, saying that "the exiguity and restraint of external action is overborn by the weight of revelatory meaning that the novelist, through his preparations, juxtapositions, and use of a post of observation has read into it."[2] (Whether it actually does so, and, if so, at what cost—the sacrifice of a significant segment of story, a flagrant ellipsis—will be something to examine later.)

In *The Portrait,* James felt that his concentration on inner consciousness had even overcome the minimal interest that might be thought to derive from his choice of protagonist—"this slight 'personality,' the slim shade of an intelligent and presumptuous girl" (2:1077). This was more than a formal decision. James understood that a sheltered young woman, realistically speaking, could hardly expect to live, in the 1880s, a life of conspicuous adventure such as a young man might hope for. Her sequestering from visible, from "public" action—the life of politics or business—was an issue for emergent feminists—and James could even identify with female sequestering, acknowledging his own exclusion, along with the mass of women, from those masculine Americas, the world of "downtown" and the world expressed in the Capitol at Washington.[3] He had had to decide that "uptown"—the female domestic world—would have to do for him, personally and artistically. Daisy Miller and Catherine Sloper had been adequate to occasion brief studies, but could such a "frail vessel" sustain "the high attributes of a Subject" through appropriate doing in a novel? The technical-thematic aspiration to make this possible corresponded to that of the real women excluded from socially significant action.

"The novel is of its very nature an 'ado,'" James wrote—using another odd word, his substitute for the "nefarious" word "plot"—"an ado about something, and the larger the form it takes the greater of course the ado. Therefore, consciously, that was what one was in for—for positively organizing an ado about Isabel Archer" (2:1077). The ado—motion of some sort, if not the relentlessly forward motion implied by "plot"—would arise from her relations with others as perceived from her own viewpoint. "Place the centre of the subject in the young woman's own consciousness and you get as interesting and as beautiful a difficulty as you could wish . . . Make her only interested enough, at the same time, in the things that are not herself, and this relation needn't fear to be too limited" (2:1079). And James concludes, making his ambiguous term for action, "doing" (already compromised by his "ado"), take a third sense, that of the artist's own efforts: "To depend upon her and her little concerns wholly to see you through will necessitate, remember, your really 'doing' her" (2:1080). The "ado" about Isabel and also the artist's "doing"—plot and the art of narrative—will begin with the question, as he sees, of "What will she *do*?" (2:1081).

The novelist himself will begin by giving his character motion, however, by that initial act which had started off American characters in earlier fictions—*Roderick Hudson, The American,* "Daisy Miller." "The first thing she'll do will be to come to Europe." But this will be movement mental as well as physical. As a perceptive young pilgrim, James had found his own high adventure of the mind in the encounter with Europe. It might seem as much adventure for Isabel as all those traditional narrative excitements she is denied. He uses the word "independence"—Isabel's most frequently noted attribute—to remark upon her "independence of flood and field, of the moving accident, of battle and murder and sudden death" (2:1083); her independence, in other words, from the old plots of physical action.

Making her story an adventure of perception would allow his feminine protagonist to enter into the realm of the novel. *The Portrait of a Lady* does not employ the services of the distant observer-narrator who tells the tale in "Daisy Miller" and *Washington Square,* an impartial, ironic presence, positioned well outside the consciousness of the heroine. The "Daisy Miller" narrator is content to participate, with reservations, in the limited perceptions of Winterbourne, knowing no more than this observer about Daisy's inner being. The Jamesian persona who tells Catherine Sloper's story is a historian of manners whose own masculine sophistication so exceeds the simplicity of her mind that he can only treat it by coming perilously close to her father's condescension. But the "ado" about Isabel Archer involves a sympathetic though urbane participation in her thoughts; she is by nature and intelligence closer to her maker than those earlier heroines, as though his sense of the artist's special empathy with the condition of women is now more conscious. It was precisely this discovery that made him proud of this work's advance of design upon his previous efforts, "a structure reared with an 'architectural' competence, as Turgenieff would have said, that makes it, to the author's own sense, the most proportioned of his productions after 'The Ambassadors'" (2:1080).

James exaggerates the consistency of his centering—the traditional self-conscious narrator who stands well away from his
favorite character is not banished altogether. The narrative consciousness still seems, as previously in his fiction, to be male, and to
resemble the author himself more than Isabel. And not only does he
often reveal his separation from the heroine, he participates in the
inner thoughts of others—particularly Ralph Touchett, who may be
closer to his own viewpoint, being also a tolerant and affectionate,
as well as richly perceiving, sponsor of her development. While
Isabel *is* the center, she is so not only because she is seen from
within her own consciousness but because she is the object of
observation by the other characters as well—who either try to
understand or to manipulate her, like generous or tyrannic novelists. As a result, the social uncertainty of female selfhood is reflected
in the novel's formal irresolution, its subjection to relativism.
James's compensatory conversion of the inner life into a substitute
field of action for his inactive protagonist is haunted by the knowledge that she is excluded from action in its physical and social sense
as men are not (unless, like Ralph, they are invalids).

Isabel is always a subject for a portrait—the occasion for the
effort of perception—rather than the portrait promised in the title.
Perhaps the title simply declares that the novel's subject is the *effort*
to achieve such a portrait, such a single view, and it asks to the last,
"Who is Isabel, what is she?" All the other characters, along with
the narrator and the reader, as well as Isabel herself, are engaged in
the *attempt* to define her, but no fixed image emerges from this play
of perceptions—though in the end, it may be said, she does for a
moment become something else than herself, the generic type she
has resisted, the "portrait of *a* lady." And yet, though James argues
that Isabel's encounters make a drama of perception and feeling, it is
not, of course, only perception and feeling that are brought into play
at her entrance into Gardencourt or her first meeting with Madame
Merle—the examples he offers. On these occasions she also enters
the domain of plot in the sense he disdains, entrained in a story with
plenty of motion. The heroine will be loved by four men and marry
the worst; she will be victimized by both a well-intentioned secret
plot to endow her with money and a wicked one to marry her for
that money; the belated revelations of both designs and of the concealed prehistory of her false friends, and various subsidiary actions,
all make for melodrama, plot at its most egregious. But these events

are not the doing of a heroine whose drama, James would insist, is not what happens to her but how she takes it.

That Isabel is the victim rather than the perpetrator of "plot"— those plots of action to which her "motionless seeing" is opposed— has, exactly, a double sense. In showing how such a narrative is a menace to the "free" character, James gives us reason to reflect on the cause of that ambiguity in language which makes us look with suspicion on the very act of structuring implied in the general sense of "plot," essential though such structuring, whether of temporal or other phenomena, may be to human thought. One is reminded that such words as "design" and "scheme" and "contrive" carry, also, the suggestion of malicious intent. And even the neutral "doing," the word we have heard so much of from James, gains a sinister meaning as it reverberates from the moment Ralph asks his mother, "What do you want to do with her?" (III:54), to the later occasion of Madame Merle's remark to Osmond, "I don't pretend to know what people are meant for, I only know what I can do with them" (III:345).

So, she is plotted against—in the sense of the word that is certainly "nefarious"; the novel invokes the meaning of plot as machination enforcing some undesired end in the spring laid for the innocent maiden by dark conspirators who take advantage of her good nature to rob her of her fortune and imprison her in the dungeon of marriage. But—more important—she is the victim of narrative ideas of what she will be and do, which others seek to impose upon her. The example of their own lives and personalities, to which she finds herself attracted, will press upon her alternate possibilities of development, of projected life stories. In their place she will only have her own aching sense of potential brilliance, her undenotable personal utopianism. In rejecting the marriage-plot of early nineteenth-century fiction she will become, unwittingly, a character in the plot of conspiracy as her false friend and her hypocritical Gothic suitor "make" her marriage after all. In this struggle the two senses of "plot" conflate; both plots are schemes of entrapment, though it is from only the unconcealed and seemingly unthreatening marriage-plot that she (vainly) tries to escape.

The reader is implicated by the force of literary tradition in this plot against Isabel, as is the writer in his awareness of reader expectation, despite his desire to keep his character free. Isabel can become the person she must be in the end only by choosing, like

Jane Austen's Emma, Mr. Knightley. Her qualifications as a possible wife and the relation of her personal charms to her possession of a fortune are exactly the sort of situation that constitutes the ground of female growth in an Austen novel. In such a novel, marriage is the act which will unite her to the social world and give her role, and it is out of the competition among her suitors that the heroine's difficulties arise, that her character is tested, and final success is to be achieved. James's story promotes our expectations of such narrative development by a familiar structure—the initial presentation of the heroine—young, attractive, economically helpless—and then, commencing immediately, the parade of suitors whose claims she must weigh. She is not asked to consider the other alternatives present for a man. (If she were a man other kinds of choice might prove equally or more disastrous than a mistaken marriage—a wrong choice of profession, of political affiliation, religious belief, social group, even environment, all of which had become matters of option for men in the new industrial age.)

It is not merely literary tradition, then, that dictates this plot. What other scope for choice did the real Isabels of her day—any more than the real Emmas—have? Nothing can be more quixotic, realistically, than Isabel's "Why should I necessarily marry?" The response of radical feminism—Olive Chancellor's, as we shall see in the next chapter—is simply unavailable to her. Practically speaking, hers is the dilemma of the upper-class girl who cannot survive by entering the market of wage-earners, but only by making the right marriage. Only her aunt's fairy-godmother intervention and her cousin's equally fairy-tale bequest keep her situation from becoming that of Madame Merle, who had realized in her own younger days that money is everything and that without it she cannot hope to marry freely.

The example of Isabel's friend, Henrietta Stackpole, seems to argue that independence without marriage is really available to Isabel—does not this sprightly character earn her own her living "by her pen," and even support some of her relatives? Henrietta's example is a proposal of plot, that of the independent woman who, as a Brontë heroine might have, could demonstrate her self-sufficiency, however exposed and solitary she might find herself, before accepting the protection of a freely chosen mate. James introduces this literal version of Isabel's "independence" into the novel for a while, but he never allows it to be more than a comic parody of

Isabel's transcendent yearning. In the end he collapses Henrietta as the representative of independence by marrying her off to a member of the species Isabel rejected—a rich Englishman.

Isabel wants to discard the plot offered her and to write another of a new form, but there is no form available except union with one of her suitors. Isabel must marry; her desire to find a plot that would free her from any aim but the fulfillment of her own nature must submit itself to the conditions of a world which only permits her to imagine—falsely—that she has found this opportunity in marriage to a man who would have been rejected unhesitatingly by an Austen heroine, a man whose lack of "position" and income alone would make him ineligible, and whose only "romantic" appeal is precisely in his having no role in society. She thus entraps herself even more securely in the marriage-plot; she simply marries the wrong man. It is not clear to anyone except herself—not even to the sensitive Ralph Touchett—that marriage to Lord Warburton or Casper Goodwood would not have provided her story with a satisfactory closure. But Isabel's marriage is not the end. It occurs in the middle of the story as part of the new plot which was becoming available to novelists in the 1880s, which revealed that marriage was only the discovery of new sources of stress and disappointment. *Middlemarch* and *Daniel Deronda*, important intertexts for *The Portrait of a Lady*, may not only have suggested to James the character of his own heroine, with her unrealizable personal longings, but showed how one could place centrally in a novel the spectacle of a failed marriage. Yet James, as we shall see, elides Isabel's post-wedding history—refusing, after all, to make marriage itself his subject. He presents the reader only with the Isabel who has already passed from happiness to misery. And he does not avail himself of the delayed marriage closure which returns in *Middlemarch* with the removal of the wrongly chosen mate by death and remarriage to the right one.

Aside from death, of course, there was divorce. Practically speaking, divorce was still an alternative nearly unavailable to someone like Isabel when James wrote his novel. It was a recourse that upper-class women, in particular, were not supposed to reach for, however outrageous the offenses of their husbands, and it was even legally difficult—not until the 1870s and 1880s did English law make provision for women as the injured party. Few novelists were ready to modify the marriage-plot so far as to include the peripeteia of divorce. Only Meredith went so far as to take a positive view of divorce in *Diana of the Crossways* or *One of Our Conquerors,* published shortly after James's novel. Isabel, in any case, had, as we shall note later, *no specific* outrage to charge Osmond with—he was neither an adulterer or a wife-beater. What lies ahead for Isabel, however, is not made clear; James simply refuses to reduce her potentiality a second time. When her two rejected suitors offer themselves again after the evident failure of her first choice, she does not seem to forsee a recovered future with either of them.

James makes Isabel's personal watchword "freedom" and also allows her, as a character, as much freedom as he can to struggle against the rigidities and reductions of social and literary formula. Her own appetite for freedom is closely related, as Richard Poirier has pointed out,[4] to James's belief that the literary character should be allowed the same unpredictability we would accord to those we love in real life. In James's handling of her we can feel that "respect for the liberty of the subject" he praised in Balzac. In his 1905 essay, "The Lesson of Balzac," he quoted Taine's remark, "Balzac aime sa Valérie," and contrasted this attitude toward the wicked Valérie Marneffe with "the marked jealousy of [Becky Sharp's] freedom that Thackeray exhibits." (2:131). James in his turn is tenderly permissive of Isabel's self-contradictions, and he encourages her to escape the determinism of the fixed and limited character. His attitude is represented within the novel by Ralph, who renounces any desire other than to give her the power to be whatever it is that she wants to be, to put wind into her sails. He merely wants to see what she will do with herself, like a novelist experimenting with the possibilities latent in his characters. Yet it may be said of the novelist, as of Ralph, that because he exercises no authority over her direction, he leaves her subject to the arbitrary impositions of others. Ralph, we must remember, is someone whose illness forbids the normal exercise of masculine force, as though James suspects in his own abstention a disability—obscurely linked to sexuality—to carry out the novelist's proper role. But Ralph, however benevolently, is one of those who "plots" against her—and this suggests that James understands, too, that a plot is something he cannot help making. He would like to create a character free of the obligation to determine itself in limiting action; he would prefer to believe in the immanence of personality and its unquenchable potentiality. Yet there is no other way to tell stories than to suppress some of the infinitude of human possibility. Putting wind in the sails of his characters, he looses them upon a particular course, as in the end Isabel's story is written by Ralph's very act of trying to grant her freedom.

Looking back from the hindsight of her later history we are likely to view her own desire to express herself freely in the medium of life as egotistic as well as naive. But James encourages us to feel sympathy for the "presumptuous" notions of this young and ignorant, though intelligent and honorable, woman. There have been readings of the novel which make her out to be the object of her creator's scorn,[5] but it is plain, I think, that James allows us to see that her dreams are also serious expressions of an ancient view of the self as an inviolate essence not always manifest to mankind. He has dared to make her a spokeswoman for the powerful romantic strain in his native culture expressed in Emerson's exaltation of the singular self with its scorn for "circumstance."[6] James could write of Emerson, "No one has had so steady and constant, and above all so natural, a vision of what we require and what we are capable of in the way of aspiration and independence"—to which Harold Bloom has added, "No one, that is, except Henry James, for that surely is the quest of Isabel Archer towards her own quite Emersonian vision of aspiration and independence."[7] It is because we must take her callow expectations seriously, because her errors are the consequence of noble conceptions of the human, that James allows her her right to our appreciation.

Yet Isabel's search for expression of her boundless self is doomed in a philosophic sense, for no manifestation can ever be adequate to such expectation. James shows the weakness of Emersonian idealism in its inability to take account of the force of evil—moral or socioeconomic—"the ripe unconciousness of evil . . . is one of the most beautiful signs by which we know him," James wrote in 1887 (1:254). Ralph's warning to Isabel that she is too fastidious is James's judgment of Emerson. "You want to see, but not to feel," Ralph says after she has told him that she doesn't "wish to touch the cup of experience . . . It's a poisoned drink! I only want to see for myself" (III:213); this is echoed in James's remark that Emerson "liked to taste but not to drink—least of all to become intoxicated" (1:265).

But however vulnerable, even to James, Isabel's idealism may also be seen as a contention against that very model of realism which, in James's own day, insisted that the novel accept the dominion of the visible fact over mere thought or feeling and accept the idea that these latter are simply the effects of facts. That model derived from realist-naturalism. James resisted it not only ontologically but morally, for himself and in the person of Isabel. He knew the precariousness of such idealism. As Arnold Kettle has written, *"The Portrait of a Lady* is one of the most profound expressions in literature of the illusion that freedom is an abstract quality inherent in the individual soul." James, says Kettle,

> though he sees the tragedy implicit in the Victorian ruling-class view of freedom, is himself so deeply involved in that illusion that he cannot escape from it. His books are tragedies precisely because their subject is the smashing of the bourgeois illusion of freedom in the consciousness of characters who are unable to conceive of freedom in any other way. His "innocent" persons have therefore always the characters of victims; they are at the mercy of the vulgar and the corrupt, and the more finely conscious they become of their situation the more are they unable to cope with it in positive terms.[8]

In social terms, post–Civil War America had made "individualism" a suspect principle; the pioneer and revolutionary dream of untrammeled individuality seemed reduced to ruthless entrepreneurism. But the sweetness of an earlier ideal lingered in the American imagination with its attachment to life, liberty, and the pursuit of happiness, terms so frequently on Isabel's own lips as she expresses her personal hopes. The ambiguity of her expectancy, which is her salient characteristic, is of course, that it is dependent for its fulfillment on her having, like Dickens's Pip, "great expectations," a legacy of money from an unknown benefactor. Yet she is protected from this realization for most of the story. Her ardent sense of futurity remains uncorrupt.

I said at the beginning of this discussion that Isabel is more tragic—because of her own complicity in the frustration of her expectations—than Daisy and Catherine, but whether the novel as a whole can be called a tragedy because its heroine's flaw contributes to her fall is questionable. In one of the best commentaries on *A Portrait of a Lady*, A. N. Kaul calls it a "a comic novel laboring under an imposed sense of tragedy."[9] He reminds us that Isabel resembles Emma Woodhouse or Dorothea Brooke—but also many masculine protagonists in nineteenth-century novels—in being a superior young person who is guilty of taking a romantic, too theoretical view of herself and the world. Seeming to belong to such a "novel of education," she is launched upon a story that should end with her discovery of the discrepancy between reality and her theories. But this change, as Kaul is correct in observing, actually fails to arrive for Isabel. The promise of comic resolution is mocked by Isabel's own mistake in thinking she has resolved her dilemma by marrying Osmond, and when knowledge of the truth about him comes at last, it does not mark so decisive a turning point as one might suppose in the resolution of her diverse attitudes.

But perhaps James's novel must not be read as the fulfillment of any *one* of its own proposed or potential designs. The element of comedy of manners, for example, is maintained to the end by the presence of "typical" characters like Casper Goodwood, Lord Warburton, Pansy Osmond, and Henrietta Stackpole, who is Isabel rendered as caricature. But Isabel herself is never the "flat" character who cannot ever surprise us; on the contrary, it may be thought that she surprises us too much; she maintains the essential indeterminacy of the tragic character whose actions arise from some mysterious depth. Isabel falls short of enlightenment because in this, too, she must resist the closure of conventional plot, must remain a potentiality. It is true, as Kaul says, that the early chapters contain the promise of comic resolution. When, after the narrator has said something about Isabel's contradictory views of Lord Warburton, he remarks, "She was a person of great good faith, and if there was a great deal of folly in her wisdom those who judge her severely may have the satisfaction of finding that, later, she became consistently wise only at the cost of an amount of folly which will constitute almost a direct appeal to charity" (III:144-145). Such a statement, midway in the first volume, seems to promise progression toward final enlightenment. But though some wisdom does come to her, it seems qualified and its persistence uncertain—and this may be seen as a maintenance of the possibilities of her still-unresolved destiny.

Few readers will be willing to accept the view of Manfred Mackenzie, who argues that Isabel is merely a melodramatist, guilty of "hideous insincerities," who acts out contrary roles as convenient. He holds her to be closer to Mrs. Penniman, in *Washington Square,* than to Catherine Sloper, to whom I have compared her.[10] But there have been others, like F. R. Leavis, who have been put off by her self-contradictions while admitting that James persuades us of her "ardent good faith."[11] But Isabel may not be intended as a psychological study. Her confusions make for a maximization of her; her multiple reasons, her self-contradictions, may be seen as a dramatization of an unresolvable contention of personal and cultural possibilities. That the reader recognizes the gestures of various traditions of story-telling—marriage-plot, novel-of-education, comedy, tragedy, melodrama, realism, and romance—is not surprising, for Isabel's search for plot involves a consideration of various ways of thinking about herself—and therefore various formal structures in the traditions of literature. If Isabel herself, as Richard Chase wrote, is a romancer,[12] then one can say that she is compelled to try to write romance in the medium of the world of materialist determination, the world of the realist novel—and her sense of romance reaches toward a freedom even from the coercions of romantic convention. *The Portrait of a Lady* may, among its other formal discords, contain a dialogue between *Middlemarch* and *The Scarlet Letter*. Isabel is related to Dorothea Brooke; she also retains a connection with Hester Prynne, Hawthorne's scourged yet unrepentant dark heroine of expanded female selfhood.

This is not so much to deny structure to *The Portrait of a Lady* as to discover that its structure is an open one which thematizes uncertainty. Its notable "failure" of closure and striking ellipses exhibit contests of plot which propose themselves from page to page. Leavis noted that the "inconsistencies" or, as he called them, "moral uncertainties" in the book "pass undetected at first because of the brilliant art with which James, choosing his *scènes à faire*, works in terms of dramatic presentation."[13] But it is just this dramatic presentation that is the essence of the novel, the inner as well as outer secret of its refusal to draw all its baggage along a single track toward an inevitable destination. In the end what we lack is, precisely, a "portrait," a spatial arrangement of our impressions, something arrived at by a hundred strokes of the brush, but finally stable.[14] If character is fate and fate is character, then Isabel's character is incompletely defined by a fate that remains always indeterminate. "What will she do?" remains an obsessive and unresolved question, while the verb itself sounds insistently throughout the text, becoming more rather than less problematic. That the contention of potentialities will not come to rest is the reason for the ending which has puzzled so many; James does not end his character's search for the destiny she has always "affronted."

In the foregoing discussion of *The Portrait of a Lady*, I have bound together issues too often held apart by critics—the role in the novel of transcendental individuality, with its belief in the limitless extension of personal being; the practical issues of personal self-definition in the social world, particularly as these presented themselves to nineteenth-century women; and the formal-aesthetic contest of openness and closure, which might be said to express both of these themes. In her astute and valuable discussion of the differences between James's early (1880) text and its revised (1908) version, Nina Baym has argued that an older, more conservative James drew back from his early interest in the theme of marriage versus female independence. His textual changes, she demonstrates, transform the novel into a more abstract study of romantic idealism.[15] I would only qualify this conclusion by insisting that James, from the start of his career—even in more rudimentary studies like "Daisy Miller" and *Washington Square*—invokes both the philosophic and the social contests at once and expresses them together in the structure of his fictions, and that this joint presence is fully active in both versions of *The Portrait*.

James's statement that the first thing he will make Isabel "do" is come to Europe has a certain disingenuousness about it, for this initial act is nearly suppressed out of the narrative. Not until the third chapter do we get a brief view of that moment when Mrs. Touchett descends upon Isabel in her grandmother's Albany house. The house is described in a curiously detailed way. Some of these details are autobiographical, corresponding to James's recollections—set down long afterward in *A Small Boy and Others*—including the adjoining primary school and the taste "of accessible garden peaches"[16] associated with his own grandmother's house in Albany. As tokens of an infantine time, which James remembered as also an age of innocence in American culture, the description must have functioned in the writer's mind in a symbolic way, and does so for the uncommon modern reader who happens to recall certain pages of the autobiography, which was published thirty years after the novel. There are a few more bits of the past of Isabel-James, farther on—her (his) father's "aversion" to unpleasantness, and the educational theories which had induced him to transport his daughters (sons) three times across the Atlantic before Isabel-James was fourteen. And when we read that, as a girl, Isabel had "an immense curiosity about life and was constantly staring and wondering" (III, 45), we are reminded of the way James describes himself as a boy who was always "gaping." These bits of description will remind us of the autobiographical passage in *Washington Square* to which I have already drawn attention, but with the difference that it is not to the narrator that this lost American past belongs but to Isabel herself. As a glimpse of Isabel's own childhood it signals James's secret identification with her, something which reinforces his concentration upon her consciousness, making for an authorial attachment more intimate and tender than his fleeting, skeptical identification with Winterbourne in "Daisy Miller."

But these associations, to which one is helped by adding to the text something unavailable to the contemporary reader, are hardly enough to give either Isabel's earlier history or the culture that has produced her a dramatic presence in the novel. The fact that she is an orphan, responsible to no one but herself, completes the severance from her antecedents. She herself feels that her situation makes her belong "quite to the independent class"—that is, the class of those "independent" of customary plots—when she insists to Casper Goodwood that she is disqualified for the role which conducts the heroine to the marriage-ending. "I'm not in my first youth—I can do what I choose . . . I've neither father nor mother; I'm poor and of a serious disposition; I'm not pretty. I therefore am not bound to be timid and conventional; indeed I can't afford such luxuries. Besides, I try to judge things for myself; to judge wrong, I think, is more honourable than not to judge at all. I don't wish to be a mere sheep in the flock; I wish to choose my fate and know something of human affairs beyond what other people think it compatible with propriety to tell me" (III:228–229).

Merely as a reminder of influences or models which Isabel rejects, James permits us the briefest of backward glances at her two sisters, her only surviving relatives, now remotely behind her across the sea—one married, not brilliantly, to an Army officer posted "in the unfashionable West," the oldest, Lilian, the mother of two "peremptory little boys," to a lawyer in New York, where she is "the mistress of a wedge of brown stone violently driven into Fifty-third Street" (III:38). James's crisp phrases express the finality of these fates, and Lilian's view of Isabel's own necessary consummation might have been uttered at the opening of one of Austen's novels: "I want to see her safely married—that's what I want to see"

(III:39). It is clear that James understands the exact nature of this expectation when he summarizes in the most compact way all Isabel's preparation. Like his own sister Alice, who paced the cliffs of Newport and dreamed of an inaccessible life of action during the Civil War,[17] Isabel is said to have "passed months of this long period in a state of almost passionate excitement, in which she felt herself at times (to her extreme confusion) stirred almost indiscriminately by the valour of either army." James's empathetic feminist irony is felt in the comment which follows almost directly: "she had had everything a girl could have: kindness, admiration, bonbons, bouquets, the sense of exclusion from none of the privileges of the world she lived in, abundant opportunity for dancing, plenty of new dresses, the London *Spectator,* the latest publications, the music of Gounod, the poetry of Browning, the prose of George Eliot" (III:45–46).

Isabel's developmental possibilities are not ones Lilian or her husband can imagine, however; her "originality" bewilders them. "I've never kept up with Isabel—it would have taken *all* my time" (III, 39) says this sister. Her husband "hope(s) she isn't going to develop anymore" (III, 40), and observes, exactly as though she is a novel, that he cannot read her, she's "written in a foreign tongue" (III, 39); the kind of story she might figure in is quite beyond him.[18] James thus introduces but brings into doubt the naturalist scheme of prediction as well as the traditional marriage-plot model, letting the reader know that his heroine is not to be "explained" by her class, type, upbringing, and, above all, by her past. In effect, she has no past and her future is obscure.

She herself accepts her aunt's invitation with "a desire to leave the past behind her and, as she said to herself, to begin afresh" (III, 41). And much later, when she is about to meet Osmond, she still considers that the past has no hold upon her: "It was in her disposition at all times to lose faith in the reality of absent things . . . The past was apt to look dead" (III, 322). Her attitude toward others, too, is to assume that they have no past, or to prefer not to inquire about it. This must explain her lack of curiosity about the previous relationship of Ralph and Madame Merle—which is hinted at, but which we never learn about. "With all her love of knowledge," we are told, "she had a natural shrinking from raising curtains and looking into unlighted corners. The love of knowledge coexisted in her mind with the finest capacity for ignorance" (III, 284). More dangerously for herself, she is incurious about Osmond's past: "His life had been mingled with other lives more than he admitted . . . For the present she refrained from provoking further revelations" (III:383). And so she never really understands what would seem obvious until, as the Countess Gemini says, the i's are dotted for her—"*ça me dépasse*, if you don't mind my saying so, the things, all round you, that you've appeared to succeed in not knowing" (IV:365).

Isabel's gap of beginning is one of the functions of the international situation which, in so many of James's fictions, introduces a lately landed American whose qualities are to be tested in the European world. She seems newborn when she steps onto the lawn of Gardencourt in the opening chapter. And even before she appears, Mrs. Touchett's telegram has attached to her that description, "independent," which she soon uses of herself. In a paradoxical sense, of course, this also makes her the symbolic representative of her nation's ideals—her own declarations never cease to echo the language of the American Declaration. But in its absolute sense independence means the right to be free even of a culture committed to freedom. When Isabel wonders at the fact that her aunt's own point of view doesn't seem particularly American (it is one of the moments when she sounds like her friend Henrietta), Mrs. Touchett exclaims, "My point of view, thank God, is personal!"— which Isabel thinks "a tolerable description of her own manner of judging" (III:81).

Isabel's independence might, for a moment, be thought of as a hereditarily determined as well as determining quality, for Mr. Touchett immediately recognizes it as a "family trait," which Isabel shares with his wife. This is hardly implied, however—the resemblance between the two is something else. It is a hypothetical prediction of a destiny that Isabel's very rejection of models implies. We learn just enough about Mrs. Touchett herself to be provided with a glimpse of the history of someone who is so "fond of her own way," as Mr. Touchett says, or who, as her son adds, "likes to do everything for herself and has no belief in anyone's power to help her" (III:13–14). At their meeting in Albany, the older woman seems to recognize the kinship when her niece refuses to promise to do everything she is told. Mrs. Touchett then responds, "You're fond of your own way; but it's not for me to blame you" (III:35). Another term applied to both women by Ralph is "natural"

(III:58)—a term also applied, as we have seen, to Catherine Sloper. Implying a certain freedom from the modes and manners of ordered society, it signifies freedom from those deterministic "natural" laws which make the idea of the natural seem the very reverse of free in later nineteenth-century thinking. The "nature" referred to is not Darwin's but the Nature of Emerson's essay. Such a concept belongs especially to American culture before 1850 but is persistently American, a dream we have never entirely surrendered to naturalistic determinism. The one fault Isabel was to find with Madame Merle in the time of her great admiration for that accomplished woman was, "she was not natural—she had rid herself of every remnant of that tonic wildness which we may assume to have belonged even to the most amiable persons in the ages before country-house life was the fashion" (III:274). This is an unmistakable reference to Thoreau, who says in *Walden:* "We need the tonic of wildness."[19]

Of course, there is nothing very wild about the elderly Mrs. Touchett, who holds Isabel to a stricter propriety than the girl is used to when she wishes to linger downstairs with the gentlemen after her aunt has retired. Mrs. Touchett extends her benevolent sponsorship to Isabel only for the most conventional of enterprises—acquisition of European culture and of a husband—her viewpoint being exactly the same as Mrs. Ludlow's; she is openly disappointed when Isabel rejects that great *parti,* Lord Warburton. Yet she is in her own person, nevertheless, a warning. In the old woman's sterile eccentricity, her wandering which knows no resting place, and her emotional distance from the husband and son who have not seen her for a year, we are given the outcome of Mrs. Touchett's independence. It is an exhibition of what might even be Isabel's fate, an alternative of existence embedded in the text as one anticipation of the outcome of her views and qualities. Since she must marry, as everyone but she feels, she would only be able to preserve her independence by becoming someone like her aunt. In the end, this does not seem impossible if her marriage to Osmond should remain an undissolved formal connection in the years to be imagined for her beyond the closing pages. As unlike her dry, elderly aunt as she seems, the reader should not forget that Isabel reminds Mr. Touchett of his wife as a young girl.

This method of presenting Isabel's alterity is one James extends to most of the other characters, who are not only independent

forces acting upon her but represent other lives she might live. Ironically, since it is her determination to resist models as much as she
can, James expresses through the characters that surround his heroine the idea that a life is a path with many forkings; in traveling
past these we have only the illusion of treading a single, inevitable
course. Forecasting in the novel may be admonitory or optative as
well as predictive. It is only after her marriage that Isabel feels that
her alterity is exhausted. As she broods before the fire upon the
mistake the marriage has been, she reflects, "She had taken all the
first steps in the purest confidence, and then she had suddenly found
the infinite vista of a multiplied life to be a dark, narrow alley with a
dead wall at the end" (IV:189).

Two representatives of her American origins follow her to
Europe and continue to exhibit that side of herself which is unmodified by foreign experience. Henrietta Stackpole is Isabel without
her grace and superior intelligence but with something of her freshness and American insistence upon self-determination. There will
be moments, as already noted, when the two friends sound very
much alike. Henrietta's alterity to Isabel is that she has achieved her
"independence" without modifying these qualities. She is an
example of an alternative to marriage, which is not the role of the
old maid dependent of Victorian families, but the working woman's
proud self-support. That it is Henrietta who does, after all, marry an
English gentleman while Isabella refuses one, is James's joke played
on a "new woman" about whom he had mixed feelings. Another
joke is the fact that this free American is the very representative of
categorical thinking. She is always looking for "types" to figure in
her articles for the newspapers and insists on the niceness of
national distinctions; Ralph annoys her by not being clearly either
English or American—but she decides he is a type, after all, "the
alienated American," of which he is "a beautiful specimen"
(III:120).

Casper Goodwood also represents something important in
Isabel's past, but James does his best to repress it from view. His
name is not even spoken in the early description of Albany, though
he is unquestionably the "person from whom she was looking for a
visit" when she hears her aunt's footstep outside her door. We
know nothing at all about him until Henrietta mentions in Chapter
11 that he has come over in the steamer with her—and charges
Isabel with being "faithless" (III:135). Whether the charge has

foundation, however—what exactly has been the previous history of her relations with Goodwood—we are never told, though her relations with Lord Warburton and Osmond, his rivals, are given to us from their beginnings—and this shutting off of any backward view of him is still another index of that suppression of beginning which has kept most of Isabel's American past over the horizon. The character of Casper is treated somewhat summarily by James, who does not seem to want to remember, any more than does Isabel, just what Casper has been to her. Yet, in another novel, he might be a hero—someone not unlike Christopher Newman—a resistant American masculinity. He, also, is a "new man," having made a fortune in industrial America, and also comes to Europe with the view that he can have what he wants—in this case, Isabel.

Neither Henrietta nor Casper, who are allied, succeeds in modifying Isabel's history. Yet Casper's pursuit is nearly successful. His urgency is answered to powerfully in Isabel's nature. This may be interpreted sexually—and her evasion of his suit put down to sexual fear.[20] But it may be more in harmony with James's intention to see that the American "freedom" Casper offers her is only another design which she strives against—though one that is closely related to her own desire for freedom from old forms. He resembles her (is one version of her) in his very American self-sufficiency, being the "self-made man" in material terms as she would be a self-made personality, owing nothing to others. When he tells her at the last that the world is very large, and asks, "To whom under the sun do we owe anything?" (IV:435), he seems to be voicing her own principles—as well as the proud solvency of the successful entrepreneur—though by this time she has come to understand the limitations of the independence she was once so proud of. Still, marriage with this suitor remains potential in the narrative like so many other potentialities, and the narrator remarks that there were moments when she said to herself that "she might evade him for a time, but that she must make terms with him at last." Though she has rejected him as well as Lord Warburton she still feels, toward the end of the first volume, that she "might really . . . come to the end of things that were not Casper (even though there appeared so many of them), and find rest in those very elements of his presence which struck her now as impediments to the finer respiration. It was conceivable that these impediments should some day prove a sort of blessing in disguise—a clear and quiet harbor enclosed by a brave granite breakwater" (III:323).

This is so powerfully put—with the image of the granite break-water representing Casper's restrictive yet, protective nature—that one may, if one is distressed by such a misleading implication of the outcome, protest that the writer does not seem to know how his novel will end. One answer is that we are in the mind, after all, of Isabel, who does *not* know what happens in the next chapter—that she meets Osmond. But another is that James wishes to keep all possibilities open even against the logic of a plot that seems to be reducing them one by one. Casper's persistence in her life will continue to suggest an alternate outcome. He does not succeed, within the bounds of the novel, in doing what he wishes—uniting himself with Isabel—yet it is representative of his nature as well as hers that he believes in an unquenchable futurity in himself and others, and presses his suit to the end. It is typical of him that he even seems to think that Ralph's death from tuberculosis can be prevented when he visits him in Rome after Isabel's marriage: "He couldn't bear to see a pleasant man, so pleasant for all his queerness, so beyond anything to be done. There was always something to be done, for Goodwood, and he did it in this case by repeating several times his visit to the Hôtel de Paris" (IV:296) Isabel is left "free" after his electric kiss, finally. Henrietta's last encouragement to Casper, "Just you wait!" implies a closure beyond the last page of the 1882 text, but James subdued this ambiguity in the New York Edition, and the revised ending maintains the openness of the novel, its gap of ending, and is in harmony with Casper's own stubborn refusal of finality. In the later version, James added, "but only to guess from her face, with a revulsion, that she simply meant he was young. She stood shining at him with that cheap comfort, and it added, on the spot, thirty years to his life. She walked him away with her, however, as if she had given him now the key to patience" (IV:437–438).

Madame Merle is another possible outcome for an Isabel who might remain poor, growing older in Europe, and come to the point of having to say, in her turn, "My dreams were so great—so preposterous." Madame Merle also says, "the dreams of one's youth, why they were enchanting, they were divine! Who had ever seen such things come to pass?" (III:286). She, too, we must remember, is an American, and "the breezy freedom of the stars and stripes might have shed an influence upon the attitude she there took towards life" (III:250). She seems, at first, also to be without a past, having had a husband who is never mentioned by her and of whom Ralph only says that he "would be likely to pass away" (III:252). She has had time to acquire a significant history, in fact; it has changed her, and remains present in her life in Pansy, but this history is quite invisible to Isabel.

What Madame Merle seems to be—however arrived at—stirs the younger woman to a passion of emulation. Something of this attitude is shared by Mrs. Touchett, of whom Ralph says that "if she were not herself (which she after all much prefers) she would like to be Madame Merle" (III:251–252). As their acquaintance continues, Isabel's fascination with Madame Merle's accomplishments and charms increases, and she finds herself "desiring to emulate them, and in twenty such ways this lady presented herself as a model. 'I should like awfully to be *so*!' Isabel secretly exclaimed, more than once, as one after another of her friend's fine aspects caught the light" (III:270). The one flaw Isabel finds in her, as I have said, is that she seems to be without "naturalness"—the American quality which Isabel herself possesses and prizes. But, in fact, it may be one of the novel's numerous potentialities that although she discovers this admired model to be someone who has deceptively plotted against her, Isabel may be nevertheless (as Leo Bersani has suggested) in the process of absorbing the example of Madame Merle in the end—that is, mastering the art of appearances.[21]

Even Pansy is a variant Isabel, another female innocent upon whom others work their designs, though her innocence is that of Nature, from which all tonic wildness has been bred out in a convent garden. In the final move to the role of sponsor and protector of Pansy—by which she assumes Ralph's role in relation to herself—Isabel acts to recover possibility for a younger self. Pansy's story provides, in the novel's late stages, a doubling back to her stepmother's own early condition, and gives one the feeling that the possibilities latent then have not, after all, disappeared; Pansy's promise of happiness keeps Isabel's alterity alive. In enacting Ralph's role toward herself in her own relationship with Pansy, Isabel again confirms her identity with him. She shares with him the imaginative qualities which make possible a donation of one's own expectations to another, a surrogateship both generous and fatal. His donation to Isabel—not merely of money but of personal expectations—is duplicated not only in her relationship with Pansy but in her earlier relationship with Osmond himself.

This implied cyclicity also threatens the expectation that Pansy may turn out to be happier than her sponsor, multiplying for us even further the alternatives which vibrate beyond the novel's final page. As we remember the fatality of Ralph's gift we see the darker side of his spectatorship, which links him unexpectedly to such a character as Dr. Sloper, who watches Catherine as though she were a character in a play and wonders whether she will show him some surprises in the next act. Ralph, we are told, is kept alive at the end by the fact that Isabel's drama is still not played out: "He was determined to sit out the performance" (IV:147). But when Isabel first meets Pansy, she too is a playgoer; Pansy strikes her as "an *ingénue* in a French play" or "the ideal *jeune fille* of foreign fiction" (III:401).

Ralph's superior mental and emotional qualities would seem to make him the only one among the men who love Isabel who is her true mate. But the relationship is closer still. It is worth pondering that James has made Ralph unable to offer her physical passion. Ralph cannot act in any way except by furthering someone else's history, though he is sometimes reminded "that the finest of pleasures is the rush of action." There is something deadly, a stillness of exhaustion, that marks Gardencourt, that beautiful garden place where if one life begins, two others are ending—the lives of the dying father and the mortally ill son who wait for Isabel in that "little eternity" of tea-time, when time has seemed to stop on the great lawn. The money of one man and the love of the other produce their intended gift of expanded life to Isabel. But the legacy is infected with their deaths.

Isabel herself is not only like the Touchetts, but like James, the motionless see-er who is an affectionate, spectatorial witness of his characters' efforts as he gives them their lives, their plots. I have referred earlier to James's recognition of his own identity with female life in a society which kept both women and the artist at the periphery of social power. Ralph, the man with the artistic sensibility, enacts a classically female abnegation. The free Isabel, who once scorned the idea that she had to marry at all, now accepts the most conventional of female plots in the abnegation of wifehood; women, *typically*, must act through men. So, it is Osmond, as I have said, in whose life Isabel first dreams of making herself potent, sponsoring the expression of *his* supposed free nature as she has been sponsored. Ralph was right in accusing her, in the beginning, of not wanting to touch or taste life. She would rather act through delegation, by marrying. Osmond will do her doing for her. If he is guilty of regarding her as an object, she is guilty, also, of thinking of him as an instrument. And James, the artist, identifies with this delegation. The "rush of action" which Ralph misses may be understood not only as that of the battlefield or of sexual intercourse but in a literary sense as the "doing" of the novel, which is James's own substitute for living action—a doing which is, in this case, an affirmation of not-doing. Just as Isabel had been seen by her Albany relatives as a book "written in a foreign tongue," so Ralph (for whom the ordinary plots of manhood are inapplicable) sees himself as "a good book in a poor translation—a meagre entertainment for a young man who felt that he might have been an excellent linquist" (III:53).

Osmond, the person most inimical to Isabel, is thus also related to her as the means by which her money can be translated into action—as she had been the intended translation of the Touchett money. The image by which she conceives of her role in relation to Osmond is exactly the same as that used by Ralph when he tells his father that he would like to "put a little wind in her sails." (III:260): "She would launch his boat for him; she would be his providence" (IV:192). Her benevolence, like Ralph's, results from her own incapacity to use money directly. This incapacity is literal; as a woman she has no way to make money "work," since women of her type and time are only consumers. Less literally it represents her reluctance to seek that "doing" which closes down her potentiality.

Osmond appeals to her precisely because he seems another self. Repeatedly the comment is made by others that he has *done* nothing. Madame Merle characterizes him as "Gilbert Osmond—he lives in Italy; that's all one can say about him or make of him. He's exceedingly clever, a man made to be distinguished; but, as I tell you, you exhaust the description when you say he's Mr. Osmond who lives *tout bêtement* in Italy. No career, no name, no position, no fortune, no past, no future, no anything" (III:281). When Madame Merle observes to the Countess Gemini that her brother "is one of the cleverest of men," his sister says, "I've heard you say that before but I haven't yet discovered what he has done." Madame Merle, who at last sees some possibility for action in Osmond's case—his marriage to Isabel—replies merely, "He has done nothing that has had to be undone. And he has known how to wait" (III:392). Osmond himself, we are told, feels that by his marriage his unexpressed self can find tongue. "The desire to have something or other to show for his 'parts'—to show somehow or other—had been the dream of his youth; but as the years went on the conditions attached to any marked proof of rarity had affected him more and more as gross and detestable; like the swallowing of mugs of beer to advertise what one could 'stand.'" Now, like Isabel, he expects to find manifestation through another: "She should do the thing *for* him, and he would not have waited in vain" (IV:12).

Unappealing as Osmond's negativity might seem, it is the very reason Isabel finds him more attractive than anyone she has known. "What has he ever done?" challenges Goodwood when he hears that she intends to marry this man, and she declares with pride, for it echoes her own abstention, "Nothing at all" (IV:47). His virtues, for her, are a list of negatives: "No property, no title, no honours, no houses, nor lands, nor position, nor reputation, nor brilliant belongings of any sort. It's the total absence of these things that pleases me" (IV:74), she tells Ralph.

Of course, one will say that Isabel is wrong to see this extreme Emersonianism in Osmond. Though Osmond declines the manifestations of action, he is a collector of objects and a cultivator of appearances; he is intensely aware, in truth, of his effect in the world—and imposes this awareness on Isabel after they are married. The most Emersonian of her wooers, despite his cotton mills, is Goodwood; "to whom under the world do we owe anything?" are nearly his last words to her. "Oh, he was intrinsic enough; she never thought of his even looking for artificial aids," Isabel reflects when Goodwood comes to see her in Rome after her marriage. His figure, she observes, had "a kind of bareness and bleakness which made the accident of meeting in memory or apprehension a peculiar concussion; it was deficient in the social drapery commonly muffling, in an overcivilized age, the sharpness of human contacts" (IV:280).

But, then, she has defined herself as "independent" of all these things in the same negative way. One recalls, again, her declaration to Madame Merle concerning a hypothetical wooer—that nothing he possessed would matter to her, just as nothing that belonged to her was any measure of herself (III:288). It is such a self, sequestered from expression in outer things or acts, that she has cherished in herself and thinks she recognizes in Osmond, the ideal lover of whom she had spoken. He actually admits to her that he has had no "natural indifference" to outward show and that his life has exhibited his "studied, wilful renunciation"—a mock enactment of the giving-up which is the heroic gesture of so many Jamesian idealists. Isabel, however, does not understand that his "renunciation" is no more than an attitude. James remarks that in her characteristic way, she had "invented a fine theory about Gilbert Osmond, she loved him not for what he really possessed, but for his very poverties dressed out as honors" (IV:75). Her imagination, writing its own story, had seen him as another character than the actual one: "she had had a more wondrous vision of him, fed through charmed senses and oh such a stirred fancy! She had not read him right" (IV:192), she later realizes.

Yet her instinct for a resemblance which makes him her ultimate and most humiliating alter-ego is not altogether mistaken. In his fastidious disdain for vulgar effort he is, again, a version of her own resistance to action; his aesthetic connoisseurship is a possibility latent in her own interest in the collection of fine sensations. He is not wrong when, after stating his personal view that "one ought to make one's life a work of art" (IV:15), he tells her that this is exactly what he believed she herself was trying to do. In what seems to be his successful fusion of American independence of spirit, disdain for "accoutrements," and European appreciation of the heritage of Western culture, he appears to represent what she aspires to. In the multitude of her potentialities even Gilbert Osmond is latent.

I have not included Lord Warburton in this review of companions who, each in his own way, enact the potentialities of Isabel's character. Warburton is, of course, the one European close to her, and he does not share with the others and with Isabel a starting point in the mythical freedom of American possibility. Representative of his country, his class, he is a type whose character and life forecast a predictable history. But James relates even him to Isabel by showing him to be a "specimen of an English gentleman," as Mr. Touchett calls him (III:90), who doesn't want to be one—he, too, is fleeing the plot he has inherited. Ralph pities him for this—"He's a man with a great position who's playing all sort of tricks with it. He doesn't take himself seriously . . . Great responsibilities, great opportunities, great consideration, great wealth, great power, a natural share in the public affairs of a great country. But he's all in a

muddle about himself . . . [and] doesn't know what to believe in."
Lord Warburton is a proprietor who is politically opposed to property. But, as Ralph says, he "can neither abolish himself as a nui-
sance nor maintain himself as an institution" (III:98).

Yet he cannot possibly escape the structure which encloses him.
He has no intention of giving up his fifty thousand acres of English
soil, his half-dozen houses, his seat in Parliament, his elegant tastes
for literature, art, science, and the new views—and the revolution
would, Mr. Touchett says, never touch him—"he's too much liked"
(III:103). Lord Warburton's is the liberal attitude toward those cultural frames and institutions that may be said to define the person;
he will, despite his "new views," leave the structure standing and
himself within it. He cannot be as radical as Isabel. Rather, he is a
good illustration of Madame Merle's belief that appurtenances
define character, are character. Henrietta later puts the matter suc-
cinctly: "He owns about half England; that's his character" (IV:4).
Despite the splendor of his offer and his personal amiability he
threatens Isabel's rejection of such a definition of self. Among all
those she knows he is the character most clearly defined by the
"system" of which he is a part—and she is forced, at the very start
of their acquaintance, to contrast him with the "young man lately
come from America who had no system at all, but who had a character of which it was useless for her to try to persuade herself that
the impression on her mind had been light" (III:144).

It is his being not a "character" in her own sense (a well of
possibility), but a "personage" that makes Isabel anticipate
Warburton's proposal with dread. "At the risk of adding to the
evidence of her self-sufficiency," remarks the narrator, "it must
be said that there had been moments when this possibility of
admiration by a personage represented to her an aggression
almost to the degree of an affront . . . She herself was a character—she couldn't help being aware of that; and hitherto her
visions of a completed consciousness had concerned themselves
largely with moral images—things as to which the question would
be whether they pleased her sublime soul. Lord Warburton
loomed before her, largely and brightly, as a collection of attributes and powers which were not to be measured by this simple
rule . . . What she felt was that a territorial, a political, a social
magnate had conceived the design of drawing her into the system
in which he rather invidiously lived and moved" (III:143–144).

Richard Chase protested that she is unfair. "Despite his being a hereditary nobleman and so, bound to the formalities and duties of his station in life, he presents himself to her with perfect candor as a man, and not a lord, who needs and desires her."[22] But this is to mistake the novel's dramatic surface for the play of its themes. Warburton *is* a man, no doubt, but he must nevertheless represent to Isabel something both more abstract and more threatening. With her personal ideal of a selfhood unbounded by cultural categories, she resists the conventional in him and imposed by him. She sees that most of the others she knows are also somehow less than "characters" in her sense. She wrongly exempts Osmond from this perception. "He resembled no one she had ever seen; most of the people she knew might be divided into groups of a half a dozen specimens. There were one or two exceptions to this; she could think for instance of no group that would contain her aunt Lydia. There were other people who were, relatively speaking, original—original, as one might say, by courtesy—such as Mr. Goodwood, as her cousin Ralph, as Henrietta Stackpole, as Lord Warburton, as Madame Merle. But in essentials, when one came to look at them, these individuals belonged to types already present to her mind. Her mind contained no class offering a natural place to Mr. Osmond" (III:375–376).

Osmond, of course, may really be as definable a type as Ralph thinks when he terms him a "sterile dilletante" (IV:71). In explaining his attraction for Isabel we must also remember that he conforms to a Romantic type, the Byronic hero-villain—he is, as William Veeder observes, "bored, indolent, aloof, misanthropic . . . he shares these traits with Grandcourt, Max, St. Elmo, and other conventional misanthropes since Satan and Byron."[23] But his pretended indifference to all commitments to convention makes him seem to her what she herself aspires to be—even though he, in a lapse into sincerity, warns her before their engagement, "I'm convention itself" (IV:21). When Ralph objects to Osmond's type, Isabel retorts—describing, in effect, herself, or her idea of herself—"What's the matter with Mr. Osmond's type, if it be one? His being so independent, so individual, is what *I* most see in him" (IV, 68).

It is in relation to these others who propose her development that Isabel tries to define those terms which are her spiritual watchwords. When she rejects Goodwood upon his first arrival in Europe, she declares, "I like my liberty too much. If there's one

thing in the world I'm fond of it's my personal independence."
Bemused, the free American man protests, "Who would wish less to
curtail your liberty than I? What can give me greater pleasure than
to see you perfectly independent—doing whatever you like? It's to
make you independent, that I want to marry you." Isabel calls his
statement a "beautiful sophism." She must suspect that his idea of
independence is in large part the material one—he will marry her
and free her of material concerns—but the implication that money
is freedom has social truth. Goodwood is correct in saying that an
unmarried woman in Isabel's time and place isn't actually socially
"independent" but "hampered at every step" (III:228). Marriage,
especially marriage to someone with money, would give her the
social role without which her selfhood cannot compose itself.
Isabel's reply to Goodwood, that *because* she is poor, among other
things, she can reject this definition of selfhood (it is the same, after
all, as Madame Merle's), is one that cannot stand the test of social
reality.

Ralph's role is ambiguous. On the one hand, he appreciates her
character. It is he who raises the artist's question, almost as James
put it in the preface: "It was a fine free nature; but what was she
going to do with herself?" He reminds himself that his question
about "doing" is "irregular, for with most women one had no occasion to ask it. Most women did with themselves nothing at all; they
waited, in attitudes more or less gracefully passive, for a man to
come that way and furnish them with a destiny" (III:87). Ralph
does not know, any more than Isabel, what new plot might be
written for her; he has the attitude of the literary experimenter who
shares her hope of discarding stale plots and finding a new one. Yet
his sense of how to put "wind in her sails" is less abstract than hers.
The economic sense of "independent" is never far from the text,
entering in that first ambiguous use of the word in Mrs. Touchett's
telegram, over which the gentlemen on the lawn at Gardencourt
ponder, uncertain whether she means that her niece is "well off" or
"fond of (her) own way" (III:14). Ralph decides to see that she has
money so that she will be able to express this fondness for her own
way *because* she is well off—the two senses of the term exhibiting
their hidden connection. He explicitly links money and imagination
when he tells his father that he wants to make Isabel rich,
explaining, "I call people rich when they're able to meet the
requirements of their imagination" (III:261).

Yet he is as vague as she will be when it comes to defining what she will be able to "do with herself." Money, after all, is itself an abstract potentiality, which does not shape the exact futurity of its possessor. He is only able to think of what money will *prevent* her from doing." "If she has an easy income she'll never have to marry for a support. That's what I want cannily to prevent. She wishes to be free, and your bequest will make her free" (III:261). Aside from this, the seventy thousand pounds[24] are to "facilitate the execution of [her] good impulses," in which Ralph shares her faith. Her goodness itself, he understands, is only what she will "do"; "she's as good as her best opportunities" (III:264).

When she is rich, Isabel herself—it is one of her contradictions—accepts the idea that riches make one more free than penniless idealism, though she is filled with a certain amount of fear. "A large fortune means freedom, and I'm afraid of that. It's such a fine thing, and one should make such a good use of it . . . I'm not sure it's not a greater happiness to be powerless" (III:320). But as time passes, her imagination of freedom recovers, and she pictures her future "by the light of her hopes, her fears, her fancies, her ambitions, her predilections . . . She lost herself in a maze of visions; the fine things to be done by a rich, independent, generous girl who took a large human view of occasions and obligations were sublime in the mass" (III:321). The money increases her sense of a great potential for some still unchosen action, but one which escapes the plot of femalehood; she "made up her mind that to be rich was a virtue because it was to be able to *do* and to do could only be sweet. It was a graceful contrary of the stupid side of weakness—especially the feminine variety" (III:301).

Goodwood, as we have seen, had thought she simply wanted to see the world a bit and offered to help her do so, but she told him he could only help her by putting the sea between them. When he then protested, "One would think you were going to commit some atrocity," she retorted, "Perhaps I am. I wish to be free even to do that if the fancy takes me" (III:229–230). Yes, even an "atrocity" must be included in her freely conceivable choice of lives. And "choice," of course, is another of her watchwords. The act of choice is more important than the thing chosen. One recalls the scene at Gardencourt when, following the discussion about remaining downstairs alone with the young men, her aunt says, "You're too fond of your own ways": "Yes, I think I'm very fond of them. But I always want to know the things one shouldn't do." "So as to do them?" asks her aunt. "So as to choose" (III:93), said Isabel.

Such declarations make Isabel sound like a flaming rebel—except that we know that she has never done an improper thing in her life. It is the theoretical right of choice that she cherishes—to the point, indeed, of making no choice, and so preserving choice still longer. Yet she begins to see that her abstention from choice, her withholding from action, may be an evasion of life. Osmond is successfully wooing her by describing himself as someone who has always rejected action, yet he correctly identifies his rule of life as "negative," as "wilful renunciation." At the end of the novel's first volume, as she is already, unconsciously, preparing to break out of her resistance to marriage, she admits to changing her plans and projects every day. "It seems frivolous," she says, "One ought to choose something very deliberately, and be faithful to that" (III:381).

As for Isabel's visions themselves, they remain unspecified from first to last. James stresses her determination to be more responsive to her own imagination than to anything else. "Her imagination," we are told, "was by habit ridiculously active; when the door was not open it jumped out of the window" (III:42). The energetic motion of the image points up the paradox that imagination is, after all, "motionless," and does not of itself produce action. Yet her fine imagination is crowded with images drawn from literary models. In the beginning, Isabel agrees with Ralph that she brings romance with her, and has "brought it to the right place" (III:62). When introduced to Lord Warburton she childishly exclaims, "Oh, I hoped there would be a lord; it's just like a novel!" (III:18). So one of Austen's marriageable heroines—or her mother—might have fluttered at the approach of an attractive, titled gentleman in quest of a wife, "hoping to fall in love," as Warburton is supposed to be. Isabel "scarce fell short of seeing him—though quite without luridity—as a hero of romance" (III:91). But this does not turn out to mean that she will figure in a tale in which a portionless girl marries a Darcy, though Lord Warburton, proposing to her, knows what role he is playing: "It was at first sight, as the novels say; I know now that's not a fancy phrase, and I shall think better of novels for evermore" (III:147). She also expects to find a ghost in Gardencourt—an appropriate item for romance—but though this will eventually make its appearance in her story, it will come in a symbolic way. As the reader listens to these remarks in the novel's a fifth chapter, he cannot yet tell what he is in for—and hears the music of various plots begin to sound. The novelist himself may be entertaining the idea of all of them.

Yet Isabel's vagueness, her reluctance to objectify her feelings by action, seems an inhibition of creative decision. We can look critically, again, at some of those declarations she makes on behalf of her "freedom." Her cousin senses her antideterministic personality: "I don't believe you allow things to be settled for you." She replies, "Oh, yes; if they're settled as I like them" (III:22–23). This suggests, misleadingly, that she knows clearly what she wants. She was "always planning her own development." But we have no glimpse of these plans. She herself wonders as she rejects Lord Warburton, "What view of life, what design upon fate, what conception of happiness, had she that pretended to be larger than these large, these fabulous occasions? If she wouldn't do such a thing as that then she must do great things, she must do something greater" (III:156). But what are these greater things?

In fact, it is never at all clear what she expects of life. She wants knowledge, but is it that mythic knowledge that is the fruit of suffering? From literature, again, she has learned "that the unpleasant had been even too absent from her knowledge, for she had gathered from her acquaintance with literature that it was a source of interest and even instruction" (III:42). When she refuses Lord Warburton, she explains that in marrying him she would be trying to escape "the usual chances and dangers . . . what most people know and suffer" (III:187). Her desire not to be exempted from experience is not, as one might think, a religious or a moral one—though it seems to resemble that acceptance of the whole mortal condition which is an imitation of Christ—an association that does press forward in the case of James's later heroine, Milly Theale. Isabel's is an intellectual or aesthetic interest—which is what Ralph accuses her of when he suspects that she really is not prepared to experience life fully, but wants simply to "see . . . not to feel." Though she bridles, and responds that seeing and feeling cannot be distinguished for "a sentient being," his challenge has point. Yet she seems to contradict herself when she admits that she does not suffer easily, and protests, "It's not absolutely necessary to suffer; we were not made for that"—and declares that she has come to Europe "to be as happy as possible" (III, 65). Certainly she does not choose the suffering she brings upon herself unwittingly. Rather, she will, like most people, try to be happy and fail.

If one is tempted to call her flighty and superficial on this as on other occasions, one is missing the opportunity of sharing the plausibility of each of these attitudes—to entertain them, successively, as she does. As James's narrator says, "Isabel Archer was a young person of many theories" (III:66). Rather than condemning her for their numerousness or incompatibility, James embraces the variety of possibilities which, as novelist, *he* entertains. And that openness to experience which she claims for herself, even if it is suspected to be a desire to see rather than to feel, is precisely the artist's own. In chapter 6 when he summarizes some of her virtues and defects the narrator observes, "her errors and delusions were frequently such as a biographer interested in preserving the dignity of his subject must shrink from specifying" (III:67). Yet he insists: "with her meagre knowledge, her inflated ideals, her confidence at once innocent and dogmatic, her temper at once exacting and indulgent, her mixture of curiosity and fastidiousness, of vivacity and indifference, her desire to look very well and to be if possible even better, her determination to see, to try, to know, her combination of the delicate, desultory, flame-like spirit and the eager and personal creature of conditions: she would be an easy victim of scientific criticism if she were not intended to awaken on the reader's part an impulse more tender and more purely expectant" (III:69). Expectancy is what we are required to have because she herself is conceived as always expectant, always ready for new realizations.

As I have been suggesting, her inability to forecast her own future, to anticipate the shape of her peculiar fate, is understandable if we remember that in discarding a conventional life pattern or any of the conventional plots of the novel, she asks for a definition lying outside of the stock of available selfhoods. James does not know any more than she how she might live as herself in another way than by choosing one of the fates that are offered her. Her "maze of visions" will turn out to have very little to do with her destiny except to lead her to make the most mistaken of choices, to do an "atrocity" in marrying Gilbert Osmond.

It is perfectly true that it is money, her "independence," that makes something happen when she accepts his proposal, as though it is the spring mechanism which puts this doll into motion at last.

She herself is not so much choosing as chosen, but it is the money that has given her a fate. The plot, which has been virtually stationary for most of the first half of the novel—consisting simply of repeated considerations of Isabel by means of her confrontations with others—now moves under the stimulus of her money. In a society based on a money economy, governed by the compulsions of the market, nothing, indeed, does happen except by the application of this source of all motion. And so here—Ralph had been right in thinking that money would give Isabel a plot. She is motivated to marry Osmond by the desire to make her money do something in the world, while the plot to marry her for her money—as conceived by Madame Merle and Osmond—has only been set in motion by those seventy thousand pounds.

But with her engagement early in the second volume, she may be said to have at last embraced the marriage-plot she has resisted so long. James had misgivings, as he worked on the novel, that there had been "a want of action in the earlier part," which he hoped would be made up in the chapters following his heroine's marriage. He thought of the matter technically: "The weakness of the whole story is that it is too exclusively psychological—that it depends too little on incident," but he hoped that "the complete unfolding of the situation that is established by Isabel's marriage may nonetheless be sufficiently dramatic."[25] The novel's structure, however, justifies itself thematically if it is seen that the nonprogressive character of the early half is a representation of Isabel's own deferral of action.

She now reminds Casper that she had warned him that she would do as she chose, but he reminds her that she had told him to doubt any rumor of her engagement. Has she changed with this definitive step? Ralph says, "You must have changed immensely. A year ago you valued your liberty beyond everything." Isabel seems, indeed, at this moment of her greatest happiness, to turn her back on that principle, for she answers, "It doesn't look to me now, I admit, such an inviting expanse" (IV:65). Continuing to explain his particular objections to Osmond, Ralph invokes once more those images of the free sail before the wind with which he had associated her: "You seemed to me to be soaring far up in the blue—to be, sailing in the bright light, over the heads of men." But "poor Isabel . . . wandering into the didactic," as James says, only replies, "I've never moved on a higher plane that I'm moving on now. There's nothing higher for a girl than to marry—a person she likes" (IV:69–70).

That others dislike Osmond only confirms her conviction that she has "married to please herself"—and so preserved her liberty (IV:77).

The structure of the text continues to preserve this liberty, however, by making it seem that Isabel has not acted at all, has not broken the barrier that separates her potentiality from its limiting expression. Though the scene of Osmond's initial declaration of love to Isabel is presented dramatically in chapter 29, her acceptance of him, months later, is elided between chapters 31 and 32. Her momentous moment of *choice*—so long delayed—is thus a virtual blank, permitting us to feel that her potentiality is still intact. And not only the scene of her acceptance of Osmond and the wedding itself (described in one sentence in a later chapter, (IV:137), but all that happened during the succeeding time to change Isabel far more, one might imagine, than she had changed at the time of her engagement is virtually nonexistent. The major ellipsis of the novel is, of course, the three or four years following her wedding, which fall between chapters 35 and 36. Yet this omitted stretch of life has included the virtual breakdown of her marriage, her disillusion in Osmond, the death of her infant. That her marriage has broken down, of course, is itself a defeat of the marriage-plot as a closure of female destiny. The ellipsis in the text must be explained by the breakdown of this narrative structure as well as by the breakdown of Isabel's literal marriage. We do not need to know the details of Osmond's depravities or cruelties to know that her project for the exfoliation of the free self has had no realization.

She herself insists, indeed, that she has acted once and for all. When she contemplates an open rupture with Osmond if he forbids her to visit Ralph's sickroom in Rome, she tells herself that "almost anything seemed preferable to repudiating the most serious act— the single sacred act—of her life" (IV:246), and still later she tells Henrietta, who advises her to leave Osmond, "One must accept one's deeds. I married him before all the world; I was perfectly free; it was impossible to do anything more deliberate" (IV:284). Osmond himself invokes the same principle in his attempt to prevent her journey to Gardencourt to the dying Ralph. He reminds her that their marriage was "of our own deliberate making . . . we should accept the consequences of our actions" (IV:356).

But Osmond's argument is dishonest since he knows, as Isabel does not yet, how little the marriage was her act, after all. The effect created by the ellipsis is justified for this reason, also. Though she had believed in "the spontaneity of her own career" (IV:329), she had not chosen but been chosen. "What have you to do with my husband . . . What have you to do with me?" she comes to the point of desperately asking Madame Merle, who replies, "Everything." She realizes, then, "that Mrs. Touchett was right. Madame Merle had married her" (IV:327). Yet later still, Madame Merle has her own disclosure to make, that Isabel's marriage is not so much this false friend's act as Ralph's. It is Isabel's last epiphany: "He made you a rich woman. He imparted to you that extra lustre which was required to make you a brilliant match. At bottom it's him you've to thank" (IV:388).

Isabel has resisted the coercion of formula by resisting Osmond's desire to obliterate her independent personality. But what (nearly unimaginable) form has that resistance taken? Even this element, insofar as it might represent a struggling Isabel, is more absent than present in the text. The details of her marital unhappiness, the actual incidents, remain, even in retrospective reference, abstract or obscure. His vices appear to her as negatives, just as his virtues once had done—he is a more desolating parody, now, of her own self-definition by not doing. "What does he do to you?" Henrietta asks, and Isabel responds, "He does nothing. But he doesn't like me" (IV:284). Even her solitary recollections in the famous vigil of chapter 42 are metaphor rather than drama. Osmond has "put the lights out one by one." But what exactly were the "shadows" that emanated from him? "They were not his misdeeds, his turpitudes; she accused him of nothing . . . She knew of no wrong he had done; he was not violent, he was not cruel: she simply believed he hated her" (IV:190). He had discovered one day that she had "too many ideas" and disliked her for them, while she had discovered in him a "sovereign contempt for every one but some three or four very exalted people whom he envied, and for everything in the world but half a dozen ideas of his own." He pretended indifference but lived for the recognition of society; he was the soul of convention, while she "had pleaded the cause of freedom, of doing as they chose, of not caring for the aspect and denomination of their life" (IV:195, 197, 199). The remarkable ruminative essay consists almost entirely of summary statements such as these. It has been justly praised—by James himself to begin with—but it must be recognized for what it is—a denial of presentation, a sleight of hand to cover the wide gap of Isabel's marriage, her single action and its aftermath. James claimed for it the virtue of dramatized thought, but as memory it is peculiarly unevocative of specific past action.

Perhaps this ellipsis is an ellipsis of the element of sexual union, the "act" which lies outside the terminus of the conventional marriage-plot. Since Isabel's marriage occurs at the center rather than at the end of the story, we are forced to consider the nature of the relation that has proved so disappointing to her, knowing her already as someone who once asserted that "a woman ought to be able to live to herself, in the absence of exceptional flimsiness, and that it was perfectly possible to be happy without the society of a more or less coarse-minded person of another sex" (III:71). James subtly but sufficiently suggests her sexual timidity, especially in the language almost invariably used to describe her responses to Casper.[26] One may guess, on this plane, that her choice of Osmond is partly dictated by the fact that he appeals most to her *ideas*. That she later finds that some of his ideas are "unclean" may reflect a revelation of his sexuality, which she has not anticipated.

But despite the pertinency of these hints it is more important, I think, to see Isabel's sexual history, insofar as it is implied, as representing a more general encounter with experience. Plot itself, it may be said, is describable in sexual terms. The arousal of tension, the achievement of climax, the attainment of pleasure, and the dissolution of desire itself in the subsidence to quiescence—these phrases describe the trajectory of a story. Isabel both desires and fears a story as much as she both desires and fears sexual union; both threaten the pure potentiality of the unaroused personality, which only subsists in itself. It is in this subtle way, I think, that we must at the last explain her rejection, made with such a mixture of response and terror, of Casper. The marriage closure is rejected just as the marriage to Osmond in the center of the novel has been unrealizable. Casper's kiss, the ritual gesture which ends so many novels, is present in all its power on the final page only to reveal its inability to provide an ending to the story of Isabel Archer.

Because the marriage itself does not, after all, provide that bustle or "ado" of incident lacking in the first half of the novel, the later portions require a new plot altogether, a supplementary story about another heroine. It is a new plot and yet, in some ways, a recapitulation, in parodic and miniature form, of some of the elements of Isabel's story—with Rosier, a harmless and more "limited" connoisseur-collector than Osmond, and Pansy, an innocent but modest *jeune fille*, without Isabel's grandiose appetite for freedom—though with a quiet power of resistance that reminds one of Catherine Sloper. Pansy reminds one even more of the heroine of *Washington Square* when one notices that her silent struggle is waged against a father whose cold, ironic intelligence, his disdain of his daughter's lover, is very much like Dr. Sloper's.

In chapter 36, the focus of the narrative even moves away from Isabel herself, and we see her less inwardly for a while. While her mysterious figure hovers in the background, the foreground is given over to the efforts of the collector of bibelots to acquire his Dresden shepherdess. We see Rosier and Madame Merle, to whom, while admiring the lace on her mantle and her other "good things," he applies for help in his suit of Osmond's daughter. We accompany him to Palazzo Roccanera on one of Isabel's Thursdays, when he tells Pansy he loves her; afterward he receives from Isabel only a brief, discouraging word—his suit won't please Osmond, and she can't help him. He goes again to see Madame Merle, who counsels patience, and again to a Thursday, where he has a cold reception from Osmond, and sees Lord Warburton appear. A few moments later, the last element of the new plot comes into view; Warburton looks across the room and notices "a dear little maid"—Pansy.

On this occasion, we begin to move closer, again, to Isabel, and listen to her conversation with Warburton about Ralph, whom he has brought to Rome, and who is more ill than ever. And, for a moment, we even get an interior glimpse of her state of mind as she measures the signs of Warburton's recovery from her rejection of him. As bereft of action as ever, "she gave an envious thought to the happier lot of men, who are always free to plunge into the healing waters of action" (IV:130). Her exterior is impermeable, however, and she assures her former suitor that she is very happy. Framed in a gilded doorway, the mistress of the house strikes Rosier "as the picture of a gracious lady" (IV:105). This sole reference to the novel's title suggests James's meaning. Isabel has become "the portrait of a lady" by surrendering her free self; she is—for the moment—fixed in her role as Osmond's wife; framed, circumscribed, by the limitation of this definition, reduced to type.

James unites the stories of Isabel and of her stepdaughter with the greatest skill. It is Pansy who provides the occasion for, at last, a visible demonstration of Osmond's implacable ambition, which converts all human relations over which he has control to instruments of his pride. Out of the story of these others will issue Isabel's final trial, and the return of the dying Ralph is a signal that we will share with this early witness the task of watching and interpreting the novel's real heroine. He has had, since her marriage, no intimate view of her, only the social aspect shown to all: "The free, keen girl had become quite another person; what he saw was the fine lady who was supposed to represent something. What did Isabel represent? Ralph asked himself; and he could only answer by saying that she represented Gilbert Osmond." It is to Ralph's insight that we owe the realization of what Osmond's new way of life means: "under the guise of caring for intrinsic values Osmond lived exclusively for the world . . . He lived with his eye on it from morning till night, and the world was so stupid it never suspected the trick" (IV:143–144).

At last, with almost all of Isabel's companions gathered together as in the first volume (Madame Merle is back after an absence and Henrietta and Casper will soon join Ralph in Rome), we reach chapter 40. With Madame Merle's return, Isabel has had occasion to reflect on the guilt—if it was one—implied in Mrs. Touchett's charge that this supple person had "made" her marriage. "It might have been written, after all, that there was not so much to thank her for (IV:159). But she tells herself, "the sole source of her mistake had been within herself. There had been no plot, no snare; she had looked and considered and chosen" (IV:160). Yet she is hard upon the very moment when, looking through a doorway, she sees her husband and her friend "unconsciously and familiarly associated" (IV:205)—and has her first intimation of a plot of which she has been oblivious.

It is still the Pansy plot, however, that we continue to hear most about. Madame Merle lingers on this occasion to talk about Warburton's interest in Pansy, and to urge, with a certain insidious familiarity, that Isabel use her influence. Osmond, in the next chapter, insists more coarsely, still, on her ability to bring the man she refused to marry "to the point." That Isabel is willing to do so has puzzled some readers—why, knowing of Pansy's love for Rosier, is she ready to assist in such a project? The answer—that she wants to please her husband, to be the wife he expects her to be—is offered, but it is not entirely convincing. Isabel, as always, finds no outlet of action; her ineffectual potentiality has become a burden to her. She longs for some "form of positive exertion" to relieve her unhappiness. "She could never rid herself of the sense that unhappiness was a state of disease—of suffering as opposed to doing. To 'do'—it hardly mattered what—would therefore be an escape, perhaps in some degree a remedy" (IV:173–174). Her immediate "act" is reflection, the long, elaborated rumination of Chapter 42, which reviews her present problem and serves to repair the text's ellipsis of her married years. It is a silent dramatization of thought which discloses a history curiously bare of recollected incident, a history of attitudes and inner responses. Her real offense to Osmond, she finally perceives, has been nothing she has done; it has been simply her unenacted selfhood—"having a mind of her own at all" (IV:200). Yet now he accuses her of acting, of "working against [him]" by keeping Warburton from proposing to Pansy (IV:263) and even of having intercepted the letter Warburton had promised to write to Osmond! Madame Merle will make the same accusation, saying bitterly to Isabel, "Your work's done" (IV:324). But Isabel has done nothing of the sort; she has failed to do anything. It is Pansy herself who has let Warburton know that he ought not propose to her. And Madame Merle, though it now seems little to boast of, has not been been able to resist the temptation to tell Isabel that even her marriage was not of her own making. To Osmond she confesses that she had been jealous of Isabel, who had seemed able to do so much good for this former lover: "I want it to be *my* work," she tells him (IV:338).

It is almost the close, as we must realize from the fact that Ralph, the witness most closely identified with the author and the reader, is ready to go home to Gardencourt to die. Bound still to the sterile inertia of her marriage, Isabel can do no more for him than delegate Casper and Henrietta, her American surrogates, to conduct him home. All three—Ralph, Casper, and Henrietta, the "spectators" of the comedy, as Isabel calls them (IV:303), have discovered the secret of her unhappiness. Casper, before he leaves, asks only to be told that he may pity her, "That at least would be doing something. I'd give my life to it" (IV:320). For herself, Isabel must tell Henrietta, vaguely, "There are many things I mean to do" (IV, 303) but leaving Osmond does not seem to be one of them—and no alternatives suggest themselves.

Yet the call to action does come; she must go to Ralph, who is on his deathbed at Gardencourt. James's narrator says that she feels "all the joy of irreflective action—a joy to which she had so long been a stranger" (IV:357), until, of course, Osmond's prohibition falls upon her. She does not dare to act alone: "They were perfectly apart in feeling as two disillusioned lovers had ever been; but they had never yet separated in act" (IV:356). But she is freed for this act, nonetheless, by the Countess Gemini. It is she who finally discloses to Isabel the secret of Pansy's birth, the long relation between Osmond and Madame Merle, the motive of the plot to marry her for her money, the motive for Madame Merle's wish to make a "great marriage" for Pansy.

The book's ending has often seemed to be an expression of James's pessimistic view of Isabel's illusions of freedom; she has at last realized the error of her faith in her own infinite possibility. It is for these reasons, it would seem, that she rejects Goodwood, whose final appeal is an appeal to that faith, to the American sense of inexhaustible futurity, expressed in Miltonic language: "The world's all before us—and the world's very big." "The world's very small" (IV:435), she tells him, and goes back to Rome. One reason we snatch at, in the obscurity of her purpose, is her promise not to abandon Pansy. It may be that she has surrendered some of her cherished independence in her intenser realization of her bond with Ralph. In her resolution to do something for Pansy she accepts some burden of action. But even this may be only a new delegation, replacing her delegation of her potentiality to Osmond. Will she attempt this again, by means of her money? It has been suggested that she provide Pansy with the *dot* that will make it unnecessary for her to marry a rich man, which would be a duplication of Ralph's fatal endowment. In one way or another she will help to float the vessel of Pansy's and Rosier's happiness.

For herself, however, she has not really surrendered, yet, her, unquenchable sense of free potentiality:

> She saw herself, in the distant years, still in the attitude of a woman who had her life to live . . . Deep in her soul—deeper than any appetite for renunciation—was the sense that life would be her business for a long time to come . . . It couldn't be she was to live only to suffer; she was still young, after all, and a great many things might happen to her yet. To live only to suffer—only to feel the injury of life repeated and enlarged—it seemed to her she was too valuable, too capable, for that. Then she wondered if it were vain and stupid to think so well of herself. When had it

ever been a guarantee to be valuable? Wasn't all history full of the destruction of precious things? Wasn't it much more probable that if one were fine one would suffer? It involved then perhaps an admission that one had a certain grossness; but Isabel recognized, as it passed before her eyes, the quick vague shadow of a long future. She should never escape; she should last to the end. Then the middle years wrapped her about again and the grey curtain of her indifference closed her in.   (IV:392–393)

This remarkable paragraph, coming before the actual dramatic close—her farewell to Ralph, her final rejection of Goodwood—is, perhaps, the novel's true conclusion. Isabel remains what she has always been, with her faith in her own potentiality only dimmed, not quenched altogether by the lessons of experience. Her fate, still uncommitted, must, by the structure of the novel itself, remain open. Her gestures, as in the case of other Jamesian protagonists, have been, one might charge, more renunciatory than anything else, but what she renounces has been in every case a temptation to terminate her own story. It is true and false, James felt himself, that he leaves Isabel "en l'air." "The whole of anything is never told,"[27] as James wrote in his notebook, and while, as he said, the artist must make it "appear" that relations end somewhere, his truthful art also lets it be known that they do not.

That character can maintain itself without appropriate outcome in plot, remains, however, problematic. Henrietta had warned Isabel that she must leave Osmond "before [her] character gets spoiled" (IV:304). Madame Merle declares that her own soul, "which was a very good one to start with," has been destroyed by her association with Osmond. It is only Osmond, the worst spokesman for such a view, who says, probably cynically, "Don't you know the soul is an immortal principal? How can it suffer alteration?" (IV:334).

The Determinate Plot:
The Bostonians

ISABEL ARCHER'S most open declaration of essentialism, "Nothing that belongs to me is any measure of me," is provoked by some remarks by Madame Merle which are not generally recognized for what they are—James's insertion in his text of a powerful statement of philosophic positivism. What Madame Merle argues is also the expression of the viewpoint of the realist novel—particularly in its naturalist phase—that all reality, including the reality of human experience, is found in the evidential.

> When you've lived as long as I you'll see that every human being has his shell and that you must take the shell into account. By the shell I mean the whole envelope of circumstances. There's no such thing as an isolated man or woman; we're each of us made up of some cluster of appurtenances. What shall we call our 'self'? Where does it begin? where does it end? It overflows into everything that belongs to us—and then it flows back again. I know a large part of myself is in the clothes I choose to wear. I've a great respect for *things*! One's self—for other people—is one's expression of one's self; and one's house, one's furniture, one's garments, the books one reads, the company one keeps—these things are expressive.   (III:287–288)

Madame Merle may well be considered to have a stronger argument than Isabel—one that accords with modern views such as Erving Goffman's about the dependence of the configurations of personality upon social gesture. Her very image of the "shell" of circumstance seems to anticipate Santayana's words, which Goffman uses as an epigraph to *The Presentation of Self in Everyday Life:* "Living things in contact with the air must acquire a cuticle, and it is not urged against cuticles that they are not hearts . . . Words and images are like shells, no less integral parts of nature than are the substances they cover, but better addressed to the eye and more open to observation."[1] Goffman's own discussion is more concerned with the enactment of social roles than with "things" in the sense of material objects, but it is to be noted that house and garments are, after all, the role-player's choices of scene and costume, and that books and "company" are not merely dramatizations of his ideas and tastes but their mode of being.

The statement that "things" are "expressive" of the self is, more precisely, a statement of literary method, and of that literary method which James praised in Balzac. In words that resemble Madame Merle's he had pointed (in his 1875 essay on Balzac) to the description of Madame Vauquier, the *pension* owner in *Père Goriot,* noting with admiration that her "whole person . . . is an explanation of the boarding-house as the boarding-house is an implication of her person" (2:52). Isabel refuses to be a character in a realist novel when she replies that none of her "accoutrements"—not her house, nor her clothes, nor her social furniture generally—express her. Implicit is the converse, that she is not the expression *of* her surroundings. And James, sustaining her belief in a self which does not flow in and out of things, expressing them and expressed by them, does not describe her appearance very particularly and does not attach to her that visible environmental signification which he admired in Balzac's novels.

It has often been noted that sight is a dominant metaphor in *The Portrait of a Lady.* As Dorothy Van Ghent has pointed out, the title asks us to see, and the handling of the story is deliberately "scenic," set in a "symbolic construct of things to be seen by the physical eye" as it moves through the "errors and illuminations of the inward eye."[2] Thus, the "look" of things represents both externalities and the reflective consciousness which, in impressionistic painting or literature, seems to register them passively, unanalytically. But the eye, which registers surfaces, is (paradoxically) also the symbolic organ of *in*sight, which does not remove the mind from the world, but makes the higher claims upon it of Emerson's "transparent eyeball." It performs the "motionless seeing" of Isabel's night-vigil in chapter 42. What is externalized for the physical eye, what is witnessed by it, is evidence of the sort to which Isabel's "motionless seeing" is opposed. Her contempt for visible "signs" reminds us how easily the eye is the source of that delusive "ocular proof" Othello asked for and received. Yet physical sight establishes that irrefutable evidence loved by the realist.

As I have argued, James tries as much as possible to further Isabel's refusal of self-exhibition through plot, her desire to remain independent of what happens to her and even what she herself does, her rejection of the idea that one *is* one's story. I have noted that an effect of Isabel's Americanism is to divorce her from any determining past. She is set free of the naturalist plot which establishes human beginning in initial conditions of birth and upbringing and traces their evolution into personal behavior, and their final consequence as destiny. She is also free, anti-naturalistically, from her present circumstances—the alien European environment, which provides no explanation of what she now is or does. By contrast, Lord Warburton, the novel's only major character located in his natural *milieu,* is an illustration of character socially explained. It is necessary for us to see Lockleigh to understand him. Isabel's visit there might be compared to Elizabeth Bennett's visit to Darcy's estate—after which Austen's heroine understands the character of the man she will marry and the character she will assume as his wife. But Gardencourt, against which Isabel's figure is first drawn for us, does not explain James's heroine (it does not even explain the Touchetts, its latest proprietors after a long history with which they have had nothing to do). The brief backward glance at her native Albany does not remedy this lack.

James's structural subscription to anti-naturalism, his belief in personal essence, may be contested in his story just the same. I have, so far, done too little justice to the fact that the novel can be read as a fable in which the free spirit is shown, at the last, to have been pressed into history by nature and the social mold as much as by the manipulations of other persons. James amuses us, as we have seen, with Isabel's confusion over whether the limiting circumstances of the poor person are a greater or a lesser guarantee of freedom. She thinks, at first, that she is freer because she is a penniless orphan, less trammeled by society's expectations. She rejects the plot of naturalism which, in so many novels, is the history of the particularly helpless *female* victim not only of biology (and to her own passions a woman, feebler in rational restraint, was assumed to be more subjected!) but of material deprivations, with which women were less equipped to cope. In *Adam Bede* Hetty Sorrel dreams of an elopement with the young squire; it is the only plot her imagination supplies. But, instead of what she expects, she is seduced, becomes pregnant, and is abandoned. Eliot comments, "Hetty had never read a novel . . . how could she find a shape for her expectations?"[3] In fact, her expectations *are* novelistic—belonging to a tradition of sentimental romance, like the expectations of Emma Bovary, who does read novels—though Hetty may simply have acquired them from the general atmosphere of her culture rather than from reading. What her culture has not provided her with, however, is an anticipation of the *new* destinal shape that Eliot herself is creating in her book, soon to be the prescribed destiny for dozens of other heroines of nineteenth- and twentieth-century novels—Hardy's Tess, the Goncourts's Germinie Lacerteux, Moore's Esther Waters, Crane's Maggie, Dreiser's Jennie Gerhardt. This new destiny is a reading of life—and especially female life—as a sequence determined to its inevitable close by natural and social forces.

Ralph reasons naturalistically when he resolves to protect Isabel from this plot. He knows better than Isabel that a poor woman has no choice but to marry, and to marry prudently. In making her rich, however, he inserts her into another kind of plot, that of the poor person who is unexpectedly revealed to be wealthy, by reason of suppressed princely origins or the fairy gift of Fortune or an unforeseen benefactor. In this Cinderella role, of course, Isabel's defiance of the naturalist plot is never brought to the test. Still, necessity may be said to return in another form. We can say that Isabel was really right in the beginning in thinking wealth to be a source of restriction, since it is her wealth that makes her attractive to the fortune hunters, and so the view that material conditions make one's fate holds. In addition, despite her struggle to keep her fate open, Isabel learns that the past of her own actions reduces her potentiality.

Thus, the novel works both to support Isabel's belief in freedom and to refute it. It expresses, in this way, one of James's persistent themes—the old question, conceived in modern terms, of the freedom of the will. James was not a religious man and would not have been burdened with the sense of *divine* predestination; for this very reason he felt the force of the nineteenth-century positivism of Darwin and Comte, which substituted a new predestinarian viewpoint for the old. But it is, paradoxically, religious tradition that offers in the novel's several Miltonic echoes an expression of this modern determinism along with a suggestion of the survival of free will. Just before her marriage, Isabel thinks, "the world lay before her. She could do whatever she chose" (IV:36). She is both right and wrong. When she resolves to accept the limiting consequences of her action, she is like Adam after the Fall: "One folly was enough, especially when it was to last forever" (IV:161). But Casper still insists, "The world's all before us," (IV:435), echoing her earlier thoughts, and even though she denies the idea, it is well to remember that it is of Adam and Eve *after* the Fall that the same statement is made at the end of *Paradise Lost*. Human freedom survives the predestined event.

It is Osmond who says, with Satan's sad knowledge of irremovable limitation. "I don't mean to say I've cared for nothing; but the things I've cared for have been definite—limited" (III:382). He is himself, like Madame Merle, an illustration of the naturalist theory of life, in which they both believe. It is Madame Merle, of course, who has been the dark heroine of that naturalist novel of female destiny which Isabel thought to escape. From the crude determining cause, lack of money, has come all her history—her inability to marry the man she loved, her illegitimate child, even her plot against Isabel. James will contrast again, in *The Wings of the Dove*, the blighted heroine of a naturalist plot—Kate Croy—with the rich, free girl who thinks she can defy it. In Milly Theale's case, the limitation of impending death will express the absolute limits of nature, yet Milly's will to freedom is not altogether frustrated. Determinism is also a major motif in *The Ambassadors*, which pivots upon the assumption that Strether's life has been a tin mold into which consciousness has been poured, taking its inevitable form once and for all. To the end, James finds in this issue of freedom and necessity the source of disruptive and cohesive forces which surge within the form of the novel.

When James wrote *The Portrait of a Lady*, he had in mind not so much Eliot's Hetty as her Gwendolen Harleth, who marries a rich man to save her mother and herself from destitution, as well as Dorothea Brooke, coerced neither by poverty or biology but still fatuous in her resolution to seek for herself a free character and history, and making a constricting marriage in the very process. When she is permitted to make a second marriage, Dorothea makes one which leaves many readers disappointed, and this suggests that Eliot did not really find the marriage-plot a satisfactory closure for *Middlemarch*. She left her heroine with a large measure of unrealized selfhood still on her hands—an ending more open than the writer may have consciously intended. James is more true to the conception of his character in allowing Isabel to reject such a recovery, yet at the cost of some sacrifice of probability as well as of the reader's hopes for the heroine.

James was also fresh from the lessons of Flaubert and of Zola and his followers, absorbed not only from their recent writings but from the heated conversations he had listened to in Paris in the winter of 1875–76. He saw them all again in 1884, and gained a more intense sense of their views and example. This time, he wrote in rapid succession two long, ambitious novels, which respond to the challenge of the naturalist viewpoint more directly than any others of his works—*The Bostonians* and *The Princess Casamassima*. Both, though they are quite different from one another, and really not very comparable to the French examples, have been generally described as James's attempts to write in the new mode.[4]

James's responses to the French naturalist group and particularly to its leader, Zola, were initially as much negative as positive, and always remained guarded. *Nana* aroused his repugnance for the "indecency" of the subject when he reviewed it in 1880, though he conceded that "the system on which the series of Zola's Rougon-Macquart has been written . . . deserves a great deal of respect" (2:867). With time, he seems to have been readier to concede that "we must grant the artist his subject," as he wrote in *The Art of Fiction* (1:56). He recognized that their enlargement of the scope of the novel remained, in the long run, the great contribution of these writers who had first shocked him. In 1888 James declared, in an essay on Maupassant, that "almost all the works of Zola and of Daudet, the best of Flaubert's novels, and the best of those of the brothers De Goncourt—treat of that vast, dim section of society" lying between the world of wealth and luxury and "the darkness of misery," and he observed that the English novel had failed to explore "that thick twilight of mediocrity." He added, "May it yield triumphs in years to come!" (2:547), perhaps thinking that his own recent pair of novels had begun that process already. Nevertheless, he seems to have retained the feeling he expressed in the *Nana* essay when he declared that "the human note is completely absent, the perception of character, of the way people think and feel and act, is helplessly, hopelessly at fault" (2:870). Though he continued to admire Zola's prodigious realistic particularity, especially in *l'Assommoir* and *Germinal*, the feeling persisted that the naturalist system was inadequate in its representations of the reality of inner being, the hidden life of character.

Some of his admiration for the naturalist achievement is expressed in his response to Daudet's *Evangéliste*, which seems to have even provoked his impulse toward emulation in *The Bostonians*. In 1883, while in Boston, James wrote his publisher and transcribed into his notebook his first idea for this novel, and remarked, "Daudet's *Evangéliste* has given me the idea of this thing. If I could only do something with that *pictorial* quality!"[5] What he meant by "pictorial quality" is suggested by a more native example, which may have exercised a still more powerful "anxiety of influence" on James's imagination, Hawthorne's *The Blithedale Romance*. The correspondences between the novels, with the trio of chief characters in each and the similar subject of the city of Boston and the movement for women's rights as well as other reform agitations, has been much remarked upon.[6] It has not been sufficiently observed that what James envied in Daudet he undoubtedly sought to repair in modifying the example of Hawthorne. In his *Hawthorne* (1879), James complained that in *The Blithedale Romance* we "get too much out of reality, and cease to feel beneath our feet the firm ground of an appeal to our own vision of the world, our observation" and regretted the "absence of satire" in the depiction of Brook Farm, whose "brethren should have held themselves slighted rather than misrepresented" (1:422).

His urge to a greater social realism than Hawthorne had attempted was perhaps, as Sandra Gilbert and Susan Gubar have recently noted, a revision made necessary, to James's mind, by American history. It is partly the result of the change in the role and power of a "separatist" women's movement in American society and may represent his correction of Hawthorne concerning a movement no longer "utopian" in its aims.[7] But his interest in the realist-naturalist aim is testified to, at the same time, by his application of its lessons to a completely foreign subject in the novel written immediately afterwards, *The Princess Casamassima*, which registers his response to the utopianism which was now energizing a rising working-class movement in England. Lionel Trilling was correct in saying that the two novels "are set apart from James's other novels by having in common a quick responsiveness to the details of the outer world, an explicit awareness of history, of the grosser movements of society and civilization."[8] In both James seems to reverse his redefinition of realism as the reflection not of external, material reality but of the impalpable realities of consciousness.

But there is another side to his double intertextual response to his French and American precursors. At almost the same time as he expressed his desire to emulate the "pictorial quality" of *l'Evangeliste,* he noted, in a published essay on Daudet, that the novel's Protestant zealot (the suggestion for Olive Chancellor) struck him "as quite automatic; psychologically . . . a blank. One does not see the operation of her character. She must have had a soul, and a very curious one. It was a great opportunity for a piece of spiritual portraiture; but we know nothing about Madame Autheman's inner springs" (2:225). It was the very kind of opportunity he would seize in the case of Olive Chancellor's curious soul. Furthermore, his analysis of *The Blithedale Romance* already had expressed a reserve on quite other grounds than its insufficient social realism—a dissatisfaction of the same sort as that inspired by *l'Evangeliste,* on the grounds of inadequate psychological depths; he protested that the "least felicitous" aspect of Hawthorne's book had been the "mysterious relation" of Priscilla and Zenobia. His own novel would explore the bond between Olive and Verena, making it more deeply and exactly penetrative of such a relation than any novel had ever done before. *The Blithedale Romance* may have offered a provocation not so much to difference as to a more intense development of something only hinted by the earlier American writer. In changing the "mystery" of the concealed sisterhood of Hawthorne's two women—of which Zenobia is unaware—to the probably unconscious lesbian feeling which underlies Olive's attachment to Verena, James find a way of converting rather than rejecting Hawthorne's example. What is simply hidden in the folds of the earlier novel's melodramatic intrigue is now the part of human nature hidden even from the conscious self.

A still more covert yet important influence of *The Blithedale Romance* on James may derive from the one character who seems to have vanished altogether from the scene of *The Bostonians, Blithedale*'s narrator, Miles Coverdale. A central sentient consciousness within the novel is not, of course, part of James's objective method in *The Bostonians.* Instead, he employs a roving omniscient presence that subjects all to its surveillance—a feature that may be attributable, as Peter Buitenhuis suggests, to the example of "the Gascon Daudet's fundamentally unsympathetic attitude towards his northern Protestant characters,"[9] rather than to Hawthorne's subjective, first-person focus. If James's novel accepts the pattern of Zenobia-Priscilla-Holgrave as an inspiration for Olive-Verena-Ransom, it conspicuously (as though *there* the influence must be withstood by might and main!)—excludes Hawthorne's inactive, yet imaginatively participant, narrator, who is as "Jamesian" as the narrator of the late *The Sacred Fount*. In the long run, the personality of Miles Coverdale was, for James, the most important Hawthornian precedent of all. His exclusion of such a subjective witness was only temporary, however. In *The Princess Casamassima*, James embraced quite deliberately again (as he had as early as *Roderick Hudson)* a form which grows out of the impressions of such an observer—despite his desire to respond objectively, still, to contemporary society, to the worsening division of the English classes, with the sense of a dangerous explosiveness beneath England's social surface.

James's two novels, written one upon the heels of the other in 1885–86, show a fundamental yet unresolved quarrel with the realist-naturalist tradition. In their curiously ironic structures, they record James's struggle with the whole problem, once again, of formulating life according to a design—and forming novels. Novelistic models of various kinds enter the text at one point or another, as I have just suggested. Naturalism appears to be the most important of the ideas he puts to the test; he toys with it parodistically and even exposes its factitiousness.

It is a commonplace to say that James's American girls have a family resemblance. But their qualities, even when similar, look different in the different fictions they inhabit. They bear a special relation, in each case, to the novelist's changing problem of enclosing life, like a portrait, in its frame, its structure of significance. Thus, Isabel's desire to escape the marriage-plot looks very different when it becomes the enterprise, also a failure, of Verena Tarrant. Yet Verena is similarly the heroine of a story in which the fairy-tale three young men are in love with her. In a sense that can only be taken as ironic, Verena is captured by the romantic plot from which Isabel manages at the last to escape, for the third suitor does sweep her onto his horse and gallop off with her on the last page. Isabel is also a victim of the marriage-plot, but this is only the midpoint of her story; on her last page she is released by marital failure to the frail hope that some potentiality remains to her. In this likeness and difference we can see James's pessimistic reflexivity, a response to his own previous novel, which intersects with the intertextuality with Hawthorne and Daudet—especially with Hawthorne's novel, which ends not only with a prospect of shadowed marriage for Priscilla but of death instead of merely defeat and humiliation for Zenobia, who is at once a more verdant figure than Olive (more like Verena, that is) and more tragic.

Matthias Pardon resembles none of Isabel's young men; Isabel is pursued by no such venal representative of the press, which is present in the earlier novel only in the person of the genuinely loyal and only mildly ridiculous Henrietta. But Mr. Burrage, a good-natured, rich young gentleman of leisure, an American patrician of liberal sentiments, might be the native equivalent of Lord Warburton if he did not also suggest Gilbert Osmond. He is like Osmond in his lack of social function and his somewhat effete aestheticism; he too is a collector, and tells Verena that she pleases him "for the same reason he liked old enamels and old embroideries."[10]

There is no Ralph to sponsor, with loving selflessness, Verena's free flight. But Olive likes to imagine herself as enacting such a role, and in her presumption that one may interfere with the best of motives in the life of another person she really only makes Ralph's error more visible. Wealthy and intelligent, just as he is, she is also drawn to alter the fate of a girl who has neither money nor, really, parents. (The Tarrants are negligible and indifferent, and when Olive virtually buys their daughter from them, she only makes evident the fact that Verena is another orphan, like Isabel.) Olive, like Ralph, is herself incapable of direct action. She is physically timid and she has no expressive "gift" like Verena; she is a version of those languid Jamesian characters who, from Rowland Mallet in *Roderick Hudson* to Lambert Strether in *The Ambassadors,* wish to sponsor the creative person or active doer, themselves disabled for creating or doing, and implicitly, perhaps, even disabled sexually. That she is, after all, also in love with Verena, fits her into the progression of the fairy-tale suitors, but she does not make a fourth contestant. Her femaleness is a kind of disability, like Ralph's illness; it makes it impossible for her to marry the heroine, and her love, if accepted, would abort the marriage-plot.

More precisely, however, Casper Goodwood and Basil Ransom have something in common, though seemingly of such different class and regional types. Surprisingly, the Northern inventor and cotton mill owner is like the Southerner, who has left his ruined cotton plantation to seek his fortune in New York. In both, male will is strongly felt as social and sexual force, as it is not in their rivals. Unlike Osmond, who boasts that he "never tried to earn a penny," Casper is a man who has strenuously tried to make money and succeeded, and Basil Ransom, though his success has not yet been great, hopes to make it. The love of both of these men is peremptory and possessive as well as sexually exigent. It is so powerful a force that Isabel just barely succeeds in resisting it, and Verena succumbs.

In the earlier historical moment pictured in *The Portrait of a Lady* the feminist movement has not yet been born, and Isabel has, as we have seen, no way of discovering a history for herself except by marrying—the example of Henrietta somehow not counting. In *The Bostonians*, however, Isabel's question, "Why should I necessarily marry?" has become a political challenge. The Civil War had so reduced the male population that spinsterhood was inevitable for some women—Ransom's own widowed or unmarried sisters, in all probability, face the prospect of remaining unmarried. But principle as well as necessity caused a great many women less peculiar than Olive Chancellor—young women like Verena herself—to reject the actual institution of marriage. As Verena reminds Ransom, "women marry—are given in marriage—less and less; that isn't their career, as a matter of course, any more" (319). So, the search of James's heroines for an unconstricting form of being, the struggle against the bonds of plot observed in the earlier novels, has, in *The Bostonians*, achieved its historic expression in the agitation aimed at real restrictions of social custom and sexual convention. When she tries to compel Verena to promise never to marry in the climactic scene in chapter 16, Olive is motivated—quite unpolitically—by a possessiveness and passion comparable to those same qualities in her political opponent, Basil Ransom. We know that her personal resistance to marriage is temperamental. "There are women," says the narrator, "who are unmarried by accident, and others who are unmarried by option; but Olive Chancellor was unmarried by every implication of her being. She was a spinster as Shelley was a lyric poet, or as the month of August is sultry" (17–18). This sounds more acidic than it should until we recall that James thought of himself, too, as constitutionally a bachelor.¹¹

He knew what the decision not to marry entailed socially. The unmarried male was somehow doomed to a marginality that made him able to identify with the woman who remained unmarried,[12] though bachelorhood was a role one might embrace without embarrassment, even in late Victorian society, while there was no such thing as a spinster who was not queer or at least ridiculous, like Hawthorne's Hepzibah Pyncheon. The unmarried or widowed and childless woman could escape such a character only to a degree by becoming an unpaid assistant mother-and-wife in a relative's household, like his own Aunt Kate—or Catherine Sloper's Aunt Penniman. Even if a woman had an income of her own this tended to be so. She might, of course, accept her singleness as a vocation in itself—and become that occasional eccentric or proto-feminist whose example stands behind Olive. Such women, however, were, to the popular eye, even more extravagantly peculiar and ridiculous. And the tradition of the novel did not offer any program for regarding them in a different fashion, did not offer any plot that would allow them to be serious or heroic. Even at the end of the century, George Gissing, attempting in *The Odd Woman* to depict sympathetically a feminist who rejects marriage and its compromises, manages only to show her as an unpleasant enemy of sexuality.

James came as close as he could to depicting the single woman by conviction in the character of Olive, who is also grotesque, though appealing to our sympathy. But there is a curious almost excessive quality of detachment in *The Bostonians*, which argues not that James had no private investment in its themes but that he felt compelled to keep himself more hidden than ever. This work, which deals more directly with the "position of women" than anything else James wrote, is the least representative of his favored method of centering upon a chosen sensibility whose inner drama makes the story. James's reversion to a more traditional narrative voice and his relinquishment of narrator-identification with any one of his characters results, in part, from his interest in naturalism, his desire to see all his characters with an equal, scientific, coolness. But part of the explanation may lie in the fact that his personal investment in his theme was more intimate and complex than he could confess; his deliberate detachment, his refusal to choose a single source of interpretation among his characters, could have been due to his own difficulty in choosing an attachment either to Ransom or the feminists. I have already mentioned the peculiarity that the character in *The Blithedale Romance* who must have interested James most is suppressed out of the configuration of *The Bostonians*—yet Coverdale is precisely that witnessing subjectivity who could be said to be closest to James himself, as he was to Hawthorne. Coverdale is ambiguous in his political views, his fascinated hate-attraction to Zenobia, his unconvincing sentimental love of Priscilla, his conflicted—implicitly homosexual—bonding with Hollingsworth.

James's own personal issues may have given him a source of empathy with women, with their exclusion from power and with the fear of marriage many, like his female characters, felt. On the other hand, as Elaine Showalter has suggested,[13] he could have felt, as Ransom does, a fear of female power, which is expressed not only in his male character's feeling for the Civil War dead of both sides, but in his desire to silence Verena's expressive power (so like Zenobia's, which Hawthorne punished by death!)—a fear prompted by his own limited literary success in a market dominated by successful women writers. His novel itself silences these rivals by appropriating, albeit ironically, their favorite marriage plot.

Aside from Olive's and his own personal sources of disinclination for marriage, James does view the problem sociologically and philosophically. Olive's radical feminist rejection of marriage is consistent with her ideology. It is dreadfully true that Verena is only free if she rejects marriage and so maintains her uncompromised and unrestricted capacity to be. The dreadfulness of this truth is shown in the novel by the total absence in it of any model of successful or happy marriage—neither that of Mrs. Farrinder, about whose husband nothing can be stated but his name, nor that of her own parents (a revolting contract between a charlatan and his accomplice) can be said to offer inspiration. Mrs. Tarrant, herself, has little connection with the marriage-plot; she is, in this respect, quite unlike Jane Austen's mothers, however limited they may be. "She supposed Verena would marry some one, some day, and she hoped the personage would be connected with public life—which meant, for Mrs. Tarrant, that his name would be visible, in the lamplight, on a colored poster, in the doorway of Tremont Temple . But she was not eager about this vision, for the implications of matrimony were for the most part wanting in brightness—consisted of a tired woman holding a baby over a furnace-register that emitted lukewarm air" (93–94). Before that "sterner fate" descends, she is quite content that her daughter accept the version of connubiality offered in Olive's cosy parlor.

And yet, being "made for love," as Basil says (315, 349), the destiny of marriage is the only one available to Verena after all. Olive recognizes at the start that Verena's talk of "free unions" represents no radical dismissal of marriage, but is "mere maiden flippancy." The word "free," which for Isabel Archer meant freedom from predictability, here represents utopian longing for a social form which does not constrain. It implies, as James notes "that unions of some kind or other had her approval" (114–115)—but what imaginable form, free of the dominion and use of one partner by another, can give fulfillment to that longing? The novelist does not provide any prevision of such a condition, for his reformers themselves cannot really foresee it.

The challenge of feminism, as James sees it, is not directed simply at marriage, a plot of personal history, but at the old plots of general history. As Verena discovers, "Miss Chancellor was historic and philosophic" (131). She would rewrite the past, providing a new account of the participation of women. We are told, in chapter 20, that the two ladies, settling down behind the drawn curtains of Charles Street during winter evenings, "read a great deal of history together, and read it ever with the same thought—that of finding confirmation in it for this idea that their sex had suffered inexpressibly, and that at any moment in the course of human affairs the state of the world would have been so much less horrible (history seemed to them in every way horrible), if women had been able to press down the scale" (166). The Jamesian narrator's tone is dry; it is clear that he thinks this new historic narrative as forced as that which it would replace. His ideological skepticism is reinforced by that persistent Jamesian suspicion of narrative which we have been observing from "Daisy Miller" on.

It should be noted, moreover, that though Olive would rewrite the past, she has no scenario for the future. She dreams of a vague triumph when "the last particle of expiation" will be exacted from men, and of the beginning of "a new era for the human family" (36), but her concept of the future is strangely unspecific. The cause she and her fellow workers labor for is the "emancipation of women," but the phrase delusively echoes the program for the abolition of slavery; no single change in legal status can be said to promise freedom from woman's invisible bonds. Olive is nowhere said to envision a better state in which there will be an ultimate reconciliation between the sexes when man will have learned to treat woman as his equal. Even Verena, who pleads gently that men are not always and altogether wicked, and who finds herself sympathizing with a man whose views she detests, can only plead that the feminine element—defined in a quite traditional way—should be allowed to do something in the world. "Why shouldn't tenderness come in? Why should our woman's hearts be so full of it, and all so wasted and withered, while armies and prisons and helpless miseries grow greater all the while?" is her vague appeal (59-60). Her word for the desired future is Isabel's, the abstraction, "freedom": "We require simply freedom; we require the lid to be taken off the box in which we have been kept for centuries" (255). The female liberation that these two zealots envision is strangely without a sense of more concrete futurity.

This curious emptiness of the space that should be occupied by a vision of the future explains the fact that James's reformers seem little occupied with political proposals for change. Olive and Verena are, in effect, reformers without causes, though their Cause is the advancement of women; changes in the structures of law and institutional privilege—suffrage, the rights connected with property, free entrance into higher education and the professions, all the specific issues of the early women's movement—seem hardly to interest them, or, at least, James chooses to give little report of their thinking in reference to them. Just once, as she undertakes to show Harvard University to Ransom, Verena remarks that it is closed to women, and explains to him that she advocates "equal rights, equal opportunities, equal privileges" (217). But she adds that she is not sure that what Olive wants as much as justice is not vengeance.

Olive and Verena's idea of the future of relations between the sexes has the same vagueness as Isabel Archer's early dreams of the fine projects that will fulfill her selfhood. It is significant, perhaps, that there is a curious similarity in their *personal* dreams of futurity. Isabel's early "wish that she might find herself in a difficult position, so that she should have the pleasure of being as heroic as the occasion demanded" (III:69), resembles Olive's hopes of heroic sacrifice, about which the narrator comments, "It was not clear to this interesting girl in what manner such a sacrifice . . . would be required of her, but she saw the matter through a kind of sunrise-mist of emotion which made danger as rosy as success" (36). The effect, in both cases, is to reject specific eventualities.

Basil Ransom's own attachment to the marriage-plot is more than the natural consequence of his romantic passion and his belief that only as his wife will Verena serve her proper purpose. He, too, is concerned with history, but chooses not so much to rewrite it as to enforce its repetition. He tells Verena, when he first speaks with her in Boston, "I think I should be able to interpret history for you by a new light" (87). It is this new-old story of the human past and future that is expressed in the articles which, he is told by the editor who rejects one of them, are 300 years behind the age—and which Ransom would like to think contain ideas that are really not too old but too new. (181). He wishes to recover a plot that has recently been rendered defunct, the plot which places one portion of mankind in the hands of another as slaves. James appears to have thought at one time of making his male outsider a westerner but then decided on the more appropriate character of Ransom as a Southerner, and it is not difficult to see why. The former slave-owner would illustrate in the most extreme form the mode of typological thinking exhibited in "Daisy Miller" 's Winterbourne.

Ransom complains of the "feminization" of society, but a more correct description of America in the post–Civil War period might be that it had become so divided into sexual absolutes that while masculinity became isolated in the worlds of business and politics, from which women are excluded, femininity dominated the world of the home, the church, and even the arts.[14] But what seems as important is that one effect of the Civil War had been to remove certain supports of masculine definition. The definition of white male selfhood had been made problematic by the abolition of slavery. The division between slave and master or white man and black no longer defined human qualities as fixed typological traits, and white men were no longer held together so securely by the sense that they were superior to males of other races. It is into this breach—this collapse of those conventions of character and personal history which sustain the fictions of life and literature—that feminism entered with its still more threatening challenge to definition by difference.[15]

Ransom would, of course, have been correct in recognizing old enemies in the feminist leaders. As a matter of actual history, early feminists had discovered their voices and learned the techniques of popular agitation on abolitionist platforms. The earlier struggle against slavery was the great cause which had first enrolled women like Miss Birdseye on behalf of a group even more enslaved than themselves. But it is also plausible that for the former slave-owner like Ransom, the sense that slavery and female bondage were the same issue arises from a deep need to prevent this further, psychic damage. Now that slavery had been abolished, all the more necessary for the restoration of what he calls the masculine tone in society (318)—and the general principle of typological thinking—is the secure domination of women by men.

It is appropriate that James's story should be full of references to the Civil War—above all in the crucial scene between Ransom and Verena in Harvard's Memorial Hall—a place not only paying tribute to the war his side had lost but to the *men* on both sides who had spilt their own and their enemy's blood. But more hints are given of the union in his mind of his feelings for Verena and his nostalgia for slavocracy; not for nothing does he feel himself carrying out the mission of John Wilkes Booth when he enters the Music Hall in his desperate resolution to recapture Verena, the runaway slave.[16] That Olive, the abolitionist of female bondage, *purchases* Verena from her parents is the intensest sort of irony in that it likens her to the slaver and to Ransom.

James was no feminist in the political sense, but he does not find it possible, even in this novel, to subscribe to the marriage-plot. The story seems to come to its traditional conclusion on the last page, the third suitor melodramatically "rescuing" the maiden from her imprisonment by a female dragon. But the famous last sentence of the novel guarantees that tears will be Verena's lot in the spurious "happily ever after" that Ransom promises. And long before this final moment, the hero is proven to be less and less of a romantic figure; he is a hard man who will have what he will have—the woman whose feminist voice has been silenced, even if he must use force. As the language that reflects his thoughts shows after her triumphal lecture at Mrs. Burrage's: "if he should become her husband he should know a way to strike her dumb" (306), or, at Marmion, "however she might turn and twist in his grasp he held her fast" (382).

Nor does the figure of Olive fulfill the role of wicked jailor very well, for she is seen with a surprising degree of sympathy as the novel progresses. If we have disliked her or considered her simply morbid at the start, we cannot withhold sympathy all the way, especially in those scenes at Cape Cod when she waits and searches for Verena during the long day the lovers spend in their boat. What has happened, in fact, is that another plot altogether has made itself felt—that of the rivalry of two persons for the love of a third, with the final triumph of one rival. When she has a moment's vision of the body of a drowned "unknown young woman, defaced beyond recognition, but with long auburn hair and in a white dress" (391) we are thrown back, again, to Blithedale, and Zenobia's terrible end, but it is not Verena but Olive who reenacts Hawthorne's terrifying vision of a suicide as she casts herself, in a nearly equal despair of disappointed love, into the sea of human rage in the Music Hall.

But the prevailing tone of the novel is more comic than sentimental most of the time. Especially in the first half of the book, James makes spirited use of the witty "set" portrait, which actually blocks narrative advance while, like a seventeenth-century character writer, collects for us a basketful of ridiculous traits, as in the famous satiric profile of Miss Birdseye (26). The narrator does not seem to weary of taking off the Tarrant family in particular, devoting most of chapters 10 and 13 and a large part of the following two chapters to simply describing Verena's mother and father, their history, and their Cambridge home. There remains, it is true, some Gothic sinisterness about Selah Tarrant; the reader who recognizes an allusion to Hawthorne's Westervelt in the description of this practitioner of a shady, theatrical mesmeric skill (both, also, show their teeth, like vampirish fangs, when they smile) will expect him to struggle for possession of Verena. Instead, however, he retreats before Olive's checkbook.

But whether viewed as a stereotype of romance or as a contemporary comic type, Selah is the subject of a narrative consciousness that is irrepressibly categorical. Like the narrator of *Washington Square* and like Dr. Sloper, he has a prompt and expert recognition of types, especially when, as in the earlier novel, he seems to borrow his vision from this novel's own categorizer, Basil Ransom. He often goes beyond what Basil could be thought capable of, and uses materials of historic understanding as well as direct perception unavailable to Basil—who could not, after all, have seen so much cultural symbolism in the mere appearance of poor Miss Birdseye.

In the case of Miss Birdseye, James appears to have regretted his nasty wit, since she was taken to represent (and perhaps did represent) that beloved Boston monument, Elizabeth Peabody. As the novel advances she grows more endearing, and even seems wise instead of dotty; at the last her death stirs the narrator to speak of "that unique woman's majestically simple withdrawal" (387). In general, again like the narrator of *Washington Square,* the narrator of the later work also ends by treating his chief Bostonians, Olive and especially his heroine, Verena, with a simple respect that matches the heroine's own simplicity, surrendering his satiric, categorical habit.

Olive and Basil are presented at the outset in strong comic outlines. The dress and the physical appearance of the dark, saturnine young man, the pale, sharp-featured young woman are, as Madame Merle would say, "expressive." The narrator does not hesitate to offer at once defining traits which can be expected to produce characteristic behavior. The young Mississippian is always that—his nature as a Southerner is never for a moment forgotten, just as Olive's spinsterhood and her ingrown New Englandism are visible in every line of her person. On the whole, even these major characters remain to the end what they have always been, like the characters in a comedy of manners, despite the emotions that mount in each as their contest rises to its climax.

It may be possible to think that Olive's character does, after all, change in the collapse of her dreams. As she paces the beach at Marmion and scans the horizon for the lovers' boat, it comes home to her "that Verena had been more to her than she ever was to Verena," and the narrator even hints at more devastating realizations—that Verena, after all, "had been only the most unconscious and successful of humbugs" and that her friend's defection showed "that it was no use striving, that the world was all a great trap or trick, of which women were ever the punctual dupes, so that it was the worst of the curse that rested upon them that they must most humiliate those who had most their cause at heart" (389). But from these further speculations the Jamesian narrator draws back, professes "incompetence," saying, "these are mysteries into which I shall not attempt to enter," refusing to give Olive any total epiphany. Her moment of truth does not significantly alter her; she recovers her nerve and carries her struggle against Ransom to the end. Yet there is enough hint of moral depth in James's portrait to give some justification to the directors of the Merchant-Ivory film of 1985, who make their Olive, without warrant from James, tell the disappointed Music Hall audience that the Cause must still hold their interest—to suggest that she may be able to rise above personal emotion.[17]

As I have already noted, the novel's tonal changes have puzzled some readers, and it may be that there is a certain disunity in it, though it is not merely the effect of the shift from the early satiric mode to the "intrigue plot" created by the Verena's concealment of her meeting with Ransom, as Alfred Habegger has charged.[18] Insofar as there is such disunity, we may consider that James allows it willingly. We may not be able to state exactly what the writer's view of his created persons finally is—he may not be on anyone's "side." He may intend to mortify our appetite for a fixed position. On the one hand he allows us to feel that everyone is a clear case and that initial definitions hold unaltered in a consistent satire, which tends to exhibit a change of relationship among human types, exposing folly and making good sense triumph, but illuminating and transforming only the reader. Yet his modulation of narrator voice allows us to question all typologies and to progress through a variety of alternative views of the story.

Verena is surrounded by examples of typological being—and invited to become one also. She strives to resist the marriage-plot, as I have said; she also resists the attempts of the narrator's comedy to include her as simply a type of the reluctant virgin waiting to be tamed. To a degree, she *is* the innocent maiden of romance, and accommodates to the sentimental mood of the later part of the book when we enter in the struggles of her tender nature between fidelity to Olive and the Cause and her attraction to Basil—a contest between Duty and Love which was familiar in the fiction of the day. And, of course, she arouses certain expectations in the reader by resemblances to Hawthorne's Zenobia—chiefly, her identification with female eloquence. But James invokes this reminiscence only to deflect it. Verena is not the "dark" heroine of experience belonging to a romance in which her opposite is maiden innocence; she *is* maiden innocence, she is also Hawthorne's Priscilla, while Olive, who inherits something of the tragic fate of a Zenobia, is devoid both of Zenobia's blooming beauty and her gift of public speech.

Perhaps in part because of her association with romantic plots, Verena differs from the other characters because the determining forces of the social world have no real significance in her case. Though subject, ultimately, to the marriage-plot, she is immune to naturalist definition, the most serious threat to the claims of the free spirit to make its own fate in this novel. Like Isabel Archer, she is given a character that maximizes her bid for freedom. In *The Bos-*

tonians, it is not the typological propensity of either romance or satire but the idea of determinant destiny which is, finally, the most serious threat to the claims of the free sprit to make its own fate.

In this novel, even more than in *The Portrait of a Lady,* the idea of ineluctable forces which refute the protagonist's dreams of freedom is present, intertextually, in the felt model of naturalist fiction. The very title, of course, announces a work which is not simply about individuals, but about individuals who are defined by their origins and surroundings—"Bostonians." Here we have more than the mere gesture in the direction of the realist tradition (with its emphasis upon setting) made by the earlier place-title, *Washington Square.* In this far more ambitious work, the sense of locale is more serious, in accordance with James's intention to write "a very American tale."[19] The typological characterization which tends to confine the characters is, after all, a way of saying that they are the expectable products of local circumstances. And most of the persons observed by the sharp eye of the narrator in *The Bostonians* are related to those circumstances.

He observes, on behalf of Ransom, that "there was culture in Miss Chancellor's tables and sofas, in the books that were everywhere, on little shelves like brackets (as if a book were a statuette), in the photographs and watercolors that covered the walls, in the curtains that were festooned, rather stiffly in the doorways" (16), detecting in Olive's somewhat overfurnished parlor the tradition of genteel Bostonian culture which has made her. The abstract, dehumanizing character of Miss Birdseye's reformism is suggested by her underfurnished dwelling—more meeting-hall than home—in the South End; the long, bare parlor furnished mostly by chairs, and lit "by a small hot glare of gas, which made it look white and featureless," "told that she had never had any needs but moral needs" (28). The shoddy Tarrants, with their history of degenerated radicalism which has thinned the strong abolitionist impulse into the quackery and quirkery of eccentricism and faddism are expressed in their rather ramshackle house in ramshackle Cambridge, "a sightless, soundless, interspaced, embryonic region," where "wooden houses, with still more wooden door-yards, looked as if they had been constructed by the nearest carpenter and his boy" (224). In the case of these characters it seems, at times, that James is only enacting by his description of their home environments that ambiguity expressed when he reports that Mrs. Tarrant was delighted, after Verena's visit to Charles Street, "with her daughter's account of Miss Chancellor's interior" (93). James's preference as a novelist was, in the long run, for what Willa Cather would call the novel *demeublé*, but in this novel the furnishings of life, the "accoutrements," are present for their semantic function—sometimes as mentonymic signs of the larger reality that explains the characters, sometimes symbolic of what they are.

And yet, *The Bostonians* is a curiously qualified and self-mocking naturalist novel, if it is a naturalist novel at all. At the heart of the book is Verena. As though to provide a basis for naturalist explanation of her, James provides her with a fully exhibited context of family, even parents whose own histories are sketched. In contrast with our exact view of the Tarrants, we are given no picture at all of the family Ransom has left behind him in the South; it is he who is the transplanted character and not the heroine, while Olive is another one of James's orphans whose remaining relative, her sister, is so absolute a contrast as to actually raise the question of how such different beings could have arisen from the same sources. Nevertheless, both Olive and Ransom are expressions of their contrasting social worlds, whereas Verena is not.

Ransom, who applies the vision of satire to everyone else he encounters, is romantically captivated by the "damsel," and the "strange, sweet, crude, absurd, enchanting improvisation" of her speech. To him, Verena is something out of a different kind of novel than the one he himself inhabits, one in which girls are called damsels; she reminds him of Victor Hugo's Esmeralda, the dancing girl who is hanged as a witch in *The Hunchback of Notre Dame* (56). Olive sees her, in much the same way, as belonging "to some queer gipsy-land or transcendental Bohemia" (75). Both these observers, are, of course, in love—this qualifies their judgments—but the narrator, though he is alert to the limits of vision of his characters in other instances, never "corrects" their portrait of someone who is an outsider to conventional typologies. The lens which has applied so brilliant a light elsewhere suddenly is focused more softly. Even though Dr. Prance suspects that the young lady who looks as though all her blood had gone into her red hair eats too much candy, no one else finds her so material. She remains for the reader a somewhat mythicized figure—one of James's American girls whose virgin freshness remains unsullied by the reality, the ground they tread. Her "fantastic fairness" reminds Ransom "of unworldly places . . .

convent cloisters or vales of Arcady" (213). He sees her as a mythic creature, made "to shake her braided locks like a naiad rising from the waves" (59).

Verena's character is the chief mark of James's skeptical interest in the naturalist plot, for she is curiously *un*explained by her heredity and environment, and her accoutrements do not express her. So, Verena's non-naturalistic freedom from circumstances makes her clothes tell nothing about who she is. Olive perceives, "Miss Tarrant might wear gilt buttons from head to foot, her soul could not be vulgar" (76). We recall that Isabel's reply to the statement by Madame Merle quoted at the start of this chapter particularly denied that her style of dress had personal meaning: "Certainly the clothes which, as you say, I choose to wear, don't express me; and heaven forbid they should! . . . My clothes may express the dressmaker, but they don't express me. To begin with it's not my own choice that I wear them; they're imposed upon me by society" (III, 288). This is as much so if she dresses "well" (which Isabel does) or with inferior taste, like Catherine Sloper, whose showy red dress, emulating some general idea of elegance, is both gawdy and inappropriate to her nature, like Verena's buttons.

The reference to clothes in both the cases of Isabel and Verena is more than a minor aspect of the essentialism which James allows them; the old metaphor of clothing as a covering and disguise of the "naked self" is, as for Carlyle and other writers, a way of representing the whole of the social habiliment of behavior and role. Clothing had a literal as well as symbolic significance for feminist women in the nineteenth century; female costume was literally a restricting, even imprisoning envelopment, hindering easy movement, barring a woman from many activities. Neither Isabel nor Verena is a "bloomer girl," of course, but their clothes would have been, in real life, practical impediments to their freer self-expression; when—as in the later novel—feminist protest is the main subject, this issue is necessarily latent. Feminists like Olive or Verena might have campaigned for dress reform—the discarding of bustle and train and the waist-pinching corset—for practical reasons.

But not only was this a practical issue. Clothing was also a representation of the social selfhoods which society imposed on women. It made them feminine in a particular way, defining femininity as physical helplessness while exaggerating the outlines of the body as a sexual object or adorning it in such a way as to signify the social and economic status of the parents or husband who had paid for the clothing. Feminists wanted to cast aside conventional female dress in order to prove that biology was not destiny; in effect, they saw clothing as the symbolic representation of the lives, the plots, women were destined to enact in the society of their day. James's essentialism may be identified with his empathetic feminism.

It may also be identified with his pessimistic view that there were no roles, not even those that the feminist movement offered, which could liberate a woman into a self-determined life. Madame Merle's rejoinder to Isabel's denial of her relation to her clothes, "Should you prefer to go without them?" is not as flippant as it sounds. How can the naked self clothe itself and remain still unconstrained? The symbolic sense of the metaphor of clothing gains force in Verena's case when she is wrapped and covered first by Olive, who in that early Cambridge scene, throws her cloak around the girl while exacting a promise that Verena will not marry, then by Ransom, who covers Verena's head with the hood of her own cloak before sweeping her off into marriage with him, in both cases obscuring the image of the essential girl.

James's ambiguous but ultimately resistant response to the argument of naturalistic determinism maintains itself in Verena's case. She may have "queer, bad lecture-blood" (237) in her veins, but nothing about her—not even her lectures, of which James gives us specimens—is "bad."[20] Even her speech—spontaneous, idealistic, but not strident—is a "gift" that expresses the discrepancy of her character from those of her mother and father, as different as possible from the lecture-hall world she has been brought up in. "She had been nursed in darkened rooms, and suckled in the midst of manifestations; she had begun to 'attend lectures,' as she said, when she was quite an infant, because her mother had no one to leave her with at home. She had sat on the knees of somnambulists, and had been passed from hand to hand by trance-speakers . . . " Olive feels vertigo at the revelation of these things in her friend's candid descriptions. "They made her perceive everything from which she should have rescued her" (79).

But, in fact, Verena is not in need of rescue, as Olive realizes. She "was perfectly uncontaminated, and she would never be touched by evil" (79). Olive's act of separating Verena from her parents has a narratological force; she hopes to impose on the younger woman an "effectual rupture with her past" (104). Taking his cue from Olive's thoughts, the narrator records that Verena's genius seemed at the very start of their relation "a mystery; it was impossible to see how this charming, blooming, simple creature, all youth and grace and innocence, got her extraordinary powers of reflection . . . her precious faculty had come to her just as her beauty and distinction . . . had come; it had dropped straight from heaven, without filtering through her parents" (78). The "perpetual enigma," to Olive, was "of such people being Verena's progenitors at all. She had explained it, as we explain all exceptional things, by making the part, as the French say, of the miraculous. She had come to consider the girl as a wonder of wonders, to hold that no human origin, however congruous it might superficially appear, would sufficiently account for her; that her springing up between Selah and his wife was an exquisite whim of the creative force" (108). In sum, she was one of those special persons who could not be explained by the naturalist, "holding from far-off ancestors, or even, perhaps, straight from the divine generosity, much more than from their ugly or stupid progenitors" (109–110).[21]

Readers have sometimes found Verena insufficiently interesting precisely because she seems so open and selfless; she appears merely passive, the empty vessel which others want to fill.[22] "What *was* a part of her essence was the extraordinary generosity with which she could expose herself, give herself away, turn herself inside out, for the satisfaction of a person who made demands of her" (361). Olive, rejecting the category that had so much appealed to the male categorizer, Winterbourne, in his study of Daisy, will not think her a flirt, "only enchantingly and universally genial." Though the narrator humanizes her a little by identifying her geniality as the product "of the subtle feminine desire to please" (113), this desire makes her less herself than the expression of others. Verena's generosity—or flirtatiousness—which allows her to express herself through fulfilling the desires of others, may be looked at as the essential sign of her stereotypic femininity, of course; James, in seeing these qualities so favorably, may be convicted of sharing Basil's conservative male viewpoint about female character.[23]

Yet these qualities can also be seen as the representation of her uncompromised potentiality. Her passivity seems an Emersonian "wise passiveness" when she declares, in a transcendental way, that her inspiration comes from some source beyond herself. "It's not me," she is always modestly saying (52, 53, 75). James undercuts the serious meaning of this statement by making it a shibboleth of her circle, especially offensive in the prating mouth of Selah (53). The practical-minded politician, Mrs. Farrinder, rejects with distaste the spells of the charming "miracle-monger" (54), and even Olive wonders for a moment whether her disclaimer is "sincere . . . or only a phrase of the lips" (75). But Olive concludes by seeing her as a young prophetess with a divine instinct for heavenly truth, the Joan of Arc to whom the girl has half-seriously compared herself (80). In Verena's pure utterance, "It's not me" recovers its transcendental verity. What her father claims for her becomes true; she is a mouthpiece of Spirit. Ransom, in quite an opposite way, separates her from what she says: "It made no difference; she didn't mean it, she didn't know what she meant, she had been stuffed with this trash by her father" (59). He "is steeled against the inanities" (58) she utters, but the charm of her personality is not at all diminished by them, and he will be ready to echo her own statement—in *his* own sense.

Nevertheless, it is necessary for her to become, in the end, more than a medium of the universal, to acquire a particular selfhood. When she leaves her parents' household to live with Olive, she substitutes her friend for the fount of transcendental inspiration, and, her modesty continuing, now says, "It's not me," again. (This time she is referring to the speeches which have been written with Olive's help, or even at her dictation; "It's Miss Chancellor as much as me," she tells Ransom in chapter 24.) It is ironic that her effort to discover a selfhood of her own means only that she must accept someone else's view of her. But this is only to say that selfhood cannot be anything *but* the self as defined in the language of social forms, that Verena is non*existent* otherwise. In her union with Olive in a "Boston marriage," she is already submitted to the stamp of a confining definition. Even with Olive, she is already on the way to embracing the very destiny she has fled from, that of a woman who marries, because this is the only plot that will enable her to go from non-being to being in the world. Yet union with Olive is a precarious, unsanctioned form of marriage, after all. It is significant that the first half of *The Bostonians,* like the first half of *The Portrait of a Lady* seems static; the narrator's essayistic style and set descriptions of character seem to hold back the unfolding of narrative. Yet in the second half, the action takes on motion as the heroine is subdued to the true marriage-plot even as she struggles to resist Ransom; before he attracted her, there was no plot at all.

My argument that *The Bostonians* is a deliberately qualified realist or naturalist novel might extend beyond a discussion of its contradictions of structure, its deliberate generic shifts, and the lapses of the naturalist plot in particular. The texture of the writing exhibits, more frequently than I can take space to illustrate, an ironic awareness of the dubieties of the novel's own realist style. One may take, as a sample only, a look at some of the descriptions which serve to set the action into a significant scenic context—and sometimes deny their own significance in doing so. Despite his resistance to naturalism, James's desire to write a "very American novel" was genuine, born of his need to come to terms with his native reality. More than twenty years later he would write *The American Scene* as an expression of the need to *look,* literally and figuratively, at his own land, but in *The Bostonians* he already anticipates the impulse to hold a mirror to local views of Boston, Cambridge, New York, and Cape Cod, and, at the same time, to make the scene represent his sense of the culture implied in the title of his later report. James's pictorial impressionism is never more active than in his glances at a reality which also functions to characterize the nature of American culture. An example is that passage in chapter 20, which describes the view from the windows of Olive's drawing room in a realist fashion that makes it a critique of a charmless modern world:

> The long, low bridge that crawled, on its staggering posts, across the Charles; the casual patches of ice and snow; the desolate suburban horizons, peeled and made bald by the rigor of the season; the general hard, cold void of the prospect; the extrusion, at Charlestown, at Cambridge, of a few chimneys and steeples, straight, sordid tubes of factories and engine-shops, or spare, heavenward finger of the New England meeting-house. There was something inexorable in the poverty of the scene, shameful in the meanness of its details, which gave a collective impression of boards and tin and frozen earth, sheds and rotting piles, railway-lines striding flat across a thoroughfare of puddles, and tracks of the humbler, the universal horse-car, traversing obliquely this path of danger; loose fences, vacant lots, mounds of refuse, yards bestrewn with iron pipes, telegraph poles, and bare wooden backs of places. (165)

The description encompasses not only the look of things literally framed in Olive's window at sunset, but the facts of New England society in the seventies—industrialized and hastily fabricated without regard to traditions of amenity or art, its lingering church steeples and the industrial chimneys almost indistinguishable "extrusions" from the bleak disorder, as James saw it.

But if James, writing in the manner of Dickens or Balzac, sees this congruence between visible reality and social meaning, between environment and life, he also refuses to rest in this view. At an earlier moment, looking out of the same window at the same time of day, Ransom had also seen the chimneys and spires and the rest across the "brackish expanse of anomalous character, which is too big for a river and too small for a bay," and found the prospect "picturesque" and "almost romantic" (15). And at this later moment Verena's interpretation also contradicts the narrator's:

> Verena thought such a view lovely, and she was by no means without excuse when, as the afternoon closed, the ugly picture was tinted with a clear, cold rosiness. The air, in its windless chill, seemed to tinkle like a crystal, the faintest gradations of tone were perceptible in the sky, the west became deep and delicate, everything grew doubly distinct before taking on the dimness of evening. There were pink flushes on snow, "tender" reflections in patches of stiffened marsh, sounds of car-bells, no longer vulgar, but almost silvery, on the long bridge, lonely outlines of distant dusky undulations against the fading glow.   (165-166)

Who is to say, James implies, that the realist-naturalist view of environment, the Zolaesque description of the cityscape, is more true than Verena's sense of its transcendental communications, the heritage of an older view of humanity in nature?

It is perhaps worth remarking that these window views are instances of that device of framing which James used repeatedly in other works to represent *subjective* vision, the person or scene contained and interpreted by the view of a watcher who looks through a doorway or from a window, as Isabel repeatedly by others in *The Portrait of a Lady*. Such an interpreting window view is, later, the view of Paris in the vision of Strether, or his view of Chad and Madame de Vionnet on the river, which is conceived as a framed picture. Here, in *The Bostonians*, these scenic window views are the only sign of James's acceptance from *The Blithedale Romance* (which otherwise so conspicuously replicates itself in the novel) of the limited, distanced viewpoint of Miles Coverdale, who watches the world from a high-placed vantage point or a window.

A few pages later, at the start of his second volume, James still more openly challenges the sense of the environmental and objective which might have been taken to govern his pages. He begins by offering a genre-painting description of Basil Ransom's New York boarding house and its neighborhood. But he turns from his colorful enumeration of picturesque street details, including a "Dutch grocery" with its overflowing stalls and fragrant odors, to say, "I mention it not on account of any particular influence it may have had on the life or the thoughts of Basil Ransom, but for old acquaintance sake and that of local color; besides which, a figure is nothing without a setting, and our young man came and went every day, with rather an indifferent, unperceiving step, it is true, among the objects I have briefly designated" (177-178).

The "old acquaintance sake" to which he refers may be biographical—like those references to his own childhood recollections which we have noticed in each of the works so far discussed—and it may also refer to another description strikingly like it in James's apprentice novel, *Watch and Ward* (chapter 9). Such self-reflexive references, however, disrupt the realist surface, which would assume the appropriateness of the description for the sake of the present narrative. The statement that "a figure is nothing without a setting" is the very height of novelistic self-mockery, a reference to the conventions of realist novels.

At the beginning of the novel he had described Ransom in terms that already identify him as a Eugène Rastignac: "He surrendered the rest of his patrimony to his mother and sisters and, at nearly thirty years of age, alighted for the first time in New York, in the costume of his province, with fifty dollars in his pocket and a gnawing hunger in his heart" (13). The intertextuality of James's language, with its reference to his young man's "costume," "patrimony" and above all to his "province" (that is, the state of Mississippi) alludes to a strictly European context. Now, near the end of the novel, he makes the boarding house where Ransom lives, in the great American city to which he has come to make his fortune, slyly recall the Maison Vauquier. The reminiscence has point—for it is by sexual conquest in a world ruled by women that Basil, like Rastignac, makes his way. That his young man is still not at all like Rastignac—any more than New York or Boston is like Paris—is also a reminder that the novel he is writing is only intermittently and ironically an attempt to write an American *Père Goriot*.

· 5 ·

The Determinate Plot:
The Princess Casamassima

In December, 1884, James visited Millbank prison to gather details for the early scene in *The Princess Casamassima* in which Hyacinth Robinson visits his dying mother. "You see, I am quite the Naturalist. Look out for the same—a year hence," he wrote Thomas Sargent Perry.[1] But his identification with naturalism may have been only half-serious. He does not claim to have composed the novel by the naturalist method when, a quarter of a century later, he introduces the revised novel in the New York Edition. He offers his recollections of its composition but does not mention the research of that long-ago morning in the London prison and makes no explicit reference to naturalism or its proponents. His language *is,* however, full of covert references to the arguments he had heard in Flaubert's atelier in Paris. He talks a good deal about "notes" and taking them, and the reader may be reminded of those notes set down by Zola and his followers, who sedulously collected data and transcribed into their novels what they had recorded, like newspaper reporters, "on the spot." But James's use of the word is ironic, contained in invisible and sometimes even visible quotation marks, and so he suggests that his practice is really different from those of the Paris group.

Only the year before writing *The Princess Casamassima* he had, in "The Art of Fiction," dealt in this same subtle way with Walter Besant's recommendation that the novelist should maximize "truth of detail." He had admitted the virtue of "solidity of specification" by which the novelist

> competes with his brother the painter in *his* attempt to render the look of things, the look that conveys their meaning, to catch the colour, the relief, the expression, the surface, the substance of

the human spectacle. It is in regard to this that Mr. Besant is well inspired when he bids him take notes. He cannot possibly take too many, he cannot possibly take enough. All life solicits him, and to "render" the simplest surface, to produce the most momentary illusion, is a very complicated business. His case would be easier, and the rule would be more exact if Mr. Besant had been able to tell him what notes to take. But this, I fear, he can never learn in any manual; it is the business of his life. He has to take a great many in order to select a few, he has to work them up as he can. (1:53–54)

In 1908, he was still aware that he could never have made a claim to the sort of knowledge Zola would have required to write of the London poor as he had written of the Paris poor in *l'Assommoir,* or to depict the hidden stirrings of social revolt among them. Yet this was the territory James focused on for the first time in his career. And, thinking back, James is prompted to wonder at his own confidence, given his personal remoteness from the conditions of life he referred to in his novel and "given the extreme, the very particular truth and 'authority' required at so many points." Systematic field-work and research, indeed, would seem to have been called for. Nevertheless, it was by quite a different mode of notation that he actually "felt in full *personal* possession of [his] matter" (2:1100). His description suggests a process more instinctive, a process of accumulated feeling and thought rather than of gathering facts.

The very plan of my book had in fact directly confronted me with the rich principle of the Note, and was to do much to clear up, once for all, my practical view of it. If one was to undertake to tell tales and to report with truth on the human scene, it could be but because "notes" had been from the cradle the ineluctable consequence of one's greatest inward energy: to take them was as natural as to look, to think, to feel, to recognise, to remember, as to perform any act of understanding . . . Notes had been in other words the things one couldn't *not* take.   (2:1101)

James, in fact, resisted not only the naturalist example of a deliberate and exhaustive notation of reality but also naturalism's self-conscious systems of meaning, the scientifically predictable types and life histories of the human species generated by circumstance, as suggested by the analogy of plant and animal life. London, which he calls, poetically, "a great grey Babylon," is described in the

preface in familiar naturalist metaphors for human society; he calls
the city "an immense illustrative flora" or a "thick jungle," out of
which figures and stories "rise . . . like startled game" (2:1086)
before the observer. But here too, his tone may be ironic. The novel
makes only a qualified use of determinate "environment" and the
precise taxonomy of naturalism. These, James seemed to fear, failed
to explain the rich confusion of human experience. It was on this
basis that he would contrast the note-taking Zola with the greater
artist Balzac, calling the younger writer's method,

> the most extraordinary *imitation* of observation that we possess.
> Balzac appealed to "science" and proceeded by her aid; Balzac had
> *cadres* enough and a tabulated world, rubrics, relationships and
> genealogies; but Balzac affects us in spite of everything as person-
> ally overtaken by life, as fairly hunted and run to earth by it. He
> strikes us as struggling and all but submerged, as beating over the
> scene such a pair of wings as were not soon again to be wielded by
> any visitor of his general air and as had not at all events attached
> themselves to Zola's rounded shoulders . . . Zola "pulled it off,"
> as we say, supremely in that he never but once found himself
> obliged to quit, to our vision, his magnificent treadmill of the
> pigeonholed and documented—the region we may qualify as that
> of experience by imitation. His splendid economy saw him
> through, he laboured to the end within sight of his notes and his
> charts.   (2:895–896)

Zola, he also wrote,

> had had inordinately to simplify—had had to leave out the life of
> the soul, practically, and confine himself to the life of the instincts
> . . . to the impulses and agitations that men and women are pos-
> sessed by in common, and to take them as exhibited in mass and
> number, so that, being writ larger, they might likewise be more
> easily read. He met and solved, in this manner, his difficulty—the
> difficulty of knowing, and of showing, of life, only what his
> "notes" could account for. But it is in the *waste,* I think, much
> rather—the waste of time, of passion, of curiosity, of contact—
> that true imitation resides; so that the most wonderful adventures
> of the artist's spirit are those, immensely quickening for his
> "authority," that are yet not reducible to his notes.   (2:129–130)

James uses Balzac not only to deprecate the naturalist's claims of a
privileged notation, but to deprecate also the presumptions of natu-

ralistic conceptions, the confinement of characterization to simplified types which exhibit those "impulses and agitations that men and women are possessed by in common." Zola's was only an imitation of the observation practised by the genius who was "fairly run to earth . . . struggling and all but submerged" by the flood of life. One can, of course, quarrel with James's distinction between the realism of Balzac and that of his naturalist "son." It is the very opposite of the contrast drawn by Georg Lukacs in his well-known essay, "The Ideology of Modernism," in which the Marxist critic finds in Balzac a "hierarchy of significance," which is surrendered to the accidental in naturalism.[2] James never ceased to refer to Balzac's fortunate inheritance of a cultural scheme of ordered types and classes. Yet in Balzac's creative variety, in his more freely "constructive" art, James finds a justification of his own method.

A different way of distinguishing Balzac from Zola in James's terms is to say that the former allowed for that ingredient of "romance" which is the essence of the desiring and unprivileged vision of Hyacinth Robinson, the hero of *The Princess Casamassima*. In his New York Edition preface to *The American*, James defined the romantic as standing "for the things that, with all the facilities in the world, all the wealth and all the courage and all the wit and all the adventure, we never *can* directly know; the things that can reach us only through the beautiful circuit and subterfuge of our thought and our desire" (2:1063). In this definition, as Peter Brooks has observed, James, in 1907, "recognized, and stated more clearly than previously, the romantic element inherent to all his work, and his need for it"—an element that helped to account for his exaltation of Balzac above that novelist's naturalist followers.[3] The things "we never can directly know" are those that reach us by the imagination.

But there is still another way to define those inescapable "consequences" that were better than deliberate record, worked-up factuality, naturalist analysis, or "act(s) of understanding." In his preface to *The American*, James calls the "real" the "things we cannot possibly *not* know, sooner or later" (2:1063), a phrase echoed in his description in connection with *The Princess Casamassima* of the "notes . . . one couldn't *not* take"—that intake, which differs from the disengaged romantic fancy, which renders "the things . . . we never *can* directly know." These Jamesian "notes" were "impressions," a word which already, in 1886, had a particular aesthetic meaning. In a discussion which expresses his profoundest view of the relation of observation to the imagination, James explains,

> My notes on the much-mixed world of my hero's both overt and covert consciousness, were exactly my gathered impressions and stirred perceptions, the deposit in my working imagination of all my visual and all my constructive sense of London . . . I recall pulling no wires, knocking at no closed doors, applying for no "authentic" information; but I recall also on the other hand, the practice of never missing an opportunity to add a drop, however small, to the bucket of my impressions or to renew my sense of being able to dip into it. To haunt the great city and by this habit to penetrate it, imaginatively, in as many places as possible—*that* was to be informed, *that* was to pull wires, *that* was to open doors, *that* positively was to groan at times under the weight of one's accumulations.   (2:1101)

As I have said, James's language is at once suggestive of the naturalist method and a denial of it. He insists that in this instance the start of his novel had not been one of those plucked anecdotes about which he feared to know too much, fearing the irrelevance that full actuality might thrust in the way of artistic development. Rather, he had welcomed a certain saturation. His novel had proceeded "quite directly from the habit and interest of walking the (London) streets" (2:1086), the word "direct" suggesting the eager and total receptivity of the "roving" reporter. James *had* rambled in London and even put together an essay for the *Century*, in 1888, in which he mentions various pedestrian tours, those of an imagined "government-clerk" who lived in a Pembridge villa and worked in Westminster and took "a rustic walk" through the parks all the way, or a winter walk past the shopfronts of the Strand and Oxford Street, the British Museum, the clubs in Pall Mall. But these street scenes *imply* rather than show. Here is the spectacle of the West End in the "Season":

> For half an hour, from eight to nine, every pair of wheels presents the portrait of a diner-out. To consider only the rattling hansoms, the white neckties and "dressed" heads which greet you from over the apron in a quick, interminable succession, conveys an overwhelming impression of a complicated world. Who are they all, and where are they all going, and whence have they come, and what smoking kitchens and gaping portals and marshal led flunkies are prepared to receive them, from the southernmost

limits of a loosely-interpreted, an almost transpontine Belgravia, to the hyperborean confines of St. John's Wood?[4]

The essay makes use of an impressionistic directness which renders only exterior glimpses, preserving a certain indeterminateness ("who are they all?") and adding only subjective figuration. It is a process he describes in the *Princess* preface as "the assault directly made by the great city upon an imagination quick to react" (2:1086) The readers of the essay are not taken through the opened doors to interiors where we might view and listen at close range to the inhabitants, learn the workings of their world. And the same can be said about the descriptions in the novel, which only seems to be what F. W. Dupee called James's "ambitious study in the *vie de Londres*."[5] The essayist seems to be an outsider who can understand the position of those children of the poor who collect "wherever the strip of carpet lies, to see the fine ladies pass from the carriage or the house"—as Hyacinth Robinson might have done. In describing the way he had developed his novel, James declared that to walk as he did through London "was to receive many impressions, so the impressions worked and sought an issue" (2:1086). These are not the "notes" of the naturalist observer bent on discovering the laws that govern life, but the random harvest of what Baudelaire, in "The Painter of Modern Life," had called "le parfait flâneur, l'observateur passionné," who sets himself up "dans l'ondoyant, dans le mouvement, dans le fugitif et l'infini. Être hors de chez soi, et pourtant se sentir partout chez soi; voir le monde, être au centre du monde et rester caché au monde."[6]

We can suspect, then, that if the naturalist model was much before James in the seventies and eighties, so was that opposite viewpoint represented in painting by the new way of looking at scenes—as, for example, one looks at a city street in Monet's "Boulevard des Capucines," exhibited in the first Impressionist exhibition in 1874. Monet's painting is not a presentation of significant details, not an analysis of the urban subject—but a rendering of the effect of color, light, and movement conveyed to the eye at a single moment to which the painter has responded. As Gerald Needham observes,

> The plunging view down into the street gives us a feeling of the busyness of the boulevard, the flow of people, but it is a generalized impression of movement, and of the vivacity of the city

street. We cannot distinguish individuals; there are no little scenes played out to concentrate our attention, which moves through the picture following the line of trees and cabs. We are attracted by the spots of pink and red, and respond to the different directions and weight of the brushstrokes. We realize that it is not a picture *of* the boulevard—we cannot see the architecture properly, the angled view prevents us from seeing the boulevard as a whole, and we have no idea of what stores or cafes are located on it. Nothing could be further from a novelist's description of a boulevard.[7]

But one must qualify this statement and observe that Monet's "description," while it does not resemble the description Zola would have given the scene, is congenial to James's method.

As we know, Zola, despite his own analytic realism, in which everything is located in a fully identifiable world—and one that implies a story, is an evidence of cause-and-effect—was the friend and defender of the new painters and actually boasted that he had translated them into literature in his descriptions.[8] But though the loose association of Impressionism with the naturalist notation of perceived details is now often made,[9] the crucial difference remains. One has only to compare Monet's painting with Gervaise's window view on the Boulevard de la Chapelle, which opens *l'Assommoir*, to realize that an unsleeping interpretive viewpoint is active behind Zola's observations. James, as we have seen, declared the value of "truth of detail" to the novelist, who, he said, "competes with his brother the painter in *his* attempt to render the look of things." But the "look" so rendered is not, for James, so directly subject to the forward drive of story, to novelistic *meaning*. We need not assume that James saw the "Boulevard des Capucines" when he arrived in Paris in 1875. But Impressionism was talked about as much as naturalism by James's Paris friends, and James might have found some interest of his own—rather different from theirs—in such new ways of seeing.

In any case, as I have argued in the first chapter of this book, James's impressionism is best understood as the consequence of more general intellectual changes in modern culture in the last decades of the century, changes which had produced the sensationalist views of Pater as well as Impressionist painting. It is for this reason as much as for the impact of the painting itself that certain attitudes implied in Impressionism could have affected the development of *The Princess Casamassima.* One of these attitudes is the modernist deprecation of the realist subject in favor of effects which remind the viewer of the process of vision itself.

Can we suspect such a principle at work in a novel so conspicuously concerned with contemporary history, with classes, with social movements—the objective social world? The choice of subject seems peculiar for James. He recalled realizing that his vision of Hyacinth Robinson's "occult affiliations"—his involvement in an anarchist secret society—might be challenged by readers with more knowledge of such things. What he had observed in his London walks and what he had imagined of the invisible side of London life could never hope to fall into some "authentic" design. But was the subject in this case less important than the mode of its perception— or was the perception itself the true subject? He insisted upon the value of his own relativist notation. "Knowledge, after all, of what? My knowledge of the aspects I more or less fortunately rendered *was* exactly, my knowledge. If I made my appearances live, what was this but the utmost one could do with them?" (2:1102).

His defense for the presentation of such dubious "knowledge" lay "in the happy contention that the value [he] wished most to render and the effect [he] wished most to produce were precisely those of our not knowing, of society's not knowing but only guessing and suspecting and trying to ignore, what 'goes on' irreconcileably, subversively, beneath the vast smug surface" (2:1102). He points out that his own ignorance is, after all, the condition of the public in general, which only guesses at what is going on in the darkness of the "underground" hidden from the law, unreported by the newspapers.

James was certain such a subterranean world existed. Writing Charles Eliot Norton in 1886, just after *The Princess Casamassima* had appeared in the *Atlantic Monthly,* he compared the position of the English ruling class to that of the French aristocracy before the Revolution or the Roman empire before the barbarians came down upon it. "In England," he predicted, "the Huns and Vandals will have to come *up*—from the black depths of the (in the people) enormous misery." He felt that England had become "grossly materialistic and want(ed) bloodletting." Who the bloodletters would be was hardly clear. "I don't think the Attila is quite yet found—in the person of Mr. Hyndman," he said, mentioning a prominent evangelical proto-Fabian of the day.[10] But international anarchism was in the air; James could have known all about Bakunin from Turgenev, who had met Bakunin; Turgenev even met Kropotkin in Paris in 1878, and could have told James about this famous anarchist leader as well.[11] It can be argued that James's sense of what anarchism—a very different thing from Fabian socialism—was about was remarkably on target. Lionel Trilling, in his classic essay on *The Princess Casamassima,* insisted that in the preface James merely "throw(s) us off the scent" of his informed understanding of the "hierarchical and secret" organizations of Bakunin. Our present weak sense of the nature of this pre-Marxian radicalism misleads us, Trilling says, into underestimating the realism of James's novel.[12]

But we cannot really dismiss, in this way, James's sense of his own and the public's "not knowing" the reality of anarchist conspiracy. "Not knowing" is his very subject. In arguing this I would distinguish my view from that of Irving Howe, who, disagreeing with Trilling, doubted that the vagueness of James's treatment was "quite the pondered choice he would later claim in his preface," and deprecated James's interest in politics. Howe viewed the book as a technical diversion for its author, "an experiment in craft and imagination: how well could he survey an area of life he had never explored?" Conceding that the novel contains "brilliant political insights into political character," Howe insisted:

> *The Princess Casamassima* seems almost designed to evade its own theme. Everything is prepared for but little is revealed, doors open upon doors, curtains onto curtains. The elaborate skirmishing around the central brute fact of the novel—I mean, of course, the nature and power of social radicalism—is probably due to James's hesitation at taking it firmly in hand as he had taken other subjects in hand. He is skittish in his treatment because he is uncertain of his material; and he is uncertain of his material not merely because he does not know it intimately, but more important, because he vaguely senses that for a subject so explosive and untried something more is needed than the neatly symmetrical laying-out of his plot or the meticulous balancing of his characters.[13]

Howe, I think, exaggerates James's political indifference, underestimates his genuine sympathy with the sufferings of the poor. Though the book does *not* describe urban squalor and anguish in graphic terms, Hyacinth's response to these is expressed in a number of powerful passages such as that in which "the deep perpetual groan of London misery seemed to swell and swell and form the whole undertone of life" during the hard winter which prepares him for his great offering (V:343).[14] But James did not undertake to write a protest novel—and his disinclination for that task may be expressed in Hyacinth's dream, after he had seen Venice, of bringing to birth literary productions of his own which would not "have anything to do with a fresh deal of the social pack" (VI:155–156).

James's suspicion of his own story-making is the source of a philosophic theme mixed in with his concrete social one. The conditions which prevent his subject from falling into a scheme of ready comprehension promote a vision of *all* social reality as failing to conform to conventional definitions, as being full of mysterious opacities and blanks. "Plot" in its doubled sense—both the intrigue set into motion by the novel's "plotters," that is, the anarchists, and narrational plot—is undermined by these conditions. In the almost totally unillumined "given" of the anarchist conspiracy, James also exhibits an idea of inaccessible general truth—truth which must remain occulted.

The worldwide anarchist movement, with its branches in various countries—even the structure of the English secret network to which Hyacinth's friends at the "Sun and Moon" putatively belong—is never displayed. It is only partially, fitfully, visible to Hyacinth. And the readers, as James arranges things, see no more of the larger picture, understand things no better than the hero, since the novelist chooses to limit *our* knowledge, for the most part, to Hyacinth's perceptions. Indeed, far from being given the full advantages of authorial omniscience, we are fated to know even *less* than Hyacinth. When he comes face to face with the source of truth, the mysterious chief, Diedrich Hoffendahl, we are not allowed to accompany him but are reduced to surmising. The effect of Hyacinth's limitations of knowledge upon the reader is intensified by this suppression of his one moment of illumination. Yet this has been his only glimpse of "the real thing," as Muniment calls it (V:361), using James's own phrase, in his famous story, for a dubiously accessible reality).

It is interesting to observe how James deftly placed this particular ellipsis at the center of the novel, in a gap between the physical divisions of its pages. Serial publication, as he would remark in the preface to *The Ambassadors,* had often seemed to prompt him to experiment with the effects produced by discontinuities between chapters: "I had been open from far back to any pleasant provocation for ingenuity that might reside in one's actively adopting—as to make it, in its way, a small compositional law—recurrent breaks and resumptions" (2:1313). In the case of *The Princess Casamassima*, James utilized the break between Book Two and Book Three, between the twenty-first and twenty-second chapters (which was also to be the break between the two volumes when published in book form in 1886 and again in the New York Edition), to separate Hyacinth's midnight cab ride to his meeting with Hoffendahl from his morning awakening—weeks later—at Medley. The meeting that determines his fate, as well as Hyacinth's immediate responses, are elided—and the elision serves to reinforce the idea that reality is full of lapses which balk our effort at story-making.

But it is not only the "underground" which remains shadowy. Hyacinth's encounters with the visible, objective structures of society, the institutions which embody its value, the scenes with their human actors which illustrate the habits and functions of classes—as one witnesses these things in the realist novel—are severely limited. There is surprisingly less particularity in James's descriptions of Lomax Place than we might expect, though here "local" color is most evident. Even the prison scene, where we might look for the results of James's "direct" observation, is subjective in the extreme—the register chiefly of Amanda Pynsent's confusion and fright.[15] But a real vision of upper-class life is even more absolutely out of Hyacinth's longing reach than the truth of the anarchist movement, and is excluded from the novel—and this exclusion cannot be explained by James's inability to picture scenes which, unlike the underside of society, he knew well.

Trilling suggested that the novel belongs to the line of works—*Le rouge et le noir, Père Goriot, l'Éducation sentimentale, Great Expectations*—whose hero may be called the "Young Man from the Provinces," an analogy which can also be made in the case of Basil Ransom. Such a hero arrives from some outer place far from the center of power, whether that outerness is geographic or social, and, chiefly by means of his relationships with women, makes his way into the very center, gains his place there, *knows* its secrets. But, unlike Julian Sorel or Rastignac—or even Basil Ransom—Hyacinth never gets much past the threshold of the world he imagines. His own high-born paternal family remains forever unknown to him.

His acquaintance with a Princess and an English Lady does not really bring him close to the milieu to which they belong.

The Princess, though he sees her as the very embodiment of aristocratic grace, opens no doors into the glittering world she has inhabited. Significantly, his first meeting with her is at the opera, where the society of wealth and rank is displayed in its tiers of boxes, very much as though it were another fantasy of the stage. One has only to consider the elusive evocation which stands for upper-class life at Medley on the occasion of Hyacinth's visit there to realize how James, himself already a habituated country-house visitor, declines the opportunity to depict a familiar world. When the Princess receives Hyacinth at Medley, he finds it to be a museum of symbols of cultivated living, an "enchanted palace," "peopled with recognitions" (VI:41, 7) But it is literally unpeopled; she receives him alone, and during his stay has almost no visitors. His subsequent intimacy with her is conducted in Madeira Crescent, the make-believe parody of lower-middle-class vulgarity where she has whimsically removed herself from her aristocratic associations. It is no accident that his relation with her has only the erotic meaning of sublimated, unsatisfied desire on his part; her feeling for him is erotically indifferent and coldly curious—at best, vaguely maternal. Unlike Ransom, Hyacinth has none of the sexual power that stands for the penetrative energy of the provincial *arriviste*.

His only other possible door-opener to the social upper world is Lady Aurora, but she is more interested in *his* level of society than in her own, and, stripped of all personal as well as class glamor, she is vainly in love with her class enemy, Muniment. When Hyacinth first meets Lady Aurora it is also out of her "normal" context, in the Muniment flat, and when he sees her in her family's London house in Belgrave Square, it is only to find her also, like the Princess at Medley, alone. Indeed, on two of these visits, she is virtually camping there, "amid a desert of brown holland" (VI:190), the furniture shrouded in dustcovers in the off-season. On his third and last visit, he finds the house occupied and a party going on, but she receives him in a small room apart for a quarter of an hour before she goes out to dinner.

Thus, though the novel gives some sense of James's concern about the old problem of England's "two nations" now more completely alienated from one another than ever, it is the observer—more than the worlds he may or may not fully discover, or the worlds only as he imagines them—that counts most. It is not really what James saw as he rambled through London during his first year there that gave him inspiration. Even his recollections of those vague visual "impressions" that supply a sense of scene in the novel did not supply its essential element. James's impressionism draws out the subjective paradox at the heart of the impressionist attitude, which, beginning as a "scientific" method of recording objectively the shapes and forms that we perceive before we know *what* we perceive, ultimately makes of the perceiving subjectivity the only reality. James's interest is in the stroller himself. James says that Hyacinth "sprang up for me out of the London pavement," but admits, in the next breath, "I had only to conceive his catching the same public show, the same innumerable appearances, I had watched myself, and of his watching very much as I had watched" (2:1087). His hero could share some of James's own sensibility; his sensibility would in fact, make the story, as nothing else would.

The *Princess* preface is one of James's most distinct declarations of the value of a central fictional consciousness of high perceptiveness, and expresses his preference for a story that evolves out of the drama of that consciousness in its response to outer things. "I have ever found rather terribly the point—that the figures in any picture, the agents in any drama, are interesting only in proportion as they feel their respective situations." The consciousness of those who are "most finely aware and richly responsible, he says, *"makes* absolutely the intensity of their adventure" (2:1088). The "notation"— and the persisting reference to "notes" is significant—goes forward, in this case, he says, "in the mind of little Hyacinth, immensely quickened by the fact of its so mattering to his life what he does make of things" (2:1094). Hyacinth, who is described as wandering through London desiring not so much to enjoy as to know—very much as James pictures himself having done—is "a youth on whom nothing was lost" (V:169). The characterization echoes James's own idea of literature as gaining its quality from the quality of the mind perceiving rather than from the things perceived. In "The Art of Fiction," he had just urged the novice writer not only to "write from experience" but to "try to be one of the people on whom nothing is lost." He had described the artist for whom it was more important "than any accident of residence or place in the social scale" to have "the power to guess the unseen from the seen." Using again that loaded aesthetic word, "impressions," James had said in the essay, "If experience consists of impressions it may be said that impressions *are* experience" (1:53).

But restriction to a single observer enforces ellipses. However fine and responsible the central consciousness, fiction that depends upon it displays, by that very reliance, the incompleteness and relativity of its evidence. In building a novel out of the consciousness of one person, the restricted viewpoint surrenders the "panoptic" view of older realist or of naturalist fiction. However keen the individual notation operating within such a fictional world, it is without privilege. Here I differ from Mark Seltzer, who recently has connected *The Princess Casamassima*—perhaps because of the early prison scene—with Foucault's symbolic use of Jeremy Bentham's panopticon (a prison-plan which places all its inmates under scrutiny from a central observation station and which, in fact, determined the design of Millbank prison). Foucault's panopticon society of universal surveillance is reflected, Seltzer believes, in James's emphasis upon vision in the novel, which corresponds in some way with the London spy and police system of the day. I would argue, on the contrary, that personal perception, here (as in others of James's fictions), is unconfirmed by a watch-tower overview which sees all.[16]

This is true even though the novel does not restrict itself to Hyacinth as the observational source of every scenic moment. There are important occasions, from the opening during his childhood when Amanda Pynsent discusses him with Mrs. Bowerbank, to the final scene after his death, that take place out of his awareness—for example, chapter 39 (between Paul Muniment and his sister and then between Paul and the Princess) or the next chapter, between Madame Grandoni and the Prince. Yet these do not modify seriously James's characterization of his own novel as an "ordeal of consciousness" which is always Hyacinth's; the inner drama—which is all the drama—is only his, while his companions remain relatively opaque, their thoughts hidden from us. We share Hyacinth's frustrated effort to understand these others.

It might be argued that James is nevertheless privileging his chosen observer in this as in other works because of that "power to be finely aware and richly responsible" which he bestows upon him. In fact, these capacities do not make absolute knowledge accessible; they only make the observer's efforts more interesting. The case of Hyacinth provokes James to observe in the preface that the observing and finely feeling character must not know too much or feel too much, must not be "too *interpretive* of the muddle of fate." He must, instead, "fall into traps and be bewildered." He adds, "It seems probable that if we were never bewildered there would never be a story to tell about us; we should partake of the superior nature of the all-knowing immortals whose annals are dreadfully dull so long as flurried humans are not, for the positive relief of bored Olympians, mixed up with them" (2:1090). "Bewilderment" is that condition of pause between interpretations—between assumptions of meaning once unquestioned and those alternatives that the mind struggles to establish in their place. It is precisely such a condition which most interests James. Indeed, as I have been saying, it is by reproducing this process in the reader, by the production of bewilderment and then of the effort of recovery from it, that James's fictions themselves progress.

Hyacinth is not identically James, not the master mind who knows everything because he has created the fiction and everything in it. Yet, as he has done before with his observing characters or narrators, James identifies autobiographically with his hero's sensitive observation of the London spectacle; he even permits Hyacinth to cherish the ambition to write as well as bind books: "In secret he wrote—quite as for publication; he was haunted with the dream of literary distinction" (V:91). But Hyacinth only aspires to authorship, and is without that access to the social world that James enjoyed.

> So far as all the swarming facts should speak of freedom and ease, knowledge and power, money, opportunity and satiety, he should be able to revolve round them but at the most respectful of distances and with every door of approach shut in his face. For one's self, all conveniently, there had been doors that opened—opened into light and warmth and cheer, into good and charming relations; and if the place as a whole lay heavy on one's consciousness there was yet always for relief this implication of one's lucky share of the freedom and ease, lucky acquaintance with the number of lurking springs at light pressure of which particular vistas would begin to recede, great lighted, furnished, peopled galleries, sending forth gusts of agreeable sound. (2:1087)

It is James, who in the winter of 1878-79 noted in his engagement book that he had dined out in London 140 times,[17] who is the "young

man from the provinces," the "provincial" American who had successfully made himself a social favorite in the most impregnable
English circles. Hyacinth's inferiority to the author is what the
novel is about; his story is the story of someone who shares James's
aesthetic nature but is forbidden to enter the inner city of luxury
and cultural opportunities.

James understood that knowledge and power are connected, that
privilege in the intellectual sense is the consequence of economic
and social advantage, that the "privileged" class possesses the
money and leisure which provide the conditions for the development of an intelligence such as his own. Without the opportunity to
know which the educated mind enjoys, the preceiving person is
deprived. Hyacinth surmounts his handicaps to a degree. He makes
a short leap out of the working class by means of a hereditary inclination to refinement, aided by the alertness to style of his dressmaker foster mother and the lucky encounter with a displaced representative of cultivation, Mr. Vetch. This start is promoted by his
meeting the Princess and his travel abroad. If he is not an artist, he
is almost one; his exquisite nature vibrates in response to beauty.
But the class barrier stands fast.

On the other hand, not even the socially privileged writer, such
as James, is so placed as to have a *fully* privileged view of human
truth. It is no accident that the reference to doors shut and opened
in the passage just quoted is echoed in James's antinaturalist boast
that he had pulled no wires and knocked at no doors in quest of
"authentic" information. James identifies, after all, with his
bemused and restricted hero when he makes no claim for the
"authentic" in his novel. Having wondered what would be the effect
of being like Hyacinth, and "having so many precious things perpetually in one's eyes, yet of missing them all for any closer knowledge,
and of the confinement of closer knowledge entirely to matters with
which a connexion, however intimate, couldn't possibly pass for a
privilege," James goes on, "There are London mysteries (dense categories of dark arcana) for every spectator, and it's in a degree an
exclusion and a state of weakness to be without experience of the
meaner conditions, the lower manners and types, the general sordid
struggle, the weight of the burden of labour, the ignorance, the
misery and the vice" (2:1088). Hyacinth's "bewilderment" is a representation of the novelist's.

A novel, as it is so often said now, is about nothing so much as its own coming-into-being. *The Princess Casamassima*, literally the story of a man who tries to make the journey from his original restrictions to what lies outside them, employs a method which makes a single, limited consciousness dynamically assimilative. Hyacinth may be said to suffer from the effect of an acute sense of his lack of perceptual privilege as much as from his longing for certain kinds of social opportunities and sensual rewards. His heritage, which combines aristocratic sensibility with proletarian indignation, suggests a capacity to live in two worlds, but his mixed nature results in an inability to reach, finally, the absolute of either. His hopeless love of the Princess is that romantic desire which cannot see its own object except in the haze of fantasy. His revolutionary passion comes out of dreams of a primal family wrong more than out of the miseries of the poor folk among whom his youth has been spent. Nevertheless, his vision is his achievement. His imagination, which springs from no certain basis in knowledge, is like James's own, which is not rooted in any claim of mimesis but depends simply upon being "finely aware and richly responsible."

It is for this reason that Hyacinth's likeness to James himself is so important, and that he is literally a maker of books and a writer by inclination. His literary imagination does all the work of supplying what observation fails to supply. Even if Lady Aurora's house in Belgrave Square is empty when he visits her there, he imagines her—from his readings—to be "just rising from dinner," though in reality he finds her making a meal of a "a scrap of fish and a cup of tea served on a little stand in the dismantled breakfast parlor" (V:314). When he sees the Princess at Medley, he is denied any glimpse of the social scene which all its elegance implies and customarily frames, but finds a connection with the purely aesthetic, which detaches itself from its social causes. As one of the princess's servants fills his glass, he is reminded of Keats' "Ode to a Nightingale," and as he wanders about the great house it is in the library that he finds himself most ravished, significantly, by the equipment of the writing table. Later, in the Princess's saloon, he finds her playing the piano in a room "littered over with books, newspapers, magazines, photographs of celebrities slashed across by signatures," and the Princess places in his hands "the last number of the *Revue des Deux Mondes* . . . calling his attention in particular to a story by M. Octave Feuillet"—while the Princess herself strikes him as "a sudden incarnation of the heroine of M. Feuillet's novel" (VI:16). Hyacinth is the writer whose observation is inescapably intertextual.

It is Hyacinth who represents in the book, finally, that tendency, inherent in impressionism, to promote the medium to a primary interest, to subordinate the subject of art to its form, which we call aestheticism. It is, after all, to the *beautiful* that his nature infallibly turns. He may miss altogether the social truth about the Princess, but her status as an image of romantic beauty remains persistent. At Medley, he glimpses in the inacessible world of privilege objects that send him messages not so much of social authority as of beauty to be loved for its own sake. It is the beauty of Paris that wins him as he sits at his table and takes "stock of his impressions" (VI:119) outside of Tortoni's—Tortoni's, which he knows about "from his study of the French novel" (VI:120), particularly Balzac and Alfred de Musset. Though he meets up with the ghost of his Republican grandfather, he takes him along on his rambles through the arcades and avenues, bridges and quays, and above all, the Louvre, for "all Paris struck him as tremendously artistic and decorative" (VI:123). In Venice, he finds himself intensely happy, wishing in a Paterian mood for nothing more than "the present hour" as he wanders about "that enchanted square of St. Marks which resembles an immense open-air drawing-room, listening to music and feeling the sea-breeze blow in between those two strange old columns of the piazzetta which seem to make a doorway for it" (VI:144). It is at this climax of aesthetic appreciation that he loses sight, as he confesses in his letter to the Princess, of "the Sacred Cause," not so much forgetful of human misery as adoring the achievements, "inestimably precious and beautiful," of which man has been capable despite them (VI:145).

If Hyacinth personalizes James's own romanticism and his impressionist-aestheticist tendency as a novelist, it is a different sort of novelistic mind that is represented by Rosy Muniment. Rosy, who has often been recognized as a Dickensian character in the mold of Jenny Wren, has a realist artist's ability to bring the true social world into her sequestered imagination. Rosy resembles James's invalid sister, Alice, whose interest in politics, fed by newspapers and the reports of her visitors, was stronger, probably, than his. Rosy makes of her sickroom a little theater to which the other characters come to exhibit themselves, and she can accurately visualize their lives outside. She goes nowhere, yet she *imagines* everything in the world outside her room. She knows to the completest exactitude how Lady Aurora lives ("She talked of Inglefield as if she had stayed there"; (V:129) as well as what the scene at Greenwich will be like when Hyacinth and her brother go there for a Sunday outing. Her imaginative vision makes the most of slight hints and puts her into full possession of remote realities, as though she were that literary sensibility upon which nothing is lost to the end of producing a veritable account of reality. Rosy would have found less play for her hallucinatory fancy in America, one can guess. Like the artist who relishes the *cadres* of social distinction, like Balzac, whom James envied for the world he found to his hand in nineteenth-century France, she needs for her purpose the expectable features of an organized social world; she does not concur with her brother's hopes of a social leveling which would eliminate all distinction. "I don't want to see the aristocracy lowered an inch," she says, "I like so much to look at it up there" (V:146).

Rosy, however, like Hyacinth, is denied actual access to these scenes; her invalidism in addition to her poverty, prevents her from taking "direct" notes. The naturalist attitude toward life, the note-taking and classifying method of apprehending and representing it, is more fully represented in the novel by the Princess herself. It is not the first time that James employs a character to enact this view-point and technique which most challenge him to emulation and to difference even as he writes his book. Scientific or naturalistic observation and analysis were the intellectual methods of Dr. Sloper, of whom the narrator says, "he was never eager, never impatient nor nervous; but he made notes of everything, and regularly consulted his notes" (34). Dr. Sloper turned out to be both right and wrong in his conclusion that human beings can be studied like animal species. He was right in his classification of Morris Townsend, but Townsend was right in objecting that the doctor's daughter doesn't "marry a category . . . she marries an individual whom she is so good as to say she loves" (63). Townsend's careful statement avoids a direct refutation of Sloper's identification of his type—it is Catherine's desire, her romantic vision of this "beautiful young man" that counts, The story, of course, exposes the fallacy of romance by means of Mrs. Penniman's grotesque parody. But it also exposes the limitations of Sloper's science. In the doctor, James had already tested the tradition of realist observation and taxonomy which is the alternative to romance.

In *The Princess Casamassima,* he internalizes this tradition in the Princess, who is a scientific note-taker and analyst of the social scene, particularly of its lower depths. We need to see her in this way to fully account for her motives for action in the novel. She is partly explicable, of course, as a victim of the nineteenth-century disease of boredom—"wretched," as she confesses to Paul Muniment, "about nothing at all" (VI:225). Her *ennui* causes her to seek sensations not offered by the routines of middle-class or upper-class existence, and she can be compared to Ibsen's Hedda Gabler in her desire to relieve herself by somehow affecting another life, however destructively. In anticipation of the "radical chic" of Park Avenue hostesses entertaining the Black Panthers, she says, "Why shouldn't I have my bookbinder after all? In attendance, you know—it would be awfully *chic* (V:298). At the same time, she wants to shock the society to which she belongs. She claims to be motivated by a desire for revenge upon the upper class, into which she was married through no choice of her own, a class which has imprisoned and humiliated her since her marriage.

Hyacinth gathers from her that "the force of reaction and revenge might carry her far, make her modern and democratic and heretical *à outrance*—lead her to swear by Darwin and Spencer and all the scientific iconoclasts as well as by the revolutionary spirit" (V:295). She has become an adherent, it seems, of the new scientific principles which underlie naturalism as a way of looking at human life—and also embraced its viewpoint of social criticism. In Madeira Crescent the Princess is seen reading "a heavy volume on Labour and Capital" (VI:220)—perhaps *Das Kapital*, which was translated into English in 1886, while James was writing his novel. She has become—or likes to think herself—the new intellectual of advanced ideas.

She is, even more specifically, the naturalist novelist. It is in this role that she is to be observed when she explores the slums and tries to meet its inhabitants in her quest for "copy." Captain Sholto appears to be her "leg-man," her researcher on the lookout for descriptive data and for human "specimens." He has managed to insinuate himself among the anarchists on her behalf, as she admits, to "make friends with some of the leading spirits; really characteristic types" (V:216). His visit to the Muniments' flat is motivated by this same naturalist mission. He has told Paul that "he'd give the world to see a really superior working-man's 'interior' " (V:257), and when he arrives there asks, "Should you call it a fair example of a tenement of its class?" (V:260). His example stimulates Hyacinth, who has no natural inclination to this mode of thinking, to respond to Sholto's own invitation with the thought that he should "embrace an occasion of ascertaining how, as his companion would have said, a man of fashion would live now" (V:263).

Muniment calls Sholto a "patient angler," but he calls the Princess a "monster." She has an obsessive naturalist appetite for mud and misery, for the conditions which exhibit the uttermost of human degradation. When she more or less engages Hyacinth as a guide to working-class London, it is because he is a citizen of that netherworld himself; he supercedes Sholto for this reason above all, and not merely, as it superficially seems, because the *capricciosa* has exchanged one admirer for another. "I expect you to take me into the slums— into very bad places" (V:298), she tells Hyacinth when he visits her in her London house. Looking about her in Camberwell, where the Muniments live, she asks eagerly, "Is this the worst part?" to which Paul replies tartly, "The worst, madam? What grand ideas you must have! We admire Camberwell immensely" (VI:166).

When she assumes a lowered social identity for herself and moves to Madeira Crescent, she does so with the descriptive thoroughness whose consistency of detail signifies a naturalist art. Not for nothing does Hyacinth notice "the stuffed birds at the window, the alabaster Cupid, the wax flowers on the chimneypiece, the florid antimacassars on the chairs, the sentimental engravings on the walls—in frames of papier-mâché and 'composition,' some of them enveloped in pink tissue paper—and the prismatic glass pendants attached to everything" (VI:181). She walks with him past shops where her eye infallibly identifies "abominable objects . . . selecting them from a new point of view, that of a reduced fortune and the domestic arrangements of the 'lower middle class' " (VI:177), and she insists that Hyacinth conduct her to that class's ungenteel entertainments in music halls or coffee taverns. There seems no question that James means us to see her as a literary researcher on the French model; despite her personal repugnance for common and ugly things, "her discoveries in this line diverted her as all discoveries did, and she pretended to be sounding in a scientific spirit—that of the social philosopher, the student and critic of manners—the depths of the British Philistia" (VI:177).

Her view of persons is typological, of course. As their acquaintance proceeds she protests that Hyacinth must not think that she only wants to treat him "as a curious animal" (V:288), but she continues to find his atypicality a disappointment. "The only objection to you individually is that you've nothing of the people about you" (V:292), she complains. She wishes that he were wearing his work clothes when he comes to visit her at Medley, and can't get over his knowing Schopenhauer. When she learns that he has already met one aristocrat—Lady Aurora—she regards him, disappointedly, as "less fresh" than she had first thought. She admits that "he would take a great deal of accounting for" (VI:60)—it is more than her scheme of categorical realism allows.

Ultimately Hyacinth proves a reluctant guide to the reality she wants to encounter, and, for all his authentic proletarian experience, too unrepresentative of it. Even Lady Aurora, the upper-class do-gooder, is more useful. "Her ladyship practised discriminations which she brought the Princess to recognize, and before the winter was over Mr. Robinson's services in the slums were found unnecessary" (VI:261–262).

> "I thought you had promised to let *me* be your guide in those explorations," Hyacinth promptly pleaded.
> The Princess looked at him a moment. "Dear Mr. Robinson, Lady Aurora knows more than you."
> "There have been times surely, when you've complimented me on my knowledge."
> "Oh I mean more about the lower classes!" she returned. (VI:187)

But it is Paul Muniment who is the final successor, as Madame Grandoni calls him (VI:233), to Hyacinth, superseding him as Hyacinth himself had once superseded Captain Sholto. Muniment is a more authentic source of the vigor—political but also sexual and literary—with which she seeks to infuse herself. Muniment's proto-Marxian determinism makes him think typologically, and he speaks of "the pampered classes [whose] . . . bloated luxury begets evil" (V:230), while Hyacinth argues, "there may be unselfish natures; there may be disinterested feelings" (V:232). Muniment's idea of social change is based on the simple naturalistic idea that "conditions" account for character: "The low tone of our fellow-mortals is a result of bad conditions; it's the conditions I want to alter" (VI:216).

In the end, Hyacinth is "chucked" by the Princess in favor of Muniment, who subordinates his friend's uniqueness to a plot (life-history and intrigue) conceived by others. But even Muniment may be superseded by Hoffendahl, who is less a human being than an invisible, impersonal force whose plot bears no relation at all to the individualities it makes use of. What we do hear of him confirms him as the ultimate naturalist, "moving ever in a dry statistical and scientific air" (VI:137). We are told: "Humanity, in his scheme, was classified and subdivided with a truly German thoroughness" (VI:55). Naturalism, James is saying, not only reduces the indeterminate reality of personality to a genus-species simplicity, but it is guilty of coldness of heart, leaving no hope for the character's escape from a foreordained story.

In *The Princess Casamassima,* as in *Washington Square* and *The Bostonians,* the narrator seems committed to the attitudes of heartless analysts and categorizers, but brings himself into some acknowledgment of his limits in the end. Even more than *The Bostonians,* this novel is an ironic experiment. No case would seem more precisely defined in terms of the determinants of hereditary influence than that of Hyacinth Robinson, the bastard child of an English nobleman and a Frenchwoman of the lowest class. He comes "naturally" by that "air of race" (V:17) which Amanda Pynsent observes even in the little boy. Yet this view is not unchallenged; Mr. Vetch accuses Amanda of *making* him a little gentleman (V:30) by imposing the *idea* of gentility upon him, "tell[ing] him every three minutes that his father was a duke" (V:33). The old fiddler, his surrogate father, is for giving the child a "dose of the truth" about his mother, to show him, at least, that his heredity is mixed.

This other derivation is visible in the fact that he "look[s] like a Frenchman" (V:75) and also in the fact that he has picked up French "with the most extraordinary facility" from a French fellow worker at the bindery, speaking the language, "he believed, by a natural impulse (V:76). James's way of putting this detaches the narrator from subscription to a literal genetic interpretation, though the idea that such an ability might be due to a kind of national genetics was a common one in the nineteenth century.[18] Nevertheless, the idea of "the two currents that flowed in his nature, the blood of his passionate, plebian mother and that of his long-descended, supercivilized sire" (VI:264), is insistently put forward in the narrative. It operates to represent a struggle of incongruities within Hyacinth himself. "Come now, who are you?" Millicent asks, and though he answers, "I'm a wretched little 'forwarder' in the shop" (V:91), the sense of being complexly determined is present to his mind. It is also the narrative theory by which one may interpret his tragic history as governed by the contrary impulses of a divided nature. That is, one can say, his exposure to the "splendid accumulations" which privilege has made possible awakens the aristocratic strain in his innate character, negating the revolutionary anger which is his maternal heritage. But this naturalistic reading is not securely enforced by the novel. Indeed, when one considers how imperfectly the language of naturalism fits the novel as a whole, it seems more appropriate to say that Hyacinth's conflict is a conflict of ideologies, which is simply represented metaphorically by his supposed genetic elements. The unresolvable claims of a political morality which requires human equalization and an aesthetic which "privileges" exceptionality—for this significant conflict of philosophies the conflict in the blood may be only a figure.

James does not surrender altogether in this novel the mechanism of character typology and social class and the determinism that goes with them. But he is interested—romantically—in the way class and type and predictable destiny are transcended. Even Millicent Henning and Amanda Pynsent, each quite convincingly authentic representatives of the world of Lomax Place, are romantic aspirants to another character than their own—Pinnie, of course, not so much for herself as for her protégé, Hyacinth. Muniment is more intelligent than most chemical workers, but this is explained by the accident of natural genius. The narrator says, "he probably . . . had a large easy brain quite as some people had big strong fists" (V:114). Paul's sister Rosy, describing their parents, says that they "had jolly good brains at least to give us," to explain how Paul "would learn more from a yellow poster on a wall or a time-table at a railway station than many a young fellow from a year at college" (V:144, 143). Yet there is something beyond natural probability in Hyacinth's prediction that someday Muniment might be Prime Minister (V:244)—or rather, it is a prediction of a possibility still in the historic future for talented young workingmen. When James's novel was appearing young James Ramsay MacDonald, a laborer's son, was working as a clerk in London for twelve shillings, six pence a week. History itself is the destroyer of categorical types in the transmogrifications of class.

Millicent, similarly, will convert romantic envy to real social mobility. She is is called "a flower of the clustered parishes, the genius of urban civilization, the muse of cockneyism" (V:62). But she is far from accepting the idea that she is a representative of the "lower orders," and when Captain Sholto explains the kind of interest the Princess takes in Hyacinth and herself, she demands indignantly, "The lower orders? Does she think we belong to them?" (V:203). We can foresee that she will escape the naturalist plot of the female, victim to the forces of poverty and sexual susceptibility, and "make it" from the provinces of the working class to upper-class status. Hyacinth is probably correct when he tells Pinnie that this child of his poverty-stricken neighbors will marry an alderman.

The view of character—particularly the character of poor persons—as cast from the mold of class is disputed by Lady Aurora. When Hyacinth observes that "centuries of poverty, of ill-paid toil, of bad insufficient food and wretched housing hadn't a favorable effect on the higher faculties," even though "Paul is a splendid exception," she replies that she has often been struck by the "great talents and . . . quick wit" of the poor, and points out that he himself is an exception. When he then tells her "I've blood in my veins that's not the blood of the people," urging biological determinism against environmental, she still replies, "You're all the more of an exception—in the upper class" (V:246–248). She repudiates the class associations of "vulgarity"; for her, the vulgar are *not* "the poor, the unhappy, the labouring classes" (V:319). She also repudiates the conventional idea of the "gentleman" in her acceptance of Hyacinth, who reflects that "he shouldn't have occasion to say to her, as he had said to the Princess, that she regarded him as a curious animal" (V:316–317). Like Isabel Archer, she takes the essentialist view of personality: taking "all sorts of equalities and communities for granted [in] homage to the idea of his fine essence" (VI:191). Lady Aurora herself is perhaps an example of a type the English have always had some examples of, the upper-class eccentric, "one of the caprices of the aristocracy." But this antitype is a defiance of type. She is said tŏ have "few of the qualities of her caste" (V:128, 127). She is a refugee from her own class—its habits, its dress, its attitudes.

We have seen how Hyacinth's own exceptionality in the place of typicality and naturalistic predictability is precisely what irritates the Princess. But she herself, of course, is only a theatrical version of aristocratic type, even though she seems to the dazzled Hyacinth (who first encounters her, significantly, in the theatre) the finest flower of aristocratic culture. Unlike Lady Aurora, who is an aristocrat born, the Princess's title, we must not forget, is her husband's; her own origins, unlike Hyacinth's, are purely plebian. If we recall her early history as indicated in *Roderick Hudson,* we remember that she is the ambiguous product of an Italian and a displaced Anglo-American, even perhaps illegitimate, like Hyacinth himself.

Medley, which accurately represents, for Hyacinth, the "accumulations" of English upper-class culture, is a property which the Princess has *rented* from its proprietors. She takes him about the estate, offering expert commentary, in the tone of a cultivated cicerone, and one expects to see velvet ropes across the doorways to rooms containing precious furniture. The one intrusion into the scene of its proper sort of inhabitants—the visit of Lady Marchant and her daughters for tea—is a comic interruption about which we learn merely that the Princess puts the Lady "through her paces" by "trying to appear dense," while Hyacinth, for his part, wonders if his own lowly character is detectable; both of them are, after all, intruders and masqueraders. The Princess is as much a *poseur* there as in Madeira Crescent, another rental, where she shows her ability to create a *similitude* of typicality of an opposite kind—her finer appurtenances being placed in storage, like theatrical props.

In her role as naturalist *novelist* rather than as a character illustrating the naturalist idea, the Princess serves to expose the fictionality of the naturalist system and to assist the naturalist plot to abort itself. And like *The Portrait of a Lady* and *The Bostonians,* the novel is haunted as well by older plots which propose themselves and are aborted, just as Isabel's story might be—but isn't—the traditional marriage-plot of the English novel, and Verena's story realizes it ironically. The Princess is already in the position of Isabel who has married the wrong man and realizes her mistake; she, too, has found herself in the prison house of conventionality, though the poor Prince is not to be compared with Gilbert Osmond. Who, indeed, might the Princess marry now, if she should part from Casamassima? Not Hyacinth, certainly, not Paul Muniment. The novel does not even consider the question.

There is a tragic side to the Princess, even if James's tone in treating her represses it. Though it is not she, but Hyacinth, who ends life's insoluble contradictions by suicide, certain aspects of her personality—her beauty and brilliance, her restless energy, her theatricality, and her interest in radical movements into which she enters as a kind of upper-class interloper—remind one of Hawthorne's Zenobia. In an essay of 1897 on Hawthorne James speaks of Zenobia as "the passionate patroness of causes who plays as it were with revolution, and only encounters embarrassment" (1:464). His use of the word "revolution" to designate Zenobia's radicalism suggests that he has his own era in mind. But this intertextuality is complicated by another. The Princess has her origins, to begin with, in *Roderick Hudson;* she is the only character in James's fiction who is carried over into a new work from one of his own earlier books. But she also relates, unexpectedly, to others of his feminine protagonists. One may wonder why James gives to her the title of his novel—rather than to his acknowledged "center," Hyacinth. Perhaps it is because she is another in a procession of heroines which we have seen begin with Daisy Miller—young women whose resistance to a preconcluded definition is the essence of their ordeal.

The Princess obviously haunted James as someone whose destiny could not be easily concluded, and even in this novel she remains unconcluded. James writes in the preface that he felt he still had her on his hands after depicting her in his early novel; his language characterizes not only his artistic desire to make something more of his idea but her own predicament: "She had for so long, in the vague limbo of those ghosts we have conjured but not exorcised, been looking for a situation, awaiting a niche and a function." Speaking of her as both an unfinished character whose completer history he wanted to write and as a woman in quest of a fulfillment of self that life seems to deny, he says: "To continue in evidence, that had struck me from far back as her natural passion; in evidence at any price, not consenting to be laid away with folded hands in the pasteboard tomb, the doll's box, to which we usually relegate the spent puppet after the fashion of a recumbent worthy on the slab of a sepulchral monument" (2:1098). James's images are indeed suggestive—that of the doll taken out for play and put back, like Ibsen's Nora, confined to her play role, and that of the carved figure on a tomb, of the dead, the absolutely finished woman. Despite the negative aspects of her world-weariness and her imposture, her resemblance to James's other heroines is evident once we realize that she is, as Howe has astutely noticed, "James's 'heroine of all the ages' in her aspect of ugliness, as Isabel Archer from *The Portrait of a Lady* is that heroine in her aspect of loveliness."[19] But it is important to notice that her boredom is not so different, after all, from that disinclination to accept what life offers which Isabel feels; like Isabel she is in search of some adequate employment of her superior character, and cannot find it.

The disaster of her marriage to an Italian nobleman is interestingly centered in the sequence of James's fiction between an earlier and a later example—the very early story, "The Last of the Valerii" and, at the other end, his last great novel, *The Golden Bowl.* In these examples the old and the new worlds succeed finally in achieving a happy union, whereas in this novel the Princess has cast behind her a marital failure. James, of course, deliberately turns our attention away from Christina's marriage, an ellipsis, one might say, between her appearance in *Roderick Hudson* and her reappearance in *The Princess Casamassima* which is greater than the ellipsis that obscures the marriage of Isabel and Osmond. And, indeed, this theme of failed marriage is an element that threatens the organization of the book around Hyacinth. Most of the scenes that concern the Prince occur out of Hyacinth's view and are distinctly a break in the continuity of awareness which James wanted in this novel. It is as though James feels that the Prince's relation to the Princess belongs to a different story than the one he wants to write—and yet that story intrudes a little, continues to propose itself. Regarded for himself—aside from the needs of James's chief interest—the Prince is not so different from the Conte Valerio or Prince Amerigo. He may also be handsome and decent, as the wife of the Conte thinks of her husband in the early story—"good and strong and brave," though, as the narrator says, "perhaps a little stupid."[20] But the subject of Casamassima's marital difficulties has no constructive issue. Madame Grandoni, *his* Fanny Assingham, can extend no real encouragement to his desire to recapture his wife. He exists only to provoke her capriciousness, to help to explain, somewhat, her curious presence among the anarchists.

But in fact, like Isabel—or Verena—the Princess is not explained by her past or her present experience or environment, and while, as we have seen, she gives revenge as a "motive" for her role, James is not really interested in this idea and we do not see its operation in her. She is a *capricciosa* by nature—and she has always bean one, if we remember Christina Light and her entanglement with Roderick

Hudson, an episode never recalled in this later history. Origins and environment, in fact, as represented by description in the novel, bear little relation to character; there are only a few instances—like that of Amanda and her little workshop—of the Balzacian correspondence of scene and person, of the pension and Madame Vauquier. Most of the characters are displaced in some way. It is significant that even the bindery workers—Poupin, Schinkel—are refugees from somewhere else, though they may be types of the worlds they derive from. Vetch is someone who was born far from Lomax Place, a declassed gentleman. The Muniment flat is no explanation of the Muniments, with their exceptional heredity, but it is particularly not an explanation of Rosy, who lives not so much in her real circumstances as in the worlds her imagination brings to her, such as Lady Aurora's family circle and its entertainments. Looking upon "the shabby, ugly, familiar paper of her wall," she can think "of the far-off fields and gardens she should never see" (VI:204).

For Hyacinth, too, as we have noticed, there are alternate plots at work besides the naturalist one. Trilling's "young man from the provinces" story *is* initiated; it is directly referred to when Hyacinth himself reflects that "being whistled for by a princess presented itself to [him] as an indignity endured gracefully enough by the heroes of several French novels in which he had found a thrilling interest" (V:203). Yet this plot is discarded as Hyacinth finds the citadel of power impenetrable. More suggestively, one is led to expect the fulfillment of the story of the foundling or orphan whose relation to high-placed parents will be revealed at last. One of the oldest of plots, of course, is that of the fairy tale or myth of the child raised as a commoner who turns out to be the royal heir. The history of the English novel offers at its outset the example of Tom Jones, a foundling who only at the last discovers his connection with wealth and authority. Tom, like others of his kind, can finally put aside those wanderings and adventures which challenge the social order—permissible in a person with no social identity—and take his place as Squire Allworthy's nephew. For this conservative closure the reader of novels is so thoroughly prepared that he expects, for a time, to see Hyacinth somehow rejoin his father's family. If he were to do so he would fulfill the conservatism of the foundling plot by a realliance which repudiates his attachment to the forces of social insurrection, the attachment which has its sources in his imaginative sympathy with his commoner mother and with the working-class world which has nurtured him.

In a sense, of course, that *is* what happens, but in a way which substitutes for his recovered paternal relation a discovery of the culture which is the fruit of his father's class advantages. One can say, if one wishes, that Hyacinth does end up like Tom Jones after all, even though this realization of his "heritage" is never, at all, an acquisition of social place or power. His privileges, so gained, are only the privileges of culture. Perhaps, in this light, it is more than accidental that James actually contrasts his hero with Fielding's in the preface, speaking of Tom as "but as 'finely,' that is but as intimately, bewildered as a young man of great health and spirits may be when he hasn't a grain of imagination" (2:1094). Though James does not make exactly this point, it is not unfair to say that the contrast between Hyacinth and Tom is made the more striking by the way the history of James's hero both repudiates and accepts the Tom Jones story. In this transposed sense, Hyacinth *is*, one may even say also, the successful young man from the provinces, since he does gain access to the citadel of art and refinement. But his curious deficiency of sexuality—the fact that he never seems to want to make love to the Princess and that she never considers him as a possible lover, the fact that he seems a child among sexual adults, is thus explained. It distinguishes him from the young man who climbs into the palace by the ladder of sexual conquest. The man who could do this is Paul Muniment, who fascinates Princesses and English Ladies, and has a plot of his own, to be realized when someone like him will fulfill the prediction that he might become Prime Minister.

The discarded foundling plot is, nevertheless, cherished within the novel by Amanda Pynsent, the foster mother who sees in the child the unmistakable signs of his high origin. With her sentimental proletarian worship of the ruling classes, she expects that her little gentleman will some day reach his proper station. Her preparation of the little boy for this realization begins promptly. "I suppose we oughtn't forget that his father was very high," she tells Miss Bowerbank, who replies bluntly, "The less said about the poor child's ancestors the better! . . . As for pride of birth, that's an article I recommend your young friend to leave to others." It is, of course, in a novel that Miss Pynsent has read such stories: "What endeared [the boy] to her most was her conviction that he belonged 'by the left hand,' as she had read in a novel, to a proud and ancient race" (V:8–10). And so, from the start, she conveys to him, without telling anything directly about the dreadful Lord Frederick, "that there was a grandeur in his past" (V:11). Not only does she see signs of his aristocratic parentage, but she keeps his modest clothes neatly "repaired for all the world like those of a little nobleman" (V:18) and serves him his tea "like a real little gentleman" (V:8), as though to prepare him for a future beyond Lomax Place.

It is in accordance with this plot expectation—and not merely because she fears the shock to his delicate nature—that she recognizes no signs, on the other hand, of his working-class parent, gives him no hints of the alternate self that might arise from this heredity, taking him only reluctantly and without explanation to the bedside of his dying mother. (That she cannot altogether suppress this true maternity, that it will remain a disturbing memory to the growing boy, will provide the seeds of his oppositional identity with the woman who murdered her nobleman lover.) Misunderstanding a remark by Mr. Vetch that Hyacinth would in time "dress [her] up," Hyacinth's adoptive mother is ready to exclaim, "Do you mean that he'll have the property—that his relations will take him up?" (V:35–36). Poor Pinnie dies in the illusion that Hyacinth, having made a grand new friend, a veritable Princess, is on the way to this end. Vetch tells Hyacinth, "She has made up her mind that you've formed a connexion by means of which you'll come somehow or other into your own. She has done nothing but talk about your grand kindred. To her mind, you know, it's all one, the aristocracy, and nothing's simpler than that the person—very exalted, as she believes—with whom you've been to stay should undertake your business with her friends" (VI:93–94). Her last words refer to the relatives she imagines he is about to rejoin: "They'll make it up, they'll make up everything" (VI:111).

But by the time she dies, her conception of Hyacinth's destiny, which has seemed plausible to the reader in the early chapters, is exposed as sentimentality. At the very end, only Millicent Henning still cherishes such a view. On the one hand, for herself, Millicent converts the romance foundling plot into its nineteenth-century realist version, the expectation of upward social mobility. Unlike Pinnie, who sews the clothes of the wealthy in her workshop, this modern working girl actually wears them, as a model—enacting even beforehand the elevation that modern society promises to the ambitious and the lucky. She disdains working with her hands, and is shocked to discover that Hyacinth wears an apron in the bindery. Unlike Hyacinth, she will succeed in transgressing the boundaries of class, and needs no rediscovery of aristocratic antecedents to do so. But she subscribes to Pinnie's plot when she insists to Hyacinth, at the very end, that his "bloated" relatives ought to have recognized him long before—and that he might have brought himself to their notice. "*She* wouldn't have drudged out her life in Soho if she had had the blood of half the Peerage in her veins!" (VI:342).

The plot that Hyacinth himself embraces, of course, is not one of oedipal reconciliation but its opposite, when he undertakes to murder his aristocratic father as the aristocrat targeted by his anarchist friends, and to repeat, in vengance for the wrongs done his mother, his mother's crime. But this "revenger's tragedy," another handed-down plot, is also, of course, aborted. Hyacinth has promised to conclude his own story—accepting death in accepting this commission. But he ends it, actually, in another way, killing himself rather than fulfilling his promise, and, at the same time, aborting the conclusion of "Hoffendahl's plot."

Like Isabel Archer, Hyacinth remains fixed in potentiality, and even dies rather than realize by action this or any of his conflicted possibilities. His complex alterity brings him to the point of embracing death rather than continuing a life which must commit him to one choice or another. It is worth noting that when he initially takes his vow in the scene in the "Sun and Moon" with which the second book of the novel ends, he does not even know to what action he offers himself. "I'm ready to do anything that will do any good; anything, anything—I don't care a damned rap" (V:360). The undenoted quality of his commitment keeps his own sense of his future open even though the nature of his promise allows for any consequence chosen by others rather than himself.

When the assignment comes to him, though we *know* it must be an assignment to commit an assassination, it comes in the form of James's favorite device for an ellipsis—a sealed letter which is never shared with the reader. It is then that those who have unreflectingly launched him upon this plot cry out and wish to stop its momentum. "We want you to do nothing because we *know* you've changed" (VI:370), says Poupin. Mr. Vetch, who had long ago shown him an example of radical attitudes—which he now rejects as though he wishes to abort the consequences in action of his own younger convictions—makes Hyacinth promise "never, under any circumstances whatever [to] 'do' anything." " 'Do' anything—?' " "Anything those people expect of you." The quoted "do," that iterated word in the preface to *The Portrait of a Lady,* has now the most sinister of senses. Hyacinth promises. "Do you take your oath to that? Never anything, anything, anything?" "Never anything at all" (VI:391).

· 6 ·

"The Aspern Papers":
The Unvisitable Past

JAMES'S PREFACES to his revised fiction in the New York Edition constitute curious, framing second thoughts. These self-interpretive comments sometimes extract an original intention only partially evident in the writings they introduce, sometimes even add a perspective which gives prominence to an idea that is only subordinate—when it is not contradicted—by the story or novel standing alone. Sometimes they even neglect to mention what the reader is likeliest to identify as the work's most evident theme. And yet the distortions of the prefaces, if one may call them that, disclose latencies in the prefaced fiction that one would not otherwise have noticed; we read again to discover these as well as the themes suggested by the unaided text.

In no case is this more striking than in that of "The Aspern Papers." In his preface to the revision of 1908, written twenty years after the original publication of the story, James relates how his "germ" came to him as gossip about a modern manuscript hunter who discovered the astonishing survival in Italy of Claire Clairmont, the half-sister of Mary Shelley and the mother of Byron's child. The story James wrote turns upon the very hinge of this anecdote—that the letters the researcher sought were finally offered to him on the condition that he marry the niece of Miss Clairmont, a price he was unwilling to pay. The dilemma of the would-be biographer of the fictitious Jeffrey Aspern is the dramatic center of James's tale, which seems to belong to a whole family of Jamesian stories illustrating moral and emotional defection in the aesthetic personality. But James gives no indication in the preface of how this situation must have fascinated him, and does not discuss his narrator, this bemused anonymous person who relates his own misadventure.

James speaks instead of the effect upon his imagination of

185

another aspect of the situation described to him. What aroused his interest most, he says, was the fact of Miss Clairmont's survival, her "having testified for the reality and the closeness of our relation to the past" (2:1175). It would seem that "there had been, so to speak, a forward continuity, from the actual man, the divine poet, on; and the curious, the ingenious, the admirable thing would be to throw it backward again, to compress—squeezing it hard!—the connexion that had drawn itself out, and convert so the stretched relation into a value of nearness on our own part" (2:1177). The dead Romantic past of the great English poets, the age which might have produced a Jeffrey Aspern, is one with which he is thrilled to make connection: "I delight," he says, "in a palpable imaginable *visitable* past—in the nearer distances and the clearer mysteries, the marks and signs of a world we may reach over to as by making a long arm we grasp an object at the other end of our own table." A vast, farther past may lie quite out of reach. But there is that glimmering recent time which has "the poetry of the thing outlived and lost and gone, and yet in which the precious element of closeness, teiling so of connexions but tasting so of differences, remains appreciable" (2:1177).

But does his story take advantage of the lingering light of a past that might still, more than half a century later, be thought of as recent? James both invites the idea that he can "visit" the Romantic age—and denies it. He calls his own first engagement with his story a moment when "history, 'literary history' . . . had in an out of the way corner of the great garden of life thrown off a curious flower that I was to feel worth gathering as soon as I saw it" (2:1173). Yet, having plucked his idea, he has a horror of knowing more of the garden from which it comes. He insists on preference for the "bare facts of intimation" and no more. The manuscript hunter's handicap had been that he had wanted more history instead of less, and that he had insisted on meeting Miss Clairmont, whereas James had *fortunately* missed her.

James's fear of an excess of real record is, of course, made on aesthetic grounds; as we know, he held that the free imagination of the artist should nurture only a "germ" of reality into art, for life, with its disorder and "waste," richly provocative as it is, is the enemy of form. As *The Princess Casamassima* illustrated, James felt that reality is often more obscure and undecipherable than we realize. If this is true of the present, how much more so might it not be of the past? James had less confidence than the preface expresses in the project of "visiting" the time of the great Romantic poets. The story he wrote is the story of his difficulty. The preface subject as he confronted it emerges as the attempt of a man engaged precisely in such a doomed project, a man who hopes—but fails—to write a true biography of a great dead genius of a vanished time.

The distance of the generation of Byron from his own seems to have struck James as allowing not only for a "romantic" relation— "romance" being, as he had defined it in the preface to *The American*, the balloon of the imagination cut loose from the ground of reality (2:1064). As an early reader objected, moreover, probability is challenged by making Aspern an American, when history doesn't exhibit an American Byron or Shelley in the early eighteen hundreds. Not quite convincingly, James insists in the preface that the problem of supposing Aspern was the difficulty inevitable when one assigns public distinction to an invented character; it made for the same difficulty as supposing an English Rachel, Miriam Rooth of *The Tragic Muse*. He seems to want to believe that he *could* have justified his figure in the presentation, even if he hasn't actually done so: "My last word [is], Heaven forgive me, that, occasion favouring, I could have perfectly 'worked out' Jeffrey Aspern" (2:1181).

But the real difficulty was not just lack of an actual model. It was that James postulated a great poet who had overcome the very disadvantages he was on record as believing inescapable for an American writer. The story's narrator says,

> His own country after all had had most of his life, and his muse, as they said at that time, was essentially American. That was originally what I had prized him for: that at a period when our native land was nude and crude and provincial, when the famous "atmosphere" it is supposed to lack was not even missed, when literature was lonely there and art and form almost impossible, he had found means to live and write like one of the first; to be free and general and not at all afraid; to feel, understand, and express everything. (XII:50)

The description of the native circumstances above which Aspern had risen recalls James's indictment of Hawthorne's America (as well as Hawthorne's own complaint in the preface to *The Marble Faun*).¹ "The moral" of Hawthorne's case, James had written in 1879, "is that the flower of art blooms only where the soil is deep, that it takes a great deal of history to produce a little literature, that it needs a complex social machinery to set a writer in motion" (1:320). That James was himself determined to escape these limitations is implied in his decision, which hardened into a fixed resolution in the eighties, to live permanently in Europe. James's *Hawthorne* is, of course, drenched in an "anxiety of influence," and it is possible that he felt the need to justify his own expatriation—which may have had more obscure causes—by a crippled forerunner.

But he may not have felt secure in his condescension; Hawthorne also remained for him the genius who had escaped all strictures. Much later, looking back at his beginnings from nearly the final moment in his long career, he recalled how he had felt in 1864, when Hawthorne died:

> His work was all charged with a *tone,* a full and rare tone of prose, and . . . this made for it an extraordinary value in an air in which absolutely nobody's else was or has shown since any aptitude for being. And the tone had been, in its beauty—for me at least—ever so appreciably American; which proved to what a use American matter could be put by an American hand: a consummation involving, it appeared, the happiest moral. For the moral was that an American could be an artist, one of the finest, without "going outside" about it, as I liked to say; quite in fact as if Hawthorne had become one just by being American *enough,* by the felicity of how the artist in him missed nothing, suspected nothing, that the ambient air didn't affect him as containing. Thus he was at once so clear and so entire—clear without thinness, for he might have seemed underfed, it was his danger; and entire without heterogeneity, which might, with less luck and to the discredit of our sufficing manners, have had to be his help.[2]

In its enunciation of a more positive "moral" proposed by Hawthorne's career, this less-known passage in *Notes of a Son and Brother* seems James's reply to his more negative earlier judgment. His anxieties of identity long overcome, he could accept Hawthorne without a distancing pity as "one of the finest" or, as the narrator says of his hero in the strikingly similar passage in the "The Aspern Papers," "one of the first." And already, in 1888, the declaration that the fictional Aspern's very Americanism had been his strength anticipates the 1914 tribute to Hawthorne. James may well have detected, even then, a certain disingenuousness in Hawthorne's self-deprecation. Hawthorne was ever and again at work at the fabricating of his own romantic myth of the melancholy artist-self, and in choosing to write his last, most ambitious novel about Italy, he chose to ignore the fact that all his past work deals with the American scene, even with its antiquity (in *The Scarlet Letter*) and with a "picturesque and gloomy wrong" (in the *House of the Seven Gables*). As though recognizing this, James would, in 1896, praise those stories of Hawthorne's that were "products of the dry New England air," and call *The Scarlet Letter* "the most distinguished piece of prose fiction that was to spring from American soil" (1:460).

His view of Hawthorne's achievement remained conflicted. For himself, he could not conceive of anything but expatriation; it would always be hard to understand the triumph of Hawthorne over the same—perhaps the even more acutely deficient—native circumstances James had rejected. In 1888, in writing "The Aspern Papers," he could postulate but not bring into direct imaginative view the Hawthorne-Aspern who found greatness without "going outside" for it. And this inability is duplicated in the vain effort of the story's narrator to write a story of his own about a heroic literary age—making, "self-reflexively," the story reflect upon the enterprise of writing it. One may say that the narrator is a "plotter" whose "plot" is a scheme to find and write the story—that is, the plot—of the past. But his is a failed intrigue, and he does not succeed in discovering the history he hopes to make into literature. The narrator never succeeds in wresting from the death-hold of time the dead poet's love affair with a woman now so old as to be no more than a ghoul out of the grave. The relation of Aspern's life to his genius remains a bare proposition, an immaterial ghost of thought. How the poet had lived to write his great poetry is unimaginable. Similarly, James, himself, has failed to write the story of "the rich, dim, Shelley drama" which would have been the romance of the poet and his "Muse." And the modern reader, it is likely, also cannot write romantic poetry or love as romantically as Aspern did. The reader is compelled to share the frustration of both James and his character. So, the confinement of the first-person point of view, which keeps us from knowing what the narrator doesn't, is functional.

Even to reach for a nearer past—to recall his own Italian hours, contemporary with the late hour of Captain Silsbee—could only be verbal sleight-of-hand:

One must pay oneself largely with words, I think, one must induce almost any "Italian subject" to *make believe* it gives up its secret, in order to keep at all on working—or call them perhaps rather playing—terms with the general impression . . . So, right and left, in Italy—before the great historic complexity at least— penetration fails; we scratch at the extensive surface, we meet the perfunctory smile, we hang about in the golden air. But we exaggerate our gathered values only if we are eminently witless . . . Off the ground, at a distance, our fond indifference to being "silly" grows fonder still; the working convention, as I have called it—the convention of the real revelations and surrenders on one side and the real immersions and appreciations on the other—has not only nothing to keep it down, but every glimpse of contrast, every pang of exile and every nostalgic twinge to keep it up . . . So it is at any rate, fairly in too thick and rich a retrospect, that I see my old Venice of "The Aspern Papers," that I see the still earlier one of Jeffrey Aspern himself, and that I see even the comparatively recent Florence that was to drop into my ear the solicitation of these things. (2:1173-1174)

Not the recovery of lost time but the longing for it is represented in James's tale, which expresses the very reverse of a Proustian confidence in personal or historic memory. To assume the possibility of such a recovery is only a "convention" we subscribe to. James speaks of his story as showing "the rich dim Shelley drama played out in the very theatre of our own 'modernity' " (2:1176-1177). But "The Aspern Papers" enacts no "Shelleyan" theme; it is "our modernity" itself that is its real subject. James's storyteller fails in his aim not merely because his strategy in pursuit of the papers has blown up in his face. We are locked, James seems to say, into our own time.

James's own artistic drive, directed upon the discovery of story, exalting that effort as a service to art and life, would seem to be represented in the narrator's claim that he is sustained by the same high motive as his idol. "I felt," the narrator says, "even a mystic companionship, a moral fraternity with all those who in the past had been in the service of art. They had worked for beauty, for a devotion; and what else was I doing?" (XII:43). Of course, he is not an artist like Aspern—or James. He is a mere editor, a grubber among the manuscripts left behind by his god, and James distinguishes himself from such a man when he contrasts himself in the preface with Captain Silsbee, the "Shelleyite" who "waked up in time" to run down Miss Clairmont. Silsbee had been only a parasite upon historic fact. But James may still have wondered whether a modern could hope to be creative in the grand Romantic way. In his relation to active life and love James may have felt himself closer to his fictional researcher than to Shelley or Byron—or even the domestic Hawthorne. His own life, so circumspect, so little involved with passion—or with great public causes or active adventure—was no Romantic poem.

I referred at the start of this chapter to the "frame" of interpretation provided by James's preface. But the preface is only the outermost frame around a story which is itself also a frame that asks to be filled by another story—Aspern's. This inner frame, however, remains empty. The researcher never sees the papers burnt in the Bordereau kitchen fire, and it is even possible to doubt, as some readers have,[3] if they ever existed. Destroyed or suppressed—or even only putative—unread letters stand generally, in James's fiction, for a gap in the narrative, and announce the inaccessibility of some story or part of a story.[4] James's own obsession with the posthumous power of letters in the revision of reputations is relevant here; he himself burnt many of his own accumulations of others' letters, feeling that the truth of the past must be irrecoverable.

Using the image he employed in describing how he plucked his idea from the garden of history, James seems to call history a *mise en abîme* of receding accessibility when he says of the effort to see the past, "The charm of looking over a garden-wall into another garden breaks down when successions of walls appear. The other gardens, those still beyond, may be there, but even by use of our longest ladder we are baffled and bewildered—the view is mainly a view of barriers" (2:1177). The barriers also prohibit excessive curiosity about the past—and recall a moment in James's actual garden at Rye, when he reproved his brother William for climbing a ladder to peer over the Lamb House wall into the neighbor's garden. The Bordereau garden within the story internalizes the garden image of the preface, and its "high blank wall," which the intruder hopes to scale, is a historical blankness "figured all over" with a mysterious but indecipherable writing that may represent the private past history he is trying to read—"patches . . . repaired breaches, crumblings of plaster, extrusions of brick that had turned pink with time" (XII:10–11).

His eagerness to get inside is born not only of a desire for knowledge but of admiration to the point of envy of the mysterious Aspern's amorous past. He is the excluded third person in a triangle of desire. Voyeurism, of course, is a sexual perversity, and the curiosity of the narrator of the "Aspern Papers" is implicitly sexual—a rage to impermissibly "penetrate"—to ransack drawers, break into cabinets in order to seize hold of papers that are arguably love letters. So, James suggests that curiosity about others—even about others in the past, about history—is a temptation to a perversity *both* sexual and intellectual. Here, again, the sense of Hawthorne's presence in "The Aspern Papers" returns to mind. The voyeuristic curiosity which James represents in the "Aspern Papers" narrator is like Miles Coverdale's impotent, prying observation of the passions of Zenobia and Hollingsworth, his sexually diffused fixation on another man and the woman in love with him.

The configuration of the story even more directly establishes a connection with *The House of the Seven Gables*.[5] It is, indeed, startling to place alongside James's story the situation of Holgrave, the lodger who presents himself under a false name with the aim of learning secrets contained in ancient documents guarded by an elderly lady, the mistress of the house, and her younger female relative. Like James's character, Holgrave is tempted to make love to the younger woman in order to get closer to the secrets, and only by the miracle of love is he saved from the crime of heartless curiosity to which James's character succumbs. Details multiply, as we compare the story to Hawthorne's novel. The shabby Venetian palazzo of the Bordereau ladies, analogous to though different from the old Salem house, also possesses a garden which the Holgrave-like lodger cultivates. A miniature of a beautiful young man is Juliana's token of her lover of long ago, as it is Hepzibah's token of her adored brother in that remote time before his prison burial. James's subsurface reference to Hawthorne's two novels is the more striking because James does not acknowledge his indebtedness in his preface which, like all the New York Edition prefaces, claims to search out the sources of the author's inspiration. Admitting so frankly the donnée from life—the story of Silsbee and Miss Clairmont—he is silent about the blossom plucked from the past of literary example. Yet some of his story's details can be explained only by the fact that they were already in Hawthorne—like the Venetian garden, which the narrator claims to love for its very improbability (it is explicable only because it has been transported from Salem to Venice!). But Hawthorne, for all his insistence upon a dark theme of perpetuated wrong, had written an optimistic fairy tale in *The House of the Seven Gables*. The ending in which love reconciles the past and the present in the marriage of Holgrave and Phoebe is precisely what cannot take place between James's narrator and Tina Bordereau. Unlike the Aspern papers, Hawthorne's irrecoverable old document is blithely forgotten. James cannot repeat Hawthorne's story to its end any more than he can be another Hawthorne.

The would-be biographer of Jeffrey Aspern is another voyeur; his greatest desire is to possess another's love story. For himself, such a narrative is out of the question. If he has ever loved anyone, we do not hear of it, though he uses the word "love" to express his feeling for the dead Aspern. Only once, perhaps without recognizing it, he feels the faint breath of love, when a transfigured Tina seems beautiful—before she becomes again (after he learns of the destruction of the papers) the plain person she has always been. Tina Bordereau, were she lovable and he loving, like Phoebe and Holgrave, might have enabled him to live again, and so know the love of Aspern and Juliana—and so recapture the past.

Before this moment, any duplication he feels when he thinks of himself as paying court to her is only an ironic parody of Aspern's ardent courtship of her aunt. All his gestures toward the Bordereau women—the melancholy watching and waiting for the sight of them, the tributes of flowers, the studied gallantry—may seem to fulfill his early declaration to Mrs. Prest that he would, to get the papers, "make love to the niece" (XII:14). But his later self-justification, that he had *not* actually made love to Tina, has this ground: his love-making is so perfunctory a gesture that justly, when he assumes a tone of romantic hyperbole, calling the older lady "inhuman," she mocks him with, "That's what poets used to call women a hundred years ago. Don't try that; you won't do as well as they" (XII:72).

James speaks of the visitable past as "palpable"; it is no accident that the thing his narrator seeks is an object he longs to touch, while he is deficient in the sensuous awareness of a lover. The narrator, as he dreams of the papers he hopes to obtain, says, "they made my life continuous, in a fashion, with the illustrious life they had touched at the other end" (XII:43). But he will never achieve that continuity by literally touching the papers at his own end. It is significant that the elderly Juliana refuses to shake his hand. It was not the custom in her day, she reminds him. He is, thus, symbolically speaking, never to touch the past this ghostly relict represents. As Adrian Poole points out, the revisions in the New York Edition multiply the references to the papers as palpable or visible objects ("material," "documents," "literary remains," "relics and tokens," "tangible objects," "mementoes," "spoils," etc.).[6] But James's narrator never touches—or even sees—them. And all the time he is numb, one may say, to the presence of love at his side in the person of Tina Bordereau. It is true that in the end he does grasp a palpable object—though it is only another artist's image of the lost reality. It is the miniature of Aspern which Tina gives him, evidence of *her* loving sympathy, which serves only to remind him of his "intolerable" loss. As he looks at the face of the poet, "so young and brilliant and yet so wise and so deep" (XII:131), he knows that he can write no story about him. The portrait is an authenticating token of the past, which may be compared to the scrap of the scarlet letter found in the attic of Hawthorne's custom house. But it has not enabled him to go on to write its story as Hawthorne's narrator writes the story of Hester Prynne.

In the place of the history he misses the narrator toys with plots which are openly hypothetical. Three-quarters of a century earlier, Aspern addressed verses to the twenty-year-old Juliana. The narrator's colleague, Cumnor, speculates that she may have been a governess in some family which the poet visited, and that their relationship had a clandestine character—a stock plot in which, as in *Jane Eyre* or James's own "Turn of the Screw," a well-bred governess might hope to attract a man of higher station. The narrator himself "hatches" an alternative plot according to which she was Aspern's social equal though somewhat *déclassée,* the daughter of an American artist, a widower, who had brought up his daughters to share his life of "queer old-fashioned expatriated artistic Bohemia" (XII:48). He gathers from somewhere the "further implication" that she had had a "perverse and reckless, albeit a generous and fascinating character," and suggests that she might have had a foreign lover and "an unedifying tragical rupture" (XII:48) before she met Aspern when he came to her father's studio for his portrait. About their relationship he is unable to imagine much. There is "an impression" that Aspern "treated her badly," but the would-be historian defends his hero: "no man could have walked straighter in the given circumstances" (XII:7)—whatever these were. Such uncertain theories cannot fill the hollow of the frame; we have *only* the frame, the story of the plausible lodger who turns out to be a criminal.[7]

There will be moments when the view of himself as an aesthetic idealist put forward by James's narrator seems as consciously deceitful as his feeble impersonation of a harmless eccentric bachelor. We may see him as a confident and deliberate schemer who conceives from the first the wrong he will commit, even though he offers some explanations or justifications of his role. The idealist who only wanted to serve the high gods is subjected to the reader's increasing skepticism. As he schemes to get hold of the poet's letters, he is "writing" a story that differs not only from the one he seeks but from the one he pretends to be enacting. Nevertheless, at moments, his sincerity seems indisputable. He himself never surrenders altogether his self-vindication—and we remain unsure whether he may not have some claim upon our better opinion.

Having failed to recover the story of the past, he also fails to give coherence to his own peculiar adventure. At the end, he knows that his quest has failed, but does he really know the nature of his failure? Gazing at Aspern's portrait he concludes (in the story's 1888 text), "When I look at it my chagrin at the loss of the letters becomes almost intolerable."[8] In editing the early version for the New York Edition, James changed this to: "When I look at it I can scarcely bear my loss—I mean of the precious papers" (XII:143). The alteration suggests that James wanted to strengthen the story's telic thrust by implying that the narrator glimpses the true nature of his loss—which is of something more precious than the papers— but this progression to enlightenment is not dramatized in the story.

James made other revisions, also, and the question to be asked is whether these clarify the issue, reduce this story's "undecidability." In the opening pages of the early version the narrator speaks of Mrs. Prest's perception that his "interest in the papers had become a fixed idea" (12), but this is changed to "she had found my interest in my possible spoil a fine case of monomania" (XII:5)—"spoil" and "monomania" already suggesting forcible seizure and obsession. Where the story's first readers heard him tell his friend, "Hypocrisy, duplicity are my only chance. I am sorry for it, but for Jeffrey Aspern's sake I would do worse still" (17), we now hear, "there's no baseness I wouldn't commit for Jeffrey Aspern's sake" (XII:12); where the narrator first says that at Juliana's death he "could seize her papers" (25), James makes rapacity literal: "I could pounce on her possessions and ransack her drawers" (XII:24). The "tremor" (72) of his fingers when he holds Aspern's portrait becomes "the intensity of their clutch" (XII:94). And when he is caught at the old lady's secretary, her eyes "made me horribly ashamed" (88) he says, until James rewrites, "They were like the sudden drench, for a caught burglar, of a flood of gaslight" (XII:118)

But despite such changes, which seem to strengthen our impression of his malice aforethought, the forward movement of the text toward a verdict of deliberate guilt is still halted repeatedly by lateral movements compelling our indulgence; the narrator remains at once a villain and an idealist with potentialities for taking another direction. Moments succeed moments which are unsubdued by the concatenation of significances drawing them toward a final verdict of condemnation. When Mrs. Prest jokes at the outset, "One would think you expected from it [his spoil] the answer to the riddle of the universe," he takes her hyperbole seriously, and observes of Aspern, "he's a part of the light by which we walk" (XII:5). For some readers, the man who is so sensitive to poetry and its illuminations as well as to the poetry of beautiful old places and old histories cannot be the thief who wanted to ravage Miss Bordereau's secrets and was willing to arouse her niece's affection to serve his purpose. Wayne Booth has argued that the "evocation of Venice" by the narrator's sensitive aesthetic observation is unreconciled to the plot of the "Shelley fanatic," and that this creates an uncomfortable "double focus."[9]

A more subtle psychological reading can explain the narrator's protestations of elevated aim as rationalizations and self-deceptions. And a still more modernist view of character allows for the coexistence of contradictory elements; James himself was always fascinated by the paradoxical combination, in particular, of refinement and intelligence with moral callousness. This combination is also to be found in Gilbert Osmond of *The Portrait of a Lady* and Mrs. Gereth of *The Spoils of Poynton*. But even this sophisticated reading proposes a stable ambiguity, which is false to the dynamics of the story which *successively* rather than simultaneously makes us think one way or another about the narrator, so that we participate in a making and unmaking of plot, a composing and decomposing of character. This is more evident if we read for the first time, or *as* for the first time, uninfluenced by the ironies of "final" truth. As we read we make the discovery that nothing is more important than the *location* of a suggestion along the track of our reading. When, on the threshold of his adventure, the narrator declares that "there's no baseness [he] wouldn't commit," this will sound to us like merely the comic hyperbole of social persiflage—and perhaps, at this point, this is all that it is for the speaker himself, who cannot know what lies ahead. His remarks that "hypocrisy, duplicity are my only chance" (XII:12) and that he might even find himself prepared to "make love to the niece," seem light-hearted exaggerations at this point when he has no idea, yet, how far duplicity will take him, or how unlikely it is that Tina Bordereau will arouse his amorous feelings—"Wait till you see her," Mrs. Prest rejoins, entering into the joke with him—and only the second-time reader can interpret them as ironically predictive, after all. His remark to Mrs. Prest that he is prepared to wait out the hot Venetian summer to accomplish his end, "I'm prepared to roast all summer—as well as through the long hereafter, perhaps you'll say" (XII:14), is jocular, rather than a premonition of his temptation to mortal sin. To read his words literally is to give a false gravity, an exaggerated Faustian solemnity, to the story at this point.

As he begins his campaign we share with the narrator his genuine appreciation of the old palace where the Bordereau ladies live—so that his protestations of admiration to Tina Bordereau do not seem mere calculation. When he babbles to her crazily about his need of a garden, we think we are reading a light story about a light man—and perhaps this impression should be allowed to persist; it may be that what happens to him is nothing other than the consequence of taking things lightly that are strange and grave, thinking the dark puzzles of life easily understood. The impossible Venetian garden always threatened by the sea, as all fictions are threatened by life, may signify that he is wrong.

It is lightness, in a pejorative sense, that he seems guilty of as he responds to the woman before him in a way to make her a non-presence, seen chiefly in negatives: "Her face was not young, but it was candid; it was not fresh, but it was clear. She had large eyes which were not bright, and a great deal of hair which was not 'dressed,' and long fine hands which were—possibly—not clean" (XII:17). Yet this condescending masculine appraisal does not prevent him from making his "suit" for lodging, though he scrupulously observes of his success, "I did count it as a triumph, but only for the commentator—in the last analysis—not for the man, who had not the tradition of personal conquest" (XII:22), leading us away from the idea, after all, of a readiness to "make love to the niece."

In the opening chapter the narrator had observed that he and his colleague had failed to find anyone alive who had known Aspern: "We had not been able to look into a single pair of eyes into which his had looked or feel a transmitted contact in any aged hand that his had touched" (XII:8). Face to face with Juliana, he finds that her eyes are hidden, and she forbids him to touch her hand. She seems already dead, the green shade hiding "a grinning skull," with empty eye sockets. His voyeurism directed toward the past is further reproved by the revelation that Aspern's divine beloved is a hard-headed old lady who means to make use of *him* by charging a thousand francs a month for rent. The poet's Juliana is as inaccessibly vanished as the poet himself. The narrator's entry into the palazzo has gotten him nowhere. Employing military as well as sexual imagery, he says, "you may push on through a breach but you can't batter down a dead wall" (XII:38), reminding us once again of the Bordereau garden wall and the wall images of the preface. As he waits in the garden for some response to the flowers he sends, the shutters of the ladies' rooms remain drawn, like "eyes consciously closed" (XII:44)—eyes, again, like Juliana's, into which he is forbidden to look.

And then, another ghost appears who does look into his eyes with the promise of eventual success: "That spirit kept me perpetually company and seemed to look out at me from the revived immortal face—in which all his genius shone—of the great poet who was my prompter" (XII:42). This gracious specter advises gentleness and patience, and, as though strengthening the narrator's conviction of fraternity with Aspern, confirms their spiritual identity: "Meanwhile, aren't we in Venice together, and what better place is there for the meeting of dear friends? See how it glows with the advancing summer; how the sky and the sea and the rosy air and the marble of the palaces all shimmer and melt together" (XII:43). The narrator's moral and aesthetic self-confidence seems justified by this invitation from another time. He rejoices purely, it would seem, in being under the same roof as the "sacred relics"—a phrase that deliber-ately links his quest with the Romantic worship of beauty, and with older traditions of Christian quest.

How far does this identity go? When he sits in the garden in the evening the very air reminds him of the greatest version of the myth of romantic love: "It was delicious—just such an air as must have trembled with Romeo's vows when he stood among the thick flowers and raised his arms to his mistress's balcony," and he knows that "Juliana might on the summer nights of her youth have murmured down from open windows at Jeffrey Aspern." But he cannot really replay that scene: "Miss Tina was not a poet's mistress any more than I was a poet" (XII:52–53). Still, when the middle-aged Tina comes down to the garden at last, he is ready to enact some part of the romantic story, telling her the flowers have been for her as well as for her aunt, asking for her trust and help—while trying to keep it off his "conscience that [he] might pass for having made love to her." He says, "Nothing less should I have seemed to do had I continued to beg a lady to 'believe in me' in an Italian garden on a midsummer night" (XII:62), his sense of the parodic expressed not only in the phrase put overtly in quotation marks but in the components of scene which invoke another tale than his own.

Can we yet convict him of "trifling" with Tina's "affections," as it might have been put in Aspern's time? One may pick one's cues to conclude in favor of his discretion or on the side of judging that he already knows and takes advantage of an unworldly spinster's vulnerability. Or one can say that his sense of difference from Aspern, his inability to match the poet's passion, is what is the matter. But at this point the plot is taken out of his hands by old Juliana, who orders him to take her niece for rides in the gondola and turns about the piazza—like the suitor he does not mean to be. He seems to resist the imposed role, to hold on to his stance of disinterestedness. Over ices at Florian's he explains his desire for the papers: "It isn't for myself or that I should want them at any cost to any one else. It's simply that they would be of such immense interest to the public, such immeasurable importance as a contribution to Jeffrey Aspern's history" (XII:82). (The 1888 text reads, "There's no personal avidity in my desire" [64]—this time James softens rather than makes more suspect the speaker's choice of language.) The persisting claim of high-mindedness still carries conviction.

And yet, as time passes and he fears the destruction of the letters by old Juliana, his impatience mounts and he feels, not quite legitimately, that Tina owes him loyalty: "I almost read it as her duty to keep me informed" (XII:87). It is no longer clear proof of his own refinement that the old lady's expectations that he will pay more for his rental reveal "a false note in my image of the woman who had inspired a great poet with immortal lines" (XII:88). Instead of duplicating romance in himself, he has duplicated modern materialism in Juliana, and the dead story is doubly dead. Yet, "there is no more money to be made by good letters" (XII:89), he reminds the old lady when she asks him whether his books have sold—and there is a pun, probably, on the "letters" by which she may think he wants to profit.

If it is not money he is after, then, what is it? What he wants is the "truth," which investigators like himself "lay bare." For this he is "avid." To crave the truth is likely to seem admirable. But the reader who thinks so has to reckon, suddenly, with the sibylline voice that speaks out of the mouth of the old woman: "The truth is God's, it isn't man's: we had better leave it alone. Who can judge of it?—who can say?" We have heard no such religious reference in the story before this, only the Romantic transposition of religious terms in "sacred relics." The direct mention of God is the rarest of notes in James. How seriously is it meant? At the very least it can remind us of that central suspicion of human certainty that we have encountered, differently put, elsewhere in his writing. The startled truth-seeker can only stammer out a claim of the virtue of his *attempt* to know the unknowable: "We're terribly in the dark, I know, but if we give up trying what becomes of all the fine things? What becomes of the work I just mentioned, that of the great philosophers and poets? It's all vain words if there's nothing to measure it by!"—to which she replies, "You talk as if you were a tailor" (XII:90). The issue joined is a profound one. Despite the seeming flippancy of Juliana's remark, she has challenged the very idea of an absolute "measure" which can be established by human inquiry. The theme that makes itself felt at this juncture is more important than the question of the narrator's "sincerity"; his voyeurism is now condemned on philosophic and religious grounds.

But even at this moment of deep seriousness the contest of the manuscript hunter and his antagonist continues on a lower plane as she teases him into paying his exorbitant rent, shows him Aspern's portrait as an object she might like to sell—but perhaps also to raise his concealed hopes. He suspects that she suspects him; his politeness is forced; their remaining exchanges are without dignity. Then, at the dying woman's bedside, he "turn(s) his eyes . . . all over the room, rummaging with them the closets, the chests of drawers, the tables" (XII:105), his voyeuristic vision, his intellectual curiosity, made equivalent by James's language to physical violation. His wish to be thought a gentleman cannot restrain him from expecting Tina to keep him posted. "I'm afraid it's proof of the grossness of my anxieties that I should have taken in some degree for granted at such an hour, in the midst of the greatest change that could fall on her, poor Miss Tina's having also a free mind for them" (XII:107). In fact, she has looked for the papers, but can't look more. "It isn't decent," she cries. And he feels "reprimanded and shamed." "Let the poor lady rest in peace," he says (XII:111). For a moment, we expect him to surrender his quest, now grown maniacal, under the influence of the gentle Tina; he goes so far as to shed his disguise and tell her his real name, as though desiring to shed a false self that has taken hold of him.

But any hope that she will prove his good conscience is dispelled. He imagines her sanction for his stealthy intrusion into the old woman's darkened bedroom, his approach to the secretary where he thinks the treasure is hidden, extenuating these violations at each step by the idea of Tina's complicity:

> I had no definite purpose, no bad intention, but I felt myself held to the spot by an acute, though absurd sense of opportunity. Opportunity for what I couldn't have said, inasmuch as it wasn't in my mind that I might proceed to thievery . . . I had no keys, no tools and no ambition to smash her furniture. None the less it came to me that I was now, perhaps alone, unmolested, at the hour of freedom and safety, nearer to the source of my hopes than I had ever seen . . . If Miss Tina was sleeping she was sleeping sound. Was she doing so—generous creature—on purpose to leave me the field? . . . If she wished me to keep away, why hadn't she locked the door of communication between the sitting-room and the sala? That would have been a definite sign that I was to leave them alone. If I didn't leave them alone she meant me to come for a purpose—a purpose now represented by the super-subtle inference that to oblige me she had unlocked the secretary. (XII:116–117)

Super-subtle inferences indeed!—although there have been readers who have wondered whether Tina has not done what he suspects, whether she has not been the manipulator instead of the manipulated. This remarkable passage suggests a mind that has projected its own desires upon someone else, but we cannot be sure. As in "The

Turn of the Screw," the first-person narrative imprisons us in indeterminacy, and any speculations about the "unconscious" may be out of place. There is no distanced narrator to tell us "the truth"— what we do have is interior to the story, the dreadful judgment of Juliana, as her eyes meet the manuscript hunter's for the first time: "You publishing scoundrel!" It is impossible to say how much he admits to when he says, with a deprecating shrug we can almost see, "Certainly I did publish and no less certainly hadn't been very delicate" (XII:120). If he decides, after all, to hold fast to his purpose, he believes himself to be acting, still, for Tina: "I said to myself that after all I could not abandon Miss Tina."

But how far will this take him? When he returns to Venice to find that the *vecchia* is dead and that her niece does not treat him as though he is a murderer, he is uncertain how much he has taken on. He senses that she would accept any motion on his part to "somehow look after her," and he even says something about arranging a little excursion of some sort, "to give her a change" (XII:124). He hasn't, at all, forgotten about the papers, however. What if they have been destroyed? In that case, "I couldn't linger there to act as guardian to a piece of middle-aged female helplessness. If she hadn't saved the papers wherein should I be indebted to her?" (XII:126). It would seem, after this statement, that his oscillations between disinterested benevolence and self-serving calculation are over—and that the narrative oscillations, which prevent the reader from making a fixed judgment, are ended as well.

But are they? She has, in fact, saved the papers, and for him. She tells him she could conscientiously share them with him if he were "a relation" (XII:133). If Aspern's divine Muse has turned out to be a shrewd bargainer, so has the niece, and the price, this time, is beyond the narrator's means. Our view of Tina as gentle and helpless wavers even as our view of the narrator has done, though, as with Juliana, the narrator has to wonder whether he has not been responsible for arousing such an expectation of payment: "Did she think I had made love to her even to get the papers?" As though to remind the reader that *intention* maintains its earlier status in the text, he sends us back to the first pages of the story: "I had said to Mrs. Prest that I would make love to her; but it had been a joke without consequences and I had never said it to my victim. I had been as kind as possible because I really liked her; but since when had that become a crime where a woman of such an age and such an appearance was concerned?"

(XII:136–137). Maybe he is merely, as I observed in the beginning, a "light" man—he seems to condemn himself to that degree when he concludes that he had "deplorably trifled."

He now feels ready to give over the search for the Aspern-Juliana story—he and Cumnor have enough material for their book without it. Yet after another night, his mood swings back to a passion for his "goods," and he goes to see Tina again. When he does, an "optical trick," *or* her own mood of forgiving renunciation, *or* his revived longing for the papers—we cannot tell which of these—makes her image bloom before his eyes with a "phantasmagoric brightness." And he thinks, "Why not?"—but only for as long as it takes her to tell him she has burnt them all. Once more she is "a plain dingy elderly person" (XII:143).

Tina's temporary transformation in the view of the narrator is a last instance of the relativity that has governed all judgment throughout the story. It also has in it some suggestion of the supernatural, of a fairy tale by which the ugly person is made beautiful by love. The miraculous transformation is offered and quickly withdrawn, though. Tina's change is shown as a possibility to the reluctant lover, who fails to understand that her love has already made the ugly princess beautiful but only *his* will make her appear so to him permanently. One can also say that "The Aspern Papers" is a folktale quest narrative (for "sacred relics"), in which the questing hero strives to penetrate a stronghold, a moated castle,, in order to seize a treasure. The guardian of the castle is ancient and formidable, possessed of dark powers against which he invokes the aid of a ghostly patron. But the paradigm does not hold to the end. "Get out of it as you can, my dear fellow," Aspern's portrait says, abandoning the seeker to his failed story.

If the narrator's story is one of failure it is possible to shift our emphasis sufficiently from him to consider that Tina's story may represent a modest triumph. The ending encloses her in old-maidhood as conceived by the masculine imagination—pitiable, solitary, without sexual charm. But, like Catherine Sloper's repudiation of the returned Townsend, she may have imposed a modest story of her own upon her experience—and created her "morsel" of narrative needlework. Juliana's plot to provide a marriage-ending for her has been as much a failure as the narrator's effort to capture the papers. But in destroying them, Tina, no longer the victim of either, has acted on her own behalf.

· 7 ·

The Disengagement from "Things":
The Spoils of Poynton

EDITH WHARTON protested that James tended more and more, as he reached his final phase, to "sever" his characters "from that thick nourishing human air in which we all live and move." She even demanded of him, "Why have you stripped them of all the human fringes we necessarily trail after us through life?"[1] What she found objectionable, it is clear, is his rejection of the realistic element of "nourishing"—i.e., explanatory—scene, and of those expressive "fringes" or "appurtenances" which Isabel Archer disdained. His art opposed itself, as his characters did, to the tradition that required these, especially after he had put it to the test in *The Bostonians* and *The Princess Casamassima*. Madame Merle's declaration, "I've a great respect for *things*!" is, as we have seen, a perfect statement of the oppositional attitude which figures dramatically in James's fiction.

The importance or inconsequence of "things" is, as my previous discussion will have suggested, a question not only literary but philosophical and sociological. It is involved with James's speculation concerning the relative importance of material, visible reality and impalpable thought—and the reason for his development of a primary psychological reality established by narrative point of view. "Things" also are involved in the question of "conditions" in the social sense, and with the consequences of the possession of money or the lack of it. Isabel's early notion that she is *more* free when she is poor is a defiance of naturalism—yet it turns out that when she is rich, she is really less free than she expected. For riches, although they seem to release one from the pressure of material conditions, also can be said to enclose one in a thicker material "shell" in the form of possessions. Isabel's inheritance makes it inevitable that she will acquire a fuller wardrobe of self-defining "clothing" in the broadest sense. Her marriage—the consequence of her money—envelopes her not only in a destiny but frames her like a portrait of a lady in the richly furnished house she occupies in Rome, and at the same time implicates her in the social rituals of the society of which she becomes a member.

The respect for "things" is also confounded in James's fiction with aestheticism, which James regards with some reserve. James was alert to the contemporary argument over the Paterian worship of the beautiful as an "end in itself"—and seems to defend this cult against its narrowly moralistic detractors in his terrifying story of 1884, "The Author of Beltraffio," in which a mother destroys her own child to protect him from his father's ideas of this kind. But in "The Aspern Papers," less than four years later, he was perfectly ready to imagine a keeper of the aesthetic flame who is morally culpable even without realizing it. His aesthetes are no more likely than others to be ethically fastidious. Perhaps they are even less so. The *collectionneur* as an aesthetic type is a particularly ambiguous figure, for in him the taste for beauty is combined with the desire to *possess* beautiful things. His appetite for such possession can be said to express the principle of capital accumulation and exploitation upon which bourgeois society is built, and is the reverse, perhaps, of the highest kind of disinterested admiration.

The lust for beautiful objects can be read in quite another way as a representation of psychological displacement, that "fetishism" which substitutes inanimate objects for the bodily zones as a source of satisfaction. In this last connection it becomes plain why sexual blockage or deflection is involved in James's stories of aesthetic collectors. Of course, the morally perverse Osmond is a collector of *beautiful* objects, his wife being one of them. But so is the innocuous but ineffectual Rosier, who fetishizes his adored Pansy as a Dresden shepherdess; so is even the noble but invalid Ralph, who seems to have had a "considerable collection" of bric-a-brac. Those later collectors from America, the millionaire Ververs of *The Golden Bowl*, acquire museum pieces for some future donation to the unfurnished American scene, but may be, no less than Osmond, mistaking persons for objects when they regard Prince Amerigo as the most exquisite of their finds; the regressive incestuous attachment of Maggie and her father, which ennervates their marriages to others, is related to this fetishism.

In contrast with the collecting and possessing impulse James also extracts from aestheticism its valuation of the *sensation* of beauty over the beautiful thing itself; Lambert Strether's resolution, in *The Ambassadors* "not to have got anything" except what Maria Gostrey calls his "wonderful impressions" (XIII:326) is the Paterian triumph of passive beholding. Renunciation of possession is an aesthetic as well as moral gesture. And yet, the two sides of aestheticism, its valuation of the ownership of beautiful things and its substitution of sensation for possession, are not, perhaps, so separated as they seem. James's suspicion of aestheticism—even though it attracted him—was profound enough to lead him to suspect self-aggrandizement in the cultivation of even the most idealized and detached aesthetic feeling. Though it seems a recoil from vulgar materialist accumulation, aestheticism may be viewed as only a more subtle mimicry of what it rejects. It is only superficially a historical movement arising from the rejection of bourgeois economic values; in a deeply "unconscious" way, aestheticism is inescapably acquisitive. The refusal of sexual possession also, however noble, is a subtle exercise of control over the other, a denial of the other's satisfaction along with one's own.

These issues are all present in complex combination in *The Spoils of Poynton*. Even James's account of the origins of this work seems to bear upon them. In the New York Edition preface to "The Spoils" James observes that art requires of life only a "tiny nugget, washed free of awkward accretions" (2:1138)—rather than a "slice," as the naturalist would say, of life as it comes. His original donnée of the real case of the mother and son embattled over furniture had been, he remembered, an idea almost submerged by the "fatal futility of Fact" (2:1140). There had been, certainly, more melodrama than he needed in the actual events—as, for example, the claim by the mother that her son was illegitimate and not entitled to the disputed inheritance of house and furnishings. James wanted only his motif, however, and refused to transcribe his story from the actual legal case reported in the press and set down in court records. His information came from a less authentic source than these—mere dinner-table gossip—but even this threatened to be too loaded with irrelevant authenticity. His preference for the "rich bare little fact" (2:1140) of the parent and child in conflict is, of course, an assertion—such as he was always making—of art's general independence of reality, his view that art makes its own forms. James's language suggests that his interest, simultaneously, is

in stories of a kind that made them independent of a crowded context of exact circumstances. They would have no need of full cir-
cumstantiality, of a plenitude of described "things" in the mode of
the realist novel.

Actuality had pressed upon his imagination more, even, than he
admitted, for, as Bernard Richards points out, there was not just this
one, but another donnée from real life for this story.[2] A few months
before the dinner party he mentions in the preface, he had, his notebooks reveal, stayed in a particularly ugly country house and conceived of "the strange, the terrible experience of a nature with a
love and passion for beauty, united by adverse circumstances to
such a family and domiciled in such a house."[3] James, nevertheless,
does not copy Fox Warren for his description of Waterbath, any
more than in presenting Poynton he resorts to exact particulars
gathered from a gracious house he was familiar with. However specific his actual memory of one or another place, he preferred to
suppress rather than exploit its details.

The very theme of the tale, moreover, is concerned with the
choice, in life, between an embroilment or a disengagement from
material objects; at the same time, the method chosen for its narration is a resolution of the problem of embracing or rejecting realist
description. James saw, as he recalled in his preface, that the true
story that pricked his imagination had, as its obvious center of
interest, "the felt beauty and value of the prize of battle, the Things,
always the splendid Things, placed in the middle light, figured and
constituted, with each identity made vivid, each character discriminated" (2:1144). The contest over them could be made significant
because of

the sharp light it might project on that most modern of our current passions, the fierce appetite for the upholsterer's and joiner's
and brazier's work, the chairs and tables, the cabinets and presses,
the material odds and ends of the more labouring ages . . . On the
face of it the "things" themselves would form the very centre of
such a crisis; these grouped objects, all conscious of their emi-
nence and their price, would enjoy, in any picture of a conflict,
the heroic importance. They would have to be presented, they
would have to be painted—arduous and desperate thought; something would have to be done for them not too ignobly unlike the
great array in which Balzac, say, would have marshalled
them. (2:1141-1142)

James, in this regard, drew back from the example of Balzac, however much this master's visionary realism impressed him. In 1875, he had written that he had often "prefer[red Balzac's] places to his people. He was a profound connoisseur in those matters; he had a passion for bric-a-brac, and his tables and chairs are always in character [though] in his enumerations of inanimate objects he often sins by extravagance" (2:50). James admired Balzac's art of the "connoisseur"; the word has here the connotation which connects the collector of fine objects, which Balzac quite literally was (compulsively furnishing his own house in Paris with real and expensive bric-a-brac, tables, and chairs[4]), with the realistic furnishedness of his style. But James developed a fictional method of the kind Willa Cather was later to call that of the novel "démeublé."[5] In *The Spoils of Poynton*, the "arduous and desperate" undertaking of describing the "beautiful things" of Poynton is rejected. That James refers to them repeatedly merely as "things"—not even mentioning any particular object—is a signal of how abstractly he conceived of them. It is surprising to see, in the photographic illustration by Alvin Langdon Coburn which James approved for the New York Edition volume containing this short novel, some "grouped objects" of virtue from the Wallace Collection. They are somehow too actual.

We hear only vaguely, as Fleda first wanders admiringly among them, of "brasses Louis Quinze might have thumbed . . . Venetian velvets just held in a loving palm . . . cases of enamels . . . cabinets (X:22)—and that is all. When she tours the house again to assist Mrs. Gereth in the selection of objects for Ricks, the "dowerhouse," she notes just as vaguely, "the old golds and brasses, old ivories and bronzes, the fresh old tapestries and deep old damasks" (X:58). When she sees them at Ricks, she discerns some undescribed tapestries, which had been the "most uplifted pride" of the collection, and slightly more precisely a "great Italian cabinet" and brocaded sofa, and she finds herself put to bed in a room all "sweetest Louis Seize" (X:71, 78). Mentioned for the first time, though never exactly visible, is the carved ivory "Maltese cross." Perhaps only the "Venetian lamp" in the form of Atlas hunching his back under his globe makes a picture for the inner eye.

James had preferred this more allusive method, he claims in the preface, because, for one thing, he had promised the editors of *The Atlantic* a *short* story, and though it had grown to 75,000 words, it was still *nouvelle* length; the Balzacian style would have demanded the scope of a still longer novel. The shortness of *The Spoils of Poynton*—its very *spareness*—was determined as much by a "commercial austerity" (2:1142) as by aesthetic preference for a parsimonious form. But his subject, after all, was not Balzac's kind. When first published in the *Altantic Monthly* in 1897, his story had been called "The Old Things." James changed the title because it wasn't, he thought, really about "cabinets and chairs and tables," and what became of them—"a comparatively vulgar issue"—but about *character*, and particularly about Fleda Vetch (who, it should be noted, was born free in James's imagination, having had no place in the original mother-son story; she was therefore a creation uncontaminated by the distracting actuality which clung to his other two figures). Fleda's character was a subject that could be dealt with reasonably briefly, a subject "maintainable at less expense" (2:1145) than the subject of "the things."

The importance of Fleda's presence was, as with previous "centers," again a case of his "subject residing in somebody's excited and concentrated feeling about something." "The thing is to lodge somewhere at the heart of one's complexity an irrepressible *appreciation*" (2:1146), he wrote in the later preface. And, indeed, his story was *about* "appreciation" in the mere sense of apprehension and in its extended sense of aesthetic feeling, as well as in the economic sense of things increasing in monetary value—as aesthetic objects do with time. A narrative which enacted itself as a drama of perception, it was also a story about the value of fine—that is, aesthetic—perception, its subject and its method reflecting one another.

The unparticularity of the description of Poynton's treasures is perhaps made more significant by the fact that they would seem to have no other relation to one another than their status as the expressions of eclectic taste. They have been torn each from its own context long ago, and have diverse origins and historical associations. In their disconnection from their origins, their loss of cultural meaning, the "things" of Poynton are truly "spoils," like treasures ripped from the temples or palaces of an enemy civilization by conquering barbarians. And Poynton's "spoils" are even twice displaced when they are huddled into vans and packed off to Ricks by Mrs. Gereth; Fleda thinks of the transfer as the "spoliation of Poynton" itself (X:78). A third displacement is predicted if they fall to the Brigstocks as a result of Owen's marriage to Mona. This may be the ultimate barbarian conquest. From the point of view of the Brigstocks, "appreciation" means simply "gain." Gone are all historical and cultural associations of Poynton's treasures, which can be represented by abstract sums in English pounds. But even before this happens, the spoils, the heterogenous bibelots of a modern collector, have, like the cultures they represent, lost any meaning beyond their individual aesthetic effect upon outsiders of another time and place.

In the provision of context for the novel's characters and action, they are the very opposite of the coherent environments of objects which stand for the social sources of Balzacian character and story—they cannot be said to "explain" Mrs. Gereth, their owner, or to be explained by her—as Madame Vauquier is explained by and explains her pension in *Père Goriot*. But as symbolic objects they also lose individuality, and their exact appearance and origins are unimportant. Most flagrantly, the Maltese cross, the prize of the collection, is not the symbolic eight-pointed equilateral cross of the Knights of Malta. It is called "Maltese" because it was in Malta that Mrs. Gereth happened to hear of it: that description, "though technically incorrect," had been applied at Poynton to this "masterpiece of delicacy, of expression and of the great Spanish period, the existence and precarious accessibility of which she had heard of at Malta, years before, by an odd and romantic chance" (X:73-74).[6] This is not to say that the cross, intrinsically symbolic as any cross must be, may not be allowed to carry its symbolic hint into the story as an image for the sacrifice Fleda will eventually make. But any such significance is curiously slighted in James's telling.

As items of collection, of course, "things" are not only aesthetic objects. They can also be unaesthetic clutter. Waterbath is also a place of things, crammed with gimcrackery. Its original virtues have been "smothered with trumpery ornament and scrapbook art, with strange excrescences and bunchy draperies" (X:7). The comparison of Poynton and Waterbath shows not only the superiority of the creation of taste to the accumulations of vulgarity, but shows that they are interchangeable also—Mrs. Gereth is by no means, in her attachment to *her* things, so clearly the superior of the Brigstocks in their comfortable harmony with theirs. Even at the outset of their friendship, Fleda sees the "absurdity" in "the poor lady's strange, almost maniacal disposition to thrust in everywhere the question of 'things,' to read all behavior in the light of some fancied relation to them. 'Things' were of course the sum of the world; only, for Mrs. Gereth, the sum of the world was rare French furniture and oriental china" (X:24).

Her things have become reifications of herself; she has become one of them. Fleda, contemplating Mrs. Gereth among her transposed treasures at Ricks, is aware that "wherever she was she was herself the great piece in the gallery" (X:73). Recalling the efforts to amass them she and her husband had made, she herself says, "They were our religion, they were our life, they were *us!* And now they're only *me*—" expressing a conversion by which a lost sense of religion has given place to the worship of self expressed in matter. Suddenly turning to Fleda, as though to commit her to the same conversion, she adds, "except that they're also *you,* thank God, a little, you dear!" (X:30–31). When she is finally denuded of her collection Mrs. Gereth invites Fleda to visit her with "You'll at any rate be a bit of furniture. For that, a little, you know, I've always taken you—quite one of my best finds" (X:245).

We tend to see Mona through the scornful eyes of Mrs. Gereth, but Mona's disdain of the aestheticism of Poynton has its validity. Mona *knows* that things are things, and is contemptuous of the claim that Mrs. Gereth's possessiveness is superior in some way to her own feeling of entitlement. The implied equivalence of Poynton and Waterbath may be seen as an expression of the modern economy which has made the Brigstocks rich; it illustrates the way *all* the resources of modern society, the intellectual and the personal as well as the material, become items of abstract exchange value. What Mona does understand about the spoils is their value as a marriage gift. Owen's marriage to Mona has been delayed "because he has lost her the things" (X:128). Waterbath may be the expression of money vulgarly spent, but it is also money that has created Poynton and its things, however cleverly spent by an astute bargain hunter. Even Owen remarks, ruefully, of his "stolen" property, "They're awfully valuable, aren't they?" (X:89). He makes Fleda wince by referring to "the furniture" without which "what was the good of Poynton?"—and makes her think "of washing-stands and copious bedding"—furnishings of the bedroom—while she herself refers to the contents of the house as "the works of art." When one thinks of today's art market, which makes an investment in accredited art works "gilt-edged," Owen's innocent inquiry seems more valid than it appears to Fleda. But she is someone who has spent a year in Paris "at a studio, arming herself for the battle of life by a course with an impressionist painter" (X:14).

It is clear that Mona has made it a condition of her consent to marry Owen that he hold his mother to "the strictest accountability" of the things, while to Owen it doesn't matter "what they're called" (X:43). Fleda, in feeling that they must be returned to Poynton so that Owen's obligation to Mona can be fulfilled, reflects that "it was quite irrelevant that Mona had no intelligence of what she had lost" (X:95). And Owen himself sees the things only numerically when he suggests that his mother take "a dozen pieces, chosen absolutely at will" (X:52). His lack of individuating appreciation of them is related to his failure, as Mrs. Gereth sees it, of appreciation of his possession of herself. She complains that he acts as though "she was just his mother as his nose was just his nose," and that he fails "from the first to understand what it was to have a mother at all, to appreciate the beauty and sanctity of the character" (X:49).

Fleda herself comes, finally, to lose all her former sense of the supreme value of the Poynton things and to "hope that she might never see anything 'good' again: that kind of experience was clearly so broken a reed, so fallible a source of peace" (X:138). Though she does not herself make the comparison, the reader is left to see the resemblance between Poynton as an expression of the urge to collect and the objects "he was fond of saying he had collected" that she observes in her disreputable father's rooms—"objects, shabby and battered, of a sort that appealed little to his daughter: old brandy-flasks and match-boxes, old calendars and hand-books, intermixed with an assortment of penwipers and ash-trays, a harvest gathered in from penny bazaars." Unconscious altogether of Fleda's connoisseurship, he even asks why she doesn't "try collecting something?—it didn't matter what. She would find it gave an interest to life" (X:145). One cannot help feeling that "interest," here, like "appreciation," is a word that does not surrender its financial sense—in the reductive equivalence of a market economy, "it doesn't matter what" investment it is that yields interest. That a life without normal emotional interest requires a fetishistic compensation is also implied.

The ordeal of Fleda Vetch consists in her effort to decide her relation not merely to the Things of Poynton but to materiality in general, and to evaluate possession as a mode of relationship to life. Possession becomes a primary theme, now, for James, in these middle years of his career, when having or not having money was very much on his mind. "The Spoils of Poynton" is the first fiction to be written after an interval of several years devoted to a struggle for success in the theater and ending, so disastrously, with the failure of his play, "Guy Domville," only months before. Returning to fiction writing, he discovered that long works from him were not in demand and that he must write short fictions which would not pay as well. His own money-making efforts foundered, and the scope of his art was restricted. But, socially, he was more and more an inhabitant of the world of wealth and leisure, the world of conspicuously "furnished" houses of the English upper class, where he went to such dinner parties as the one which had provided him with the "nugget" of "The Spoils of Poynton." He was as fascinated as Balzac by the way the desire for money and what it could buy dominated the society he lived in. And he was no longer the dazzled new arrival; his sense of that world now included a less romantic view of the effects of wealth and, as *The Princess Casamassima* had shown, even an awareness of the effects of poverty.

He had, of course, as early as *Washington Square*, done a story in which possessiveness exerted against another person is paralleled with the desire simply for money. Dr. Sloper's tenacity in holding fast to Catherine parallels Townsend's desire for her fortune, and one should recall that Sloper's prototype is Balzac's literal miser, who clutches to the death both his barrels of gold *and* his daughter. Mrs. Gereth, the possessor of a more refined material hoard, is also said to be "possessing herself of a son"—whose marriage to the unworthy woman he has fallen in love with she strives to prevent. She is as clever as Dr. Sloper, while Owen, like Catherine, is an unworldly innocent whose innocence is curiously identified with lack of cleverness and poor taste. Thus, hidden in *The Spoils of Poynton* is a recollection and revision of *Washington Square*, James altering the earlier story by the introduction of a better mate favored by the possessive parent in the place of the disapproved one. It is this new character, Fleda—absent also, as has been noted, from the real-life anecdote he had been told—who is the perceiving focus of his new version of the *Washington Square* situation.

At the outset, of course, it was the "things" that engaged Fleda's interest. Immediately after her first meeting with Mrs. Gereth her vision, as she rides in the train on her return from Waterbath, is of a "future full of the things she particularly loved" (X:11)—and the word is not used here in its more abstract sense as meaning any distinguishable subject or entity, but refers to tangible, inanimate objects. As we are told immediately, "These were neither more nor less than the things with which she had had time to learn from Mrs. Gereth that Poynton overflowed" (X:12).

But at this moment she encounters Owen and "love" 's sexual sense gains a peculiar definition. Like Maggie Verver's Prince Amerigo, Owen is already grouped with the other "things she particularly loved"—an object of *virtu*; he is already seen as something to be acquired, like a fine article of collection, for like Mrs. Gereth, Fleda has the impulse of a *collectionneur*. And it is well to note, too, that she has something of the bourgeois collector's character, though she is a penniless young woman, unlike the millionaire Adam Verver or his daughter. For she finds that Owen fits her idea of a husband who would, for all his charm, "be a force grateful for direction"—which causes the narrator to remark next that "she was in her small way a spirit of the same family as Mrs. Gereth" (X:11). She is like a modern collector of aesthetic prizes who would first have had to become rich by exercising his will and intelligence upon mindless matter and the stuff of inferior men.

Yet, in the end, she must escape the Gereths. Fleda rejects Poynton more than she does Owen, but the two are linked. Her renunciation of him seems sterile until we realize that the man she loves is not only honorably bound to another, he is bound to the spoils of Poynton. Hence, of course, she rejects the marriage plot, which is always connected with the heroine's need to acquire an envelope of circumstance, a social role—and possessions, or "things." In the preface, James calls Fleda a "free spirit," and contrasts her with Mrs. Gereth, of whom James says, "as a character she is the very reverse of a free spirit" (2:1147, 1148). His explanation of this distinction is not very clear but the statement is suggestive in a number of ways which I find useful.

Fleda is free because she is sufficiently imaginative to be capable of a variety of choices; she is not determined and predictable like Mrs. Gereth with her single obsession. She is attached to her own freedom, but differs from Isabel Archer in that her attachment seems moral rather than romantic; she will not compromise her ideal of ethical behavior. The "things," though she admires them, do not govern her behavior; she has no desire to possess them—not even to guard them from the seizure threatened by Mona. But neither does her love for Owen overcome her reluctance to own him; she renounces the desire to possess him as though he were a thing to be wrested from someone else.

Yet her rejection of the marriage-plot appears to be a piece of extravagant fastidiousness. Why, readers have asked, doesn't she take the happiness available to her and "let herself go," as Mrs. Gereth is always urging. Why doesn't she help Owen to escape from his engagement to Mona, whom he no longer loves, instead of contriving, by deception, to get Mrs. Gereth to restore the ravished spoils to Poynton—and so sealing his marriage to the other girl? Her behavior has seemed at least as perverse as Isabel's in refusing Casper Goodwood. Indeed, more so—for while Isabel's response to Casper is involuntary and repudiated by her own will, Fleda knows that she loves Owen. So, we can see that she is vulnerable to the charge that she has embraced, in another form, the vice she has repudiated, the vice of possessiveness, inherent in aestheticism itself, which cherishes its own selfish "interest" even while disdaining ownership. In her disregard for the human injury inflicted upon them both, she is still a collector of her own emotions and illuminations, content to have had her moment of appreciation.

But this is only to say that she is a still more striking case than Isabel of the character who maintains her potentiality, her freedom, by rejecting circumscription. She will not marry Owen and place herself within the frame of Poynton and its things, becoming its "portrait of a lady." In conceiving her in this way James engages her, of course, in another traditional plot scheme, which his recent immersion in the theatre must have proposed to him. As Lawrence Holland pointed out, Dumas' *La dame aux camélias* is precisely recalled when Mrs. Brigstock calls on Fleda to plead with her to let Owen go so that he may fulfill his promise to marry Mona; it is the analogue of that occasion when Armand Duval's father asks Camille to break off her affair with his son.[7] Fleda herself immediately recognizes her identification with the courtesan, for when Mrs. Brigstock says, "I came, I believe, Fleda, just—you know—to plead with you," she snaps, "As if I were one of those bad women in a play?" (X:177). Yet there is a fit to the insinuation, however much Fleda rejects it. The structure of the drama James models upon this famous well-made play fulfills the identification despite the fact that her break with Owen does not come immediately, and that their mutual passion even develops further after this scene. Her final renunciation of him, however, makes ironic use of that melodramatic stage tradition by which the "bad" woman recovers virtue in a gesture of ultimate self-sacrifice. For Fleda, judged by convention, *is* bad, someone outside the marriage-plot whose status as a "free spirit" might be thought to connect her with bohemianism. Also, she is bad because she has rejected the possessive principle itself, at least in its crude material form, however much she garners a spiritual and mental profit. James understood, perhaps, that there was something subversive after all in such a rejection, that it threatened the very foundation of the society he lived in.

Unlike Camille (or Daisy Miller), Fleda does not have to die to prove her superiority of heart. Yet it is difficult to imagine her further life. The "things" are themselves destined to vanish into smoke, destroying the possibility of any future relation to them, even to the one object, the Maltese cross, which is Owen's consolatory gift to her. And in Fleda's renunciation both of "things" and of any plausible further destiny in the form of marriage, we see a consistency. The idealist aestheticism that is superior to possession of beautiful objects is like the rejection of that materialization of being which constitutes human action in the world. James suspected that life provides no role for the "free spirit." His fear of the excess of provision in the original episode which gave him his suggestion for the tale is not only an expression of his attachment to the "sublime economy of art." As he listened to his dinner-table companion, he grasped his subject in the opposition of mother and son over possession of the family treasures, but "when in the next breath I began to hear of *action* taken, on the beautiful ground, by our engaged adversaries, tipped each, from that instant, with the light of the highest distinction, I saw clumsy Life again at her stupid work. For the *action* taken, and on which my friend, as I knew she would, had already begun all complacently and benightedly further to report, I had absolutely, and could have, no scrap of use" (2:1140). The word "action," which I emphasize in this passage, refers to legal action, the suit by which, in the actual case, the son sought to recover his inheritance. But the word suggests inescapably as well action in general, that limiting reduction of potentiality which plot must impose upon character.

Fleda rejects not only the marriage-plot of novel tradition, therefore; she also rejects her fate as a representative naturalist heroine even more heroically than Isabel, who accepts a rich sponsor in Mrs. Touchett and also inherits unanticipated Touchett money. Fleda is also a poor girl, nearly orphaned, whose remnant of family only serves to remind her of the constraints of poverty. She is taken up by Mrs. Gereth, virtually "adopted" by the elder lady, who also wants to launch her into the marriage-plot by marrying her to her own son—and here too, there is some resemblance to Isabel's experience, for while Mrs. Touchett wanted Isabel to make any "good" marriage, *Mr.* Touchett, it may be remembered, suggested to Ralph that he was in love with his cousin and ought to marry her.

Fleda's situation is also much like that of Kate Croy in *The Wings of the Dove*, a novel deeply concerned with the theme of possession. Like Kate, Fleda is also dependent upon the benevolence of a wealthy older patroness, also expected to marry "well" in order to save herself from the destiny represented by her married sister, also dragged down by a disreputable, penurious father. Except for such patronage, she would be someone always "visiting", like Madame Merle; she also is said not, for the present, to "live anywhere in particular" (X:98). Kate's Aunt Maud is not unlike Mrs. Gereth. Lancaster Gate is decidedly not an achievement of aesthetic harmony like Poynton, but it is a place of "things", crammed with the over-solid furnishings of upper-middle-class taste. Kate—whose personal style is to be " 'dressed,' often with fewer accessories, than other women" (XIX:5), strives to escape Aunt Maud's overfurnishedness in the way of conventional ideas for her niece's future. But while Kate strives to escape Aunt Maud's plot, she is captured by another, and enacts the role of one naturalistically coerced by circumstances into criminality—like Madame Merle. Fleda strives for a greater freedom. She refuses Mrs. Gereth's plan for her, and even "plots" to do so—but not to gain for herself in any way. She thus remains defiant both of the sentimental marriage story and of the naturalist inevitabilities inherent in her situation.

We may hazard more speculative analogies also by saying that in sacrificing her own opportunity to embrace the plot proffered her, or to contrive any other, Fleda reenacts James's own renunciation of a fiction of realistic plenitude and undeviating and concluded story. And whether the latter renunciation is something actually available in life, or is some *imagined* possibility, some alterity not allowed to make itself felt in the finished work, something, in this process, is lost while potentialty remains more rich. It is in the same preface to this very tale of extreme renunciation that James speaks of his feeling that the artist always asks himself, "Which is the work in which he hasn't surrendered, under dire difficulty, the best thing he meant to have kept? In which, indeed, before the dreadful *done,* doesn't he ask himself what has become of the thing all for the sweet sake of which it was to proceed to that extremity?" (2:1144). The italics are James's—for the "dreadful *done*" he felt both desire and fear.

"The Spoils of Poynton" is a more ambiguous, more evasive work than James's previous fictions, though it deals superficially with some of the same concepts. I have already referred to the connection of this story with *Washington Square*—but the difference is worth elaborating further. What, indeed, has happened to the terms "natural" and clever," which established a clear opposition between Catherine Sloper and those, particularly her supremely clever father, who surround her? In the end, cleverness, with which the artist himself, in his narrative persona, seems initially identified, proved inferior to the "artlessness" (in every sense) of Catherine. But the antithetic taste-less person in "The Spoils" is not its heroine Fleda—who is certainly clever enough to please the very clever Mrs. Gereth—nor even Owen, whose simplicity is still endearing and whose chief lapse of taste, like Catherine's, is in the choice of a love-object, but rather the anti-heroine, Mona Brigstock. Mona is vulgar and mean. But the Brigstock estate has to be conceded by Mrs. Gereth, however grudgingly, to have a quality which we do not hear of in connection with Poynton: "The flowers at Waterbath would probably go wrong in colour and the nightingales sing out of tune; but she remembered to have heard the place described as possessing those advantages that are usually spoken of as natural" (X:3). Mona herself, in a way that parodies the touching inarticulateness of Catherine, is facially inexpressive, even when she chatters like Daisy Miller: "She belonged to the type in which speech is an unaided emission of sound, in which the secret of being is inpenetrably and incorruptibly kept. Her expression would probably have been beautiful if she had had one, but whatever she communicated she communicated, in a manner best known to herself, without signs" (X:9). Here the narrative tone, with its ironic use of the approbative "incorruptible," is on the side of "expression," of signification, rather than of silence.

It is Owen, though, who is more closely, if ambiguously, like

Catherine. Unlike Mona, he has plenty of "signs," but they are "all very simple and immediate. Robust and artless, eminently natural, yet perfectly correct, he looked pointlesly active and pleasantly dull" (X:9). The condescension of the narrator toward the "handsome and heavy" (X:8) Owen is exactly like that adopted by the narrator of James's much earlier short novel toward the "robust" and "dull" heiress of *Washington Square*. But this later narrator is ready to admit at once, with the aid of Fleda's consciousness, which is more morally sensitive than Dr. Sloper's, that "it was of a pleasant effect and rather remarkable to be stupid without offence—of a pleasanter effect and more remarkable indeed than to be clever and horrid" (X:10). The observation, which comes at the end of the first of the book's twenty-two short chapters, forecasts the realization with which this work ends, as does its forerunner, that cleverness and horridness can all too often combine. Mrs. Gereth is also viewable as horrid, in the end. Cleverness certainly becomes a dubious term, anyhow, by the time Fleda can say to Owen's mother, "He's ever so much cleverer than he makes any show of; he's remarkable in his own shy way" (X:217).

And the question is exactly the same as applied to art. James seems to be putting his own devotion to the principle of the crafted and organized artwork on trial when he describes Poynton as having been, with its contents, "treated as a single splendid object," even by Mrs. Gereth's husband, in willing it undividedly to his son (X:15)—a human injustice somehow perpetrated in the name of aesthetic perfectionism. The consequence of Mrs. Gereth's aestheticism, Poynton is itself a work of art, composed and entire—which is why the proposal that she should take away to Ricks such items as she "liked best" seems laughable to her: "There wasn't a thing in the house she didn't like best . . . What had her whole life been but an effort toward completeness and perfection? Better Waterbath at once, in its cynical sameness, than the ignominy of such a mixture!" (X:50). But that such harmony and unity of parts imposes itself tyrannically on life is a judgment of his own aesthetic effort which James seems willing to make.

We are inclined to be critical of Mrs. Gereth's condescension, as we are of Dr. Sloper's, notwithstanding the fact that she is *right* in thinking little of Owen's choice of Mona Brigstock. But the case *for* Mrs. Gereth is maintained; the marriage that she objects to—and that will take place despite her objections—will be a triumph of vulgarity over refinement. As I have observed, it is possible to see her repugnance as intimately meaningful to James, and James encourages this inclination to criticism of Mrs. Gereth in the face of his own horror of "vulgarity," of elements haphazardly assembled to please a low taste, which makes Mrs. Gereth shudder at Waterbath. Waterbath corresponds to the philistinism with which he was forced to compete in the magazines. Like Fleda, with whom he might have identified himself, finally, he shared her view of the usurper of his house, the house of fiction. But Mrs. Gereth herself, it turns out, is not fine but "coarse"—she admits it. She has only the one question about other persons: "were they clever or stupid? To be clever meant to know the 'marks' " (X:138)—that is, the identifying marks of fine "things." To exercise connoisseurship with such expertise reminds one, of course, of Dr. Sloper, whose cleverness enabled him to see at once the "marks" that identify the kind and quality of human types. But unlike the clever Dr. Sloper, who objected to Townsend, another clever person like himself, on moral grounds, Mrs. Gereth objects to someone who is merely less innocently and amiably stupid than her son.

The candidate she does favor, as we have seen, is as clever as she is, "a spirit of the same family" as herself. But Fleda becomes determined not to put her cleverness to base use, even though she has conceived of a possible marriage for herself in which "she should contribute all the cleverness." Fleda, the character who does not exist in *Washington Square*, resembles Isabel Archer, a young woman of high intelligence and aesthetic sensibility who is also moral and generous. Despite the expectation just referred to, she finds that her "designs" upon life (like Isabel's in marrying Osmond) have been presumptuous, and she shrinks from further exercise of her powers. She refuses to lift a hand to bring into being the marriage that would exactly answer her prescription. She does not use her cleverness to discover, as cleverness generally does, a purposive scheme which links events to an intended end, a plot, a scheme of possession. From possessions and enactments she would disengage herself as best she can.

The true alternative to Poynton, is not, after all, Waterbath—or West Kensington—but Ricks, the modest "dower-house" which had belonged to a dead maiden aunt and which is offered to Mrs. Gereth in the place of Poynton. It, too, is crowded with objects collected by its former inmate, but it "was crowded with objects of which the aggregation somehow made a thinness and the futility a grace; things that told [Fleda] they had been gathered as slowly and as lovingly as the golden flowers of the other house." The maiden aunt, they also told her, "had passed shyly, yet with some bruises, through life; had been sensitive and ignorant and exquisite: that too was a sort of origin, a sort of atmosphere for relics and rarities, though different from the sorts most prized at Poynton" (X:54–55). In one sense, what the alternative of Ricks consists of is obvious— female self-reliance even to the point of spinsterhood. It also speaks of another way of assembling one's attachments to make a harmonious life.

What Mrs. Gereth does with Ricks, however, is to try to make it into Poynton by forcibly thrusting into it as much of the spoils of Poynton—fulfilling this title as she ravages the house no longer hers—as she can crowd into its space. She thus routs from Ricks its former ghostly harmony, the harmony of things that hang together by some grace of deep personal association and feeling. But in the end the spoils are returned and Ricks recovers its own character. The ghostly maiden aunt, who seems to represent the fate Fleda has chosen, returns. The lonely older woman embraces the context of the spinster aunt and makes something of her own out of it. As Fleda says to Mrs. Gereth, "It's not the great chorus of Poynton; but you're not, I'm sure, either so proud or so broken as to be reached by nothing but that. This is a voice so gentle, so human, so feminine—a faint far-away voice with the little quaver of a heart-break. You've listened to it unawares." In the transmission of this female experience Fleda feels an influence that is precious and sustaining, and purely feminine: "It's a presence, a perfume, a touch. It's a soul, a story, a life. There's ever so much more here than you and I. We're in fact just three!" The special grace of Ricks, we now realize, is precisely that it represents the surrender of the drama, the marriage-plot, that Mrs. Gereth had envisioned for Fleda. In its mute renunciation of story, it gives "the impression somehow of something dreamed and missed, something reduced, relinquished, resigned: the poetry, as it were, of something sensibly *gone*" (X:248–249).

Fleda thus enacts, also, as radically as any of James's characters, the writer's own sacrifice, representing the "reduced, relinquished, resigned" mode of James's narration. It is a sacrifice which James may not have entirely endorsed. James's aborted story seems to renounce possession of life in favor of pure appreciation, yet that renunciation is also a loss of the intimate commitment to reality that is involved in the view of persons as bound to oneself by the right of ownership. Fleda's sacrifice *must* seem perverse, in the end, bringing as it does no happiness to herself, and James's preference for a renunciatory form may have seemed, even to himself, perverse also.

· 8 ·

"The Turn of the Screw"

"THE TURN OF THE SCREW," which James himself dismissed as a potboiler[1] and which critics worry into triviality because of its famous undecidability, is perhaps more about the real world than is usually granted. It is, after all, another story about a middle-class woman of slender means. James's governess—and how significant it is that we never know her by name, only by the occupational title to which she has been reduced—is one of those girls of "good" family but small fortune who have failed to find the rescue of marriage. She is a country parson's daughter—like the Brontë sisters, who turned to teaching school or educating at home the children of more fortunate women. The profession of governess was one of the few available to gentlemen's daughters in the Victorian world, a niche somewhere above the servant class, which sheltered women who were not necessarily inferior to their employers in education or "gentle" manners.[2] Even the ruined Miss Jessel was "a lady" (XII:207).

It is worth noting that until the time he wrote "The Turn of the Screw," James did not interest himself in a heroine forced to earn her own living. Isabel Archer is given shelter by her wealthy aunt and made rich by her cousin before she can consider any alternative (such as Henrietta Stackpole's self-suppporting journalism) to the marriage Casper Goodwood is pressing upon her. Save for such unlikely intervention, marriage is, quite realistically, the only survival available to her. Verena Tarrant, who might have become a professional orator and propagandist—Matthias Pardon sees good prospects of it—passes without intermission from the protection of the well-to-do Olive to the marital state, however unpromising, that Ransom offers. Fleda Vetch is likewise one of those "nice" women who have no alternative but to accept the patronage of wealthier relatives or friends until marriage offers permanent security—or to subsist on such patronage permanently, like Madame Merle, who knows so well all the etiquette of visiting (not to bring too much luggage, not to get ill, etc.). It should be noted, also, that dependency is the uneasy status of Tina Bordereau, whose aunt, Juliana, can only provide for her, it seems, by leaving her the papers which might be bartered for a marriage offer. What she will do—how she will live—when that legacy is destroyed, we cannot imagine. Madame Merle's exact basis of life is not really very clear, after all, and it is not inconceivable that even Fleda, with her fastidious taste for refined living, might become a governess.

In *What Maisie Knew,* published just a few months before "The Turn of the Screw," there are *two* governesses (though neither is the heroine). There is Mrs. Wix, already an "old maid" with that half-pitiful, half-grotesque defect of poor eyesight which links her to Hawthorne's Hepzibah (she is actually a poor widow who has lost her only child). And there is the glamorous, well-bred Miss Overmore, of whom Maisie's mother says, "a lady and yet awfully poor. Rather nice people, but there are seven sisters at home"; Maisie, comparing her to Moddle, the nursemaid who had previously cared for her, observes, "Miss Overmore never, like Moddle, had on an apron, and when she ate, she held her fork with her little finger curled out" (XI:16).

Miss Overmore, who is as ambitious and sly as Thackeray's Becky Sharp, succeeds in getting the father of her pupil to marry her. In actuality, Victorian governesses, isolated from their own supportive background, especially when they came from impoverished but genteel families, were likely enough to hope for rescue from the nearest source—the male members of the families that employed them. Now and then they probably succeeded in marrying back into the employing class. There is an authentic nostalgia of class exile, at any rate, in the romantic improbability of Charlotte Brontë's dream of feminine self-realization and wish-fulfillment. One may well ask what the meaning is of the condition imposed by the children's uncle in "The Turn of the Screw"—that the governess may never, under any circumstances, communicate with him once she has accepted her position. Is it that between the rich man and the poor young woman there stands a class barrier that cannot be breached by romance? *Jane Eyre* is unquestionably James's principal intertext for "The Turn of the Screw," but this is an intertextuality that denies its model, compelling us to see the dreams of the governess at Bly as illusion and futility.

What was the consequence, in life, of such illusion? Were governesses prone to the neurotic consequences of their peculiar situation—and did their cases illustrate the poor single woman's predicament in a way apt for representation not only as romantic heroines in need of rescue but as sinister, witch-like, or lunatic? Contemporary records indicate that in the 1840s—the period in which the story seems to be set—governesses accounted for the single largest category of female patients in English asylums for the insane,[3] which gives a certain basis to the theory that attributes the extraordinary visions of James's governess to the fact that she is a victim of strain and repression.[4] In a lesser-known story, "The Middle Years," published only three years before "The Turn of the Screw," a female dependent on a wealthy dowager's patronage possesses "a queer stare, naturally vitreous, which made her remind [a young man who meets her] of some figure—he couldn't name it—in a play or a novel, some sinister governess or tragic old maid" (XVI:84). The description suggests that James may have already conceived a story about such a figure.

Even if a governess's dream of recovered status through marriage is to be frustrated there is, of course, one intimacy with her employer family to which she has special access—that with the child or children in her care. In James's fiction, moreover, such children are generally, themselves, the victims of displacement or abandonment of some sort—sharing with the governess her exile from affection—like Miles and Flora, orphans given over to the authority of an uncle who refuses to assume direct responsibility for them, or like Maisie, whose parents first see her as a "bone of contention" and then, that role no longer interesting them, cast her off. The forced coupling of the child and the employed caretaker gains, from this situation, an intensity we are likely to feel as almost sexual, as we do in the case of the governess and Miles. Something very similar happens, indeed, in James's illustration of the governess situation in a male version—that of the tutor, Pemberton, "the poor young man," a "gentleman" without resources, who finds himself drawn so feelingly toward little Morgan Moreen in "The Pupil."

That "love between the classes" is the forbidden vice obsessionally present in "The Turn of the Screw" has been interestingly suggested by Bruce Robbins, who has brought to bear on the story the evidence in Victorian life studies that upper-class men were routinely "initiated" by maids or governesses.[5] He does not, however, suggest what logically follows from this evidence, that Miles—and perhaps Flora—were themselves sexually initiated by Miss Jessel and Quint; instead, he emphasizes the violation of class distinctions involved in the relation between the adults, the well-bred Miss Jessel and a man distinctly "below" her in social rank. He suggests that knowledge of this *social* perversity constituted the children's initiation. More evident is the fact that the living governess's own relationship with the children, and especially with Miles (and perhaps the relationship she later has with Douglas) has erotic overtones. That sexual feeling should unite the children of the upper-class household with the governess violates not merely the taboo against sex between adult and child but the barrier of class, and provides an unmentionable outlet—erotic and social at once—for the frustration of her forbidden desire to unite with her employer and his class.

This doubled sense of the illicit may have been reinforced by other suppositions that must have come to the mind of the late Victorian reader of "The Turn of the Screw" as readily as did adultery or the seduction of children as the unspecified transgressions of Miss Jessel and Quint, and even of the governess herself. Richard Ellmann has suggested that "The Turn of the Screw" deals centrally with the theme of homosexuality, a subject so full of fear and fascination for the turn-of-the-century reader. According to Ellmann, Miles's unmentionable offenses with other boys at school were understood to be homosexual, something, as the governess says, "revoltingly, against nature" (XII:295); the relationships between Quint and Miles and between Miss Jessel and Flora were also understood to be homosexual.[6] Here, too, one must say that it is the offense against the rules of class separation which is felt most fundamentally and given a more threatening, more illicit quality by conflation with an even less mentionable sexual crime.

In reading "The Turn of the Screw," however, one must guard against a too-literal psycho-historical interpretation, though the issues of sex and class surely lie behind the more abstract configuration of the story, its play of style, and its intertextual reference. The governess's frustration can be seen as a frustration of plot—the romantic resolution of the Brontë story is, for James, doomed from the start, even though there is some early promise of its realization.

Her struggle to find self-definition and destiny of a romantic sort just the same—to be some kind of heroic person—may be related to the similar efforts of other Jamesian heroines. As Leo Bersani has said, the governess is "the Jamesian character idealized to the point of parable, that is, to the point where the essentially conventional distinction between character and author disappears and the character, released from the obligation of having to operate within a clearly and distinctly given world of fictional events, assumes the function of novelizing. The governess is in pursuit, but she is, quite literally, in pursuit of the story itself."[7] Like Isabel Archer, then, she strives to find an enacting role, but also to compel others around her into the drama in which she would figure. In this she is not only Isabel but those who "plot" against or on behalf of Isabel; she is determined to impose story upon others.

The governess, like Isabel, is a reader of novels, even of gothic novels. Isabel, though she raises the possibility that she might enter a romantic fiction when she first sees Gardencourt, does not really expect to encounter a ghost—and Ralph assures her that she will not. She rejects Warburton's moated castle, which might have provided her with an appropriate setting for a gothic romance. Her aim is to escape such stories. Ironically, of course, she is attracted to the gothic-Byronic hero-villain, romantically misanthropic and with a mysterious past and a little child as a token of it, just like Rochester, and this Rochester type immures her in his own fortress-like house. And she does see the ghost in the end.

Unlike the rational Isabel, the governess expects to figure in a gothic romance. She sees her entire experience at Bly in terms of such a romance, and views herself as its heroine. She is no Catherine Morland to be cured of her anticipations of ghosts and evil forces; one suspects that *Northanger Abbey* would not have been among her favorite books. The reader, too, is prompted to generic expectations. Like the group of guests in the prologue who have gathered to exchange ghost-stories on a winter's night in an old country house, the reader is prepared to surrender himself to a tale of supernatural possession and haunting. Moreover, the governess has also read and adored *Jane Eyre,* and she dreams of marrying a Rochester—the mysterious master, with no visible wife but with children on his hands, who has placed the children in her charge at Bly. So powerful are the suggestions of generic repetition, indeed, that some readers will want to believe that they are *his* children, and perhaps even the children of

Miss Jessel, who preceded the governess at Bly—as Rochester's wife and mistress had preceded Jane—even though we are expressly told that they are the children of his younger brother, and have been sent to him from India.[8]

From the first, the governess's reveries of the reenactment of *Jane Eyre* are forbidden dreams. She is never to call upon her employer, and violates his prohibition even in imagining that he will reward her fidelity by loving her. Yet this and other romance plots direct her actions just the same. If she cannot be Jane Eyre, who marries the master, she can be be a valiant female knight embattled against monsters. With joy she seizes this role: "I was there to protect and defend the little creatures in the world the most bereaved and the most loveable. . . . We were cut off, really, together; we were united in our danger. They had nothing but me, and I—well I had *them*. It was in short a magnificent chance (XII:199). In crafting her story she is like the writer in her efforts; she is also like the reader, who seeks, by interpretation, to organize impressions of her and of what she perceives into a continuous narrative with a single meaning.

A mass of critical commentary has accumulated to illustrate this reader compulsion, but the prolonged debate about the reality or irreality of the ghosts in the story, the principle pivot of controversy, seems finally to have come to a halt in the acceptance of the idleness of such a question. From the reader's point of view, the story remains "fantastic" in the sense formulated by Tzvetan Todorov.[9] The governess's reports cannot be proven to be either supernaturally valid *or* her illusion, and our hesitation is the source of the peculiar *frisson* of the story. Our epistemological quandary, our inability to be positive about how to take her observations, is, of course, rooted in our inability to verify or refute her first-person account; we cannot escape the enclosure of her mind, and all efforts to find internal clues of veracity or distortion in what she tells us are baffled because of this. The confidence she inspires in her fictional editor, Douglas, does not really help, for he, too, is a possibly compromised speaker over whose shoulder the first-person narrator of the framing introduction regards us with neither reassurance nor skepticism. James does not intervene to direct us either. Having given her, as he says in the New York Edition preface, "authority" (2:1186), the writer who liked to be called "cher maître" covertly refers his own attitude to that of "the master" in the story, who has given her the "surpreme authority" (XII:154) which forbids any recourse to himself. James, the master, gives this first-person narrator that "long rope for acting herself out," by means of which, he believed, Balzac gave freedom to his favorite characters. James's abstention from intervention in the governess's narrative allows him to disclaim intention—he goes so far, even, as to deny that he had *any* serious intention, and calls his fiction, "perfectly independent and irresponsible . . . of the very kind, as it happens, least apt to be baited by earnest criticism" (2:1181–1182), giving us, his readers, whatever authority *we* want to take. As a work that consciously pretends not to interpret itself, "The Turn of the Screw" becomes James's most notorious demonstration not that truth cannot be established, but that earnest criticism can be baited.

A peculiarity hardly remarked upon, however, is the fact that the hesitation essential to the fantastic is not shared—as in most fantastic tales—by the narrator-protagonist. Her version of events seems to be unequivocally on the side of the marvelous from the moment she seizes upon the conviction that she has seen the dead Peter Quint and Miss Jessel. Her uncertainty is of another kind. She strives to resolve indeterminacy by establishing the *moral* meaning of the mysterious world of Bly. It is not the existence of the ghosts of the two dead household servants that the governess needs to establish, but a cosmic plot of the struggle of evil and good. In her determination to read the world this way she also offers the reader a warning example. James called his tale "a perfect example of the imagination unassisted . . . unassociated, a fairy-tale pure and simple" (2:1183). But the vision of fairy tale is not so much the author's as it is his character's; it is the governess who sees those around her in fairy-tale terms and sees herself as a heroine engaged in a struggle against demons. When James says, "I cast my lot with pure romance" (2:1187), it is not merely because dramatic strategy causes him to leave so much to the reader's imagination—to refuse to "assist" it by the provision of complicating particulars. The simplifications of fairy tale are a clue to the governess's fatal habit of simplification. She has no need of the realism that might obstruct her simplifying vision.

Romance sees the world composed of opposed purities, allowing only for ideal virtue and unqualified viciousness, for heroes and heroines, villains and villainesses diametrically opposed, for evil and good in so complete a state that no reality of experience can fully express them. Implicit in such a view is the Manichaean mythos of Christianity which, while according responsibility for creation to one sacred being, also suggests that God and Satan contest the world and are equal sources of the divine and the demonic in human life. In the Calvinist version of Christian doctrine, human souls, also, are unalterably distinguished as good or evil. The governess is the writer of a Calvinist romance which shifts alternately from a view of Bly as a garden of innocence to one which perceives it to be permeated by corruption. Life appears to her as one of those designs which we have been taught by Gombrich to see as a representation of the exclusiveness of visual illusion.[10] We are allowed to see either rabbit or duck, a flock of white birds crossing a black sky from left to right *or* a flock of black birds crossing a white sky from right to left—but never both at once. Her mind—subjected to this alterity of opposites—cannot sustain ambiguity, which allows opposites to exist together.

The condition of romance depends upon absence (as realism does upon presence) not because romantic narratives do not contain details but because the details are never enough; no amount of them will ever fill the void of the absolute, supply enough wicked deeds to fully justify our view—at the very outset—of Cinderella's wicked sisters, or fully account for our sense of Cinderella's own perfect goodness. The ghosts—creatures of fairy tale or romance— convey to the governess a powerful "tone" of evil without her ever knowing the nature of their crimes. James was determined not to make her perception of their badness "shrink to the compass of some particular brutality, some particular immorality, some particular infamy portrayed: with the result, alas, of the demonstration's falling sadly short." He asked himself "What, in the last analysis, had I to give the sense of? Of their being, the haunting pair, capable, as the phrase is, of everything . . . What would *be* then, on reflection, this utmost conceivability—a question to which the answer all admirably came. There is for such a case no eligible *absolute* of the wrong." So, he boasted—in language that has a deconstructionist ring to the modern ear—"There is not only from beginning to end of the matter not an inch of expatiation, but my values are positively all blanks save so far as an excited horror, a promoted pity, a created expertness—on which punctual effects of strong causes no writer can ever fail to plume himself—proceed to read into them more or less fantastic figures" (2:1187–1188).

We can and do perform this reading in of "figures" more or less fantastic. James's ellipses invite various kinds of filling-in, some of which I have already practiced in dealing with suggestions of sexual and sociological implication in the story. However, James's ellipses must be permitted to maintain themselves even as they provoke our own constructive efforts. He observed that readers would provide the reparation of his gaps, but did not fail to point out that these would be made of each reader's own inner stuff of experience or conception: "Only make the reader's general vision of evil intense enough, I said to myself—and that already is a charming job—and his own experience, his own imagination, his own sympathy (with the children) and horror (of their false friends) will supply him quite sufficiently with all the particulars. Make him *think* the evil, make him think it for himself, and you are released from weak specifications" (2:1188). This passage, often quoted merely to illustrate James's technique of ghost-story scarification, should be noted as a reminder of his probable readiness to subscribe to the modern critical view that the individual reader provides interpreting structures.

The "gaps" that provoke this process are not limited to the sexual and social. The difficulties which depend on restriction to the governess's own account of things will tempt us generally to "explain" what she does not. One has only to think again of the critical argument concerning the verifiability of her visions of Quint and Miss Jessel; her veracity has been denied for lack of confirmation from others or sustained because of the accuracy of her descriptions. Instead of ingeniously arguing that she learned what Quint looked like from one of the villagers (though we are never told this),[11] or (as in *The Innocents*, the 1961 file scripted by William Archibald and Truman Capote) that she had come upon a miniature portrait of him in the attic of the house, we should probably allow the unexplained to maintain its power to unsettle us. No doubt such extrapolations beyond the text are inescapable; the austerity of New Critical suspicion of such flights by the reader probably overlooks the process by which the reader invariably inserts explanations into the gaps, small or large, of all stories. At the same time, this admission reminds us that we are also obliged to admit the hypothetical and individual nature of our additions.

But if we are asked by this story to consider and evaluate the governess's way of imposing design on the palpable life around her—*her* intrusions of meaningfulness into the gaps and obliquities, the true occultation of experience—we have a different sort of subject altogether, and the story does not collapse into themelessness. The reader's difficulties in establishing the "truth" of the story are a warning against the governess's quest for one or another certainty of her own. From her point of view it is not only the ghosts whose evil need not be specified; her romance or Calvinist view of life causes her to postulate in little Miles and Flora an undenotable absolute, whether of evil or of good. She seeks to validate this view of them without seeking particular facts; what she wants from the children is a revelation not of their actual history or present behavior but of their essential selves in a condition of damnation or salvation. She does not really look for narrative "proof," which would be trivial—as human works are no demonstration of divine intention—but yearns for some confession by them of what they essentially *are*—angels or fiends.

Her fastidious disdain of facts is anticipated in Douglas's observation, at the start, that her story will not "tell . . . in any literal vulgar way" (XII:151) whether she was in love. Her having fallen in love with the master, which she admits to Mrs. Grose as soon as she she arrives at Bly, is the expectable spring which sets the plot into motion, but in no literal (that is, "vulgar") way. The introductory glimpse of her interview in London with the wealthy bachelor who struck her as so "gallant and splendid" seems to promise a close in which we will see the two united. As Douglas's friend remarks, with conscious reference to literary tradition, the master was "such a figure as had never risen, save in a dream or an old novel, before a fluttered, anxious girl out of a Hampshire vicarage" (XII:153). Here, again, we think, is the mysterious, glamorous proprietor of an old country house with a crenellated parapet,[12] a house set in a park from whose tall trees the rooks fly over the lawns, as at Rochester's Thornfield. Here is the conscientious and intelligent young governess. She has taken charge of children who are not the master's own but for whom he is responsible, as Rochester is for his ward, Adèle. She will discover that the house is haunted by the ghost of her predecessor (as Rochester's is, in a sense, by the hidden presence of his living wife—who will be Jane's predecessor in such a marriage as James's governess fails to achieve). The governess herself is aware that her situation resembles that of a character in a gothic romance or of Charlotte Brontë's heroine when she arrives at Bly and wonders if there is a "secret" in the old house, "a mystery of Udolpho or an insane, an unmentionable relative, kept in unsus-pected confinement" (XII:179). She expects someone—probably the master—in narrative terms, as she reflects that "it would be as charming as a charming story suddenly to meet someone [who] would appear there at the turn of a path and who would stand before me and smile and approve" (XII:175).

That the marriage–plot fails to fulfill itself, however, is an example such as we have already seen of James's abstention from this convention of personal closure. But the governess is no resigned "old maid," content, like Catherine Sloper to compose her own "morsel" of fancy in solitude. Instead of a consummation she cannot realize, the governess embraces a view of life as an endless, unprogressive contest between opposed possibilities which she struggles, alternately, to embrace. It is a contest with neither resolu-tion nor enlightenment as its outcome. So the characters in the story she tells exist as a series of repeated pairs who are alternate versions of each other. (Only Mrs. Grose, significantly, has no double, her admirable "grossness" making such a division impos-sible). The governess sees herself duplicated twice, in opposing ways, in Miss Jessel and little Flora. She sees the master alternately as a figure of grace or malice, expressed in little Miles and Quint. Quint is an inversion of the God-like owner of Bly who has sent the governess upon her mission there; with his red hair and beard he reminds some readers of traditional association of redness with the devil,[13] and may be named in the dying Miles's ambiguous last words ("Peter Quint—you devil!"; XII:309). But he is also the master's evil double, taking his place at Bly.

Her romantic idealization of the master is accompanied by a counterview, deriving from a feminist critique of masculine power such as Charlotte Brontë had expressed in her heroine. The master's sexual magnetism, which has caused the governess to be "carried away" in London, has exercised itself before, and perhaps resulted in the destruction of women like the former governess. Mrs. Grose says, "Well, Miss, you're not the first" (XII:162); her words may refer to Miss Jessel, just as "young and pretty" as the governess, who remarks, "He seems to like us young and pretty." But the master's sexual behavior is confused, in this conversation, with that of Quint in the housekeeper's stammered reply, "Oh, he did . . . I mean that's his way—the master's" (XII:169), which already suggests to the governess the presence at Bly of someone else. Of course, Mrs. Grose may not be referring to anyone but the master—but, by her suspicions of masculine power, the governess is plainly prepared to meet the *Doppelgänger* who had had his "way" with Miss Jessel and others, as Mrs. Grose later suggests. Quint may be responsible for Miss Jessel's mysterious end (pregnant, perhaps; perhaps a suicide) as representative of the master, while the master may or may not have "carried [her] away" to the point of seducing her.

Quint—the objectification of the master as a source of fear—appears just when the present governess imagines her employer's sudden arrival. Despite his warning that she will not see him again, she longs for a reprieve from the abortion of the *Jane Eyre* plot. With the illogic of romance, its penchant for reversal of expectation, she daydreams of his smiling approval of her management, the gift of his presence being the reward of her submission to his interdict of communication. Instead, she sees Quint, who wears his "better's" clothes but no hat (and so is not a gentleman), who "looks like an actor" (and so is an impersonation of someone else), who is her intuition of threat in the masculine authority that has possessed her erotic fancy (XII:191). Her decision to do nothing about the letter from the head*master* (another inscrutable masculine power who cannot be appealed to) is itself, of course, a way of maintaining the alterity of her view of both the master and Miles. She is unwilling either to establish the nature of Miles's offense or to clear him of guilt, retaining her capacity for alternate visions of this further representative of the master.

Her attachment to Miles is, by this same division of mind, a representation both of her attachment to the master and her suspicion of him. The ten-year-old is an exquisite "little gentleman," referred to by Mrs. Grose, by the accident of convention, as *Master* Miles. He is dressed, like Quint, if not in the master's clothes, at least by the master's tailor. To the governess he is as seductive as the man in Harley Street, calling her "my dear," or "a jolly 'perfect' lady" (XII:249–250). In the scene after Flora's departure when they dine together, making the governess think of them as a pair of newlyweds, young Miles fulfills for a moment the marriage-plot glimpsed in her meeting with the master. But if he is the master's real nephew, he is also a nephew of Quint, who as a sort of surrogate uncle ruled the household in the master's stead, making "too free" with the maids and "with everyone" as a representative of the master's callousness and lust. One can say that the governess fastens her sexual longing, frustrated of its object in the master, upon the child, but it should be noted that Miles has enacted for his own part the master's seduction. And as its sequel, he will abandon her by his resolution to go back to school. This is such an abandonment as she knows she might expect from the master—who would also want to go back to his "own sort" (XII:251), as Miles puts it—that is, to his own class—and whose admonition that she must never appeal to him gives a warning of his ultimate dismissal. Miss Jessel, as I have said, may be assumed to have been used and abandoned, if not by the master *in proprie persona,* then by his alternate, Quint, as a representative of masculinity's destructive potential.

Miss Jessel is the governess herself, and in imagining her fate the governess projects for herself or, rather, we are invited to project for her, neither gothic romance nor the marriage-plot but that nineteenth-century discovery, the naturalist plot of the seduced and abused lower-class female victim of biology and circumstance. This predecessor is to be seen by the governess in postures that even she recognizes as her own. When she is about to write to the master she is confronted by the sight of a figure like herself at her own desk, occupied in writing like "some housemaid who . . . had applied herself to the considerable effort of a letter to her sweetheart" (XII:257); that is, writing such a letter as our governess might write to the master if she had become his mistress. She has collapsed at the foot of the steps in the lonely house after her return from her conversation with Miles outside the church—the conversation in which he tells her definitely that he must leave, as the master might be imagined to tell a mistress of whom he had grown weary. She realizes that it is exactly there, identically bowed, that she has seen "the spectre of the most horrible of women" (XII:256). Her own emotions at this moment are those of guilt and shame; she has deserved Miles's reproach that he is kept from school and his proper company by her possessive surveillance. And, perhaps, in the haggard and terrible Miss Jessel, she sees the alternate self which could deserve to be cast off by the master.

Flora completes the symmetry of the three couples—the governess and the master, Miss Jessel and Quint, and the two children. Though there is no sexual relationship between the children, she, too, stands in a slighter way for the governess. In her original beauty and innocence she is an absolute of the governess's virtue, more perfect because presexual. She, too, is to be abandoned by Miles for the education and future career which are not open to her, and for his "own sort," which is the world of men and even boys from which she is excluded as absolutely as the governess is divided from the master's and Miles's world, not only by class but by sex. In the end, when the governess has lost her own innocence altogether, the child's beauty becomes ugly and hard, like Miss Jessel's, and she seems crazed and an "old, old woman" (XII:279), anticipating the destiny of lunatic or "tragic old maid" which may await the governess.

I have elaborated this pattern of duplicates to emphasize the structure of mirroring and reversal in the story. That all the characters represent potentialities of either the governess or of the master as she fears or hopes to know him is a technique of doubling that we have already seen at work in *The Portrait of a Lady*. In the present story these potentialities are the projections of the governess's own way of seeing things. One can seem to say almost the same thing as I have been doing by identifying all these paired figures, or at least Miss Jessel and Quint, as hallucinatory projections of the governess's repressions.[14] But this is to give a psychological literalization to the poetic design of James's fable and to diminish its thematic interest. These paired characters, as the substance of the governess's own schematic vision, express a view of reality which is ultimately false.

It is a view of a world of absolute division, just as the paired figures are purities of good and evil. If such perfection of beauty, goodness, and heavenly grace as represented by the children exists in the world, then the opposite of these qualities, according to such a view, is implied by them. The governess is tossed between love and hate, trust and fear, the desire to save and that to destroy. She knows no middle ground, recognizes no human mixtures. Nothing is more significant in the story than her response to Miles's appeal that she allow him to be ordinarily bad. Miles can only be either angelic or satanic, like Satan himself for whom there could have been no half-way halting place between Heaven and the Hell to which he fell. If she surrenders her belief in his perfection she must insist upon his capacity for some unspeakable act of wickedness.

To read the story as the drama of this situation is to see how the narrative is a kind of binary permutation in which alternatives maintain their exclusiveness. The plot is not a progression to revelation but an endless succession of reversals. Repeatedly, the governess's language reinforces the effect of a viewpoint in which assertions can be read backward to mean their opposites. Such effects can be summarized in the governess's own phrase when she starts her tale: "I remember the whole beginning as a succession of flights and drops, a little see-saw of the right throbs and the wrong" (XII:158). And, immediately, the seesaw rhythm is initiated. She has somehow dreaded her arrival at Bly, but is delighted by its beauty—the "bright" flowers, the "golden" sky, the perfectly named Flora—and finds herself received there "as if I had been the mistress" and placed in a grand room with a great "state bed" (XII:159), a seeming fulfillment of her dream of marriage to the master. But there is a "drop" in Mrs. Grose's eagerness to see her which seems to imply another reading of appearances. Doubt invades her language:

> But it was a comfort that there could be no uneasiness in a connection with anything as beatific as the radiant image of my little girl, the vision of whose angelic beauty had probably more than anything to do with the restlessness that, before morning, made me several times rise and wander about my room to take in the whole picture and prospect; to watch from my open window the faint summer dawn, to look at such stretches of the rest of the house as I could catch, and to listen, while in the fading dusk the first birds began to twitter, for the possible recurrence of a sound or two, less natural and not without but within, that I had fancied I heard. (XII:160)

There could be no uneasiness, yet uneasiness is precisely what the image of Flora provokes in her. And during the night she thinks she hears the cry of a child. These "fancies," she goes on, were thrown off immediately, yet she gives them significance a moment later by saying that "in the light, or the gloom, I should rather say, of other and subsequent matters" (XII:160), these negative impressions would return. In the morning she denies, yet her language seems to admit, a ground of fear: "What I felt the next day was, I suppose, nothing that could be fairly called a reaction from the cheer of my arrival; it was probably at the most only a slight oppression produced by a fuller measure of the scale, as I walked round them, gazed up at them, took them in, of my new circumstances" (XII:162).

As Flora conducts her from one part of the house to another she anticipates alternatives of plot for the story she has entered:

> I had the view of a castle of romance inhabited by a rosy sprite, such a place as would somehow, for diversion of the young idea, take all colour out of story-books and fairy-tales. Wasn't it just a story-book over which I had fallen a-doze and a-dream? No; it was a big ugly antique but convenient house, embodying a few features of a building still older, half-displaced and half-utilized, in which I had the fancy of our being almost as lost as a handful of passengers in a great drifting ship.   (XII:163–164)

And so the first chapter ends with its ambiguous invocation of the patterns of fairy tale or legend—the last, the image of Bly as a "drifting ship," a kind of Flying Dutchman, is an alternate to the fairy castle where all wishes are granted. The next begins with a "this" whose referent is, presumably, the second view, which is said to have come home to her after she has met "the little gentleman" but in the evening been "deeply disconcerted" by the letter from his school. The letter, she reports, says nothing but that he cannot be kept on—but she interprets it to mean "that he's an injury to the others" (XII:166). She asks Mrs. Grose if the boy has ever been bad, and the housekeeper, who thinks *some* badness only normal, assents vigorously while rejecting the governess's leap to absolute terms—"contaminate," "corrupt." For the governess, he is not capable of venial fault, only of absolute depravity. Yet he is by every sign exquisite innocence itself.

And since the seesaw play of alternatives must be kept up, she never does the obvious things that might resolve her choice. She never writes to the school to find out why the boy was sent down; she does not write to his uncle, who might act to shed light on the matter; she does not question Miles. But the perfect trust on which her attitude seems based is all too ready to yield to its opposite. The gentleness of the children is called "a trap" to put her "off [her] guard" (XII:173); the peacefulness of the succeeding days is "the hush in which something gathers or crouches" (XII:174). After she identifies the twice-seen mysterious male figure as the dead valet, and hears, with a "sickness of disgust," that he had been "too free" with Miles, she watches the child for signs of corruption. Yet he astounds her by his perfect goodness—which she scrutinizes, none-theless, for evidences of its opposite: "If he had been wicked he

would have 'caught' it, and I should have caught it by the rebound—
I should have found the trace, should have felt the wound and the
dishonour. I could reconstitute nothing at all, and he was therefore
an angel" (XII:182–183).

Yet she "knows" that there has been something between Miles
and Quint, and that the specter is trying to continue his wicked
relations, though she will not confirm or dismiss her hypothesis by
questioning the boy directly. She begins to watch the children with
a suspiciousness she calls a "service admirable and difficult," though
her own words betray her self-doubt: "I began to watch them in a
stifled suspense, a disguised tension, that might well, had it continued too long, have turned into something like madness"
(XII:199). She is "saved" from this madness—the madness of being
unable to move from the pole of trust to the pole of suspicion—by
the apparition of Miss Jessel and Flora's appearance of pretending
that she does not see this figure of "unmistakable horror and evil"
(XII:203). Still, she does not confirm or dismiss her theory by questioning the little girl.

The alternatives are always exclusive. If Flora meets Miss Jessel
willingly, is it not, asks Mrs. Grose, "just proof of her blest innocence?" But the governess counters, "If it isn't proof of what you say,
it's proof of—God knows what!" (XII:205). And she moves from her
belief in perfection to its ever-undenoted opposite; "it's far worse
than I dreamed. They're lost" (XII:208). She has also begun to
describe herself in the same self-contradictory language that suggests
negation even as it affirms: "To gaze into the depths of blue of the
child's eyes and pronounce their loveliness a trick of premature cunning was to be guilty of a cynicism in preference to which I naturally
preferred to abjure my judgement." In the presence of the children,
however, the "see-saw" is again in motion, and "everything fell to
the ground but their incapacity and their beauty," until, as it swings
back to the negative side, she feels "obliged to re-investigate the certitude" of Flora's "inconceivable communion" (XII:210–211).

From Mrs. Grose she believes she learns that Miles had known
about the relation between Quint and Miss Jessel and in concealing
this knowledge had been corrupted by it. It is no use for Mrs. Grose
to cry, "If he was so bad then as that comes to, how is he such an
angel now?" (XII:214). Everything the governess thinks she learns
about the relations of the children and the dead pair suits "exactly
the particular deadly view [she is] in the very act of forbidding

[herself] to entertain" (XII:215). And once again, the effect of her pupils' appearance gives a "brush of the sponge" to her convictions, and she begins to "struggle" against [her] new lights" (XII:217). The children's charm seems "a beguilement still effective even under the shadow of a possibility that it was studied." Their responsiveness to her succeeds "as if [she] never appeared . . . literally to catch them at a purpose in it" (XII:218).

It is then she has her third encounter with Quint and finds that Flora, at the window, denies that she has seen or looked for anyone but the governess herself—who reflects, "I absolutely believed she lied" (XII:225). And when she finds the little girl at the window once again, she declares with conviction, "She was face to face with the apparition we had met at the lake and could now communicate with it as she had not then been able to do" (XII:228). The governess sees only Miles in the garden on this occasion, but she is convinced that he is gazing up at the tower above her head, the tower at the top of which, standing in the same spot as Miles, she had first seen the valet's ghost. Yet her language betrays her self-condemnation when she describes how Mrs. Grose took her "disclosures." It was, she says, "as had I wished to mix a witch's broth and proposed it with assurance, she would have held out a large clean saucepan" (XII:231).

Miles's defense, as I have said, is the very center of the story, the nub of the problem I have been describing as the governess's absolutist obsession. He tells her that he simply wanted to bring down a little her conception of his unnatural goodness, to make her think him "for a change—*bad!*" He had been very naughty; he had sat up without undressing until midnight, and then he had gone out and nearly caught cold. "When I'm bad I *am* bad!" he exults. And the governess is nearly persuaded to seesaw once again, thinking of "all the reserves of goodness that, for his joke, he had been able to draw upon" (XII:235). But she returns to her conviction that the "four . . . perpetually meet." She tells Mrs. Grose, "Their more than earthly beauty, their absolutely unnatural goodness. It's a game. It's a policy and a fraud!" (XII:237). Miles's plea for a normal allowance of commingled good and bad has failed.

Yet more and more her language betrays that she, who has cast herself in the role of savior, sees herself now, in the same fashion, as damned. It is as though her inability to allow a mingled nature to others makes for her own punishment. After she sees Miss Jessel at the lake, she declares, "She was there, so I was justified; she was there, so I was neither cruel nor mad" (XII:278). Against the weak denial of the syntax these powerful epithets, "cruel," "mad," thrust themselves. The children have continued affectionate, and she says, "Adorable they must in truth have been, I now feel, since I didn't in those days hate them!" (XII:247)—and we are made to suspect that she did hate them. Miles's reasonable plea for school and his liberty arouses her opposition; *now* she will write the master and inform him of the expulsion from the old school. Again, when Mrs. Grose asks the nature of the child's offense, she—and we—are denied the knowledge, and the governess answers in terms, once more, of the paradox that governs her polarities, "For wickedness. For what else—when he's so clever and beautiful and perfect? (XII:261). Only abstract wickedness can be the countertruth of such an appearance of completest goodness.

She is driven, at last, to drop her former discretion and to ask him what happened, only to receive for answer his shriek as she appeals to him and drops on her knees, to "seize once more the chance of possessing him" (XII:267), as though he were a soul to be wrested from the devil—or as though *she* were a devil seeking to "possess" the child. He blows out the candle—or Quint does. The admission, the proof absolute, still eludes her while she reflects, "Say that, by the dark prodigy I knew, the imagination of all evil *had* been opened up to him: all the justice within me ached for the proof that it could ever have flowered into an act" (XII:269). She has, till now, wanted only the admission of essential corruption from Miles, but now she craves the revelation of "doing," the "plot" of the past which she thinks he can tell her. A belief in personal essence has been as much an obsession with the governess as with other Jamesian characters. If she aches at last for the expression of essence in "act," it is late in the day.

The children continue to seem to her suspecting mind either divine or infernal, and her language to represent her dilemma. She calls their contrivance to keep her from simultaneously observing them (Miles plays the piano for her while Flora goes off to the lake) "the most divine little way to keep me quiet." "Divine?" echoes Mrs. Grose, and the governess giddily responds, "Infernal then!" (XII:271). In her desperation she is ready now to speak out, to say, "Miss Jessel" to Flora, and point to the opposite bank of the lake in triumph and even "gratitude" that the apparition is there and the demonstrative moment has arrived, but the child seems to see nothing and says to Mrs. Grose, who also sees nothing, "Take me away from *her*!" (XII:281).

There is no more to be hoped for from Flora except Mrs. Grose's report that the hysterical child utters undenotable "horrors" (XII:289). The governess is now alone with Miles, hoping to extract his confession, though assailed by a "perverse horror" of her own efforts: "For what did it consist of but the obtrusion of the idea of grossness and guilt on a small helpless creature who had been for me a revelation of the possibilities of beautiful intercourse?" (XII:301). But the illumination passes. She asks him if he stole her letter, and Quint's "white face of damnation" (XII:303) appears to her at the window once more just as the boy admits that he has taken it. And at last she asks him what he did at school and gets only his vague reply that he "said things . . . to those I liked" (XII:306–307). Like Flora's unrecorded "horrors," these undisclosed utterances make another absence, another gap in the story. Whatever they were, the confession of words rather than deeds sounds so meager a criminality that the governess swings, for the last time, away from her conviction of his depravity and feels "the appalling alarm of his being perhaps innocent. It was for an instant confounding and bottomless, for if he *were* innocent what then on earth was I?" (XII:307).

It is *her* innocence, finally, that has, perhaps, converted itself to its opposite. The story ends on a note of alterity. When she points to the wraith she is sure she sees at the window and clasps the terrified child to her breast, Miles cries, "Peter Quint—you devil!"—but the alternate reading of his words identifies *her* as the devil he names at last. She believes that she has triumphed; it is "a tribute to her devotion"; she has named the "hideous author of our woe" (XII:308) and become the child's savior. But she herself is almost identified, in the Miltonic phrase, with the devil himself. And perhaps she has been herself named the "author" (like the literary "author" to whom the word must also apply) of the woe she has created by story-making.[15]

· 9 ·

The Language of Silence:
What Maisie Knew

THAT MAISIE IS a *female* child is, of course, important. James himself, in his New York Edition preface, noted how inevitable this choice was: "My light vessel of consciousness, swaying in such a draught, couldn't be with verisimilitude a rude little boy; since, beyond the fact that little boys are never so 'present,' the sensibility of the female young is indubitably, for early youth, the greater, and my plan would call, on the part of my protagonist, for 'no end' of sensibility." (2:1159). In reflecting on *The Portrait of a Lady,* he had already defended the special "value" of "the image of the young feminine nature," and quoted George Eliot's "In these frail vessels is borne onward through the ages the treasure of human affection" (2:1077), echoed in this remark. James seems to value Maisie's femaleness because it guarantees greater sensibility as well as innocence than an equivalent young male consciousness. His choice of the more vulnerable "frail vessel" also serves again the function of dramatizing his character's embattled potentiality, that resource of human possibility which is more helplessly subject to the manipulative "plots" of others in the case of a woman than of a man.

Sallie Sears has called *What Maisie Knew* a latent pornographic novel, comparing Maisie's situation, in which she is repeatedly seized and outraged but bounces back to receive new assaults, to that of Pauline Réage's character "O" in *The Story of O.*[1] What is certainly true is that the extremity of her helplessness and her readiness to submit and respond to her victimizing manipulators is most representatively a female condition. James's choice of the sex of his protagonist is strongly motivated, I think, by the appropriateness with which a girl more than a boy illustrates his general idea of the character who is thrown into the midst of competing plots. Maisie, more completely than any of his heroines, is the mere "shuttlecock"

243

tossed to and fro by her parents and stepparents, who use her in their contests with one another; she has *no* power to choose her location, to choose whose child she will be. That is, of course, until the very end, when she makes a momentous choice between the alternatives presented to her, having "grown up" to see the necessity of surrendering her hope that she might escape choosing. Such a submission to limitation is inevitable for this particular little girl, whose qualified options are displayed in the selfish interest in her— the insistence on writing her into their own story-telling—offered by everyone who might be expected to love her disinterestedly.

What Maisie Knew is a history of the emergence of consciousness into the condition of adult language. In "growing up" Maisie must achieve the conceptual—that is, verbal—awareness which will provide her with a selfhood framed by her culture's ideas of female character and destiny. But the novel, which takes Maisie from childhood to the brink of young womanhood, exhibits her struggle not so much to *acquire* these forms and codes as to resist them; in this resistance, in her fidelity to a presocial silence, she resembles James's older heroines who, as we have seen, hold such forms and codes at bay as best they can. Like Catherine Sloper, Maisie, in this later short work, will find herself surrounded by vociferating others who threaten her with their several species of rhetoric and narrative conception. *What Maisie Knew* is, like *Washington Square,* a dramatization of its heroine's resistance to the various styles by which the other characters express their ideas of personal definition and destiny. Dramatized by a complex reiteration of verbal references to silence and speech is her resistance to language itself—language which is inevitably an expression of the social designs which confine the essential self yet ultimately provide it with its only mode of mature being. Her attachment to silence, like Catherine's, is the expression of her vain effort to preserve potentiality against its necessary enemies.

James is, of course, the chief of these writers of story who surround Maisie, for though he declares his desire to locate his story in the child's perceptions, he insists upon the necessity of their translation into his own narrative voice:

> Small children have many more perceptions than they have terms to translate them; their vision is at any moment much richer, their apprehension even constantly stronger, than their prompt, their

at all producible, vocabulary. Amusing therefore as it might at the first blush have seemed to restrict myself in this case to the terms as well as the experience, it became at once plain that such an attempt would fail. Maisie's terms accordingly play their part—since her simpler conclusions quite depend on them; but our own commentary constantly attends and amplifies. (2:1160–1161)

The language of James's narrator thus seems to improve upon Maisie. "We simply take advantage of these things better than she herself" (2:1160–1161), James concludes.

But this choice, seemingly a technical convenience, has a thematic effect. James's narrator, this invisible adult—and probably masculine—presence, has a significant role to play, as James's narrative presences have had before. Like the similarly more sophisticated, even patronizing, narrative persona of *Washington Square*, he has lessons to learn in the process. Like that earlier Jamesian persona, who comes to acknowledge the mysterious force of Catherine's inarticulate nature, Maisie's interpreter will discover himself inadequate to compass his heroine's silent knowledge, and the reader will make the same discovery. In his respect for Maisie's very lack of interpretive means there is, of course, a reminder of James's responsiveness to impressionism. Maisie is the ultimate impressionist, dependent upon her immediate experiences, unequipped with sense-making, story-making conceptions, for worse or for better. If she has story conceptions to apply to what surrounds her they are only infantile ones, as when it is said, "Only a drummer-boy in a ballad or a story could have been so in the thick of the fight. She was taken into the confidence of passions on which she fixed just the stare she might have had for images bounding across the wall in the slide of a magic lantern" (XI:9).

The voice which addresses us in the novel is James's wittiest, abounding in sophisticated imagery by which appearance is converted into social statement. Its function is to remind us to use our adult perceptions in going beyond what Maisie can see—or say. Maisie herself, for example, could hardly describe her mother, Ida Farrange, as "some gorgeous idol" with "huge painted eyes—they were like Japanese lanterns swung under festal arches," or say that her "face was like an illuminated garden, turnstile and all, for the frequentation of which [her lover] had his season ticket" (XI:143, 144). This is not to observe merely that James is making a conspicuous distinction between the most accomplished speech of adults and Maisie's own speech. There is a separation between Maisie's infantile narrative mind and ours. It makes her curiously *unutterable* knowledge about the adults she "knows" a thing to which we have no access. James implies, in this novel, I think, a distinction which separates *all* language from knowledge more primitive or pure. Maisie is originally helpless to "know" the story enacted about her, lacking concepts and terms to apply to it. But it would be wrong to think that we are improving on Maisie's ignorance by our superior verbal or constructive powers. This would be to define her condition negatively, and James wants us to consider doing the contrary.

Maisie's ignorance of "facts" about her elders makes for narrative ellipses which the narrator does not directly fill—giving us none of the scenes that might reveal the exact nature of their relations with one another. Even when she overhears their conversations or bears their messages, she is unable to interpret these, though her elders are not chary of mutual interpretation. As a witness to the expressive verbal interchanges of Maisie's quartet of "parents"—her natural mother and father, Beale and Ida Farrange, and the stepparents who themselves become a couple, Miss Overmore-Beale and Sir Claude—she has, one might think, an interpreter in Mrs. Wix. Mrs. Wix's interpretations, however, are a pastiche of conventional formulas—melodramatic or sentimental, like the formulations of Mrs. Penniman in *Washington Square*. Her view of Sir Claude is straight out of romantic fiction, most of the time; Maisie is only picking up her governess's language when she thinks that "He looked . . . quite as Mrs. Wix, in the long stories she told her pupil, always described the lovers of her distressed beauties . . . 'the perfect gentleman and strikingly handsome' " (XI:61). Mrs. Wix's consciousness is stuffed with trite conceptions of literary plot and characterization. As the narrator observes, "She knew swarms of stories, mostly those of the novels she had read; relating them with a memory that never faltered and a wealth of detail that was Maisie's delight. They were all about love and beauty and countesses and wickedness. Her conversation was practically an endless narrative, a great garden of romance" (XI:27). These fictions fail, ultimately, to contain Maisie's experiences. When she meets her father's mistress, the narrator says, "The child had been in thousands of stories—all Mrs. Wix's and her own, to say nothing of the richest romances of French Elise—but she had never been in such a story as this" (XI:175).

But Maisie is threatened as much by the governess's "moral sense" as by her banal literary imagination. Mrs. Wix shares with that other governess embattled against evil spirits (the governess of "The Turn of the Screw") a sense of moral mission which threatens Maisie's free being as much as the cynical manipulations of the other adults. Maisie must discover that nothing can be less like "the Arabian Nights" than the real Countess to whom her father introduces her, just as she must surrender a view of Sir Claude as the Prince Charming of fairy tale. But she must also discover that in acquiring a "moral sense" she will still lose. Even Mrs. Wix is the enemy of Maisie's free spirit, for Mrs. Wix only differs from the rest of Maisie's mentors in offering to confine her in sentimentality and conventional morality.

Does she—or do we (sharing her ordeal of knowing)—gain or lose in coming, at last, to understand what *we* would call the "real story" about these persons? For a long while Maisie is witness enough to what the four say to one another to enable us to make certain deductions, yet she does not make them. And the narrator is careful not to fill in the omissions that are created by Maisie's ignorance. James observed in the preface that his "design . . . would be to make and to keep her so limited consciousness the very field of [his] picture while at the same time guarding with care the integrity of the objects represented" (2:1159). Though we feel in possession of the facts of which Maisie is oblivious—the technical facts of sexual liaisons, in particular—the narrative does not directly supply these. Though we are aware of vanity and greed and lust disguising themselves in various self-justifying ways, Maisie's ignorance of what her elders "mean" when they speak to each other makes for "gaps and voids" which the narrator does not directly fill by explanation or by exhibiting scenes out of her sight and hearing. James says,

> The infant mind would at the best leave great gaps and voids; so that with a systematic surface possibly beyond reproach we should nevertheless fail of clearness of sense. I should have to stretch the matter to what my wondering witness materially and inevitably *saw*, a great deal of which quantity she either wouldn't understand at all or would quite misunderstand—and on those lines, only on those, my task would be prettily cut out. To that then, I settled—to the question of giving it *all*, the whole situation surrounding her, but of giving it only through the occasions and

connexions of her proximity and her attention; only as it might pass before her and appeal to her, as it might touch her and affect her, for better or worse, for perceptive gain or perceptive loss: so that we fellow-witnesses, we not more invited but only more expert critics, should feel in strong possession of it.   (2:1160)

Of course, James expects that we will know what goes on around Maisie. Like himself, we have long been accustomed to putting together fragmented appearances, understanding sexual relationships without scenic exhibition, whether we are observing the behavior of real persons or reading novels. We are all too ready to translate inexplicit utterances if they do not contain such a term, for example, as "adultery," a word that does not appear in the text till very late. Yet Maisie's blindness may act as a reminder of a certain alterity even in the most indisputable factuality. The gaps in her knowledge permit not only Mrs. Wix's ideas—romantic or moralistic—to represent possible truths, but they give room for something else, Maisie's "wonder" (which is her unformulated appreciation of all of these persons), to have its own status. They permit such leaps of belief as she makes when she insists that her "unspeakable" mother is "good" or when she challenges one of her mother's temporary lovers to love Ida always. And this is the meaning of that "continuity of resistance" which James claims for her:

> Successfully to resist (to resist, that is, the strain of observation and the assault of experience) what would that be, on the part of so young a person, but to remain fresh, and still fresh, and to have even a freshness to communicate?—the case being with Maisie to the end that she treats her friends to the rich little spectacle of objects embalmed in her wonder. She wonders, in other words, to the end, to the death—the death of her childhood, properly speaking; after which (with the inevitable shift, sooner of later, of her point of view) her situation will change and become another affair.   (2:1161)

James's word, "wonder," is meant to describe a wordless state, though not without powers of communication, a state of resistant apprehension which escapes language and the conceptions it derives from. What Maisie knows at the start of her experience is a knowledge, however, that, like Wordsworth's growing child, she will be forced to surrender as language encroaches upon wonder.

Her knowledge, it may also be said, is supremely synchronic, an unprejudiced appreciation of moments uninfected by prior experience or by anticipation, that "lively sense of the immediate which is the very air of a child's mind" in which "the past, on each occasion, became for her as indistinct as the future." In this, too, her state can be compared to that of James's other singularly uninitiated characters, about whom I have already spoken. In a contest of wills demanding from her affiliation or narrative subscription, she remains, for as long as she can, unaffiliated, open to every possibility. "She was at the age for which all stories are true and all conceptions are stories. The actual was the absolute, the present alone was vivid" (XI:14). But the fact that the narrative itself is nothing else than *a* particular story represents the very separation between ourselves and Maisie which promises to disappear with that "inevitable shift" James speaks of.

At the start of her parents' divorce, sent back and forth between them with messages of insult, Maisie appeared "either from extreme cunning or extreme stupidity . . . not to take things in" (XI:15). Words reach their most undenotable futility in the abusiveness of name-calling which she is forced to hear—and at first tries to transmit. The words are imaged by James as toys to which adults give reality, the toys Maisie *doesn't* play with as she plays with her doll, the games she cannot master like the games Sir Claude brings to the nursery. This is declared in the opening of the first chapter when Maisie has difficulty grasping her father's "sufferings":

> It was only after some time that she was able to attach to the picture of her father's sufferings, and more particularly to her nurse's manner about them, the meaning for which these things had waited. By the time she had grown sharper . . . she found in her mind a collection of images and echoes to which meanings were attachable—images and echoes kept for her in the childish dusk, the dim closet, the high drawers, like games she wasn't yet big enough to play. The great strain meanwhile was that of carrying by the right end the things her father said about her mother—things mostly indeed that Moddle, on a glimpse of them, as if they had been complicated toys or difficult books, took out of her hands and put away in the closet. A wonderful assortment of objects of this kind she was to discover there later, all tumbled up too with the things, shuffled

into the same receptacle, that her mother had said about her father.   (XI:11–12)

As time goes on, some of the words take on meaning; the toys come to life, "the stiff dolls on the dusky shelves began to move their arms and legs; old forms and phrases began to have a sense that frightened her." It is then that Maisie closes her eyes and lips. "She would forget everything, she would repeat nothing" (XI:15). Her mother will accuse her of never opening her mouth to her, while chattering to Sir Claude "like a dozen magpies" (XI:89), but Sir Claude himself finds her the "perfection of a dunce" (XI:157) when he quizzes her about her mother's friend, "the Captain," encountered in Kensington Gardens.

Her elders, in contrast, are vocal, though in varying degrees. The gentlemanly Sir Claude is at least decorously silent when Maisie's mother calls him "an awful fraud and an idle beast and a sorry dunce"; unlike Maisie's father, "he never said a word to her against her mother—he only remained dumb and discouraged in the face of her ladyship's own overtopping earnestness" (XI:88). Mrs. Wix is even more closely allied to Maisie in her preference for silence, and Maisie's first parting from her is compared with the "screwed up intensity" of a dental extraction: "It was dreadfully silent, as it had been when her tooth was taken out; Mrs. Wix had on that occasion grabbed her hand and they had clung to each other with the frenzy of their determination not to scream. Maisie, at the dentist's, had been heroically still, but just when she felt most anguish had become aware of an audible shriek on the part of her companion, a spasm of stifled sympathy." Their parting hug "fortunately left nothing to say, for the poor woman's want of words at such an hour seemed to fall in with her want of everything"; Mrs. Wix is contrasted here with her rival, Miss Overmore, who "had been thoroughly audible and voluble; her protest had rung out bravely and she had declared that something—her pupil didn't know exactly what—was a regular wicked shame" (XI:29–30). Mrs. Wix's inarticulateness, even her poorly written letters, further silenced when kept from Maisie, becomes a language which, like Maisie's silence, is superior to the speech of others. Mrs. Wix's "very silence became after this one of the largest elements of Maisie's consciousness; it proved a warm and habitable air, into which the child penetrated further than she ever dared to mention to her companions" (XI:42).

In these "companions" Maisie tends to nullify speech by rendering adult realities unmentionable in her presence; they are literally "unspeakable." It is as though she enforces silence, a sacred language, upon these profane persons. When her father's friends pinch her calves and call them toothpicks, she knows that she is "deficient in something that would meet the general desire." The word suppressed out of the text may be "fat." "She found out what it was, it was a congenital tendency to the production of a substance to which Moddle, her nurse, gave a short ugly name, a name painfully associated at dinner with the part of the joint that she didn't like" (XI:10). What the calf pinchers really find wanting in Maisie's young legs is even less mentionable, however, and not so easily identified with a substance—sexuality, a special sense of "desire" that Maisie does not yet know.

Yet Maisie can sometimes make her own sense of these ellipses. "What do people mean?" her mother asks concerning insinuations touching the poor but attractive Miss Overmore. Maisie "didn't know what people meant, but she knew very soon the names of all [Miss Overmore's] sisters. She privately wondered, moreover, though she never asked, about the awful poverty, of which her companion also never spoke" (XI:16). "Wonder," as already noted, is James's term for Maisie's peculiar form of wordless knowing, her "embalming"—that is, preserving—Miss Overmore as an object of sympathy. Later on, Maisie will wonder what the "idea" is that keeps Sir Claude from meeting her new stepmother and herself at the Exhibition. It seems that he doesn't want the child "mixed up"—for which Maisie herself can supply the synonym she has often heard without understanding, "compromised." Her knowledge is just sufficient and just insufficient enough for her to be able to offer herself, as she often does, regardless of meaning—"Whatever it means, I don't in the least mind *being* mixed" (XI:168–169).

Maisie's grown-up "companions" generally debase the sacred character of silence. They use it to conceal what for them does have a name. Maisie's mother, by Sir Claude's account, now lets him do what he wants so that she may do what she wants, but Maisie is rebuffed when she asks, "What may that be?"—"I wouldn't tell you for the whole world" (XI:113). When they confine themselves to gestures and looks—Miss Overmore's "unmistakable language of a pair of eyes of a deep, dark grey" (XI:18) or the flashing of Beale's beautiful teeth—it is because they decline to utter the words in their minds. And the silence they ask from Maisie is their kind, not hers, as when Sir Claude, though he may want her to tell him about the Captain, enjoins her also not to tell her mother that he sees Mrs. Beale. Maisie "set[s] her teeth like an Indian captive" (XI:68), but her silence expresses her fidelity, not his duplicity.

Concealed language, hidden by either false silence or lying speech, is found together with true silence in the two great rejection scenes during which Maisie is cast off, successively, by her father and her mother. The first begins with her encounter with Beale and the Countess at the Exhibition, in a "bewilderment not so much of sound as of silence," when she understands what is said no more than the "indistinguishable address" her father throws at the cab driver. She reflects that "she at this point would have put a question to him had not the silence into which he charmed her or scared her—she could scarcely tell which" prevented her, while he "trembled too much to speak, and this had the effect of making her, with an emotion which, though it had begun to throb in an instant, was by no means all dread, conform to his portentous hush . . . She neither knew exactly what he had done nor what he was doing; she could only, altogether impressed and rather proud, vibrate with the sense that he had jumped up to do something and that she had as quickly become a part of it" (XI:173–175).

It is one of those moments of truth to which Maisie is attuned, the reflex of her capacity for sympathy which fills the gaps of her knowledge with its own substance. When she finds herself tenderly held on her father's knee and he shows his shining teeth and lets her inhale the fragrance of his beard, she comprehends "his difficulty in being specific to her about anything. She had such possibilities of vibration, of response, that it needed nothing more than this to make up to her in fact for omissions . . . What was this but splendid too—this still directer goodness of her father and this unexampled shining solitude with him, out of which everything had dropped but that he was papa and that he was magnificent?" (XI:180).

But immediately his mendacious speech conveys unuttered messages. Her father asks her to go with him and at the same time insists that she really doesn't want to. "She understood as well as if he had spoken that what he wanted, hang it, was that she should let him off with all the honours—with all the appearance of virtue and sacrifice on his side" (XI:187). She breaks down momentarily at the prospect of never seeing him again, and at first refuses to give him

up. Beale merely looks at her, then, "showing her a strained gri-
mace, a perfect parade of all his teeth, in which it seemed to her she
could read the disgust he didn't quite like to express"—a menacing,
sharkish silence. Then, as Mrs. Cuddon steps into the room, he
simply lies, "She won't come" (XI:192, 193).

Her mother's last message, at Folkestone, is couched, like her
father's in a misleading code, "profuse and prolonged . . . [but] not
exhaustively lucid . . . a muddle of inconsequent things. It was as if
she had asked outright what better proof could have been wanted of
her goodness and her greatness than just this marvellous consent to
give up what she had so cherished" (XI:217–218). It is a message
doubly deceptive, an ambiguous and obscure scramble of selfishness, distaste, vanity. She avows her own goodness, misusing
Maisie's tribute of that word: "I *am* good—I'm crazily, I'm crimi-
nally good. But it won't do for *you* any more, and if I've ceased to
contend with him, and with you too . . . it's for reasons that you'll
understand one of these days but too well—one of these days when
I hope you'll know what it is to have lost a mother" (XI:219). In her
evasion and insinuation she parodies true silence: "I spare you
everything, as I always have; though I daresay you know things that,
if I did (I mean if I knew them) would make me—well, no matter!
You're old enough at any rate to know there are a lot of things I
don't say that I easily might; though it would do me good, I assure
you, to have spoken my mind for once in my life" (XI:221).

"Good" and "mother," the two significant terms in Ida's speech,
are prime illustrations of the unreliability of language. Maisie has
asserted a noumenous sense of her mother's goodness, the fruit of
her illumination in Kensington Gardens, and she will retain it
despite her mother's misappropriation. She has felt her father's
"directer goodness" when he held her on his knee at Mrs.
Cuddon's. But nothing the narrator can tell *our* adult minds gives
evidence of what this means, and we can only feel irony when
Maisie's parents claim goodness themselves. The second term,
"mother," suffers protean revision throughout the novel. When
Mrs. Wix first appears, Maisie is touched, we are told, in a spot
"that had never yet been reached . . . Maisie knew later what it
was, though doubtless she couldn't have made a statement of it."
But Mrs. Wix is represented by the word "mother," previously
without adequate referent, "something Miss Overmore was not,
something (strangely, confusingly) that mamma was even less"

(XI:23–24). "Mother" and "father," also, are terms that change places along with the changing positions of Maisie's real and step-parents. "He's my husband, if you please, and I'm his little wife. So *now* we'll see who's your little Mother!" (XI:51), cries the new Mrs. Beale as she snatches Maisie from Mrs. Wix. Previously she had found her definition as Maisie's governess more than simply appropriate. It had "made it right" for her to be part of the household of Maisie's papa. Maisie infers that mamma's new friend might therefore become her tutor, similarly to "make it right," but is reproved: "I'm a real governess" (XI:40). But what is "real" here? Sir Claude, the lover of Maisie's mother, is what Miss Overmore is to her father—an inadmissible symmetry which the terminological discrimination only hides.

With her acquisition of a new title, Mrs. Beale is something different from her former self as Miss Overmore. "Shall *you* be different?" Maisie asks, and is answered, "As your father's wedded wife? Utterly!" The changes in titles and roles make a riddle of realities which have no independent stability, a condition stated like a riddle: "If she was her father's wife, she was not her own governess" (XI:53–54). When Miss Overmore becomes Mrs. Beale, she has "no connexion at all with anybody who had once mended underclothing and had meals in the nursery" (XI:123). The sense of "daughter" changes along with "mother" when, at Boulogne, Mrs. Beale tells Mrs. Wix, "Dear lady, please attend to my daughter." The narrator reflects, "She was still, as a result of so many parents, a daughter to somebody even after papa and mamma were to all intents dead" (XI:302). Later, Sir Claude proposes the new "unconventional family" they might make together: "She *is* your mother now, Mrs. Beale, by what has happened, and I, in the same way, I'm your father" (XI:334). But Maisie, called "an abominable little horror" (XI:359) by *this* mother, even as she has been called "a horror" and "a dreadful dismal deplorable little thing" (XI:225) by her original one, by this time knows that these name-callers have no name she can rely upon.

Mrs. Beale exactly reverses the truth of things when she calls Maisie a "hideous little hypocrite" and speaks of the "years that I've slaved to make you love me and deludedly believed you did" (XI:359). "Love" is the most unstable term of all. Even "intimacy," as enjoyed by her father's visitors, baffles Maisie: "Even Lisette, even Mrs. Wix had never, she felt, in spite of hugs and tears, been so intimate with her as so many persons at present were with Mrs. Beale and as so many others of old had been with Mrs. Farrange" (XI:56). Adult intimacy, with its inadmissible meanings, is ironically compared with Maisie's uncritical love. Unspecified was the "certain sentiment" about which Maisie had inquired on a return to her father's house when she asks Miss Overmore, "Did papa like you just the same while I was gone?" But her father, roaring, says, "Why you little donkey, when you're away what have I left to do but just to love her?" And snatching the child from him, his mistress declares, "I shall make him understand that if he ever again says anything as horrid as that to you I shall carry you straight off and we'll go and live somewhere together and be good quiet little girls." The only really good quiet little girl "couldn't quite make out why her father's speech had been horrid, since it only expressed that appreciation which their companion herself had of old described as 'immense' " (XI:31).

The changeable loves of adults are reflected in their attitudes toward Maisie, who is alternately seized and cast away, and after it has suited them each to claim her furiously from the other it later suits each to accuse the other of leaving her too long on the complainer's hands. Love plays at puss-in-the-corner with its opposites, hate and fear. Maisie's mother is said to be "passionately in love" (XI:68) with Sir Claude, yet her attitude toward him strangely resembles her attitude toward the previous husband she now detests: "It was because mamma hated papa that she used to want to know bad things of him; but if at present she wanted to know the same of Sir Claude it was from the opposite motive" (XI:70). Sir Claude, for his part, admits that he married Ida because he was afraid of her, and as soon as he is in love with Mrs. Beale he is afraid of her, too—as he would be of Maisie herself, if she were older.

Maisie's own idea of love is independent of verbal mutations and annihilations of meaning. When her father tells her, in their last talk, that "the other pair" are "awful," she says, "I don't care—not a bit . . . It doesn't prevent them from loving me." Her father gives definition to this "love"—you're a jolly good pretext . . . for their game." But Maisie gives her own value to what she receives: "That's all the more reason . . . for their being kind to me" (XI:188–189). And as though to plead for an impossible semantic stability she begs the Captain to love her mother always. In the end, Maisie comes to see through all these loves of the others for each other and for herself. She becomes capable of hate for Mrs. Beale (who had been her "first passion"; XI:22) and is "in love" with Sir Claude in the newly learned and unstable sense of adults.

But the most obvious verbal modulation is that which overtakes the title word, "knowledge." What Maisie knows is, at the start, different from that forbidden knowledge adults possess: "She had grown up among things as to which her foremost knowledge was that she was never to ask about them . . . life was like a long, long corridor with rows of closed doors. She had learned that at these doors it was wise not to knock." She played at the adult game of mystery meanwhile, in child-game terms, attempting with her doll "the air of shading off, like her mother, into the unknowable," since "there were at any rate things she couldn't tell even a French doll"; once she even snapped at the doll, in her mother's tone, "Find out for yourself!" (XI:33–34).

Her "finding out" is played off against her intermittent acquisition of formal knowledge, quite a different thing. When her governess becomes her stepmother, instruction in "subjects" ceases at her father's house. Mrs. Wix's attempts to "make up" at her mother's are inadequate, too, but other knowledge arrives there:

> The year . . . rounded itself as a receptacle of retarded knowledge . . . They were surrounded with subjects they must take at a rush and perpetually getting into the attitude of triumphant attack. They had certainly no idle hours, and the child went to bed each night as tired as from a long day's play. This had begun from the moment of their reunion, begun with all Mrs. Wix had to tell her young friend of the reasons of her ladyship's extraordinary behavior at the very first.

But it is not only such explanations that constitute her enlightenment. "Her lessons these first days and indeed for long after seemed to be all about Sir Claude" (XI:66–68).

This was not so much the result of Mrs. Wix's information as because of her own growing love for him, which Mrs. Wix shares. As they study the intricacies of the games he has brought to the nursery, "the answer on winter nights to the puzzle of cards and counters and little bewildering pamphlets was just to draw up to the fire and talk about him; and if the truth must be told this edifying interchange constituted for the time the little girl's chief education." These fireside conversations took them sometimes beyond the "old-fashioned conscience, the dingy decencies of Maisie's simple instructress," who would sigh, "It isn't as if you didn't already know everything, is it, love?" But what Maisie knew was not mere gossip or even factuality. The text gives us none of the particularities about Sir Claude that Mrs. Wix might have transmitted. "What the pupil already knew was indeed rather taken for granted than expressed, but it performed the useful function of transcending all textbooks and supplanting all studies" (XI:73).

Maisie's characteristic knowledge is separate from the knowledge conveyed by statements. To take another example, there is her knowledge about her mother's new friend, Mr. Perriam: "It was singular perhaps . . . that Maisie never put a question about Mr. Perriam, and it was still more singular that by the end of the week she knew all she didn't ask . . . It was extraordinary the number of things that, still without a question, Maisie knew by the time her stepfather came back from Paris" (XI:93–94). This knowledge is not only acquired but it is communicable without words: "Sir Claude never came into [the nursery] without telling its occupants that they were the nicest people in the house—a remark which always led them to say to each other 'Mr. Perriam!' as loud as ever compressed lips and enlarged eyes could make them articulate" (XI:96).

Silence continues to express Maisie's deepest responses when Mrs. Wix urges Sir Claude to detach himself from Mrs. Beale. Maisie has a "sharpened sense of spectatorship," of watching "a game of football," as she listens to their argument, "flattening her nose against a pane of glass . . . while she waited for the effect of Mrs. Wix's eloquence." The result is Sir Claude's promise never to forsake her. At this, Maisie "cried without sound" as though even sobs might express less than her silence. And her sublimity communicating itself, Sir Claude joins her, "his tears . . . as silently flowing. Presently she heard a loud sob from Mrs. Wix—Mrs. Wix was the only one who made a noise" (XI:107–108). Nevertheless, Sir Claude will soon resort to language at its most mendacious when he tells her that he does not see Mrs. Beale.

Although Mrs. Beale takes up the challenge to repair the deficiencies of Maisie's education with "courses at institutions—on subjects" (XI:133), these are not forthcoming, and Maisie finds that as regards formal education she "was to feel henceforth as if she were flattening her nose upon the hard window-pane of the sweet-shop of knowledge" (XI:137)—a repetition of the image of her silent attendance at adult argument. Such argument she listens to again in Kensington Gardens when her mother threatens her husband, "Should you like her to know, my dear?" and Sir Claude breaks out, "You damned old b---!" (XI:145), the typographical suppression standing for the most abusive of articulations.

Now, Maisie knows that Sir Claude does see Mrs. Beale, though "how and when and where . . . were just what Maisie was not to know." (XI:159) "It was in the nature of things to be none of a small child's business, even when a small child had from the first been deluded into a fear that she might be only too much initiated." Still, "patient little silences and intelligent little looks could be rewarded by delightful little glimpses" (XI:161) of the relationship between her stepfather and her stepmother. Her formal education makes progress, now, by means of books prescribed and supplied by Sir Claude and lectures attended with Mrs. Beale—as though her growing knowledge will soon be expressible in language.

At Folkestone with Sir Claude her learning accelerates. "Maisie had known all along a great deal, but never so much as she was to know from this moment on and as she learned in particular during the couple of days that she was to hang in the air, as it were, over the sea which represented in breezy blueness and with a summer charm a crossing of more spaces than the Channel" (XI:202). The crossing of spaces, of ellipses, Maisie is about to make is clearly from childhood, with its inexpressible knowledge, to the knowledge of adulthood spelled out in conventions and language. "She had ever of course in her mind fewer names than conceptions, but it was only with this drawback that she now made out her companion's absences to have for their ground that he was the lover of her stepmother and that the lover of her stepmother could scarce logically pretend to a superior right to look after her. Maisie had by this time embraced the implication of a kind of natural divergence between lovers and little girls" (XI:204). The word "lover" appears in the text now for the first time, and gone is Maisie's transcendent unawareness of "divergence." She is ready to learn what "amour" means, and "adultery"—a "crime branded in the Bible," as Mrs. Wix says.

Her knowledge of her mother's "goodness" is giving way. Sir Claude's remarks upon his wife's habit of rolling a ten-pound note into a ball makes her conscious "of how immeasurably more after all he knew about mamma than she," though with Sir Claude himself there lingered still "a sense and a sound in everything to which words had nothing to add" (XI:228-229). For Mrs. Wix, Ida's one saving grace is that she has sent them "a decent person"—herself— to stand against Mrs. Beale, "the worst person of all" (XI:247-248). Mrs. Wix's moral distinctions are precise. The letter from Maisie's father to Mrs. Beale confirming his "desertion" does not set his wife free to live with Sir Claude. When he leaves Boulogne to join her, Maisie gives him her old wordless intensity; she "chose the soft method of silence to satisfy him; the silence that after all the battles of talk was the best balm she could offer his wounds" (XI:262). But she and Mrs. Wix continue their educative communing and "what [Maisie] had essentially done, these days, had been to read the unspoken into the spoken; so that thus, with accumulations, it had become more definite to her that the unspoken was unspeakably the completeness of the sacrifice of Mrs. Beale" (XI:269).

Maisie resists: "Why shouldn't we be four? . . . Why is it immorality?" (XI:271-272). She protests, "She's beautiful and I love her!" (XI:276), and when Mrs. Wix points out that this lovely one is as bad as Maisie's father, who "pays" the Countess, Maisie demands, "Doesn't he pay you too?" Everyone pays or is paid. All morality is as much a system of payment as immorality. "Oh you incredible little waif" (XI:277), cries Mrs. Wix, dropping, like all the others, into the language of abuse before they go home in reconciliation and silence.

So now the final stage of Maisie's education has been reached. She must acquire what Mrs. Wix' calls a "moral sense." To Mrs. Wix's demand to know whether she has one, her response, in her old language of silence, is "vague even to imbecility, and that was the first time she had appeared to practice with Mrs. Wix an inaptitude to meet her—the infirmity to which she had owed so much success with papa and mamma" (XI:279). Once she had resisted the demand that she comprehend the language of evil; now she tries to resist the language of virtue. What Maisie has preserved through silence is threatened by language at its most noble, finally. Mrs. Wix, so nearly her ally, compels upon her that system of discriminations expressed in moral distinctions, rejecting the knowledge of Maisie's which dispenses with judgment. "I did lose patience," her preceptor tells Maisie, "at how it was that without your seeming to condemn—for you didn't, you remember! you yet did seem to *know*" (XI:283-284). As the two drive out Maisie begins, we are told, to strike up an acquaintance with the moral sense, "with scarce an outward sign save her surrender to the swing of the carriage," while the coachman takes them through the rich French landscape "pointing to invisible objects and uttering unintelligible sounds . . . strict features of a social order principally devoted to language" (XI:280).

It is at this point that the narrator bursts forth with a self-identifying "I" to confess his own helplessness to record Maisie's transitions:

> Nothing more remarkable had taken place in the first heat of her own departure, no act of perception less to be overtraced by our rough method, than her vision, the rest of that Boulogne day, of the manner in which she figured. I so despair of courting her noiseless mental footsteps here that I must crudely give you my word for its being from this time forward a picture literally present to her. Mrs. Wix saw her as a little person knowing so extraordinarily much that, for the account to be taken of it, what she still didn't know would be ridiculous if it hadn't been embarrassing . . . As she was condemned to know more and more, how could it logically stop before she should know Most? It came to her in fact as they sat there on the sands that she was distinctly on the road to know Everything. She had not had governesses for nothing: what in the world had she ever done but learn and learn and learn? She looked at the pink sky with a placid forboding that she soon should have learnt All. They lingered in the flushed air till at last it turned to grey and she seemed fairly to receive new information from every brush of the breeze. By the time they moved homeward it was as if this inevitability had become for Mrs. Wix a long, tense cord, twitched by a nervous hand, on which the valued pearls of intelligence were to be neatly strung. (XI:280–282)

At this climax of her education Maisie is ready to know good and evil, as adults do—to accept language and narrative. Her newly acquired moral sensibility is even keen enough to include suspicion of her own and Mrs. Wix's sources of censure. Are they not, after all, merely jealous of Mrs. Beale's possession of Sir Claude? "Was the sum of all knowledge only to know how little in this presence one would ever reach it?" (XI:288). Maisie guarantees her moral sense by the declaration that should Mrs. Beale be unkind to him, she would "kill her," and the young and the old join in the admission that they "adore" Sir Claude. This love, no longer so sacred and inexpressible, is acknowledged by Maisie's serene, "Oh I know" (XI:289).

It is the cue for Mrs. Beale's arrival to announce her "freedom," to assume the role of "mother" with its concomitant claim of fatherhood by Sir Claude, who arrives to challenge Maisie to give up Mrs. Wix. Maisie will give up Mrs. Wix if he will give up Mrs. Beale; she is willing to dispense with both sin *and* the moral sense, though what she wants most is, simply, Sir Claude. Her choice is forced as he goes, as he must, to Mrs. Beale. She goes, of course, to Mrs. Wix, allying herself to the conventions of moral tradition, with all the intermixture of unacknowledged personal·desire and spite which even Mrs. Wix has given evidence of. There is, after all, nowhere else to go. "Oh I know," says Maisie once again. But "Mrs. Wix gave her a sidelong look. She still had room for wonder at what Maisie knew" (XI:363). The wonder is shared by the narrator who has led us to the brink of mystery, and by the reader.

· 10 ·

The Inaccessible Future:
"The Beast in the Jungle"

"THE BEAST IN THE JUNGLE" may be James's most extreme expression of the theme of human character as potentiality which cannot or will not move out into the world of action, of plot. Published in 1903, the same year as *The Ambassadors,* it bears, as will be seen, a certain relation to that novel, which arises, in a much more complicated way, from the idea of the failure to "live." But the short story is a dark fable, more abstract and pessimistic than the novel. Marcher (whose name differs from hers only by an initial letter) is the farthest James would ever go in illustrating the consequences of Isabel Archer's cult of Being; but where she is heroic in resisting the reductive expectations of others that she will enact herself in some way, he waits for his narrative in mere passive expectation, and—far from being a "marcher"—in the end is trapped in the story of his vain waiting.

It is not surprising that "The Beast in the Jungle" did not appear in one of the monthly magazines which had published most of James's fiction, short and long, but was first printed in a collection, *The Better Sort.* The idea of a man so self-preoccupied that he fails to perceive, much less appreciate, a generous woman's love is easily grasped—and repeats an important element of "The Aspern Papers." But it is difficult to imagine what magazine readers would have made of this later tale's ultimate irony as non-story. It is one of the most philosophic of James's tales—crystallizing in a fable his ideas about the self disassociated from act. Aside from the obvious moral that egotism such as Marcher's deserves punishment, there is a sense in which his bleak condition becomes universal, and his waiting has a modern existential quality, as though he were waiting for Godot.

Modern as James's depiction of static—and sterile—being is,

Hawthorne had, as in other instances, provided James with a precedent. In one of the best analyses of the story ever written, Allen Tate not only reminds the twentieth-century reader that "The Beast in the Jungle" was written at about the same time as Joyce's "The Dead," but also observes that the subject of the isolation and frustration of personality may be discovered in Poe's "William Wilson" and in a number of Hawthorne's tales of ingrown egoism.[1] Hawthorne especially, I would add, seems to have been fascinated by the paradox involved in anticipations fulfilled but unperceived or quests that end in the discovery that the treasure or secret has all along been waiting at home or within the breast of the quester—as in the case of "Ethan Brand." Marcher's discovery that his doom is nothing other than his long waiting seems a variation of Hawthorne's ironic reversals, which seem to nullify the expectation that the self is known by outer demonstration—and may be an expression of the earlier writer's use of his inherited Calvinist distrust of the record of human acts as a clue to the hidden heart. Yet Hawthorne, like James, also deplores the life that does not seek to know itself better through deeds.

In discussing the structure of James's story, Tate also offered the view that the "foreground" provided by the first two of its six sections is unjustifiably long; he pointed out that in only about twice the space James prepares for the action of *The Ambassadors*. I want to argue the contrary, however. This prelude, far from being excessive, has great pertinence to the rest of the tale. It is appropriate that even before the question of his future is broached, John Marcher finds himself in a limbo from which the sense of the *past* has departed. By his own defect of memory, rather than by that narrative contrivance which excludes the sense of germinal beginning from the stories of Isabel Archer or Lambert Strether, he is launched upon a story which elides its own origins. Even the narrator's opening remark—"What determined the speech that startled him in the course of their encounter hardly matters" (XVII:61)—participates in a mood in which beginnings are as irretrievable and felt to be dispensable as endings will be seen to be unreachable.

The meeting of Marcher and May Bartram takes place in an ancient country house, a palace of the past with a mythical-sounding name that suggests the end of time—Weatherend (that is, the place where weather, or change, ends; or "*whether* [or not] end," the end of choices). In its numerous rooms are gathered "pictures, heirlooms, treasures of all the arts," to an extent or value such as to defeat any "dream of acquisition" and to make Marcher feel "disconcerted" as much by those who "knew too much" as by those who "knew nothing" (XVII:61–62). The house, with its collection that exceeds the dreams of the collector, recalls Poynton, that failed achievement of the mind which desires to assemble and retain the past. As though to recall that earlier house and its treasures, we learn, quite gratuitously, that its mistress is "the widowed mother of the new successor to the property [who] had succeeded—thanks to a high tone and a high temper—in not forfeiting [like Mrs. Gereth] the supreme position at the great house" (XVII:75). The past of the "things" of Weatherend—which he cannot hope to possess—overwhelms Marcher: "The great rooms caused so much poetry and history to press upon him that he needed some straying apart to feel in a proper relation with them" (XVII:62). It is just as he is about to make this difficult effort that he encounters May. Unlike himself, she understands Weatherend; she is a functionary skilled in explaining its history, able to "answer questions about the dates of the building, the styles of the furniture, the favourite haunts of the ghost" (XVII:63). It is her task to conserve memory.

Marcher's encounter with May reveals to him that the past is something he either doesn't remember or invents. His very first sight of her strikes the note of something lost of which the outcome is obscure. Her face, "a reminder, yet not quite a remembrance . . . affected him as the sequel of something of which he had lost the beginning. He knew it, and for the time quite welcomed it as a continuation, but didn't know what it continued." The start of the "thread" of narrative continuity—beginning, middle, end—is hidden from him. May, it is clear, hasn't lost the thread, though "she wouldn't give it back to him . . . without some putting forth of his hand for it" (XVI:62). As it turns out, it is she who not only remembers the significant past but achieves foreknowledge of the end Marcher is unable to guess. But even as regards the past, she will not, it is clear to him this early, simply hand over her own vision of connectedness. He must reach for it, must make some effort to gain it himself.

Marcher senses only vaguely that in the interval since their first meeting she has suffered "one way and another" (XVI:63)—yet he does not then—or ever—learn the early chapters of *her* story. And, since the narrator will give us only such knowledge as this center of consciousness himself possesses, Marcher's own lack of curiosity robs the reader of a portion of May's history, of *her* private tale. Marcher's masculine indifference to a separate female continuity predicts the disinterest he will exhibit throughout their coming relationship. Unconsciously perhaps, he already sees her as ripe for some sort of exploitation; he perceives her to be a mere dependent in the house and finds that this perception "satisfied [him] without in the least his knowing why" (XVII:63).

In making a story of his relationship with May, he at once proves himself inadequate— for what story can proceed upon its course without a sense that it starts somewhere? He is unable to achieve a clear sense of his own beginning with her; uncertain if "any contact between them in the past would have had no importance," or why, then, "his actual impression of her should so seem to have so much," he dismisses the problem, existentially, with the thought "that in such a life as they all appeared to be leading for the moment one could but take things as they came" (XVII:63). His efforts at recollection are ludicrously off the mark. He first thinks, as he hears her voice, that "the gap was filled up and the missing link supplied," and rejoices in being able to remove her "advantage" and subdue the irony he senses in her air of knowing more than he; he believes that they met in Rome seven years earlier when he had been with the Pembles. But May corrects him: it had been Naples, *ten* years before, and he had been with the Boyers. There *had* been an incident of thunderstorm that had driven the party into an excavation for shelter, but it had been at Pompeii and not the Palace of the Caesars. He is forced to conclude "that he *really* didn't remember the least thing about her; and he only felt it as a drawback that when all was made strictly historic there didn't appear much of anything left." The past was like a defective pack of cards; "the past, invoked, invited, encouraged, could give them, naturally, no more than it had" (XVII:65–66).

His renunciation of the shape of meaning, his impressionism, is, unlike Strether's similar mood upon his encounter with Maria Gostrey, no promise of a richer receptiveness to the present. Without a past to start with, Marcher and May are nearly unable to have a present: "The present would have been so much better if the other, in the far distance, in the foreign land, hadn't been so stupidly meagre." The "small possible germs" of their earlier encounter, says James (seeing this buried moment as a kind of literary "germ"—his favorite term for the initiating idea of a story—were "too deeply buried . . . to sprout after so many years." Marcher longs for an identifiable Aristotelian starting point—something even as modestly, tritely, dramatic as saving her from a capsized boat in the Bay of Naples, or rescuing her bag from a *lazzarone* with a stiletto in the streets, or as touching as her sympathetic attention when he had been stricken by a fever. "*Then* they would have been in possession of the something that their actual show seemed to lack" (XVII:66). Without such an initiatory episode how could any story about them be conceivable?

James's elaboration of this condition—of elided beginning—is deeply suggestive. The openings Marcher longs for are literary clichés, and James's parodic reference to them is the bored professional's negative critique of popular narrative conceptions. At the same time, it is a critique of the general state of the reader's—of everyone's—mind, which requires such conventional structures and cannot freely invent others. It is particularly significant that his ideas would constitute first steps leading in some predictable way to a marriage-ending. That there is no such overture to romance in his shared past with May is both a source of regret and a release from the conventional that would all to certainly entrap them both in a trite history. In language that expresses his identity with the literary artist, Marcher reflects, frustratedly, "It was vain to pretend she was an old friend, for all the communities were wanting, in spite of which it was as an old friend that he saw she would have suited him." Marcher, the story-writer whose stories are too familiar, "would have liked to invent something, get her to make-believe with him that some passage of a romantic or critical kind *had* originally occurred. He was really almost reaching out in imagination—as against time—for something that would do, and saying to himself that if it didn't come this sketch of a fresh start would show itself for quite awkwardly bungled. They would separate, and now for no second or no third chance" (XVII:67).

Remedying this artistic "bungling," this gap of beginning which threatens to abort their story, May retrieves the past for him, after all. He has completely forgotten what he said to her one day they went to Sorrento and, when she begins to remind him, fears it will prove to have been the most banal of initiatory gestures—that he had made some "imbecile 'offer' " (XVII:68). In fact, something unusual had happened. He had confessed his own most secret

secret—his "sense of being kept for something rare and strange, possibly prodigious and terrible" (XVII:71) that would sooner or later overtake him. Their beginning—the beginning of their story—was this confession of his expectation of an end toward which no story need make its progress, an end that would simply arrive, and when it arrived be beyond anything he could anticipate—an ending, indeed, without either beginning or middle. It was not, he was sure, any common catastrophe, not, for example, "falling in love," but something so unforeseeable that May charges him with simply desiring to be original: "You want something all to yourself—something nobody else knows or *has* known" (XVII:73)—such a story as no one has ever written before.

Such an anticipation puts all ordinary endings out of the question, of course. He had never made her an "offer," and he certainly could not now ask her to marry him; no marriage-plot can develop from his expectation that "something or other lay in wait for him, amid the twists and turns of the months and the years, like a crouching beast in the jungle" (XVII:79). The movement of James's story, which thus far has demonstrated the futility of the search for narrative beginnings, now finds a beginning, of sorts, in May's promise to watch and wait with him for an unforeseeable end.

Yet forward movement is still doomed to abortion. The end that cannot be foreseen will not draw toward itself a train of narrative episodes. "Nothing happens," as readers impatiently protest— which is just the point. Marcher's aging appearance through the years, his modest career, are only simulations of the progress of ordinary life history, and as for May, "beneath her forms as well detachment had learned to sit, and behavior had become for her, in a social sense, a false account of herself." Of course, *she* does have a story, unknown to Marcher; she is in love with him. Stepping for a moment beyond the boundary of Marcher's masculine awareness, his inability to feel the female side of experience, the narrator remarks, "There was one account of her that would have been true all the while and that she could give, directly, to nobody, least of all to John Marcher" (XVII:82).

For the eyes of the world Marcher and May pretend the history of a love affair. "What saves us, you know, is that we answer so completely to so usual an appearance: that of the man and woman whose friendship has become such a daily habit—or almost—as to be at last indispensable." For Marcher in particular their "habit" of keeping each other company "saves"; as May tells him, "It makes you, after all, for the vulgar, indistinguishable from other men. What's the most inveterate mark of men in general? Why the capacity to spend endless time with dull women—to spend it I won't say without being bored, but without minding that they are, without being driven off at a tangent by it; which comes to the same thing. I'm your dull woman, a part of the daily bread for which you pray at church. That covers your tracks more than anything" (XVII:83–84).

Literally interpreting James's story we can, if we wish, see Marcher as a man who fears the most intimate human communion and commitment, the sexual bond. At the same time, one may say, he is not unwilling to accept the protection of a woman's friendship, a friendship which makes him seem normal, helps him "to pass for a man like another" (XVII:92)—though it denies her what the appearance implies. Eve Kosovsky Sedgwick has interestingly suggested that something more positive than a mere *lack* of sexual desire is the matter with Marcher. She thinks that Marcher's "pretense" of an ordinary sexual affair must conceal an unavowable motive of another sort, and that "to the extent that Marcher's secret has a content, that content is homosexual." "The apparent gap of meaning . . . is far from being a genuinely empty one," she says. "It refers to the perfectly specific absence of a prescribed heterosexual desire." The "nothing" that is Marcher's fate, on the other hand, is "male homosexual genitality," which can only be referred to by preterition—that is, as the "love that dare not speak its name."[2] In her interesting speculative reading of the story Sedgwick goes on to see May's long patience with Marcher as an unsuccessful attempt to free him from "homosexual panic" by helping him to understand his own desires. Yet sexual nullity, rather than homosexual desire, serves as an appropriate sign of the refusal of enacted being.

But perhaps the "gap" of psychological explanation for Marcher's behavior needs to remain unfilled, however eagerly our imaginations *will* fill it, in this parable, which, like Hawthorne's tales upon which it is modeled, is an abstract moral statement without psychological depth. Hawthorne's notebooks are full of one- or two-sentence summaries of proposed stories which will fail to gain realistic substance even when he writes them; for "Ethan Brand" the writer first set down the following idea: "The search of an investigator for the Unpardonable Sin;—he at last finds it in his own heart and practice"[3]—which completely summarizes the story. Or one can say that the gap of exact knowledge about Marcher's life is like the unfillable gap of undenoted "evil" in "The Turn of the Screw," which also (and perhaps even more plausibly if we read it as more realistic than it is) can suggest the covert homosexual subject.

I have already drawn attention to Marcher's peculiar inability to discover a beginning for his relation with May, but, of course, his mysterious obsession is itself without accessible beginning; no amount of suppositious depth-analysis will reveal its hidden source. The character of Marcher has no "unconscious," no hidden selfhood. If we ask how, psychologically speaking, it originated, how he arrived at this conviction of some mysterious doom, or if we ask what part of his psyche he has repressed, we see at once that such questions cannot be answered; he is simply *the* man who somehow has been cursed in this way, having been given a prediction of destiny which he cannot elude but whose arrival he will not be able to anticipate or even recognize.

It might be insisted, nevertheless, that Marcher and May live in a real world, belong to a small social circle of the upper middle class in turn-of-the-century London, a circle whose social occasions they attend separately or together. Marcher is one of James's "poor sensitive gentlem(e)n" (2:1250)—a social type of the privileged individual who has become alienated from a world of increasingly crass competition for wealth and power. We are told that he has a minor government post of some sort, a small inheritance, a library, a house with a garden in the country; his is a representative existence, then, of fastidious bachelorhood, a life studiously lived at the margin, determinedly uninvolved in active pursuits or in marriage. One may interpret his aspiration for some tragic or heroic end as a recoil from the common goals of his society. At the same time, the story can be read as a representative Jamesian study of the selfishness and passionlessness that may accompany intellectual refinement and good breeding, a reading of fastidiousness as a mask for the evasion of social and personal responsibility.

May's own story, in so far as we glimpse it, has an even clearer realistic character. She is introduced at the start as one of those well-bred young women so often figuring in James's fiction who manage their lives by some precarious dependence, a "poor relation

. . . there on harder terms than anyone" who pays for her protection at Weatherend by guiding its visitors and explaining its treasures, "though it wasn't that she looked as if you could have given her shillings" (XVII:63). She repays her great-aunt as one might imagine Fleda Vetch repaying Mrs. Gereth. Only the death of that relative unexpectedly provides a bequest that makes her modestly self-sufficient—and frees her from the need to marry which is such a heroine's only alternative to dependence.

But such realities are given us by just a few sentences in the narrative, which consists chiefly in a succession of conversations between May and Marcher, conversations which take place as the years pass in a bare space withdrawn from the social world. It is literally May's London drawing room, but no other visitor is ever visible besides Marcher, and nothing in this private place is ever described until that climactic moments when, near death, she rises to tell him, "It's never too late." Even then we hear merely of the chimney piece against which Marcher leans, "fireless and sparely adorned, a small, perfect old French clock and two morsels of rosy Dresden constituting all its furniture" (XVII:105). These few imperishable ornaments can stand for the past preserved, that beginning with May which Marcher could not recall—though, of course, we can view them as mere items of realist description. The same double function—realist and symbolic—may be attributed to that image of preserved blossoming to which May herself is compared—an image fit to be literalized as another Victorian ornament of her chaste drawing room: "With her white petals and green fronds she might have been a lily . . . only an artificial lily, wonderfully imitated and constantly kept, without dust or stain, though not exempt from a slight droop and a complexity of faint creases, under some clear glass bell" (XVII:98–99).

The world Marcher inhabits is a chamber of eternity. Like "The Turn of the Screw," the story is a mythical and moral tale, despite its modern tone. It is not for nothing that May, in the scene I have just mentioned, is called sphinx-like. Something must happen and, she even says, *has* happened, though Marcher can discover no evidence of it in his life. The conundrum is, like the sphinx's riddles, designed to be solved in a form least expected. The correct answer cannot be anticipated by the man to whom it has been told: "He had been the man of his time, *the* man, to whom nothing on earth was to have happened" (XVII:125). His fate has arrived, it will turn out, precisely *because* nothing has happened. As allegory, the story is designed to illustrate the idea that no life escapes a destiny.

Mythically, the hero will encounter a "beast"—a figurative image which does not altogether, any more than the ghosts of "The Turn of the Screw," lose its relation to traditions of folklore—and recalls Hawthorne's "bosom serpent" (in "Egotism, or the Bosom Serpent") in its semi-literal, semi-symbolical presence in the story. A further resemblance to "The Turn of the Screw" resides in the fact that James seems to have conceived of Marcher as another absolutist who craves a fairy-tale plot of melodramatic simplicity, like the governess. Marcher, James explains in the New York Edition preface, found "none of the mere usual and normal human adventures, whether delights or disconcertments, appearing to confirm to the great type of his fortune . . . No gathering appearance, no descried or interpreted promise or portent, affects his superstitious soul either as a damnation deep enough (if damnation be in question) for his appointed *quality* of consciousness, or as a translation into bliss sublime enough (on *that* hypothesis) to fill, in vulgar parlance, the bill. Therefore, as each item of experience comes, with its possibilities, into view, he can but dismiss it under this sterilizing habit of the failure to find it good enough and thence to appropriate it." His career," James concludes, "thus resolves itself into a great negative adventure" (2:1250–1251). Marcher himself seems to suspect and fear the utter negativity of his adventure when he asks May if she does not foresee that *nothing* will really happen to him.

James's problem, of course, was the difficult one, as Tate puts it, "of dramatizing the insulated ego, of making active what is incapable of action."[4] James does not reduce this problem, however, by exhibiting as incident the succession of challenges summarized in the preface—the preface really promises more drama in the form of "descried or interpreted promises or portents" than the tale ever brings into view. What is suggested instead is simply the might-have-beens which Marcher and May both gaze into, a sweeping stream of negatives. "He knew each of the things of importance he was insidiously kept from doing, but she could add up the amount they made, understand how much, with a lighter weight on his spirit, he might have done" (XVII:81–82). Between them, nearly eventless, flows the story, the *only* story, actually lived, though it is to prove the greatest might-have-been of all.

I say *nearly* eventless for, of course, there are *some* scenic moments which suggest to the reader that Marcher is making his way along a path not only of time but of development. He *has* been launched upon a plot, and James uses the same image of a boat put into the wind and current of its course that he used to describe the initiation of Isabel's destiny by Ralph's putting "wind in her sails": "The recovery, the first day at Weatherend, had served its purpose well, had given them quite enough; so that they were, to Marcher's sense, no longer hovering about the head-waters of their stream, but had felt their boat pushed sharply off and down the current" (XVII:76). In the end the story disproves the idea that negativity can be maintained. It suggests that there is always a story, that in not writing one one writes another.

May's first assurance that something *will* happen is an occasion marked for him as a "a date" or crisis which already gives some semblance of form to time; "again and again, even after long intervals, other things that passed between them wore in relation to this hour but the character of recalls and results" (XVII:90). Marcher comes to believe that she knows what his catastrophe will be. He depends upon her for the validation, somehow, of this ultimate revelation, and when she grows ill begins to fear that she may die without witnessing it at his side, and that perhaps it is already "Too Late" for his Event. He fears that he has been "sold." "It wouldn't have been failure to be bankrupt, dishonoured, pilloried, hanged; it was failure not to be anything." Time is threatening to stop—and all possibility of story cut short; "Since it was in Time that he was to have met his fate, so it was in Time that his fate was to have acted" (XVII:97).

It is at this point that the story, which is enacting itself without Marcher's knowledge, exhibits its climax in the exquisite scene in which May seems already beyond time, mythically metamorphosed, *her* story completed and preserved like a lily under a bell jar. Their conversation convinces him that she knows his fate. She knows it as "the worst" thing conceivable, something they've never mentioned in reviewing possibilities. Her reassurance that he will not consciously suffer revives his fear that she has come back to his own early dread—that *nothing* will happen. But she can say no more. As at the start of their friendship, she cannot give him the "thread" of narrative continuity "without some putting forth of his hand for it." She stands before him with figure and face conveying her own offering before she collapses, with her despairing question, "Don't you know—now?" What has happened is "what *was* to" (XVII:107). His story-less life has just achieved its catastrophe, though, as she had warned, he won't give it the right name.

He thinks that it is her death—and the solitude it means for him—that is the promised disaster. But in their last interview she tells him that disaster has already struck, though he asks, in bewilderment, "How can the thing I've never felt at all be the thing I was marked out to feel?" (XVII:113). What he does experience, after her death, is extinction of the suspense which had filled his days for so many years. "What was to happen *had* so absolutely and finally happened that he was as little able to know a fear for his future as to know a hope; so absent in short was any question of anything still to come. He was to live entirely with the other question, that of his unidentified past, that of his having to see his fortune impenetrably muffled and masked" (XVII:117). Again, as at the start of the story, we realize that the past and future only identify themselves to the kind of vision Marcher lacks. His catastrophe, now past, is as unknown to him as when it was a thing of the future.

A diminished man, with no sense of the shape which gives meaning to a life, he comes to worry less about "whatever had happened." Revelation does arrive at last at his dead friend's graveside, where the face of another mourner, unknown to him, is "the image of scarred passion." He realizes that "he had seen *outside* of his life, not learned it within, the way a woman was mourned when she had been loved for herself." Now he realizes that she had offered him an escape from the Beast; "the escape would have been to love her" (XVII:124–126).

Yes, he had been "*the* man to whom nothing on earth was to have happened . . . That was the rare stroke—that was his visitation" (XVII:125), the story states. But James's message is more subtle— or ambiguous. Marcher *is*, after all, the victim of the catastrophe he has been waiting for; the Beast springs at last. The Beast—like the sphinx's creature who walked on four, on two, and then on three feet—is only man, who must live the life of man. Marcher, like everyone, is the man to whom something *has* happened. His is only the disaster that is the outcome of a life that disdains a history but cannot escape one.

That plot overtakes the character who resists it seemed, in the case of Isabel Archer, an acknowledgment that the "free spirit" must be overtaken by a limiting, even diminishing story. James called Isabel "presumptuous," but indulged his heroine for the nobility of her presumptions. James contrasted that nobility with the destinies that would entrap and degrade her. But to presume that one can dispense with "adventure" of some sort, to imagine that there can be a tale without a plot, is delusive. In the story James so often seems to write, the story of the mere witness to life who refuses action, or of the person for whom opportunity comes "too late," refusal itself will turn out to constitute an adventure, for better or for worse. In "The Beast in the Jungle," James redefines that word, "adventure"—a term used both for life's actual tale and for the literary narrative—and makes sense of the oxymoron, "negative adventure." More than Isabel's, Marcher's presumption amounts to arrogance in its indifference to life's best opportunities—and constitutes a critique of her attitude, from which the novel deliberately refrained.

The argument is perhaps conservative, a refutation of idealist intransigence, for it seems to say that we had better do the possible, after all. In the end, selfishly cherishing our essence, we will have acted somehow, and probably badly. To the literary artist the warning is obvious. There is no way to write stories but by resort to the old tales in the storeroom—tales of love and marriage or whatever, the stories men have been telling from the beginning of human time—stories so inescapable that they will express themselves in the most story-denying fiction we may invent.

· II ·

The Presence of Potentiality:
"The Jolly Corner"

James was certainly aware that the storyteller arbitrarily suppresses all but a few potentialities of story in his materials. He speaks of such potentialities in the already familiar preface to the first volume of the New York Edition, in which he describes life as a "vast expanse" of canvas with "its boundless number of distinct perforations . . . for the needle" of the tapestry maker. Confronted with innumerable solicitations to design, the artist-weaver feels "terror" or at least an "ache of fear . . . of being unduly tempted and led on by 'developments' " that might not, after all, contribute to the pattern he has decided upon. In actuality, "relations stop nowhere," but art pretends otherwise as the artist picks out one design or another on the canvas (2:1041). In the preface to the volume that contains "The Jolly Corner," James reflects that he found himself rediscovering in his notebooks possibilities passed by as well as some taken up, and those taken up suggesting other outcomes than he had later given them. But he feels more than the artist's tenderness for literary opportunities passed by—his language suggests James's sympathy with bypassed alternatives, with suppressed potentialities in any individual life, a theme felt again and again in his stories and novels.

The discrepancy between available social role and the self's best expectations is made more absolute in the fable of "The Jolly Corner," probably the latest work to be included in the New York Edition. In 1908, when the story was published,[1] James was already looking squarely at the kind of personal options open to the seeking self in the twentieth century—especially on that frontier of the future, his own America, which he had recently revisited after an absence of twenty years. "The Jolly Corner" is a fictional twin of *The American Scene*, with its vision of a rapidly changing New York

275

full of new opportunities for entrepreneurial energy—a scene bustling with the physical evidence of a multiplied alertness to business opportunity. The Manhattan to which Spencer Brydon has returned is a physical metaphor of finance—its numerous cross-ruled streets and new buildings are described as "the dreadful multiplied numberings which seemed to him to reduce the whole place to some vast ledger-page, overgrown, fantastic, of ruled and criss-crossed lines and figures" (XVII:439). In bringing his sensitive expatriate back to America, James confronted the idea of what such a man would have *had* to be in this place, this new age. It was an intensely personal way of thinking, which gives a special, autobiographical sense to those sentences in the preface in which he seems to be talking only about artistic projects: "We chance on some idea we *have* afterwards treated; then, greeting it with a tenderness, we wonder at the first form of a motive that led us so far and to show, no doubt, to eyes not our own, for so other; then we heave the deep sigh of relief over all that is never, thank goodness, to be done again. Would we have embarked on *that* stream had we known?—and what mightn't we have made of this one *hadn't* we known! How, in a proportion of cases, could we have dreamed 'there might be something'?—and why, in another proportion, didn't we *try* what there might be, since there are sorts of trials (ah indeed more than one sort!) for which the day will soon have passed?" (2:1261).

"The Jolly Corner" is James's final fable dealing with the presence of the unlived life in the life that is lived. It is a final settling of the problem of potentiality in its relation to act, of character and its expression, mutilating or improving, in plot. Spencer Brydon, the *déraciné* who has returned after half a lifetime away from his native New York, is assailed at first by the "great fact" of "incalculability" in the world that might have been his. Unimaginable also is the man he would have been if he had stayed at home. But in his new situation he feels compelled to imagine an alternate self, an alternate life. "He found all things came back to the question of what he personally might have been, how he might have led his life and 'turned out,' if he had not so, at the outset, given it up" (XVII:448). The mysterious other whom Brydon pursues in his old house on the "jolly corner" may be thought of as representing his growing sense of his own nature and its potentialities. But it is, more precisely, a summoning out of an imagined but possible past of a history that could have been his. The self who never was figures in the story as a ghost of a special sort, not a revenant of the dead, a spook such as the cleaning woman, Mrs. Muldoon, fears to encounter in "the ayvil hours." He is a hypothesis made visible, the unenacted alternative comprehended as a "presence"—the word used in an ambiguous sense throughout the story—because what we can or could be is always *present* in what we are, and yet it is ghostly, immaterial. In "The Jolly Corner," James exploits the "fantastic" doubt that hovers between the real absence of unenacted possibility and its ghostly, hypothetic realization.

Brydon has come back to look at his property, which consists of two buildings, the ancestral house on the "jolly corner," which still stands preserved in its antique state, and another, a row house in the middle of the block, already joined to the new times by its transformation into money-making flats. James's penchant for making houses symbolic—an outgrowth of the realist congruence between a character and its habitation—here provides a choice of expressive "envelopes" (as Madame Merle might call them) for Brydon. The empty old house on the jolly corner represents the man he knows himself to be, the man of tradition and refinement who has carefully preserved his original nature by expatriation and aestheticism—and by emptying his native past from its old habitation. But he is about to discover that he might have been—and perhaps is—another man. The "other", the aptly-termed "converted" building, with its occupied, rent-yielding flats, represents another self he finds himself capable of being as he directs the building's modernization and exploitation.

This discovery is achieved by an internal experience, literally speaking—a crisis of identity only vaguely connected to external events, though dramatized as a metaphorical ghost story. It is another example of James's method of displacing the idea of "adventure" from outer to inner experience, of which he boasted when reviewing his treatment of Isabel Archer. Of the story written twenty years after *The Portrait of a Lady*, James says:

> Odd though it may sound to pretend that one feels on safer ground in tracing such an adventure as that of the hero of "The Jolly Corner" than in pursuing a bright career among pirates or detectives, I allow that composition to pass as the measure or limit, on my own part, of any achievable comfort in the "adventure-story"; and this not because I may "render"—well, what my poor gentleman attempted and suffered in the New York house—better

> than I may render detectives or pirates or other splendid despera-
> does . . . but because the spirit engaged with the forces of violence
> interests me most when I can think of it as engaged most deeply,
> most finely and most "subtly" (precious term!). For then it is that,
> as with the longest and firmest prongs of consciousness, I grasp and
> hold the throbbing subject.   (2:1260)

Brydon's "adventure," therefore, is expressed in the vehicle of the
haunted-house story, but in that story as metaphor. It is realistically
true that hidden personal potentialities make themselves known in
his suddenly discovered capacity for mechanical cleverness and
turning a dollar in the modernization and marketing of his other
property. But we are alerted to the approach of supernatural mystery
and terror when we hear: "He scarcely knew what to make of this
lively stir, in a compartment of his mind never yet penetrated, of a
capacity for business and a sense for construction" (XVII:438). The
image of the mind as a house—with closets, cabinets, rooms, which
may be open or shut or long disused, predicts the literalization soon
to come in Brydon's final pursuit of his other self to a shut upper-
story room of the "unconverted" building.

The literalization of metaphor—or the interplay, rather, between
the metaphor as metaphor and its slippage into the main term, the
tenor of narrative—is an important semantic technique in this story.
The power of language to make what is absent present is illustrated,
in all discourse, by figurative imagery, which offers the momentary
hallucination of a reality that is withdrawn as soon as it has sharpened
our sense of the main term. So James's haunted house and its ghost
are poetic expressions of psychic reality or, alternately, literal truth.
But as the story advances, vehicle (the figurative) becomes tenor
(the literal). The figurative ghost becomes a figure actually seen.
Nothing could be more apt than such a confusion of the imagination
to make us understand how what can be conceived as a possibility is
no less real than what happens. What seems only a technical eccentricity is, in fact, a representation of the story's own theme.

Brydon's friend, Alice Staverton, has never left New York, and she
and Brydon have the memories of their youth and its "values" in
common; they share "communities of knowledge." This was " 'their'
knowledge (this discriminating possessive was always on her lips) of
presences of the other age, presences all overlaid, in his case, by the
experience of a man and the freedom of a wanderer, overlaid by
pleasure, by infidelity, by passages of life that were strange and dim to

her, just by 'Europe,' in short, but still unobscured, still exposed and cherished, under the pious visitation of the spirit from which she had never been diverted" (XVII:440). The use of words that have a more general meaning but can suggest the otherworldly—"presences," "visitation," "spirit"—initiates the slippage between the literally supernatural and the metaphoric. Brydon and Alice become a pair of privileged observers, who not only feel the continued values of what is past, but may be able to see its ghosts.

But Brydon's family home, which expresses the many lives lived there, is not actively "haunted" by his ancestral past, "that mystical other world that might have flourished for him had he not, for weal or woe abandoned it" (XVII:455), though "the mere feel, in his hand, of the old silver-plated knobs of the several mahogany doors . . . suggested the pressure of the palms of the dead" (XVII:445). The emptiness of the house is a representation of an absence that has not been filled, a past that remains invisible. Brydon has, perversely, kept his house vacant, neither living in it nor letting it be developed for profit, without, he proudly says, "the ghost of a reason," since in America "there are no reasons . . . *but* of dollars" (XVII:446)—and the cliché, "ghost of a reason," comes to life to suggest something spectral that yet declines to haunt. Without a reason or the ghost that might represent his awareness of one, he clings to a delusion that his life is what it is, and that alternatives—the alternatives that American reasons might have provided—can be kept out of it by his refusal to let it make him rich.

In its emptiness, its "absolute vacancy . . . from top to bottom" (XVII:442), the house on the jolly corner contrasts with Alice's little house in Irving Place, which is full of objects and furnishings that signify the continuing presence of old habits, a "small still scene where items and shades, all delicate things, kept the sharpness of the notes of a high voice perfectly trained." Brydon tells her, correctly, "you're a person whom nothing can have altered. You were born to be what you are, anywhere, anyway" (XVII:450–451). Born to be what she is, she is without latencies like Brydon's—her life has fully expressed her, and she has successfully kept the vulgar present from her door, not by flight to another world but by personal integrity.

She detects, however, the hollowness of Brydon's devotion to "other values than the beastly rent values." She perceives, even before he does, the other man in him. After all, he owns another, less jolly house which he has been glad to see converted into those income-yielding flats. "In short, you're to make so good a thing of your sky-scraper that, living in luxury on *those* ill-gotten gains, you can afford for a while to be sentimental here," she tells him (XVII:444). The profundity of this observation is worth noting; she implies that the freedom to be highminded and aesthetic is itself purchased at the price of concession somewhere, as a leisure-class culture conceals a real devotion to plain considerations of profit. On the personal level, too, perhaps, this may be also true; the aesthetic idealist is likely to be someone whose consciousness excludes the sources of his freedom of choice.

And indeed, Brydon's jolly corner will soon show that it is haunted not by his early past but by the later time he might have lived there, by the character of a man who would have known how to make money in the new ways. The gradual realization that "if he had but stayed at home he would have anticipated the inventor of the sky-scraper" seems to sound over "his own lately most disguised and muffled vibrations," as if some unexpected occult visitor had begun to make himself heard in Brydon's empty rooms. "This was the image under which he himself judged the matter, or at least, not a little, thrilled and flushed with it—very much as if he might have been met by some strange figure, some unexpected occupant, at a turn of one of the dim passages of an empty house"—which exactly predicts, though only as the minor term of a simile, the confrontation to come. James's teasing and self-conscious linguistic play continues: "The quaint analogy quite hauntingly remained with him, when he didn't indeed rather improve it by a still intenser form: that of his opening a door behind which he would have made sure of finding nothing, a door into a room shuttered and void, and yet so coming, with a great suppressed start, on some quite erect confronting presence, something planted in the middle of the place and facing him through the dusk" (XVII:440–441), offering a still more vivid analogical premonition of the ghostly confrontation to come.

Brydon's sense of his own alterity begins with the hypothetical or figurative imagining of himself as a "he," who, whatever "he" is, is distinctly and absolutely "other." He tells Alice Staverton, in the playful way they have of discussing his unlived life, "*He* isn't myself. He's the just so totally other person. But I do want to see him. And I can. And I shall" (XVII:451). Alice accepts the idea that he is both himself and someone else when she answers that she has seen "him" twice in a dream. She insists on the division when Brydon says, "You dream about me at that rate?" and she responds, "Ah about *him!*" (XVII:452).

After this, he begins the habit of visiting his jolly corner during the night, when he could "most intimately wander and wait, linger and listen, feel his fine attention, never in his life before so fine, on the pulse of the great vague place"—as though, indeed, the identity imaged in the house were being sounded and searched by an attentive physician. He would "watch with his glimmering light" as he passed from room to room "for the revelation he pretended to invite" (XVII:453–454). That the "pretended" waiting and the probing search take place at *night* suggests an exploration of the "nightside" of personality, which Brydon makes during the hours of sleep—or the psychiatrist makes when he reviews his patient's dreams. James could hardly have had any idea of the still-to-be-promulgated Freudian unconscious and Freud's conception of the significance of dreams—but he might well have known of his brother William's brilliant anticipations of the idea of repression. In 1891, William James had written to their sister Alice about "neurotic cases [in which] some infernality in the body *prevents* really existing parts of the mind from coming to their effective rights at all, suppresses them, blasts them out from participation in this world of experiences, though they were *there* all the time."[2] Brydon's explorations of his house become a "depth analysis" and a retreat from the waking world spent among "people who had truly not an idea of him." The analysis results in the discovery of the repressed self, which had been "there all the time," as the novelist's brother had insisted. Indeed, because of the gradual reversal of Brydon's reality-sense, the "real" world seems "some game of *ombres chinoises*," and the hours spent in his dark house, the hours of inwardness, "the other, the real, the waiting life," are where some true "he" is to be found (XVII:454–455).

That the inner life is "more real"—however problematic and invisible—than what impinges upon it from the outside is a familiar Jamesian principle, asserted in nearly every one of his fictional dramas of consciousness. If the play of mental images is "the real," then what lies within as potentiality is real even if it has failed to give visible evidence of itself. It becomes more real the more Brydon thinks of it, giving it "form" in his imagination. And James's style itself performs the conversion from idea to "form." His house seems to Brydon like a crystal glass or bowl around the edge of which one can run one's moistened finger to hear the humming sound:

The concave crystal held, as it were, this mystical other world, and the indescribably fine murmur of its rim was the sigh there, the scarce audible pathetic wail to his strained ear, of all the old baffled foresworn possibilities. What he did therefore by this appeal of his hushed presence was to wake them into such measure of ghostly life as they might still enjoy. They were shy, all but unappeasably shy, but they weren't really sinister; at least they weren't as he had hitherto felt them—before they had taken the Form he so yearned to make them take, the Form he at moments saw himself in the light of fairly hunting on tiptoe, the points of his evening-shoes, from room to room, from storey to storey. That was the essence of his vision—which was all rank folly, if one would, while he was out of the house and otherwise occupied, but which took on the last verisimilitude as soon as he was placed and posted. He knew what he meant and what he wanted; it was clear as the figure on a cheque presented in demand for cash. His *alter ego* "walked"—that was the note of his image of him, while his image of his motive for his own odd pastime was the desire to waylay him and meet him.   (XVII:455–456)

Though literal-seeming and unambiguous as the "figure on a cheque" (and what more apt symbol of materialism in twentieth-century New York could James have chosen?), the form to be taken by this alter ego is clearly, now, that of a man like himself, a ghost who "walks" to represent "all the old baffled foresworn possibilities." But the alter ego can take other forms, symbolic or spectral. Hunted, it can be imaged as a "beast"—like John Marcher's expectation of his tragic destiny; as Brydon makes his rounds of the house certain rear portions "affected him as the very jungle of his prey" (XVII:459). James is careful to preserve our sense of the "as" of simile. He shows himself possessed of a literary consciousness (the kind of consciousness which makes so many of James's characters duplicate the action of the author himself) when he is said to be searching for a "form" from storey to storey (or story to story?), "stalking a creature more subtle, yet at bay perhaps more formidable, than any beast of the forest. The terms, the comparisons, the very practices of the chase positively came again into play; there were even moments when passages of his occasional experience as a sportsman, stirred memories, from his younger time, of moor and mountain and desert, revived for him— and to the increase of his keenness—by the tremendous force of analogy." The beast is analogical, a mind-created figure for what cannot otherwise be imagined, as is made clear when Brydon considers that *he* may appear in this form to the mysterious other. His eyes sharpening in the darkness make him feel "like some monstrous stealthy cat; he wondered if he would have glared at these moments with large shining yellow eyes, and what it mightn't verily be, for the poor hard-pressed *alter ego,* to be confronted with such a type" (XVII:456–458).

Brydon knows that his game of analogies is only a literary game. Outside he sees the "hard silver of the autumn stars . . . the flare of the street lamps below, the white electric lustre which it would have taken curtains to keep out. This was human actual social; this was of the world he had lived in." But "within the walls, and in spite of the clear windows, his consistency was proof against the cynical light of New York." He *cultivates* an awareness that this light would deny: "It had belonged to that idea of the exasperated consciousness of his victim to become a real test for him; since he had quite put it to himself from the first that, oh distinctly! he could 'cultivate' his whole perception" (XVII:458–459).

So now he begins to feel the other self more distinctly, feels himself following *and* followed—as much pursuing as pursued, as much inspiring fear as fearful. Finally, the night comes when he is convinced that "he" is waiting on the top floor of the house. "I've hunted him till he has 'turned' . . . he's the fanged or the antlered animal brought at last to bay." As he goes up, he is almost pleased that this "ineffable identity" of himself is not miserably skulking (XVII:461–462). But where is he? Brydon finds a closed door he is sure he left ajar. He had left it ajar so that he might catch sight of "his baffled 'prey' " (XVII:466) as he approaches the end of a series of connecting rooms. No such perspective of vision—or of understanding—is available; only the evidence of the closed door.

He turns away, renouncing any further effort to know this hidden self. "So rest for ever and let *me!*" (XVII:468), he silently communicates to the being behind the door, like someone rejecting knowledge of the final secrets of the suppressed psyche or of what he has already termed his "foresworn possibilities." It has been enough to know without doubt that another "presence" inhabits his house. Indeed, should the door have opened to reveal it, "it would mean that the agent of his shame—for his shame was his deep abjection—was once more at large and in general possession" (XVII:471–472)—and that would have made him jump out of the window. But this does not happen. He sits by the open window, now welcoming the reality of external things, watching "as for some comforting common fact, some vulgar human note, the passage of a scavenger or a thief, some night-bird however base" (XVII:469). He has explored his irreality for the last time—and "they might come in, now, the builders, the destroyers" (XVII:473), to do what they wanted with the house.

But the specter is not finished with him after all. Downstairs he finds the inner hall door open, though he had left it closed, and this time he has the perspective in which to perceive that "the prodigy of a personal presence." Rigid and conscious, spectral yet human, a man of his own substance and stature waited there to measure himself with his power to dismay," inside the street door. James's description of this figure is extraordinarily precise—and may have been suggested by one or more of the works of John Sargent, whose art of portraiture James admired: "No portrait by a great modern master could have presented him with more intensity, thrust him out of his frame with more art" (XVII:475), we are told of the specter's appearance. One Sargent portrait in particular, that of Henry Lee Higginson, may have been in James's mind. He had seen it in the Harvard Union in 1904–05, and he anticipated "that reference [he] should like to make to the effect of Sargent's portrait of H. H., rather dimly made out in the 1st 'gloaming' at the Union," and to the "splendid portrait of H.H.—floated into the presence of *that* as one was, by the impulse to do something with one's 1st impression of the Union, and its great high Hall."[3] In *The American Scene,* published the year before "The Jolly Corner," he praised the portrait for showing the artist's ability to "interfuse . . . public acts with the personality . . . of the actor."[4]

Now, one peculiarity of Brydon's specter is that it appears to have a hand with two fingers "reduced to stumps as if accidentally shot away." This was not actually the case with Higginson, though the fingers of his left hand in the painting are hidden as he grasps the arm of his chair and, in Sargent's chiaroscuro, only the upper half of the hand catches the light. Whether the idea came from the painting or not, James's representation of the "other" Brydon as mutilated is important; it suggests what could have happened if, like Higginson, Brydon had been a Civil War soldier who had fought at Antietam and Chancellorsville and finally been seriously wounded in hand-to-hand fighting at the battle of Aldie Gap. Higginson's actual injuries, though less visible than those of Brydon's specter, troubled him till the end of his life, when Sargent painted him. As an outward sign of his sitter's war experience, the painter posed Higginson with his cavalry cloak thrown over his knees.

After the war, Higginson engaged in an experiment in cotton farming with free black labor, just as James's two younger brothers, also veterans of combat, had done. Like them, he failed at it, "[came] to anchor in State Street," as his biographer says,[5] and made a lot of money. The ghostly alter ego of James's Brydon is a man who has made money, too—"He has a million a year!" says Alice at the end of the story. Even if the Higginson portrait was not specifically in James's mind when he wrote "The Jolly Corner," its subject—or someone like him—might have been. Such a man represented that alternative American life of action and enterprise which the expatriate would have missed. If he had remained at home, Brydon would have fought in the war and then, in the Gilded Age that came after, he would have "invented the skyscraper" and become wealthy and powerful.

Higginson, for his part, had surrendered early his own dream of aesthetic dedication; as a very young man he had wanted to be a musician and had studied music in Germany—so *he* might well have had, somewhere in his secret consciousness, a lost alternate self not unlike James's Brydon. Conceiving the regrets of such a man, perhaps, James represents the self Brydon has refused to become as a thing to be pitied; that self covers its face in shame in confrontation with *its* alternative, "the achieved, the enjoyed, the triumphant life" in Brydon. But, uncovered, the specter's face reveals "a bared identity too hideous" for him to recognize as his own. "Such an identity fitted his at *no* point . . . the face was the face of a stranger . . . evil, odious, blatant, vulgar" (XVII:476–477). For Brydon, in the end, the dilemma of alterity is resolved by the triumphant conviction that this possibility is not, after all, himself. The life lived, his chosen life, *is* what he is. With infinite relief he tells Alice Staverton, "There's somebody—an awful beast; whom I brought, too horribly, to bay. But it's not me" (XVII:482). Yet this existential answer to the question of potentiality is not undisputed in the story, which puzzles us because it points in two ways, has two conclusions. Alice Staverton has also seen Brydon's alter ego—and seems to believe, like William James, in those "really existing parts of the mind" that have been "there all the time."

Alice is, again, that feminine confidante and prop who offers comfort to "sensitive gentlemen" who have problems on their hands—she is like May Bartram of "The Beast in the Jungle" or Maria Gostrey of *The Ambassadors*. Like these characters, she offers Brydon a vision that differs from his own. But her message is unlike that of these other *ficelles*—and her success is greater. May Bartram understands, as Marcher does not, that one's life—as lived—is the only fate one has; no other life lies in reserve. Maria yearns, unavailingly, to give Strether the only "living" left to him—an adventure of his own after the adventure of Chad is over. Alice, on the other hand, sees that "what might have been" is a reality not to be denied. Loving Brydon *both* as he is and as he could have been, she rescues him—and says with self-contradicting reassurance, "He isn't—no, he isn't *you*!" (XVII:485). Brydon's appreciation of what she does for him is complete, and enables the tale to close—as so few James fictions do—with a presumable marriage.

Alice is like May in one particular respect: she, too, reminds the man she has always loved of their early encounter and gives him a past he has forgotten, a beginning he has elided. She herself is one of Brydon's might-have-beens, a potentiality he had nearly forgotten during his long absence from America. There is a hint that they once shared a tentative romance to which she, at least, has been faithful, having never married and remaining, despite the changes of the years, like some "pale pressed flower" (XVII:440). This image of the past preserved rather than withered reminds one of the image that represents May as the preservation of Marcher's forgotten past—as a lily under a glass bell. Brydon's own evasive, "selfish frivolous scandalous life" in another country has made him a certain kind of person, he knows; but Alice reminds him, "You see what it has made of *me*" (XVII:450), suggesting that her present state—perhaps even her preservation of the selfhood belonging to an earlier New York—is the result of his abandonment. She has been faithful, it is implied, not only to him but to the "presences of the other age."

Having lived on in the world he left, she understands, however, what he might have come to be. She knows that the "small tight bud" which Brydon speaks of having "blighted . . . for once and for ever" might have flowered into something "quite splendid, quite huge and monstrous"—a rather different bloom, one may note, from her own pale, pressed one. But she is not repelled. She understands, as James presciently does, both the ugliness and the creative strength of the new age, and tells Brydon, "You'd have had power."

"You'd have liked me, have preferred me, a billionaire!" he exclaims, to which she responds, "How should I not have liked you?" (XVII:449–450).

She has been able to see the alternate man from the first, has dreamed of him. "What's the wretch like?" (XVII:452) asks Brydon, but she will not say. Yet it is the sight of this other a third time in a dream that sends her to Brydon's rescue after he has had his own devastating vison of it at last. She, however, does not speak of "him" any longer: "In the cold dim dawn of this morning I too saw you," she says. "Saw *me*—? exclaims Brydon. "Saw *him*," she concedes indulgently (XVII:483). Brydon cannot accept that the "wretch" is himself. Like the governess in "The Turn of the Screw," he demands a moral world of exclusive opposites, and if he is himself worthy he *cannot* be that "wretch" as well. But Alice has the necessary double vision. She has, all along, shown that she could even have loved this other. "Ah I don't say I like him *better* . . . But he's grim, he's worn—and things have happened to him. He dosen't make shift, for sight, with your charming monocle" (XVII:485). And she pities the ruined sight, the maimed hand—even as she sinks into Brydon's embrace. Brydon, in any case, has enlarged his own nature enough to love the woman who sees his alterity plain—and he is rewarded as are few Jamesian heroes. To this measure—in the form of Alice's love—he has recovered a possibility forgone.

James's ending, thus, remains ambiguous. The alternate self, the rejected potential of the man she cares for, does not altogether die out in the consciousness of the more generous and perceiving character; Alice's final italicized "you" in her "He isn't *you*," might be taken to represent her appreciation of the compound nature which includes *both* Brydons. That our personal contrarities even support one another is also implied in her acute perception of the relationship between money and culture; she unpins all of Brydon's vanity of refinement when she tells him that his jolly corner is kept empty, and "converters" at bay, only because he has profited from the other house. Yet human charity requires the concession that the restraint of some of our worse potential is a credit to our "higher nature"— there is a positive side to the idea that what we do *is* what we are.

We may also apply this sense to Brydon's about-face upon his pursuer which James thought of as the most "intimate idea" of his story, "his turning the tables, as I think I called it, on a 'ghost' or whatever, a visiting or haunting apparition otherwise qualified to appal *him*; and thereby winning a sort of victory by the appearance, and the evidence, that this personage or presence was more overwhelmingly affected by him than he by *it*."[6] The story ends once and then a second time in the hero's two encounters with his alternate self—one in which, frightened of what he may discover, he draws back before the closed door, and the other when, forced to confront it, he moves fiercely *against* the possibility he has feared. Viewed at last, the mysterious "other" does not "leap," like Marcher's beast, but flees his pursuer; the "ghost" that traditionally appalls the living person is itself appalled into retreat. This second scene, we know, had a particularly intimate meaning for James, for it derives from the dream recorded in his autobiography of a spectral pursuer who is faced and forced to flee the dreamer in the Galerie d'Apollon of the Louvre.[7] What alter ego of himself James acknowledged and yet was glad to have driven before him isn't clear—but it has some possible connection with Brydon's. Gaping at the skyscrapers of New York, the writer felt Brydon's mingled emotions, and his encounter of consciousness between pasts actual and possible, life lived and its alternatives, is reflected in the story.

We may also read this story as a fable of art. Brydon starts from a condition of willed indifference to the possibilities of any story but the one he has lived, of any character but the one he recognizes as himself. But into this void he allows his recognition of an alternative life to enter, and he hunts, with the aggression of art, for the latencies in his own narrative, the unenacted in his own nature. It is as a writer of fiction that he sees how analogy and metaphor can assist the process by which the hypothetical acquires living form. He discovers that alterity is always lurking in our structures of meaning, that narrative contains its subverting alternatives. But such alterity is also the enemy of formal art; the artist strives to rout it out of his house of fiction. Only Alice, the perceiving reader, knows that it is, in some sense, still within, a haunting part of the structure's potentiality.

· 12 ·

The Wings of the Dove

The Wings of the Dove is generally discussed as though it centers exclusively upon the "dove" of the title, Milly Theale, another in James's succession of young American women who crave a freedom—sometimes thought to be characteristically American—from the restrictions of destiny. James himself lent strength to this view by admitting that his image of Milly was born out of old memories of his cousin Minny Temple, who—like this heroine—had died in her early youth, and that his impulse to write the novel had been memorial.[1] Yet it may be argued that Kate Croy, with whom the novel begins and ends, occupies a greater space, and is seen more closely. In a letter to Ford Madox Ford written shortly after the novel appeared in 1902, James responded to the criticism that he had failed to give Milly the place and treatment of a central figure by declaring that "the subject was Densher's history with Kate Croy—hers with him, and Milly's history was but a thing involved and embroiled in that."[2]

But the truth may be that the novel does not subordinate either of these subjects to the other—that both prevail in a powerful engagement with one another. How this came to be is disclosed in James's own notebook record of his progress in conceiving his story. As he began to think of it in 1894 his ideas soon included something not at all involved with his youthful memories. He *had* first picked up the old interest in a young woman condemned to an early death. He then thought of how her case might affect a sympathetic young man who is prompted to help her even if he will lose rather than gain, "to sacrifice something in order to be kind to her, and to do it without a reward, for the poor girl, even if he loved her, has no life to give him in return." His help would be quite disinterested. How different this conception is from the situation in the finished novel. In the place of

289

unselfish sympathy, which can in no way be repaid, Densher is drawn into a relationship with Milly by Kate's and his own expectation of advantage. And, in fact, a few days after his first notation, James recorded his decision to make the young girl rich and to picture the young man agreeing with his fiancée to marry her for her fortune. Their charity, having been replaced by profit seeking, is now the attribute of the dying girl. It is she who will represent love that earns no reward, not even the briefest happiness; she will leave him her fortune *without* marrying him.

At the start, James had spoken of the girl's case using the word "have" in both its slang sexual sense and the sense of possession: "Oh, she's dying without having had it? Give it to her and let her die." Now, he finds "having" of any sort a bar to the ideal he wishes to image in his heroine. "I seem to get hold of the tail of a pretty idea in making that happiness, that life, that snatched experience the girl longs for, BE, *in fact,* some rapturous act of that sort—some act of generosity, of passionate beneficence, of pure sacrifice, to the man she loves. This would obviate all 'marriage' between *them,* and everything so vulgar as an 'engagement,' and, removing the poor creature's yearning from the class of egotistic pleasures, the dream of being possessed and possessing, etc., make it something fine and strange."[3] It is possible to misunderstand this decision as an expression of James's distaste for sex. But what James really intends is to separate the idea of "interest" from that of charity with a schematic clarity. If an engagement would bring the relation of Milly and Densher into "the class of egotistic pleasures" it is because James sees how permeated modern sexual relations are with what one may call the psychology of the marketplace. The engaged couple who will represent this condition will, in the novel, turn out to be Kate and Densher themselves. It will be Milly Theale's achievement of life through loss that makes hers a style of being of supreme contrast with these others and with their world in which, incongruously, she is placed.

But what is not predicted in James's notebook outline is what he would make of the character of "the fiancée." Having given the young man an "interest" in the heiress, James felt that the two girls, mutually jealous, should be hostile. In the novel, however, they are friends who deeply appreciate each other's qualities. Milly, of course, is deceived about Kate's relationship to Densher, but Kate, who suspects Milly's feelings from the start without disclosing her own, can admire and pity her, and yet act in terms of the most uncorrupted self-interest. The fiancée of the notebooks is too coarse, too cruelly indifferent to her victim, to be Kate Croy, and at the end, unlike Kate, she simply accepts the bequest of the dead girl—and marries "Lord X," the later Lord Mark. Kate is the special triumph of the novel, unanticipated in James's first inspiration—a character who represents a new conception of noble behavior to oppose to Milly's traditional one. Milly remains as that opposite ideal still to be identified with James's view of Minny Temple, who had a character which might have been "almost literally said to have been without practical application to life."[4] But the figure of Kate becomes of such equal—or more than equal—importance that James could overstate it in the letter to Ford. If Milly's character turns out to "have no practical application to life," Kate is the heroine of the practical. She represents a cluster of modern traditions—naturalist and pragmatist. She is the ultimate expression of a society in which "value" means the purchasing power of anything as determined by the market.

To these attitudes and this world Milly opposes an older transcendental tradition of intrinsic personal being and a principle of moral behavior which stresses sacrifice rather than gain. There are really two heroines in the novel. In the New York Edition preface James comes around, in fact, to realizing that he had made Milly only one pole in the field of his novel, or, to use his own figure, one side of a freely hanging medal, "the correlative half being the state of others as affected by her," a medal whose two faces were "embossed and figured with an equal salience" (2:1292).

I wish to speak of *The Wings of the Dove* in several ways, and I will begin by reviewing its precise reference to the social and economic world of the early twentieth century, a stratum of meaning to which its narrative language and formal design are closely attached. It is easy to see that *The Wings of the Dove* is all about money. It is all about the fact that Kate and Densher cannot be happy unless they get money. It is no use our saying they could have married without it; their personal and class premises make a grubby survival in Chelsea, like that of Kate's sister, inconceivable—and Susan Stringham's example (like Henrietta Stackpole's in *The Portrait of a Lady*) of the independent woman who earns her own living is simply not available to Kate as an alternative. Though Densher offers at the end to marry her without Milly's fortune, Kate knows perfectly well that this is impossible, and her offer to dispense with Milly's money if he can swear that he is not in love with her memory is made with the knowledge that he cannot make that avowal. But the calculus of gain has governed their relations in a more subtle way also. In this novel James presents through symbolic action and language the reflex of a commercial society in the recesses of private life. With extraordinary insight into the nature of modern experience, he recognizes that it is not sufficiently descriptive of modern man to say that he is subject to a market economy and constantly engaged in a contest for economic advantage. The competitive establishment of market value extends to those parts of a person, those aspects of behavior, once thought to have *incalculable* value.

The Wings of the Dove opens with a remarkable conversation between a father and a daughter. Kate's aunt, Maud Lowder, has made her a proposal. It is the first offered bargain in the book, to be followed by many. If Kate will give up her father, Aunt Maud will "keep" her. However altered the terms from their usual sense—Kate's father is hardly a sentimental tie—this is an offer to exchange a moral for a practical benefit. But Lionel Croy is for the transaction in terms that make them equivalents. He urges Kate to "work" the family bond with Aunt Maud to raise her "value." "If he recognized his younger daughter's happy aspect as a tangible value, he had from the first still more exactly appraised every point of his own" (XIX:12). He advises her: "I'm a poor ruin of an old dad to make a stand about giving up—I quite agree. But I'm not, after all, quite the old ruin not to get something *for* giving up." In his only half-ironic way, Croy continues, "The family sentiment, in our vulgarized brutalized life, has gone utterly to pot. There was a day when a man like me—by which I mean a parent like me—would have been for a daughter like you quite a distinct value; what's called in the business world, I believe, an 'asset'" (XIX:17). "Value" here and many times henceforth in this novel will have its strictest economic sense.

Kate has a kind of bargain in mind herself. She proffers her family loyalty to her father in exchange for the right to continue her romance with Merton Densher, who she realizes is excluded from Aunt Maud's package. And though her sense of family loyalty is sincere and her love for Densher genuine, they have been reduced to their equivalents as items of exchange. Croy, measuring their "value" against eventual expectations that attend for him if Kate goes to Maud, rejects his daughter's offer.

Mrs. Lowder, to whom Kate now goes, is the mythic divinity of the modern world, the representative of the great hidden forces of commerce underlying its events. Kate calls her "Britannia of the Market Place," a grandiose title for an ordinary middle-class dowager, but James makes us see her as the goddess of the countinghouse, "with a pocket full of coins stamped in her image." Seeing her at her accounts, with her pen behind her ear, Kate "felt that she should not be happy till she might on some occasion add to the rest of the panoply a helmet, a shield, a trident and a ledger" (XIX:30–31). Aunt Maud deserves all the trappings of Britannia—and, in addition, James slyly implies, the *ledger*, which is not included in any of Britannia's conventional images on coins or elsewhere. So, it is at Lancaster Gate that the principle of exchange value is most consciously put into practice. It is there that Kate and Milly and Densher are all "weighed," Densher hearing from the house its constant muffled hum, "What do you offer, what do you offer?" (XX:32).

Kate, the modern "free" girl, and Densher, the somewhat rootless young man whom she picks up at a party, begin their romance in that urban anonymity and publicity which denies them privacy and futurity—in the streets and the museums and railroad stations and the public parks of London where they meet because they have nowhere else to go. Under the open sky of Kensington Gardens they pledge their love, but even here a bargain has been struck. Densher has won Kate's promise by agreeing to keep their engagement secret so that they may still maneuver for Aunt Maud's money. He has been "forced to weigh his case in scales," considering the relative weight of shame in "marrying for" and "marrying without" (XIX:63) money, as if these were quantities on a shop counter.

The decision to use Aunt Maud is a plan which is promoted by the arrival of the rich young American, Milly Theale, whose friendship will possibly make a cover for theirs, her tender interest in Densher a concealment of their own romance. But finally, they resolve to dispense with Aunt Maud altogether by a still more promising plan by which Milly, who is dying, will marry Densher and leave him *her* money. How clearly even this summary suggests that perversion of affection into "use" hinted already in Kate's conversation with her father! Not only does Milly's love have a "use" in this scheme of Kate's and Densher's, but their own sympathy and respect for her, real enough, become efficacious in the furtherance of their plan. And their *mutual* love comes to constitute a commerce by which—Kate dealing with Densher, Densher with Kate—each can bend the other to his purpose.

But let us consider the image of Milly Theale in her status as the "dove" of the novel's title. This association and other images connected with Milly suggest that religious tradition is being invoked—but there is no need to see allegory in the novel. Milly is not Christ, but James wanted to introduce the powerful vocabulary of the tradition which insists on the immeasurable value of the spirit and the ethic of generous love in the place of the modernism exemplified by Kate and Densher. There is, of course, the early scene in the Alps when Susan Stringham sees her friend perched on a promontory in a posture that suggests that she is "looking down on the kingdoms of the earth" (XIX:124). If this is a significant association with Christ in the desert, it may not be so much with the second temptation as with the one following it, when Christ is challenged to cast himself off the pinnacle of the temple in Jerusalem and prove himself the Son of God when angels catch him in midair. Christ refuses to renounce his humanity, however, until he reaches the ultimate in human suffering. Susan guesses that Milly on her mountain peak rejects a "sharp or simple release from the human predicament. It wouldn't be for her a question of a flying leap and thereby of a quick escape. It would be a question of taking full in the face the whole assault of life" (XIX:125). Her identification with Christ also serves to reinforce Milly's role as the representative of disinterested love, even sacrifice. "Sacrifice," of course, is exactly antithetic to "sale" (when something is "sold at a sacrifice" it has ceased to figure in a proper market exchange). Milly is also tempted in the way of Christ's second temptation—she is tempted by the desire to possess the fullest human satisfactions, including love—and only finds her divine gesture when her dearest friends have betrayed her.

Before she comes to this, she is immersed in the marketplace world of Lancaster Gate. Lord Mark explains "Nobody here, you know, does anything for nothing" (XIX:160), and tells her that she herself is an "offering" being "jumped at" (XIX:154–155) from all quarters. Kate continues her education by explaining that "everyone who had anything to give . . . made the sharpest possible bargain for it, got at least its value in return . . . The worker in one connexion was the worked in another" (XIX:179). Maud and Lord Mark were

each "waiting for what the other would put down." Milly is quick to
see that Kate is on Maud's "counter"—and Kate agrees, "I *am* . . .
when I'm not in the shop-window . . . the essence, all of it, of my
position, and the price, as properly, of my aunt's protection"
(XIX:278–279). This education in middle-class exchange values
continues when Milly goes from Lancaster Gate to the more refined
example of the kingdoms of the world, the aristocratic ancient
country house, Matcham. There she meets Lord Mark again, and
feels his calculated interest at the same time as she contemplates the
Bronzino portrait which looks like her and reminds her of the death
which will overtake her own splendid love of life and her royal free-
doms. She knows she is ill and goes to her physician, Sir Luke Strett,
who suggests that she may "live" (even though she must die) by
open acceptance of the human lot—again the meaning of Christ's
refusal of the third temptation, with which her pose in the Alps has
already identified her. There follow the wonderful pages in which
Milly digests this message as she walks slowly home across London.
In Regent's Park she sees, as though for the first time, the world of
men and women "just in the same box" (XIX:250).

With the opening of the second volume of the novel we find
again, as at the beginning, the pair of modern poor lovers meeting to
consider their situation, and Densher discloses the ravages of an
"impatience that, prolonged and exasperated, made a man ill"
(XX:7). Sex quite divorced from sentiment appears in this volume
as it had not in the earlier one; already we are being prepared for
Kate's and Densher's conversion of it into a currency of exchange. It
is Kate who first sees possibilities in Milly's feelings for Densher
and urges him to "make something of that" (XX:18). She does not
seem to care how deeply he may become involved with the dying
girl if it will be to their advantage in the end. And so, as they begin
to pervert sexuality in relation to Milly, they pervert it in relation to
each other. In Venice, Densher will exact in payment for his
promise to proceed with the other girl Kate's promise to "come" to
him (XX:200).

Milly's Venetian palace is the "ark of her deluge" (XX:143),
the place of her hope of some sort of survival that reinforces the
Christian association of her life with the old typology that makes
the Noah story a representation of death and transfiguration. She
establishes herself there, never, as she tells Lord Mark, to come
down again, while she rejects his offer in terms of that sense of value

that he himself and Lancaster Gate have taught her. "He mustn't be mistaken about her value, for what value did she now have?" And then she realizes the terrible sense of "value" for this suitor. "Wouldn't her value for the man who should marry her be precisely in the ravage of her disease?" (XX:149). He cannot see, for his part, how she can reject him and the love he is perfectly ready to put forth so that, as she interjects, one finds oneself "forced to love in return" (XX:156). But as Milly rejects love as barter, Densher and Kate infect their own with the parlaying of the market. He feels "a rage at what he wasn't having" in which sexual impatience is combined with the irritation of one who has made a bad bargain. He "looks into their account," and finds that "whereas he had done absolutely everything that Kate had wanted, she had done nothing whatever that he had" (XX:175, 177). From Milly, on the other hand, he has got more than he has "consciously bargained" for—"her welcome, frankness, sweetness, sadness, brightness, her disconcerting poetry" (XX:184).

Milly after this appears to Kate and Densher, though she does not speak to them, at the party she gives in her palace, a scene that even more than Matcham suggests the worldliness that surrounds the sacred, as in Veronese's *The Wedding at Cana* at the Louvre, to which Susan Stringham compares it. Like Christ, luminous but remote in the background of the crowded painting, Milly is seen from a distance "diffus[ing] in wide warm waves the spell of a general, a beatific mildness" (XX:213). Yet it is at this moment that Kate's and Densher's way of using Milly's love is given explicit expression when Kate compels him to articulate, "Since she's to die I'm to marry her? . . . So that when her death has taken place I shall in the natural course have money?" (XX:225). As they still look at Milly in her splendid pearls sending them a sense of "the value of her life," he promises to "do everything"—and Kate agrees to sleep with him (XX:229, 231).

His sexual after-feelings are expressed, as we now expect, in terms of the novel's ambiguous senses of "possession" and "value." "He had in fine judged his friend's pledge in advance as an inestimable value, and what he must now know his case for was that of a possession of the value to the full . . . The quantity of the article to be supplied, the special solidity of the contract, the way, above all, as a service for which the price named by him had been magnificently paid, his equivalent office was to take effect—such items

might well fill his consciousness" (XX:236, 237). And so, in fulfillment of his contract, he begins to pay the lover-like visits to Milly
to which he has been obliged by Kate's embraces. Curiously, however, he feels strangely unguilty. Something "purges" his relationship with Milly, makes it innocent. Something "incalculable"—
how significant the word is in this fable of calculation!—is wrought
for him as he finds Milly "divine in her trust." What Milly has to
give is not an exchange—her welcome provides "a felicity—he
scarce knew by what strange name to call it—for which he said to
himself that he had not consciously bargained" (XX:184).

But when her door is closed to him Densher realizes that her
majordomo, Eugenio, has spotted him all along as a fortune hunter.
Later, when he discovers that it is Lord Mark's revelation of his
secret engagement to Kate that has caused Milly's collapse he is
wildly indignant, as though to assert that he is not, like Mark, after
Milly's money—though what else *has* he been after? And perhaps he
is altered enough to make the indignation legitimate. After a long
wait in a storm-swept "Venice all of evil," he is permitted to see
Milly for the last time. Recalling the occasion afterward he saw
himself in an image of "a young man far off and in a relation inconceivable, saw him hushed, passive, staying his breath, but half-
understanding, yet dimly conscious of something immense and
holding himself painfully together not to lose it . . . The essence
was that something had happened to him too beautiful and too
sacred to describe. He had been, to his recovered sense, forgiven,
dedicated, blessed" (XX:342–343). The language is, again, religious
in tone, and the "young man" might be the elegant worldling with
whom Susan has identified him, who holds up a glass, discovering a
miracle, in the foreground of *The Wedding at Cana*.

Back in London, he gives his report to Kate, whose easier pragmatic mercy condemns him for not having lied to Milly about themselves. His refusal suggests to Kate the truth that he has fallen in
love with the dying girl. But there is no regret in Kate's accusation.
She suspects, correctly, that Milly has loved and forgiven him, and
that she will make him rich—"Which is what I've worked for . . .
She won't have loved you for nothing," she says, confident that
Milly has received an adequate exchange for what she gives. "And
you won't have loved *me*," she adds, assuring Densher that his
reward, for his love of Kate, which has reached so far, will be given
appropriately (XX:332–333). So they wait for news of Milly's death

as the London winter—like divine judgment, or like Milly herself—grows "disconcertingly mild" (XX:344). Not irrelevantly, the season is Advent when the fallen world, religiously speaking, is approaching the promise of Paradise regained. Meeting Kate once more in a park on the shortest day of the year Densher begs her to marry him. Kate, like a business partner rather than a lover, accuses him of threatening to "desert" her when success is almost in their grasp; Densher takes in, as she talks, "her imperturbable consistency, which it was quietly, queerly hopeless to see her stand there and breathe into their mild remembering air." Of course, if he *knows* something—if he has definite assurance that Milly is going to leave her money to him, they needn't wait. "There my dear," smiles Kate, like a merchant who makes a "generous" offer, "I call that really meeting you." Densher can only "stand there with his wasted passion" and "horror of her lucidity." And Kate, as previously, acts to "save their position . . . putting her hand upon him, she made him sink with her, as she leaned to him, into their old pair of chairs, she prevented irresistibly, she forestalled, the waste of his passion" in that economy of hers which finds a "use" for love (XX:348–350).

On Christmas Day Densher passes but does not enter an "Oratory" where a service is in progress and visits Kate at her sister's, to find her surrounded, as at the beginning of the novel, by those conditions from which she must escape. He brings her an unopened letter from Milly and offers her the right to open it to pay her back for the hour she had given him in his rooms in Venice—a "sacrifice" which will annihilate what he terms her own sacrifice in submitting to him then. "Sacrifice" is not the right word for what Kate has done, of course. The right word would be "sale." Yet, paradoxically, it is Kate, though she burns the letter unopened, whose "lucidity" allows her to see Milly as one who brings spiritual renewal by an act of abundant sacrifice. At the very end she tells Densher, "She died for you then that you might understand her" (XX:403). It is Kate who calls Milly a dove and says that her wings cover them.

But their bargaining is not quite done before this happens. Another letter, which contains Milly's formal bequest, has arrived from her lawyers. Densher offers to marry Kate immediately if he can send it back, decline the legacy. Kate senses another weighting of the balance, and says she agrees if he can swear he is not in love with Milly's memory. But he is, and they will never be as they were;

their own love, once innocent, has been subdued to the "dream of being possessed and possessing" (XX:403).

I want to consider, now, how *The Wings of the Dove* dramatizes a philosophical dispute that goes beyond the description of personal relations in the modern world, and how the novel's use of literary traditions of plot and character description is involved in presenting the contention between the pragmatic calculus and "exchange" value and the idea of "sacrifice." Kate may be identified with the secondary female character—Madame Merle or Olive Chancellor in James's own earlier novels—who can be called the antagonist of the drama of intrigue in which the innocent young woman finds herself. But the split of interest in this later study is more than a matter of fair and dark ladies, those pairs that occur throughout the history of the novel to illustrate female innocence and its corrupted though fascinating alternate. Kate is a contrast with Milly because she is conceived not so much as a wicked person who plots to contrive personal gain and deceives her friend as a character who belongs to another plot of her own—that of naturalism. In the latter plot, she is, of course, only what she must be, determined by her circumstances and endowments, her own will itself a "natural" force that makes her not so much a passive victim as a creature who survives as she can. The novel's two heroines seem to belong to different worlds of cause and effect.

At the same time, the relation between them is a unitary one which refers itself back to the alterity of the earlier heroine—to that potentiality we glimpse through Isabel's resemblances to other characters who help to compose the shifting light and shadow of her portrait. What Isabel was as well as what she might have been is expressed in *The Wings of the Dove*. After beginning as the poor young woman of refined background and personal quality who seems to have no alternative but to accept the only plot available to her (the marriage-plot, which, by placing her economically and socially, will give her survival and a story), Isabel becomes, romantically, the heroine liberated from the ordinary naturalistic constraints by a fairy-tale gift of great wealth. She thus passes from being Kate (with whom the later novel begins and on whom it focuses for many chapters) to being Milly Theale, the new center of the book, the rare and beautiful rich young woman who seems able to do whatever she wishes. The rich Isabel discovers, it will be remembered, that she has not been made more free than when she was poor. Exactly in the same fashion, Milly discovers eventually that being rich has made her more subject to the imposed plots of those who now conspire against her, a consequence as inevitable as the effects of poverty.

But the refutation of the dream of self-determination will be even more absolute in her case. As James describes her in his preface, she is "possessed of all things, all but the single most precious assurance; freedom and money and a mobile mind and personal charm, the power to interest and attach; attributes, each one, enhancing the value of a future." She is the "heir of all the ages"—she has everything that might descend upon a human being as the gift of unstinting good fortune—and yet, she has only a brief futurity in which to employ these things; she is to be "balked of [her] inheritance" (2:1290–1291). It is Milly who must finally face the inevitability of her own death, must realize—sooner and more sharply than most persons—that the mere fact of being human exposes her to circumscriptions more absolute than poverty. Still, her ability to act freely persists. She asserts the survival of her potentiality, asserts James's romantic faith in the human will, acting even in her dying to fulfill her own curious prediction, "Since I've lived all these years as if I were dead, I shall die, no doubt, as if I were alive" (XIX:199).

But while Milly's career, in *The Wings of the Dove,* is an analogue of Isabel's history after she has become rich, the later novel gives us in Kate the enactment of the merely potential Isabel. Kate is Isabel as she might have turned out if she had not been made free of the usual constraints confining a poor girl's destiny. Like Isabel, she is a young woman of great personal promise who is "taken up" by her wealthy aunt and launched upon the marriage market. Like Isabel, Kate is in a position to receive proposals from prospective husbands—she, too, has her English aristocrat favored by her aunt in the person of Lord Mark, her Lord Warburton. She, too, resists by means of another possibility of her own choosing, a man she would prefer to marry. But Kate cannot marry Densher if Aunt Maud disapproves of him—whereas Isabel can marry Osmond because she has magically become an heiress as a result of Ralph's intervention in her fate.

Nothing so unlikely happens to Kate, who becomes, under these circumstances, the other female figure of importance in *The Portrait of a Lady,* its dark anti-heroine, Madame Merle. She is an expansion to major terms of that earlier character's determined prehistory as a young woman who had a lover she could not afford to marry. One can extrapolate backward to imagine a young Madame Merle, lately landed from America, who might have been someone like Isabel. (She, too, we remember, speaks of having once had such dreams as Isabel cherishes.) But she is sponsored by no one; her love affair, which once, we can imagine, burned as brightly as that between Kate and Densher, remains (as Kate's already is) furtive and without prospect. The shadowy M. Merle may or may not have existed—he seems as much an invention of Madame Merle as anything else—but the illegitimate child, Pansy, is the consequence of sexual liaison which the naturalist novel seldom omits. Kate has not come to this yet, though the consummated sexual character of her relationship with her lover is more explicit here than sex is almost anywhere else in James. Of course, she is not, within the novel, so captive to biology as to become pregnant. But she is no less a naturalist demonstration for that. Like Dreiser's Sister Carrie, Kate does not suffer the usual consequence of sexual relations—in times before birth control—because we must see her as herself a strong natural force. Susan Stringham characterizes Kate's Aunt Maud as "a grand natural force" (XIX:217), and so she is, but the description is just as appropriate to Kate. Symbolically, Kate's capacity to survive nearly dominates the forces of circumstances.

Milly's faith in freedom is seemingly sustained by the crude fact of wealth; in this irony the naturalist argument maintains itself behind the transcendental idealism of the protagonist. Material conditions—the conditions of wealth—promise to make for the freedom from material considerations which Ralph thought to donate to Isabel through his father's legacy. Milly, an heiress who has never been poor, starts with a freedom from ordinary constraints that is obvious to all. "She had to ask nobody for anything, to refer nothing to any one; her freedom, her fortune and her fancy were her law" (XIX:175). Her success in London makes Kate tell her "There's nothing you can't have. There's nothing you can't do" (XIX:228). Because she is rich and without any ties she can, it would seem, choose her husband, and so fulfill the marriage-plot in its most rosy version. Milly is, from the start, a "princess" who can live in a palace, wear pearls—and, if she wishes, marry a poor man.

But even when she receives her doctor's sentence—along with his advice to accept "any form in which happiness may come," she insists on her freedom: "I can do exactly as I like—anything in the whole wide world. I haven't a creature to ask—there's not a finger to stop me" (XIX:242–243). She undertakes to practice living by "her option, her volition" (XIX:249). Wealth does not help her—any more than it did Isabel—to be free since it serves to provoke the designs of those others, the pair who need money, and involves her with them in what James calls, in the preface, "communities of doom" (2:1292). The disappointment of Lord Mark, who, unlike Lord Warburton, wants money and sees the same opportunity in Milly that Kate and Densher do, makes for the catastrophe in which he reveals the lovers' scheme to the girl—and the plan of gaining from her while keeping her deludedly happy only causes her willingness to die. So, the plot which would have fulfilled her dream of marriage and Kate's dream also, both at the same time, is derailed. In addition, the coercion of natural forces, her mortal disease, arrives to refute the hopes of freedom of this anti-naturalist heroine, though she is young and in love with life.

More darkly, James also saw (as with Isabel) that the delusions of freedom could convert even his virtuous heroine to the role of her opposite; Milly "plots" against Kate as much as she is plotted against by Kate—thus reinforcing their twinship in another way. As we have seen, Isabel may have been as guilty as Osmond and Madame Merle in stimulating their schemes by her desire to endow Osmond with the power to act that she herself is incapable of exercising. Her passivity—which cause her to resemble naturalism's passive victim character—makes her, paradoxically, irresistible. So, Milly may, ultimately, be both dove and eagle, holding the other two chief characters in her power. Her generosity and her need as well as her wealth have created the plotters' plot as much as they themselves. Not only have these operated as temptations impossible to refuse, but it is *her* design—call it love and sacrifice—that her bequest to Densher finally imposes although it seems most to fulfill the aim that Kate and Densher have worked for. Precisely because she *does* leave them her money, the two lovers can never be united "as they were." In his New York Edition preface James describes Milly, startlingly, as a *Lorelei*. He sees her treacherous friends as "terrified and tempted and charmed; bribed away, it may even be, from more prescribed and natural orbits, inheriting from their connection with her strange difficulties and still stranger opportunities"—the new plot or "orbit" they enter upon being, thus, a result of her influence. James uses another image even more terrifying, not so much mythological as naturalistic: Milly, in her sinking, is like a great ocean vessel, "or the failure of a great business," which creates a "whirlpool movement of the waters" whose "strong narrowing eddies, the immense force of suction, the general engulfment that for any neighbouring object, makes immersion inevitable" (2:1290–1292).

But despite the alterity within each of them, Milly and Kate inhabit worlds governed by different viewpoints. This difference is underlined by James's contrasting treatment of the two. He not only makes Kate someone who enacts the viewpoint of naturalism and pragmatism, but defines her positively and naturalistically. He makes Milly someone who not only is a representative of a romantic view of human identity and fate, but who is exhibited in the text by a complementary literary mode. Kate's starting point in family connections and material conditions is exactly clear, as the realist tradition demands, while the reverse is true of Milly. The novel opens with a sharp physical description of Kate as she sees herself in the "tarnished glass" (a symbol of realist mimesis) in the shabby parlor of her father's lodging house. As she moves restlessly about the room, her glance takes inventory of her derelict father's surroundings, "from the shabby sofa to the armchair upholstered in a glazed cloth that gave at once—she had tried it—the sense of the slippery and the sticky" to "the sallow prints on the walls and . . . the lonely magazine, a year old, that combined, with a small lamp in coloured glass and a knitted white centre-piece wanting in freshness, to enhance the effect of the purplish cloth on the principal table." Her itemizing gaze gives us a swift environmental summary of the "vulgar little street" whose "narrow black house-fronts, adjusted to a standard that would have been low even for backs, constituted quite the publicity implied by such privacies" (XIX:3)—an image which crystallizes the expectation that externalities, whether of houses or persons, express what is hidden within them.

But James's parody of Balzac in the mean boardinghouse where Lionel Croy's downward-moving fortune has brought him also implies that Kate's presence is an anomaly; she is not the expression of such circumstances but of the earlier, never visible gentility and prosperity from which the Croys have fallen. Her offer to live with her father is a gesture which must be rejected—aside from her father's calculations—because the congruence between character and appurtenances, which Isabel scorned, is absolutely essential to

Kate; she is inconceivable in such a scene. As a character who must be defined by her outer circumstances—like Madame Merle, who cannot ever be imagined as shabby—she cannot exist there.

Directly after this, the reader is asked to test the suitability to Kate of a contrasted setting. At Lancaster Gate, Maud Lowder's house expresses a "florid philistinism"; Aunt Maud herself seems one of her expensive decorative furnishings, "majestic, magnificent, high-coloured, all brilliant gloss, perpetual satin, twinkling bugles and flashing gems, with a lustre of agate eyes, a sheen of raven hair, a polish of complexion that was like that of well-kept china" (XIX:31, 30). Certainly Aunt Maud is like Madame Vauquier, whose appearance expresses her house and whose house expresses her. Kate must choose between the two real worlds of Chirk Street and Lancaster Gate, but it is plain that, despite her offer to give up her aunt and come to her father, there is no question that she belongs to the world of "things"—whether philistine or aesthetically superior, like the collection of Poynton.

Lodged with her aunt, "she saw as she had never seen before how material things spoke to her. She saw, and she blushed to see, that if in contrast with some of its old aspects life now affected her as a dress successfully 'done up' this was exactly by reason of its trimmings and lace, was a matter of ribbons and silk and velvet. She had a dire accessibility to pleasure from such sources" (XIX:28). Such a statement means that Kate is "materialistic" in the usual sense; that is, she enjoys the furnishings of life that money can buy—houses, clothes, and the rest—though her taste in such matters is probably, like Fleda Vetch's, an aesthetically superior one. But it is also a statement that defines the kind of being she is, one for whom—by her nature—a certain environment is, as Madame Merle would say, "expressive." In her father's present surroundings or the meager and resentful respectability of her sister's house in "comfortless Chelsea" (XIX:33), she is placed among conditions "grotesquely inapt" for her (XX:364), as Densher recognizes. She is "made for great social uses" (XIX:212), as even Milly feels when she views this friend against the background of a great English country house.

It would be a mistake, of course, to think of Kate as wedded to things merely in a vulgar, acquisitive sense. Seen in her father's mantel mirror, she is at once visible as a person of elegant economy of means, her general handsomeness "not sustained by items and aids" (XIX:5). Her style of dress signifies that she is someone who can dispense with a good deal, someone who knows exactly what she wants and what she can afford to do without in order to have it, and knows this with such surety and intelligence that her realism has a purity, even a beauty, which compels admiration. Her outstanding and admirable feature being her "lucidity," she does not waver and collapse before unpleasant facts but acts as she must to make the best of them, knowing, without self-deception, what *must* be given up as well as what must be done to gain her ends. When Densher wonders how, caring for him, she can bear to insist that he go on to the end with Milly, she says, "I don't like it, but I'm a person, thank goodness, who can do what I don't like"—a speech in which Densher reads "a kind of heroic ring, a note of character that belittle[s] his own incapacity for action" (XX:226).

In Kate James created a representative of that modern pragmatic consciousness in which the distinction between the dictated and the freely chosen course has begun to disappear—the will fused with a conscious recognition of conditions that impose themselves and dictate the kinds of accommodation that make for survival. She sees the limits of free will in a universe dominated by objective conditions. Her practicality is confirmed by the most absolute of tests in the complacency with which she can dismiss sexual jealousy as a dispensable emotion; she does not balk at the condition necessary to success, that her own lover make love to another woman. Densher, at the end of the novel, recoils from this practicality—to which he has also been committed—in his final renunciation of the fortune he and Kate have striven for. Practically speaking, his gesture is as futile (Milly is dead and cannot appreciate his sacrifice) as it is self-mutilating (Kate will consequently be lost to him). But Kate remains to the last unregretful of her pursuit of the only course which might have married circumstance to her desires.

Kate's philosophic materialism and pragmatism account for her valuation of appearances. "Things" for her, as for Mrs. Gereth, *are* what is, and nothing else is. And things are known by their register upon the senses and then named for what they are and their usefulness is understood. Kate explains to Milly that at Lancaster Gate, to whose measure she is subdued, "one knew people in general by something they had to show, something that, either for them or against, could be touched, or named or proved" (XIX:178). Milly's lessons at Lancaster Gate become, with Kate's help, lessons in "seeing things as they [are]" (XIX:278). Kate is like Madame

Merle, again. Not only is she no believer in personal essence; she also does not believe, one feels, in spiritual essences of any kind or in the worth of things that are good in themselves instead of having a quantifiable efficacy; she is like Dr. Sloper who asks what things—and even persons—are "good for."

The denial of anything but manifestation or practical effect is, of course, one consequence of the general positivist denial of essence. In James's friend Maupassant's famous story, "The Jewelry," a husband who has lived a life of perfect marital felicity discovers his wife's deception only after her death when she leaves him a legacy of falsely "fake"—really valuable—jewelry dishonorably gotten. He then marries an honorable woman who makes him miserable. Behind this irony is the pragmatic argument that the counterfeit coin of appearances, as Edouard says in Gide's *Les faux monnayeurs*, is as good as the genuine as long as it passes current. Kate's faith in the value of the apparent makes her able to commit the same sort of crime as Madame Merle—that is, to arrange a marriage between another, wealthier woman and her own lover. In both cases, it is a crime that breaks no laws. It may even benefit (as long as she is unknowing) its victim, and violates only that imponderable privilege of self-determination which the free spirit cherishes above else. The victimizer—Madame Merle or Kate Croy—does not ever really understand the gravity of the violation exercised; to these pragmatists, anyhow, free will is an illusion.

That Kate views life like a naturalist novelist herself is, as I have been trying to show, related to James's own interest in attaching her to presented circumstances, in identifying the background to which she "belongs" as a plant or animal belongs by its nature to one appropriate environment or another. Although the whole of the first and second books—about a hundred pages—is given over to the presentation of Kate's social and economic displacement and the problems it creates for her, James still thought that he had not provided *enough* of the causative and the explanatory in setting her character before the reader. He seems to have realized that he does not show just how she has come to be the sort of person who would act as she does. Motivated by the need for money, she has also been initiated, one can guess—though not see—into the mean shifts and surrenders of scruple which have been the career of Lionel Croy. But James regretted, as he confessed in his preface, that Croy had not been more particularized. He understood that "the image of her so compromised and compromising father was all effectively to have pervaded her life, was in a certain particular way to have tampered with her spring" (2:1295). But he knew that he had not sufficiently exhibited this process. Perhaps the word "compromising" reaches back behind its sense as moral or social discrediting to the fact that between parent and child an inevitable "agreement" of character or destiny is promised. To explain Kate completely, some of Lionel Croy's dissimulation and opportunism might have been shown to have corrupted his daughter, to have "tampered with her spring."

James might have claimed more for his treatment of Croy than he seems to have realized, however. Instead of treating him as a naturalist demonstration of the relation of causes and effects, he uses him in the novel's opening chapter as an ironic illustration of the *delusiveness* of appearances, the masquerade of roles and types. The model English gentleman he has always appeared to be, recognized and admired invariably at a foreign *table d'hôte*, Kate remembers, "was so respectable a show that she felt afresh, and with memory of their old despair, the despair at home, how little his appearance ever by any chance told about him. His plausibility had been the heaviest of her mother's crosses . . . He had positively been, by the force of his particular type, a terrible husband not to live with; his type reflecting so invidiously on the woman who had found him distasteful" (XIX:11). No true alterity is implied by Croy's appearance, but only the falsity of the superficial typology which seems to contain him.

In the case of Densher, the gentleman-journalist who is Kate's accompanying case of social displacement, James felt that he had failed even more to show "the who and the what, the how and the why, the whence and the whither" (2:1296). And Densher is, indeed, not an entirely successfully realized character, belonging neither to the naturalistically comprehensible world of Kate or to the very different universe which encloses the image of Milly. In contrast to our knowledge of Kate, we know very little about his background. Though we are given a page-long synopsis of his early years—his "migratory parents, his Swiss schools, his German university," his father a British chaplain in many foreign places, his mother a "copyist" of famous paintings—and though we are told that Cambridge and London marked his return to his native environment, the summary James offers is that "he had been exposed to initiations indelible. Something had happened to him that could never be undone." He is one of those anomalous persons "various and complicated, complicated by wit and taste . . . spoiled for native, for insular use" (XIX:93–94). He escapes a standard definition of English types. Indeed, what appears to be a description of his character is really a parody of one, an exercise in non-definition:

> Distinctly he was a man either with nothing at all to do or with ever so much to think about; and it was not to be denied that the impression he might often thus easily make had the effect of causing the burden of proof in certain directions to rest on him. It was a little the fault of his aspect, his personal marks, which make it almost impossible to name his profession. He was a longish, leanish, fairish young Englishman, not unamenable, on certain sides, to classification—as for instance by being a gentleman, by being rather specifically one of the educated, one of the generally sound and generally civil; yet, though to that degree neither extraordinary nor abnormal, he would have failed to play straight into an observer's hands. He was young for the House of Commons, he was loose for the Army. He was refined, as might have been said, for the City and, quite apart from the cut of his cloth, sceptical, it might have been felt, for the Church. On the other hand he was credulous for diplomacy, or perhaps even for science, while he was perhaps at the same time too much in his mere senses for poetry and yet too little in them for art. You would have got fairly near him by making out in his eyes the potential recognition of ideas; but you would have quite fallen away again on the question of the ideas themselves.   (XIX:47–48)

James backs away from this list of non-indicators to indulge his character as still possessed of "that wondrous state of youth in which the the elements, the metals more or less precious, are so in fusion and fermentation that the question of the final stamp, the pressure that fixes the value, must wait for comparative coolness" (XIX:49). His image of Densher as a coin of fixed value—and not yet such a coin—employs what I have already discussed as one of the novel's primary images, that of monetary exchange. The "value" of Densher, as of other characters, will be appraised by Aunt Maud, the goddess of the marketplace, at Lancaster Gate, and found to have no equivalence with Kate's. What should be noted, now, however, is how the image of a coin, exactly understood to have one value and no other, is appropriate for the fixed and determinate character which can be understood by realistic typology. James's portrait of Densher excuses itself from such definition just as his portrait of Lionel Croy mocks it.

In accordance with his personal indefiniteness, Densher's, the third important point of view which figures in the book, is a temporizing, impressionistic one which avoids judgment, progressing forward as a series of disjointed conditions. James's presentation of him—unlike his dismissive and limited satiric presentation of Kate's father—is also an instance of James's allowance of alterity to this character who is, from moment to moment in the novel, *either* Kate's collaborator, as much determined upon the exploitation of Milly as she—*or* someone who accepts Milly's innocence as a measure of his own responses. Dramatically, Densher's slowness, his reluctance to perceive what Kate sees at the start as the fatal necessity to which he must come—to marry Milly in order to inherit her fortune when she dies—is a device of suspense, making him also a victim in the intrigue of which Kate is the designer. But, of course, he is an agent—his blindness is a *self*-delusion which makes his commitment possible without shock to his conscience. And yet, such delusion preserves in Densher that element of free sensibility which escapes the pragmatic calculus and allows Milly to purge his motives in their last Venice days.

It is for this reason that we tolerate without scorn his own refusal of an obvious duplication of himself in Eugenio and Lord Mark, who are both also interested in Milly for her money. He is not a stamped coin of unfluctuating value, exactly equivalent to these others. He recoils, horrified, from the realization that all along Milly's major domo has "taken a view of him not less finely formal than essentially vulgar . . . the imputation in particular that, clever, *tanto bello* and not rich, the young man from London was—by the obvious way—pressing Miss Theale's fortune hard" (XX:257). He considers that Lord Mark's revelation to Milly (that Densher and Kate have been engaged all the while) is dastardly. Certainly Mark has acted out of spiteful resentment of Densher's success where he has failed—and his cruelty to Milly is clear—but he has not lied. And yet the sense that Densher's awareness of what Milly is has grown so greatly that it matters less than it did; the story enacted by his calculated tenderness has become true. It is his alterity.[5]

Densher's doubtful self-definition places him at the center of the story between the naturalistically definable and the transcendentally undefinable young women who are both in love with him. He needs to make a choice, just as the reader does, between them—and between two self-definitions. He is poised between the two definitions of a plot, a story, that Kate and Milly represent. We are told that he has "since the day he was born," been one of those for whom the inner experience, the invisible, *un*manifested life, has been his whole adventure—as for so many Jamesian heroes: "He had thought, no doubt . . . much more than he had acted; except indeed that he remembered thoughts—a few of them—which at the moment of their coming to him had thrilled him almost like adventures" (XX:294). In Venice he meets his crisis not so much by an *act* as by becoming more and more aware of Milly. It is his great "adventure" to reach such awareness. The validation of his failure to tell Milly about his love for Kate is—however self-servingly— that he has never denied it to her because she has not asked him. What he thinks of as "the difference between acting and not acting" (XX:76) is, on the one hand, a casuistical excuse; on the other, a claim that his unenacted inner self has been preserved in his silence.

But if Densher's presentation in the novel seems to escape naturalist constraints by its deliberate vagueness, it is the complete absence of the preconditions and explanations required for the realist character that is striking in the case of the novel's second feminine center. Milly is never so closely seen as Kate in the mantel mirror, though we do get a novelistic glance in Susan Stringham's first sight of her young friend, "the slim, constantly pale, delicately haggard, anomalously, agreeably angular young person, of not more than two-and-twenty summers, in spite of her marks, whose hair was somehow exceptionally red even for the real thing, which it innocently confessed to being, and whose clothes were remarkably black even for robes of mourning, which was the meaning they expressed" (XIX:105). But of all those characters in James's novels who preserve potentiality from the determination of the past, Milly's severance from her personal past is the most drastic. Kate, of course, has lost a mother, but is all too persistently connected to her father, sisters, aunt, and a whole society, of which she is a part and to which she refers as "us" when she urges Milly, half seriously, to "drop us while you can." She is connected to "tiers and tiers of others" (XIX:281). But Milly is the most absolute of orphans, "blooming alone," as James says, "for the fullest attestation of her freedom" (2:1290). She is the solitary, transplanted individual who takes nothing from her past except her own unalterable, intrinsic character.

She is, significantly, someone who has not yet loved or been loved erotically—it is the essence of her situation that she has not, in any sense, really "lived" in an ultimate sexual sense. Kate, when we meet her, is already launched upon her love affair with Densher, which has become so serious a matter that it makes any match contrived by Aunt Maud unthinkable. We have the full sense of this London romance in its local terms—the first encounter at a party and again, by chance, in the Underground, and then the trysts, merely for conversation, in public meeting places in the great city. But Milly's encounter with the same man during his American journalistic tour is only referred to, never seen or described though it might logically have been made visible in the narrative, coming, in time, well after the opening of the novel. Susan Stringham has the impression that her friend had liked the young Englishman, but even she was not witness to their direct encounters very much, and Milly's exact feelings about him are not clear. Densher, returning to Kate and London after his American trip thinks of it, himself, as a textual ellipsis, a "parenthesis" in his life, and feels that once again "he was once more but a sentence, of a sort, in the general text . . . a great grey page of print that somehow managed to be crowded without being 'fine' " (XX:11). The omitted episode keeps the beginning of an alternate story for Densher—if it is a beginning—obscure. It is as though in the American world from which Milly starts there can be no significant precondition.

But this suppression of some early start of Milly's adventure is only an anticipation of the way James deliberately utilizes narrative gaps to make her experience mysterious to the reader at more crucial moments. The difference between James's suppression of Milly's priority and his backgrounding—even though he thought it insufficient—of Kate is also connected with James's view that Milly is someone whose inner mystery cannot be seen directly, whereas Kate is fully explicable, as a naturalist heroine must be. Let us return now to consider once more the degree with which James removes Milly from the foreground of his scene—a removal which has been commented upon by many since Ford, one of the novel's earliest critics, complained of it to James, and received the reply already referred to at the start of this chapter. James, as we have seen, defended these suppressions as the result of his greater interest in Kate and Densher—and particularly rejected the idea of a sentimental "last interview": "Hall Caine would have made it large as life, and magnificent, wouldn't he?" he wrote.[6] In his preface he does "mourn . . . the absent values, the palpable voids, the missing links, the mocking shadows" in his novel (2:1294), but these are not his omissions in his account of Milly but rather the insufficiency of his provision of naturalist illusion for Kate and Densher, as already noted. His different way with Milly than with Kate has, as I have been insisting, a more structural purpose, and one which does not diminish Milly's importance. And he seems to have arrived at a more confident justification of his procedure:

> I note how, again and again, I go but a little way with the direct— that is with the straight exhibition of Milly; it resorts for relief, this process, whenever it can, to some kinder, some merciful indirection: all as if to approach her circuitously, deal with her at second hand, as an unspotted princess is ever dealt with; the pressure all round her kept easy for her, the sounds, the movements, regulated, the forms and ambiguities made charming. All of which proceeds, obviously, from her painter's tenderness of imagination about her, which reduces him to watching her, as it were, through the successive windows of other people's interest in her. So, if we talk of princesses, do the balconies opposite the palace gates, do the coigns of vantage and respect enjoyed for a fee, rake from afar the mystic figure in the gilded coach as it comes forth into the great *place*. (2:1303)

It is, indeed, true that Milly is absent from the first two books. She appears suddenly in the third book, in the alpine scenes when we see her not from her own point of view but as an object of wonder and speculation to Susan. She is before us more interiorly in London and at Matcham in the next two books, though we are actually denied a direct view of such a crucial moment as her interview with her doctor—perceiving it only in her reflections as she walks through the city afterwards. She is absent from the sixth book, though we have Kate's and Densher's thoughts about her. It is in the third chapter of the seventh book that we see her for almost the last time from within her own mind, as she settles her thoughts in solitude in her great Venetian palace and then receives and rejects Lord Mark. But the eighth book returns us to Densher's inner thoughts and his conversations with Kate, though Milly is the constant subject of both. At her great dinner party she appears herself only as a background figure while her friends make their bargain to come together and continue their plot. In the last two books she soon becomes invisible in the text and is actually invisible to Densher when her door has been closed to him. Unexhibited, also, is her conversation with Lord Mark, who has, Densher realizes, revealed to Milly how her friends have deceived her—and the nature of her reaction is communicated only by Susan's metaphoric "she has turned her face to the wall." Finally, the tenth book opens after a gap of the greatest importance; Densher has been back in London for a fortnight, having finally been able to see the dying Milly, but this interview and his immediate reaction to it now lie in the past. Her death, when it comes, is far away from his and our view, and her last utterance to him, the letter he gives unopened into Kate's hand, is burnt in the fire unread.

Milly's own reticence as well as James's technique of scenic effacement contribute to the curious sense of absence and distance which surrounds her. In contrast with the explicitness of Kate's statements—her refusal to mince words about what must be done to obtain the prize of Milly's money but also her frank readiness to admit her own passion for Densher—Milly's love is only implied in her gentle dependence upon his company in the early days in Venice. She is reticent, too, about her illness, never letting it appear, refusing to look ill as long as she is visible; gravely ill when she last lets Densher see her, she appears "just as usual" (XX:328). To the end, as Kate has predicted, she does not smell of drugs. (XX:53). Her own reserve, of course, enforces upon others the same silence, and a certain degree of denial of the facts of her case; it promotes "suppressions which were in the direct interest of everyone's good manner, everyone's pity, everyone's really quite generous ideal." (XX:298). So strong is this refusal of exhibition that it rivals, in its willfulness, Kate's positive determination to make something happen—and is an instance, again, of the merger of their characters. The dove becomes an eagle in its "ferocity of modesty" and "intensity of pride" (XX:54).

So she will maintain herself as the image of the unexpungable feminine heroine whose exquisiteness is not subject to nature—whereas Kate, the naturalist heroine, might be expected to age or wither or be staled by custom as time goes on. We can be sure that if Kate were ill we would know exactly what she was ill of. But is Milly dying of cancer, of tuberculosis, or of what? She predicts, early, "I think I could die without its being noticed" (XIX:228)—

and, in a sense, this is what she achieves. After Milly's first consultation with Dr. Strett, Susan learns only that "she hasn't what she thought"—which was something she had apparently feared—but her case may be "something else" which the doctor is watching for, though what that is, Susan doesn't want to know (XIX:109, 111). All she does surmise is that, in some fairy-tale way, love is the "specific" prescribed for Milly's improvement (XIX:112). Her disease, which is never exactly identified, is, really, a token of James's refusal of exactness, of specific identity in Milly's "case" in the most general, unmedical sense. It is altogether appropriate to her role in the moral drama of the novel that James's representation of Milly detaches her—*narratively* speaking—from particularities, encourages the novelist to "sacrifice" these in favor of an image without much visible involvement. In making her the image of sacrificial love, James simultaneously made her surrender the density of realist art which attaches persons to things.

So, James makes Milly more problematic and inscrutable, someone whom others try, unsuccessfully, to bring to definition. It is because he wishes to propose or to test the value of her indefiniteness that she is observed and reflected upon or discussed by all the other characters, by Susan, Kate, Densher, Mrs. Lowder, Lord Mark, Sir Luke. Their problem with Milly is James's own problem, which we have seen him wrestle with repeatedly in other novels, the problem of defining human individuality in relation to its living acts and visible aspects. In *The Wings of the Dove,* no less than in his earlier fictions, the writer's problem is so self-conscious as to express itself in metafictional language. James's metaphor of a Milly seen from different windows or coigns of vantage by those who surround her reminds one of his well-known description in the preface to *The Portrait of a Lady* of the "house of fiction" as a structure from whose windows life is viewed differently by different observers. (2:1075). But even more striking is the way James's language makes his characters duplicate his own experimentation with characterization as they "read" or "write" the story of those they observe.

The effort to represent each others' characters in literary terms is universal in the novel. Milly and Densher both, in turn, look at Kate like novelists trying to fit formula to a new phenomenon. Milly's analysis of Kate fits her to the realist Victorian novel as well as to popular stereotype. She thinks of Kate as "Thackerayan" as she comes to understand "her situation, her past, her present, her general predicament, her small success up to the present hour" and sees Kate as somehow achieving a brilliant destiny. For her, Kate is the "London girl; conceived from the tales of travellers and the anecdotes of New York, from old porings over *Punch* and a liberal acquaintance with the fiction of the day . . . with turns of head and tones of voice, felicities of stature and attitude, things 'put on' and, for that matter, put off, all the marks of the product of a packed society who should be at the same time the heroine of a strong story. She placed this striking young person from the first in a story, saw her, by a necessity of the imagination, for a heroine, felt it the only character in which she wouldn't be wasted" (XIX:173, 171–172). When she meets Kate's sister, Mrs. Condrip, her sense of the tradition of the novel makes her recognize the alternative destiny so often illustrated in the lives of sisters (from Austen's novels to Arnold Bennett's *Old Wives' Tale*): "how in England, apparently, the social situation of sisters could be opposed, how common ground for a place in the world could quite fail them" (XIX:191).

But Milly knows that trying to "place" Kate is a game somewhat childish in its simplifications: "Milly, who had amusements of thought that were like the secrecies of a little girl playing with dolls when conventionally 'too big,' could almost settle to the game of what one would suppose her, how one would place her, if one didn't know her. She became thus, intermittently, a figure conditioned only by the great facts of aspect, a figure to be waited for, named and fitted"—and concludes that it is Kate's supreme quality to be marvelously adaptable rather than rigid—"it was of her essence to be peculiarly what the occasion, whatever it might be, demanded when its demand was highest" (XIX:212). If she is still thinking of Thackeray, the model might be Becky Sharp, a female pragmatist explained by circumstances, who is also, to a point, their master.

Densher, looking at Kate literarily, also, senses her newness as a type, and sees her promise of splendid action. He praises Kate for being a new kind of heroine in books still to be written when he tells her, "The women one meets—what are they but books one has already read? You're a whole library of the unknown, the uncut . . . Upon my word I've a subscription" (XX:62). Referring again to this description of her as an "uncut volume," he speaks of the pleasure of reading her, "the thrill of turning the page" (XX:222). But no more than the reader is he able, at this point, to foresee how Kate's story ends, and how her supremacy of practicality and strength as an organism fit to survive will fail, finally, to provide her with the success she seeks. But Milly, herself, if she is a book, is a text that is not so much unprecedented in its design as one that invites, being postmodernly "scriptable," each reader's imagination to write the story. To Susan, Milly seems "a muffled and intangible form," though she expects that she will be illuminated by "the light in which Milly was to be read." James adds that Milly "worked—and seemingly quite without design—upon the sympathy, the curiosity, the fancy of her associates, and we shall really ourselves scarce otherwise come closer to her than by feeling their impression and sharing, if need be, their confusion" (XIX:116).

Paradoxically, one available explanation for the difficulty of making Milly more definite is certainly her Americanness, which, while it seems to make her a "type," also allows for unpredictablenss, individuality, freedom. Milly herself knows the *restrictive* cues by which her compatriots might be inevitably identified when, on her visit alone to the National Gallery, she amuses herself by "count[ing] the Americans . . . cut out as by scissors, coloured, labelled, mounted," and identifies a particular family group with an unerring sense of "where they lived, and also how." James's own zest for typology is visible in her comprehension of a passing group which might have figured in "Daisy Miller":

> She *knew* the three, generically, as easily as a school-boy with a crib in his lap would know the answer in class; she felt, like the school-boy, guilty enough—questioned, as honour went, as to her right so to possess, to dispossess, people who hadn't consciously provoked her. She would have been able to say where they lived, and also how, had the place and the way been but amenable to the positive; she bent tenderly, in imagination, over marital, paternal Mr. Whatever-he-was, at home, eternally named, with all the honours and placidities, but eternally unseen and existing only as some one who could be financially heard from. The mother, the puffed and composed whiteness of whose hair had no relation to her apparent age, showed a countenance almost chemically clean and dry; her companions wore an air of vague resentment humanised by fatigue; and the three were equally adorned with short cloaks of coloured cloth surmounted by little tartan hoods.   (XIX:290–291)

James—with Milly—seems to be confessing to a little shame in describing anonymous and only momentary human phenomena with such dismissive certainty, like the schoolboy with his crib. The subjects of this satire are reciprocally capable of the same kind of thinking when they are overheard describing Densher as " 'the English style' of the gentleman" (XIX:292). Indeed, from the typological view Milly herself can be regarded as a "type" Lord Mark knows "from afar off," and she herself says to him humbly, "You've heard *me* of course before, in my country, often enough" (XIX:152, 162). His previous impressions of Americans had "helped him to place her, and she was more and more sharply conscious of having—as with the door sharply slammed upon her and the guard's hand raised in signal to the train—been popped into the compartment in which she was to travel for him" (XIX:157). In this, her first conversation with him, at Mrs. Lowder's dinner, she notices, however, that his assurance has faltered over the problem of interpreting Kate, and shaken just a little as a consequence his naturalist-categorical confidence, "his certainties about a mere little American, a cheap exotic, imported almost wholesale and whose habitat, with its conditions of climate, growth and cultivation, its immense profusion but its few varieties and thin development, he was perfectly satisfied" (XIX:166).

But Milly's Americanness is also the source of her *in*definiteness, her maximized potentiality. The famous American spontaneity means that she cannot be absolutely "placed," predicted and confined in a "compartment" by definition, after all. Milly, in moments of confusion or difficulty, consciously resorts to the freedom of such unconfinement. James puns on this "margin" of the unprescribed as the freedom of the text itself to escape conventional limits and at the same as a monetary extra beyond her stipulated value—as upon this occasion of her encounter with Kate and Densher in the museum: "She had long been conscious with shame for her thin blood, or at least for her poor economy, of her unused margin as an American girl—closely indeed as in English air the text might appear to cover the page. She still had reserves of spontaneity, if not of comicality; so that all this cash in hand could now find employment. She became as spontaneous as possible and as American as it might conveniently appeal to Mr. Densher, after his travels to find her" (XIX:295–296).

Densher, the journalist trained in the identification of the representative phenomenon, begins by viewing her almost as reductively, as categorically, as a latter-day Winterbourne—or as Lord Mark. On his return from his American tour, he does not find "little Miss

Theale's individual history" sufficiently distinctive to be "stuff for his newspaper," and he hasn't "invented her" for the benefit of London society, though his friends are inclined to think so. He has only been ready enough to speak of the group to which she belongs. "He was seeing but too many little Miss Theales. They even went so far as to impose themselves as one of the groups of social phenomena that fell into the scheme of his public letters. For this group in especial perhaps—the irrepressible, the supereminent young persons—his best pen was ready" (XX:10–11). It is only later that he develops a quite different view of Milly as he knows her better in London and, especially, in the weeks in Venice he spends with her alone—one more in accordance with Susan's romantic protest that her friend is "a thousand and one things" (XX:41).

Susan Stringham, a popular novelist, sees her from first to last as a romantic American heroine. The only American association who accompanies Milly into her European story, Miss Stringham bears to her a relation both close and distant; she is passionately devoted and yet a kind of employee as much as a friend, the supported companion that the solitary rich girl requires. She is a *ficelle* or "string"—as her name indicates—for the narrative convenience of the author. James can "employ" her as well. Without an integral relation to the plot, Susan is someone who is on hand—as Milly's confidante—to assist us in contemplating the heroine. She is also the representative of the novelist, sharing with other Jamesian characters those secret marks of autobiographical identification which make her problem of interpretive characterization particularly authorial. Like Densher, and also like Daisy Miller's Winterbourne, she was sent to school in Switzerland in her early youth. More importantly, she is a writer devotedly "literary," who emulates "masters, models, celebrities, mainly foreign" (XIX:107); her "rare passion of friendship" for Milly is "the sole passion of her little life save the one other, more imperturbably cerebral, that she entertain[s] for the art of Guy de Maupassant" (XX:45). She writes fiction for "the best magazines," watching "the thin trickle of a fictive 'love-interest' through that somewhat serpentine channel, in the magazines, which she mainly managed to keep clear for it" (XIX:108).

It is not surprising that it is she alone who has been allowed to perceive something of Milly's initial interest in Densher and she tries to write a story with an ending in love and marriage, just as Kate and

Densher are doing, but with a more romantic meaning, even at the last urging Densher to give the lie to the revelations of Lord Mark in order to save Milly's life—as though a corrective "happy ending" might still be written for their romance. In attaching herself to Milly and Milly's fate she has, for the time being, given over the actual writing of fiction in favor of a "reading" of Milly's living story. She has "found herself in the presence of the real thing, the romantic life itself. That was what she saw in Mildred—what positively made her hand a while tremble too much for the pen" (XIX:107). Like a typologically minded novelist Susan knows Milly's "type, aspect, marks, her history, her state, her beauty, her mystery" (XIX:125). But Susan understands the American paradox in this "subject," the unpredictability rather than determinism generated by such genealogy: "New York was vast, New York was startling, with strange histories, with wild cosmopolite backward generations that accounted for anything; and to have got nearer the luxuriant tribe of which the rare creature was the final flower, the immense extravagant unregulated cluster, with free-living ancestors, handsome dead cousins, lurid uncles, beautiful vanished aunts . . . was to have had one's small world-space both crowded and enlarged. . . . This was poetry—it was also history—Mrs. Stringham thought, to a finer tune even than Maeterlinck or Pater, than Marbot and Gregorovius" (XIX:110–111). Even as she receives her first intimation of Milly's illness—along with her "excess of the joy of life"—Susan calls her friend's situation "magnificent" and the alpine scene around them stirs her romantic sensibility: "The great Alpine road asserted its brave presence through the small panes of the low clean windows, with incidents at the inn-door, the yellow diligence, the great waggons, the hurrying hooded private conveyances, reminders, for our fanciful friend, of old stories, old pictures, historic flights, escapes, pursuits, things that had happened, things indeed that by a sort of strange congruity helped her to read the meanings of the greatest interest in the relation in which she was now so deeply involved" (XIX:132–133).

To see Milly as romantic and her history as an adventure is Milly's own view, too, when she takes from Dr. Strett even her sentence of imminent death as providing an unexpected opportunity, "a great rare chance" (XIX:245). Sir Luke promotes her venture of freedom in that same Miltonic language that James used to express Isabel's aspiration and, later, Casper's assertion of continued possibility for her when he tells her, "The world's before you." Her doctor encourages Milly to dispense with the usual idea of a life-story, and to "accept any form in which happiness may come" (XIX:242). Instead of a safe future, "the beauty of the idea of a great adventure, a big dim experiment or struggle in which she might more responsibly than ever take a hand, had been offered her" (XIX:248). Even when her death is closer, she embraces her "impossible romance" as she conceives it when she confesses to Lord Mark that she no longer goes down from the great upper floor of her palazzo: "The idea became an image of never going down, of remaining aloft in the divine dustless air, where she would hear but the plash of the water against stone," and she speaks paradoxically to him of the "adventure of not stirring" (XX:147–148). Her situation seems to signify an elevation above the restrictions of ordinary life, an adventure that is the reverse of the usual story of action, of "stirring." Of course, she is not free of these restrictions at all, as is obvious. Her adventure is achieved not by the usual acquisitions of experience but by the sacrifice of opportunities. Her freedom must contend with this recognition, as it arrives. Her romantic adventure consists in the discovery that she may "live" even though she cannot expect to live, literally speaking, much longer, and even though, in what literal life she has, the usual modes of living "to the full" are denied her.

The story of Milly Theale is, thus, a demonstration of the rescue of story from conditions which seem to prohibit it—and a demonstration of the plasticity of plots which cancel each other in the dynamics of James's narrative. Like *The Portrait of a Lady,* its most obvious structure is an intrigue—that is, a story about a story which must be uncovered beneath the apparent action. It is, then, in the most invidious sense, about story-telling, making up a story to deceive. But it subjects this process to the test embodied in Kate's pragmatic calculus, already mentioned—which is to ask how much more valid is a story that is "true" than a story which persuades us of its truth—or is there no real difference between the two? And the complement of this question is the one that asks whether the wrongness—moral as well as epistemological—only begins when the lie is exposed. Such a speculation is the ultimate in moral skepticism, pushing to the extreme that epistemological doubt which James's subjective art always invites.

James's characters are, thus, the source of plots which contend with one another for survival in the novel. I have already spoken of the way the characters contain alternatives which link them to one another, a quality James's characters have exhibited in previous novels. But the story that the novel tells is not, as a consequence, a simple linear design, but a true "garden of forking paths." Each of the major characters is the source of potentialities of plot. Aunt Maud, though secondary to Kate, Milly, and Densher, is not a goddess for nothing. She is the initiator of traditional plots, which she would impose on everyone about her, manipulating everyone to make the combinations she approves. As Kate observes to Densher, "What she had made her mind up to as possible *is* possible . . . what she had thought more likely than not to happen *is* happening. The very essence of her . . . is that when she adopts a view she—well, to her own sense, really brings the thing about" (XX:188). But Kate and Milly and Densher offer the world more than one simple vocabulary of possibilities.

Kate, to begin with, has been displaced from her original plot, that "profitable journey" (XIX:4) which would have led to a comfortable marriage. She must choose among "prescribed and natural orbits." But Kate wants it all—wants to have both love and money. Before the advent of Milly makes another way of getting money and keeping Densher seem possible, she insists that she will not "sacrifice" him and still will bring Aunt Maud around: "I shall sacrifice nobody and nothing, and that's just my situation, that I want and that I shall try for everything. . . . If we avoid stupidity we may do *all*" (XIX:73). But the two ends can't be combined in one tale. No real progress is made in persuading Aunt Maud to accept Densher as an appropriate match for her niece, and so an alternate plot must be enacted—and this seems possible when Milly makes her appearance. The new project also seems to Kate to entail the sacrifice of "nobody and nothing"—but in the end it does mean the sacrifice of Milly and Milly's own willingness, in the end, to give her own meaning to the sacrifice.

Densher's problem is that stories are written for him by others—by the three women who have their own ideas for him. In Venice he finally asks himself if has any longer a will of his own. He had done everything Kate had wanted and she had done nothing he did. He does not alter this situation by compelling Kate to "come to him." The small plot he writes for her sexual submission is over soon, and he is left alone in Venice to continue to carry out plots that still are not his. They are Kate's and also

Mrs. Lowder's, for the latter—for reasons quite different from Kate's—sees an appropriate ending also in the possibility of his marriage to Milly. How, in this situation, can Densher write his own story? He resolves, out of compunction as much as calculation, to keep the truth from Milly—and this is the beginning of his love, and the validation of the fiction Milly will embrace that her love is returned. So he doesn't leave—thus conforming to Kate's plan—but he realizes "that departure wouldn't curtail, but would signally coarsen his folly, and that above all, as he hadn't really 'begun' anything, had only submitted, consented, but too generously indulged and condoned the beginnings of others, he had no call to treat himself with superstitious rigour" (XX:183).

Densher, in general, deceives himself about the story in which he is figuring, the story of Milly's betrayal. He says that he hasn't "begun" anything in Venice—but of course he has. He takes a false—indeed a shocking—comfort, as we have seen, from the fact that it is not he but Lord Mark who has dealt Milly her mortal blow: "It wasn't a bit he who, that day, had touched her, and if she was upset it wasn't a bit his act . . . It was for all the world—and he drew a long breath on it—as if a special danger for him had passed. Lord Mark had, without in the least intending such a service, got it straight out of the way. It was *he*, the brute, who had stumbled into just the wrong inspiration and who had therefore produced, for the very person he wished to hurt, an impunity that was comparative innocence, that was almost like purification" (XX:264–265). Milly will finally alter the story for him altogether, giving him a true relation to the part he has been playing.

Milly has wanted to write a story for Kate and Densher as well as for herself all along. She believes until Mark's disclosure in a false version of the relationship between her friends and anticipates playing a part in it. Believing that Densher loves Kate but is not loved in return, she sees herself delicately "charming to Kate as well as to Kate's adorer; she would incur whatever pain could dwell for her in the sight—should she continue to be exposed to the sight—of the adorer thrown with the adored. It wouldn't really have taken much more to make him wonder if he hadn't before him one of those rare cases of exaltation—food for fiction—food for poetry—in which a man's fortune with the woman who doesn't care for him is positively promoted by the woman who does" (XX:81). "Food for fiction, food for poetry," this story is—and it is false or not false as the novel will prove. On the one hand it isn't true at all—Kate never rejected Densher. On the other hand, the plot will so change our evaluation of her love that it will be true, in the final sense, that it proves inferior to Milly's. Milly, "the woman who does," will spread her wings of the dove benevolently over Densher and the woman who almost can be said, by comparison, not to care for him.

· 13 ·

The Ambassadors

The Ambassadors is James's greatest study of a character whose life has seemingly failed to contain a degree of doing to match his intensity of being. Unlike Isabel Archer, Lambert Strether thinks it too late to find an adequate plot for himself, but engages himself in the effort to discover—and even to rewrite—the story of another man. The novel is a history of his education in the traps and delusions inherent in such an undertaking; it figures his adventure, his search, his creative effort, but becomes at the same time an exploration into his own latencies of being, his own renewal of doing, despite his conviction that the time for this is past. This double process produces James's most elaborated exhibition of the way a work of fiction may be a contest enacted from page to page among different possibilities of story, rather than *a* story proceeding with undeviating determinism from the opening page to the last. The opening paragraph, as Ian Watt has shown, does, in a sense, predict the whole of the book with its syntactical emphasis upon deferral of interpretation—its impressionism. But in saying this we say that it announces at once that no straight line will lead to disclosure and closure at the end. Yet surviving in this demolition of the idea of plot is the older view that personal being, if it is intense enough, needs no other expression than its own recognitions.

The "germ" of *The Ambassadors* is well known—the declaration of an older man to a younger that he has failed to "live." Howells, who said something of the sort to a young friend of James, probably meant he had missed a particular kind of sensuous and cultural experience, more available in Europe than in America, a sense carried into Lambert Strether's confession in Gloriani's garden. But the failure to live has also a more absolute sense in

James's novel; it is the condition of the richly endowed character who has been denied a sufficient plot, the quality of being which has found no adequate doing. James had actually conceived of something like—though not precisely the same—as this idea at least two years before October, 1895, when he recorded hearing about Howells's outburst'—and it is possible to suspect that his real start for the novel was a more personal feeling than his interest in a friend's experience.

This anticipation was "The Middle Years," published in *Scribner's Magazine* in May 1893. In this short story, James depicted a writer in those difficult "middle years" in which he now found himself (he had reached 50 and was launched upon a career in the theater which had failed to produce that upturn in his fortunes he had hoped for). Like James, perhaps, Dencombe is plagued by the thought that if he died suddenly there would be no better claim upon posterity than his still uncertain achievement. Ill, discouraged, the fictional novelist is in the act of going over and revising his latest fiction; a true James persona, he is "a passionate corrector, a fingerer of style; the last thing he ever arrived at was form final for himself" (XVI:90)—the "for himself" suggesting not only the literary but the personal revisionary compulsion, the state of mind which denies finality of form to the self as well as to literary language. Dencombe encounters a young admirer to whom he confesses that he wants "another go," he wants to "live"—by which he seems to mean a chance of writing still better. In the end, he doesn't get his "extension" yet becomes reconciled to what he has achieved. His book is received with more understanding than he expected. The "second chance" has come after all, through the better effort of readers. As for the writing itself, "there never was to be but one. We work in the dark—we do what we can—we give what we have. Our doubt is our passion and our passion is our task. The rest is the madness of art" (XVI:105).

In placing the story beside the long novel, we can see how James's interest in the dilemma of a man who feels he has not lived enough might have grown out of his own special sense of incompletion—even though he could hardly be said to have failed to exhibit his powers in fiction. "The Jolly Corner," as we have seen, suggests that James's own sense of foregone chances, as well as of personal catastrophes somehow escaped, was poignant late in life. The book which Dencombe is rewriting and for which he craves a better appreciation is itself called "The Middle Years," but the ambiguous title of James's own story may refer also to that time when a man might long to "revise" *life* by a "second chance." Dencombe confesses his sense of having "outlived," without *anything* to show for the past; exactly like Lambert Strether he has lost his wife in childbirth and their son, "at school . . . carried off by typhoid" (XVI:94). A few years later James, the childless bachelor, the withdrawn witness of other lives, confessed that "the deepest thing" about him was *"the essential loneliness of [his] life"*—deeper, he insisted, than his "genius," his "discipline," his "pride," and even "the deep countermining of art."[2] His mood was not so distant, possibly, for all his difference, from that of Dencombe—or of Strether. He admitted to a friend that one might discover in the hero of *The Ambassadors* the story of a man who wakes to the realization that he has failed to "live," "a vague resemblance (though not facial!) to yours always, Henry James."[3] James decided not to make Strether a writer, like Dencombe or himself—or like Howells, whose own "middle years" might have brought doubts of his literary achievement as well as other regrets. Strether is simply a middle-aged "man of imagination." The artist, the man of "imagination in *predominance*" was a case that would have to wait for another occasion; "the comparative case meanwhile would serve" (2:1307). But Strether, the "comparative case," is a man of artistic *sensibility* who finds his *life* to have been a story inadequately told—and must find a way of still telling it.

It was not, probably, only the lost opportunities of life which pressed upon the consciousness of the aging James. The recollection of forgotten artistic alternatives preoccupied him as he mused over each of his works and viewed their origins in retrospect. We have seen in the preface to "The Jolly Corner" how he describes himself coming, in his notebooks, upon "possibilities past by." James saw, as he looked again at *The Ambassadors*, that even the finished text of the novel, "critically viewed, is touchingly full of . . . disguised and repaired losses [of its original intention], these insidious recoveries, these intensely redemptive consistencies" (2:1320). James's revision of himself in the New York Edition, along with the still further revising prefaces, is at once an artistic act of rewriting and a revision of personal self. He is now that "passionate corrector and fingerer of style" who does find a "second chance" in this way, and above all, by the acquisition, like

Dencombe, of better readers who will revise their own earlier understanding of him.

The story the novel undertakes to tell is that of a man who embraces the same opportunity as the author—in life rather than art—to revise and to revise again, to rewrite his personal plot. And nothing could be more appropriate to such a story than the self-revising method of the text itself, which builds upon occasions each corrective of the last, proposes to the reader one after another development, aborting expectations while preserving possibilities. It is this process which is enacted both by the hero and by the reader, making for the novel's remarkable thematic integrity. The sense of loss and gain, destruction and repair which James felt as he reread his novel is what the reader will also experience without sharing precisely the author's own recognitions and regrets; the reader, too, will experience the "might haves" of the novel at each unfolding moment. As Strether moves from one attitude to another, from one view to its correction, he finds himself, as James describes in his scenario for the novel, "sinking . . . up to his middle in the Difference—difference from what he expected, difference in Chad, difference in everything; and the Difference . . . is what I give."[4] It is tempting, though not at all necessary, to give "difference" in this statement a deconstructive sense James could not have intended, as a pun upon deferral indefinitely prolonged.

James felt, rightly, that it was necessary to read the novel slowly, responding to its oscillations, and we should heed the advice he gave a reader,

> Take, meanwhile, pray, *The Ambassadors* very easily and gently: read five pages a day—be even as deliberate as that . . . Keep along with it step by step—and then the full charm will come out . . . I find that the very most difficult thing in the art of the novelist is to give the impression of the *real lapse of time, the quantity* of time, represented by our few poor phrases and pages, and all the drawing-out the reader can contribute helps a little perhaps the production of that spell.[5]

James's Strether is not only a man who has had a too limited measure and kind of experience. The structure of presentation which gives him to us at the outset of the novel suggests absence of a more extreme order by its virtual omission of appropriate beginning. As

in earlier instances, James's "international situation" inserts an oce-
anic separation between the hero's past and that moment when we
see him just landed on an alien shore where everything will be different. But the past from which this present differs is out of our
view. The novel implies a missing first chapter in the America from
which the hero has come. Woollett has sent Strether to Paris; in
Woollett waits the strong princess whose ambassador he is and
whom he will marry if his mission succeeds. But we are never
shown, even in retrospect, this starting ground. James does not
allow the narrative to turn back for the briefest direct vision of it, as
he did in the few pages that permit us to glance at Isabel Archer in
Albany.

Strether is older than Isabel—middle-aged—and, of course, he
has, literally, lived. But the novel summarizes his youthful love,
marriage, and loss with the cruel brevity of a few sentences; wife
and child do not even have names. Strether, moreover, charges himself with having failed, in grief for the mother, to cherish and preserve his boy—who thus becomes a particular "opportunity lost"
(XXI:84), a missed chapter of life. The absence of other surviving
family makes him one of those Jamesian orphans whose anteriority
is thus disposed of, as was the case (despite her surviving sisters)
with Isabel Archer, and more absolutely the case with Milly Theale,
whose many relatives perished before she came to Europe.

Strether's subsequent life has contained enough event to bring
him to the point of being ready to marry again. But Mrs. Newsome,
a widow with grown children, does not have a first name either—
and though others speak for her, we never hear her own voice or see
her. She is supposed to be a source of imperial power, exercising
authority in distant lands, but her power instantly begins to be ineffectual upon Strether's arrival in Europe; long before he renounces
his embassy he begins to betray it. Mrs. Newsome, who proposed to
write a story for Strether, is bound to fail by the very act of making
him her ambassador; by the expectation that her desires will be fulfilled by someone else, she has incurred a failure inherent in delegation in a world in which only the immediate, the present, is going to
count.

In Europe Strether seems newborn. His freshness of apprehension, his moral "innocence," while features of his character and
even his nationality, are also the consequence of this suppression of
the past. James thought he had made up for this suppression by

explanations offered in Strether's early conversation with Maria Gostrey: "Thanks to it we have treated scenically, and scenically alone, the whole lumpish question of Strether's 'past' " (2:1318), he says in his preface. But it is not Woollett that is really made "scenic" in this conversation; Maria, the mere *ficelle*, has already become an interest in herself, a representative of Strether's new life. She is the visible lady in the red velvet neck-ribbon who supersedes Mrs. Newsome in her Elizabethan "ruche," glimpsed only in a passing comparison. The *in*visible lady's identification even as one term of a comparison has already been lost when Strether, wondering at his immediate ease with Maria, reflects, "Well, she's more thoroughly civilized—!" The narrator, underlining his omission, adds, "If 'More thoroughly than *whom?*' would not have been for him a sequel to this remark, that was just by reason of his deep consciousness of the bearing of his comparison" (XXI:9).

James appears to have surprised himself by the way Maria became "a prime idea" when she was intended only as a convenience, and the way she did so causes him to observe what this novel will illustrate—more richly, perhaps, than anything he ever wrote—how narrative development permits unexpected turns and surprises, provokes us to consider variant possibilities. The emergence of Maria in his story, he says, "shows us afresh how many quite incalculable but none the less clear sources of enjoyment for the infatuated artist, how many copious springs of our never-to-be-slighted 'fun' for the reader and critic susceptible of contagion, may sound their incidental plash as soon as an artistic process begins to enjoy free development" (2:1318–1319). So, the unanticipated history of a relationship with the hero amounting to a plot of her own, which ensues for Maria, will contest for its presence in the novel with the main story of Strether's search for a vision of Chad, and with the companion story of his personal rediscovery. But Maria, it must be admitted, though she is present, still fails to have a manifest life of her own; she suffers from that insufficiency of both the hero's and the author's interest which inheres in her functionary role.

We may see, eventually, that she has her own mute story, nonetheless. She is still another of James's precariously surviving female figures, who requires some closure of personal destiny—marriage, most obviously—which she cannot achieve. Like Fleda Vetch or May Bartram, meanwhile, she is someone who makes herself useful to more fortunate friends who help her to get by; she helps bewildered fellow Americans negotiate the European scene. But for these friends—and Strether is one of them—she will not ever be sufficiently regarded for herself; she will be a convenience, a *ficelle*, as she is for the author. That she emerges simply for Strether's need, as does May Bartram for Marcher's, is suggested by the fact that Strether has the same difficulty finding any starting point for a relation with her that Marcher had upon his encounter with May at Weatherend. It seems Maria met his friend Waymarsh in Milrose, Connecticut—a place as remote from their own encounter in Chester as Woollett—and she thinks he must know *her* friends, the Munsters. But these connections produce no recollection in Strether. Without a start "their attitude remained, none the less, that of not forsaking the board; and the effect of this in turn was to give them the appearance of having accepted each other with an absence of preliminaries practically complete" (XXI:7).

This relation without beginning will have no end, and hardly a middle. Maria will suffer a fate like May Bartram's, her inability to live for herself significantly duplicating the failure "to live" of the man she cares for and takes care of. In this duplication she is a sort of twin rather than that non-self which would liberate his being into outerness by active passion—and he cannot fall in love with her. Their twinship is disclosed in their actual resemblance of age and appearance, "each so finely brown and so sharply spare, each confessing so to dents of surface and aids to sight, to a disproportionate nose and a head delicately or grossly grizzled, they might have been brother and sister" (XXI:10). Yet it is Maria who helps Strether to begin a story which can dispense with a narrative start in Woollett. "Nothing could have been odder than Strether's sense of himself as at that moment launched in something of which the sense would be quite disconnected from the sense of his past and which was literally beginning there and then" (XXI:9), he reflects as he prepares to see Chester with this new acquaintance.

If Strether already is felt to be the man who has not lived—or whose past is not worth remembering—his character has managed just the same to prevail against his fate, and he has remained "a man of imagination . . . of thickened motive and accumulated character" (2:1206–1207), of potentiality. The "deep human expertness" of the artist, Gloriani, seeing as James himself sees, flashes upon him during the garden party in book 5 "a test of his stuff" which concedes "possibilities . . . if everything had been different" (XXI:197–198). James

himself had wondered on behalf of his hero, "*Would* there yet perhaps be time for reparation?—reparation, that is, for injury done his
character; for the affront, he is quite ready to say, so stupidly put
upon it?" (2:1305). Can the ellipsis of experience be filled by the
future? Already it is evident even to Strether that though he may not
have "lived" in the usual sense, "it [is] nothing new to him that a
man might have—at all events such a man as he—an amount of experience out of any proportion to his adventures" (XXI:227). And at
this very moment the adventure Strether despairs of is beginning, as
we realize if we recall that redefinition of "adventure" that James had
made in the case of Isabel Archer. Simply coming to Europe at all, for
the heroine of the earlier novel, was "no small part of her principal
adventure," which would manage to emerge despite her independence "of flood and field, of the moving accident, of battle and
murder and sudden death". It would consist mostly and best in
"motionlessly seeing" (2:1083–1084).

Such a confidence in the fertility of perception, and of response
to the immediate may be called impressionism—and it is opposed
not only to traditional conceptions of plot but particularly to the
philosophy and aesthetic of naturalism, which, as we have already
seen, challenged James's imagination in a crucial way. Strether's
moment of crisis in Gloriani's garden contains his own admission of
naturalist inevitability. To Little Bilham, he cries desparately,
"Live," but he is more aware than James has permitted the reader to
be of all the initial and determining influences in his American
life—his probably Puritan upbringing, his materially and spiritually
straitened American circumstances: "The affair—I mean the affair
of life—couldn't, no doubt, have been different for me; for it's at the
best a tin mould, either fluted and embossed, with ornamental
excrescences, or else smooth and dreadfully plain, into which, a
helpless jelly, one's consciousness is poured—so that one 'takes' the
form, as the great cook says, and is more or less compactly held by
it: one lives in fine as one can." Yet, having offered this perfect
naturalist metaphor for the determined fate, he draws back to assert
the value of the belief in freedom. "Still, one has the illusion of
freedom; therefore don't be, like me, without the memory of that
illusion. I was either, at the right time, too stupid or too intelligent
to have it; I don't quite know which. Of course at present I'm a case
of reaction against the mistake; and the voice of reaction should, no
doubt always be taken with an allowance. But that doesn't affect the

point that the right time is now yours. The right time is *any* time that one is still lucky as to have" (XXI:218).

The desire for an adventure adequate to his own character—in that time he is lucky still to have—is implied in the impulse which prompts Strether to delay his encounter with Waymarsh at the very moment of his landing in Liverpool. "His business would be a trifle bungled should he simply arrange for this countenance to present itself to the nearing steamer as the first 'note' of Europe" (XXI:3). What is this "business?" It is not Woollett's commission—which would hardly be deflected by encounter with this reminder of New England. Rather, it is a private undertaking of new experience, implied by language which makes the character the writer who deliberates the opening "note" of his own novel, just as James must have done in writing *The Ambassadors*. The appropriate note Strether requires is "such a consciousness of personal freedom as he hadn't known for years, such a deep taste of change and of having above all for the moment nobody and nothing to consider, as promised already, if headlong hope were not too foolish, to colour his adventure with cool success." The cool success and the "adventure" implied are not to be achieved by the fulfillment of his assignment from Mrs. Newsome. Already, instead of consorting with some of his fellow voyagers, reminders of home, he had "given his afternoon and evening to the immediate and the sensible," though this might be only "a qualified draught of Europe, an afternoon and evening on the banks of the Mersey" (XXI:4).

The surrender to the "immediate and the sensible" is an impressionistic surrender of narrative preconceptions and a program not only for the hero but for the reader. Such a statement should not be confused with the idea that there is specific evidence in *The Ambassadors* of James's descriptive imitation of Impressionist paintings. Certain scenes in the novel can be said to remind one of those works, and Charles Anderson has even argued that particular paintings were in James's mind. There is the scene of Strether in the Luxembourg Gardens, when "terraces, alleys, vistas, fountains, little trees in green tubs, little women in white caps and shrill little girls at play all sunnily 'composed' together" (XXI:80), which seems to Anderson to be copied from Pissarro's *Jardin des Tuileries* (1899). Or the scene of Chad and Madame de Vionnet as Strether sees them in their boat in the country, which is, Anderson is convinced, a transcription of Monet's *La Seine à Vétheuil* (1880) or else a "fabulous coincidence."[6] My view of James's impressionism is not based on these analogies but rather on his way of making his novel a succession of moments, visually scenic or otherwise. It is James's most developed experiment in the mode of a narrative that submits itself flagrantly to successions of interpretation based on instant states.

The method of the novel is the hero's method of personal continuity. For Strether, impressionism is a personal program of perception implying an openness to chance and to a multitude of personal "impressions" as they come, to a multitude of possible responses. Paris, the scene of his adventure, will come to seem a "jewel . . . in which parts were not to be discriminated nor differences comfortably marked." He will find that "it twinkled and trembled and melted together and what seemed all surface one moment seemed all depth the next" (XXI:89). But James tests the Paterian impressionistic outlook by Strether's prompt suspension of his mission, his willing subjection to the effects of each moment immediately upon his landing in Europe. As he prepares for the inevitable encounter with Waymarsh at Chester, Maria arrives to encourage this project, to protect him from restriction to the story begun for him in Woollett. One of the first things he admires in her—and contrasts with Mrs. Newsome's unwavering sense of an ending—is her ability to respond to "the advantage snatched from lucky chances" (XXI:9). As time goes on, she promotes her new friend's project of living for the immediate occasion instead of "always considering something else" (XXI:19). It is a "plunge"—the first of several he will feel himself making, by which he divests himself of the past and abandons that double vision which keeps him always from thinking of "the thing of the moment." Strether confesses that his lingering "obsession of the other thing"—particularly the dictates of the past—is "the terror." By the end of book I he knows that his new program will cost him his past "in one great lump" (XXI:45).

Maria is ready to prepare him to think of life in a wide variety of narrative ways. It is for this reason that she is a repository of fictional concepts, narrative alternatives, "mistress of a hundred cases or categories, receptacles of the mind, subdivisions for convenience, in which, from a full experience, she pigeon-holed her fellow mortals with a hand as free as that of a compositor scattering type" (XXI:11)—a sentence which, as I have observed, identifies her with the novelistic imagination itself and puns on the word "type." In the informed epistemic awareness she possesses, in the range of her knowledge of alternatives, in her breadth of taxonomic categories of the human species, she offers Strether a certain liberation from prescribed story, though it is a liberation that Strether himself will go beyond, dispensing even with her generous choice of conceptions.

James, as though both providing for and imitating his character, writes in *The Ambassadors* a novel which considers the "receptacles of the mind" and brings them into question. In the end, its own method is more indifferent to conventional narrative linearity and makes consistency of character more problematic than it is in any of his previous fictions. James's narrative method in *The Ambassadors* has been compared to the modernist technique called "stream-of-consciousness"—which it does not closely resemble; it is too clearly structured by the continuity of logical thought governed by the narrator's analytic comment. But there is a sense in which the narrative does submit itself to merely temporary conditions of the mind of its central character, a process which can be compared to the experiments of Woolf or Joyce or Faulkner. James's determination to center his story undeviatingly upon this one mind—more consistently than in any other long work he ever wrote—maximizes the relativism of the restricted point of view. Without intervention from another source, the narrative becomes an accretion of moments kept free of final interpretation and the sense of origin and end.

So, Strether, unlike a Winterbourne, submits himself to his impressions; he will float on their stream. Inescapably, he is tempted to use those "receptacles" of character—some, at the outset, very much like Winterbourne's—by which he can seize mental hold of Chad Newsome and his new European associations. He will struggle to contain in one or another narrative preconception what he observes. But he will not be "stiff" like Winterbourne; he will surrender to the effects of new impressions, and he will do this again and again, till it seems evident that there can be no absolute and rigid conclusion about these matters. When he urges Little Bilham to "live," his conviction of wasted time is made acute by his appreciation of Chad Newsome's fulfillment. That occasion also seems to represent the end of his inquiry into the secret history of this other man. Seeing Chad and young Jeanne de Vionnet together, "was the click of a spring—he saw the truth" (XXI:220). But this very "truth" is only another in a series of hypotheses later to be rejected by Strether and the reader. Moments earlier, Little Bilham had warned him, "What more than a vain appearance does the wisest of us know? I commend you the vain appearance" (XXI:203). The gap of ignorance concerning Chad has not really been repaired, his story is still obscure. At the same time, another narrative repair has, all unconsciously to Strether, been set into motion—by the cultivation of his appreciation of the "vain appearance." His own unlived life, which he so deplores, is about to acquire what has been bypassed; his own history will be supplied with the missing element of passion. *The Ambassadors* will continue its braiding of two plots whose motive is the search for story itself.

When Maria declares that she likes Strether for not being a vulgar American success, for not having fulfilled the compulsory American male plot, which consists of a career of moneymaking, she contrasts him with such a man as his friend Waymarsh, who has done just that. She praises him for being a "failure"—"anything else is too hideous"—and notes her own twinship to him, for she also has failed to live the right story (which would be to marry someone with money) and Strether acknowledges, "You too are out of it" (XXI:44). But he is not yet quite out of it. His Woollett-instructed mission is, curiously, a version of the female plot of marriage, but this Cinderella is male. And this banal, self-suppressing self-interest must give way also to true self-realization even at the expense of the surrender of plot. Maria asks him what he stands to lose by failing in his mission, and he says, first, "nothing," then admits, "everything" (XXI:74-75). Waymarsh, the businessman, correctly understands the venture upon which Strether has been launched: if Chad returns to the family business as a result of Strether's efforts, the family interest in the business will "boom," and Mrs. Newsome and the man she marries will be richer. "You'll marry—you personally— more money." So Strether is "fierce for the boom" (XXI:110-111).

But it is Waymarsh who sees that the "rescue" of Chad is the wrong plot for Strether's character. "You're being used for a thing you ain't fit for" (XXI:109), he tells his friend—and Strether himself pauses from time to time to wonder whether, indeed, his ambassadorial role "might pass for interested" (XXI:181). Only by embracing failure in Woollett's terms does he, paradoxically, gain. His final resolution, "not, out of the whole affair to have got anything for myself," rejects any gain at all of visible kind—even the consolation offered by Maria ("the offer of exquisite service, of lightened care, for the rest of his days" [XXII:325-326])—in a recoil of severest consistency from Woollett's calculus of profit making, from the idea of getting something or somewhere "in the end." It is a refusal of futurity matching the novel's early disengagement from the past—a seeming defect of visible closure—just as his vacant past was signified by the suppression of narrative beginning. But by this foregoing of a marriage-plot "reward" Strether has been left free for an unforeseen compensation. His "making up" will be the belated height of feeling reached by his imagination and sympathy—an augmentation of his rich potentiality, which remains available for whatever still comes.

In his effort to understand at the start what has happened to Chad, Strether has brought with him from Woollett trite narrative preconceptions of the young man's likely entrapment and degeneration in Paris, conceptions compounded of Puritan prejudice and Victorian cliché. These preconceptions of plot James saw as a danger for the writer, who might himself think in this fashion, or for the reader, for that matter, with his own triggered response to the idea of Parisian temptations for the unwary Anglo-Saxon—"the dreadful little old tradition, one of the platitudes of the human comedy, that people's moral scheme *does* break down in Paris; that nothing is more frequently observed; that hundreds of thousands of more or less hypocritical or more or less cynical persons annually visit the place for the sake of the probable catastrophe, and that I came late in the day to work myself up about it." The effect of Paris upon Strether himself was to be, James insisted, of a different kind of "revolution"—"he was to be thrown forward, rather, thrown quite with violence, upon his lifelong trick of intense reflexion," which was "to bring him out . . . *in* Paris, but with the surrounding scene itself a minor matter, a mere symbol for more things than had been dreamt of in the philosophy of Woollett" (2:1312). But this does not mean that Strether does not initially embrace the "dreadful little old tradition" in his anticipations of Chad's story.

It is appropriate that he should offer this scenario to Maria during an evening at the theater in London, where melodrama on the stage accompanies his description of Chad's supposititious female attachment as "base, venal, of the streets." Maria, however, suggests that there are *two* possible stories—"one is that he may have got brutalized. The other is that he may have got refined" (XXI:55, 69). It is the second which emerges from Strether's first view of Chad's flat in the Boulevard Malesherbes. Yet in the contest of plots which continues in the text the first hypothesis, crass as it is, is never entirely forgotten and will even have a certain renewal.

Meanwhile, Strether is finding himself "in the presence of new measures, other standards, a different scale of relations" (XXI:114). Before Chad appears in the box at the *Comédie* it already seems likely that Paris has refined rather than coarsened the heir to the Newsome fortune. Strether even finds himself charged by Chad with having a "low mind" for thinking that a woman of any sort has kept him from returning home: "Don't you know how much I like Paris . . . Do you think one's kept only by women?" (XXI:158–159). Strether can imagine Woollett's skepticism about a plot *sans femme.* "He fairly caught himself shooting rueful glances, shy looks of pursuit, toward the embodied influence, the definite adversary, who had by a stroke of her own failed him and on a fond theory of whose palpable presence he had, under Mrs. Newsome's inspiration, altogether proceeded" (XXI:165). Yet if there is a woman in the story, how shall the accustomed storyteller or reader classify her? If it still seems likely that a woman does hold Chad back, she is a woman "too good to admit" rather than the "wretch" imagined by a low mind. This would explain the fine changes in Chad—only such a woman could be responsible. But such an influence might imply something inadmissible by the very exhibition of its "unnatural goodness"—a suggestion so unsettling to Strether that he can only say, crudely, "Ah then you're speaking now of people who are *not* nice." To which Maria, the adept at classification, responds, with a certain impatience, "I delight in your classifications. But do you want me to give you in the matter, on this ground, the wisest advice I'm capable of? Don't consider her, don't judge her at all in herself. Consider her and judge her only in Chad" (XXI:170). On the other hand, Chad's "disavowal" may not be gallantry: "It's the effort to sink her," Maria proposes. He wants to "shake her off." To which Strether objects indignantly, "after all she has done for him?" and Maria responds ruefully, "He's not as good as you think!" (XXI:171).

Here, before we have even reached the halfway mark of the novel, are a dozen different contending potentialities, which will thrust against one another till the end. The theory of the superior woman who had done so much for Chad and the theory of Chad as a person marvelously improved and "good" will reemerge when Strether is ready to accept the idea of his young friend's "virtuous attachment" to Madame de Vionnet. The view that theirs is just a passing "affair" and that she is a mistress whom he is ready to discard, is justified later, yet it does not rout its alternative; she is still the wonderful friend who has done so much for him and to whom he is grateful. Strether's partisanship, even on these latest terms, for the woman abandoned, is the ripest of his realizations, yet so early as this he has shown himself ready to betray Woollett's commission for her sake.

The constant generation of new plots for Chad derives, technically, from the central obscurity in the presentation of the story of Chad and Marie de Vionnet. What he *is* and what she *is* are never cleared up in the unfolding of Strether's impressions, which have no exterior verifiability. We will never see Madame de Vionnet and Chad as they are when out of the sight of this one bemused witness. We will never see them alone with each other, and never know positively how they feel about each other; we see things only from Strether's limited view, to which the narrator refrains from adding further insight. We cannot fill this hermeneutic gap except, as Strether does, by an excess of imagination. The abandonment of one romantic plot elicits another, its opposite. "It seemed somehow as if [Chad] couldn't *but* be as good [as Strether had thought] from the moment he wasn't as bad" (XXI:171). Mildness and charm mark every encounter with Chad and his circle and so frustrate Strether's expectations of "violence" that "he might almost have passed as wondering how to provoke it" (XXI:174).

For Little Bilham, the new "improved" Chad is also a text he reads with contending feelings, confessing to a preference for "the well-rubbed, old fashioned volume" he had once known; the revised Chad is "like the new edition of an old book that one has been fond of—revised and amended, brought up to date, but not quite the thing one knew and loved." Chad, by this favorite Jamesian image of man as a book,[7] becomes a fiction ordered by plot concepts or character concepts old or new. And, continuing the image, Strether asks who the "editor" is who has revised the old novel to read as a new story (XXI:177–178).

Little Bilham, this "intense American" who cannot be supposed to lie, offers Strether a reading. He says that Chad really wants to go back and take up his Woollett future, a career which "will improve and enlarge him still more," as one improves or expands a text in still another way—another example of James's way of comparing persons to books and a reference to that revisionary process in both which is the central subject of this novel. Little Bilham explains that Chad isn't happy—despite appearances—because he's not "used . . . to being so good," and being good means that he isn't free to go home because the attachment in Paris is "virtuous" (XXI:177–180). So, Strether's speculations—communicated to Maria—ensue. What narrative suppositions can be based on this fact of a "virtuous attachment" along with the news that Chad's greatest friends are a mother and a daughter whom he is anxious to introduce to his mother's emissary? The attachment may be virtuous because it is to two women rather than one, or because he has not yet made up his mind between them. The attachment must be to the daughter, considering his age; she may be old enough for marriage. But then, why doesn't he say so? Perhaps because the girl doesn't like him. Or maybe she can't face Woollett. Or maybe he's really "on terms" with the mother. If the girl's of the right age can the mother be? But maybe the girl's only a little girl. Is the mother a widow? If she isn't, maybe that's what makes the relation "virtuous." Finally, Maria refuses to say that she believes in the "virtuous attachment," anyhow. "Everything's possible. We must see" (XXI:188), she says, leaving the reader and Strether standing at a crossroads from which one might journey down a dozen divergent paths of expectation, as though the writer himself has stopped to consider every alternative story.

At this point what we have been given, again, is a bewildering review of a variety of potentialities. Some will continue to reverberate. The mother turns out to be still marvelously young and pretty, though of a respectability so distinct that she reminds Strether of the women of his Puritan Woollett. But she is not a widow—and so it may follow that Chad is in love with the daughter, who is just old enough, lovely, and plainly fond of their friend. Miss Barrace observes that "in the light of Paris" one always sees "what things resemble," a relativity of definition quite different from the one demanded by the man from America, who insists on knowing "what they really are." "Oh I like your Boston 'reallys,' " this sophisticated lady exclaims. When Strether persists in wanting to know whether Madame de Vionnet "really show[s] for what she is," he still gets no answer beyond, "She's charming. She's perfect" (XXI:207–208).

To his own mind, the exquisite lady shows for what she is.

Strether is sure that all she wants of *him* is help in working things out for her daughter. But when he asks her, "Do you want [Chad] to marry your daughter?" she answers, "He likes her too much" (XXI:254)—and Strether is again thrown into confusion. Likes her too much to do what? To take her to America where she won't be happy, perhaps? Or to use her as a cover for the other relationship? He realizes very soon that little Jeanne isn't Chad's attachment. It *is* Madame de Vionnet, even though there is no possibility that she can divorce her husband to marry him. Pressed, Chad, for his part, says that for him she is "too good a friend" to leave summarily. He "owes [her] too much"—and Strether is convinced that this declaration itself places the lady above reproach. Her irreproachableness, anyhow, is what Chad himself insists on—and we are in no position, at the end of book 5, to consider that he lies. Nevertheless, the reader is likely to have become sensitized to contrary possibilities by all the previous play of speculation. Portentously, Maria Gostrey inexplicably washes her hands of her old school friend.

Already, Strether's sympathies have caused him to forget his promise to achieve Chad's return. He tells Madame de Vionnet, "I'll save you if I can" (XXI:255)—though a little later he confesses that he is still trying to discover what his own words mean (XXI:274). More and more he is convinced that the "high fine friendship" which has done so much for Chad is worth the sacrifice, even, of Chad's American chances. He arrives at a chiasmus, as has been often noted, in the novel's exact center at the end of the first volume, passing over from being Woollett's ambassador to the side of Madame de Vionnet and the view that Chad should remain. "Let them face the future together! . . . I mean that if he gives her up . . . he ought to be ashamed of himself!" (XXI:286).

But it is less generally observed that the real crossover of plots is that it is Strether who is ready to offer Madame de Vionnet such devotion and such sacrifice. Chad, on the other hand, wants to take up the plot of Woollett, to marry a Woollett woman and make the business "boom," endings that are fast fading out of Strether's future. Strether feels still that he has no life of his own, only "a life . . . for other people" (XXI:269). In a sense this will continue to be true. But Strether's response to Madame de Vionnet begins to deserve the name of passion. Most readers of the novel continue to see him as the man who has missed his hour irrecoverably. But from the sixth book onward the text begins to express Strether's instead of Chad's love—along with Strether's acceptance of the sacrifice of gain Chad refuses to make. "What was their relation moreover—though light and brief enough in form as yet—but whatever she might choose to make it? Nothing could prevent her—certainly he couldn't—from making it pleasant. At the back of his head, behind everything, was the sense that she was—there, before him, close to him, in vivid imperative form—one of the rare women he had so often heard of, read of, thought of, but never met, whose very presence, look, voice, the mere contemporaneous *fact* of whom, from the moment it was all presented, made a relation of mere recognition" (XXI:252). That had not been the case with Mrs. Newsome; it was not the case even with Miss Gostrey. Strether's recognition of Chad's *femme du monde* has become adoration, expressed in a supreme poetic reverie:

> Her bare shoulders and arms were white and beautiful; the materials of her dress, a mixture, as he supposed, of silk and crape, were of a silvery grey so artfully composed as to give an impression of warm splendour; and round her neck she wore a collar of large old emeralds, the green note of which was more dimly repeated, at other points of her apparel, in embroidery, in enamel, in satin, in substances and textures vaguely rich. Her head, extremely fair and exquisitely festal, was like a happy fancy, a notion of the antique, on an old precious medal, some silver coin of the Renaissance, while her slim lightness and brightness, her gaiety, her expression, her decision, contributed to an effect that might have been felt by a poet as half mythological and half conventional. He could have compared her to a goddess still partly engaged in a morning cloud, or to a sea-nymph waist-high in the summer surge. Above all she suggested to him the reflexion that the *femme du monde*—in these finest developments of the type—was, like Cleopatra in the play, indeed various and multifold. She had aspects, characters, days, night—or had them at least, showed them by a mysterious law of her own, when in addition to everything she happened also to be a woman of genius. (XXI:270–271)

To create this image of absolute femininity James has invoked the highest associations of myth and poetry—she is a goddess or nymph, like Venus emerging from the sea foam, like some divinity on a classic coin—and like Shakespeare's unparalleled Cleopatra.

His relationship with her begins on a new basis after a chance meeting in Notre-Dame when he sees her first, without recognition, as "some fine firm concentrated heroine of an old story, something he had heard, read, something that, had he had a hand for drama, he might himself have written." He had recently purchased seventy volumes of Victor Hugo, and in the great cathedral, one of Hugo's subjects, wondered "where, among packed accumulations," this "fruit of his mission" might find a place. This is more than a digressive association and a reference to his thoughts of return and the literal problems of the tourist's baggage. Where, indeed, in his remainder of life, will Strether find place for the romantic kind of story Hugo wrote? He feels that his purchase is "out of proportion . . . for any other plunge," he tells Madame de Vionnet. Yet, "even as he spoke how at that instant he was plunging," for Madame de Vionnet "was romantic for him far beyond what she could have guessed." He is writing the old romantic play or story after all. During their *déjeuner* he feels that "in the matter of letting himself go, of diving deep . . . he ha[s] touched bottom" (XXII:9-13).

He has, indeed, "travelled far since that evening in London, before the theatre, when his dinner with Maria Gostrey, between the pink-shaded candles, had struck him as requiring so many explanations." He now neither seeks or requires such explanations as Woollett or even Maria would have expected—but gives himself to the "reasons" of sensation which precede "lucidity," as these might have been captured in an Impressionist painting—a moment of color and light that shimmers beyond "explanation" as they dine on the Left Bank with a view of the Seine from their window table.

He had at the time [in London] gathered them in, the explanations—he had stored them up; but it was at present as if he had either soared above or sunk below them—he couldn't tell which; he could somehow think of none that didn't seem to leave the appearance of collapse and cynicism easier for him than lucidity. How could he wish it to be lucid for others, for any one, that he, for the hour, saw reasons enough in the mere way the bright clean ordered water-side life came in at the open window?—the mere way Madame de Vionnet, opposite him over their intensely white table-linen, their *omelette aux tomates*, their bottle of straw-coloured chablis, thanked him for everything almost with the smile of a child, while her grey eyes moved in and out of their talk, back to the quarter of the warm spring air, in which early summer had already begun to throb, and then back again to his face, and their human questions. (XXII:13–14)

He has written to Woollett to report Chad's transformation and its cause. He receives in response the ultimatum to bring Chad back immediately—or, if he cannot do so, to return himself. Chad is ready to go, but—the chiasmus of plot completing itself—Strether insists that he wait, and will not heed his own recall. He will risk the Pococks, who will be sent in his place, hoping that they will appreciate the "new facts," refusing to heed Chad's warning that his replacement by Mrs. Newsome's daughter "bears upon—well, you know what" (XXII:36). For if he loses his futurity in Woollett he gains back, now, his lost past, the youth he never had, the beginning so summarily dealt with by the narrative structure of the novel. He tells Maria,

> I began to be young, or at least to get the benefit of it, the moment I met you at Chester, and that's what has been taking place ever since. I never had the benefit at the proper time—which comes to saying that I never had the thing itself. I'm having the benefit at this moment; I had it the other day when I said to Chad 'Wait'; I shall have it still again when Sarah Pocock arrives. It's a benefit that would make a poor show for many people; and I don't know who else but you and I, frankly, could begin to see in it what I feel. I don't get drunk; I don't pursue the ladies; I don't spend money; I don't even write sonnets. But nevertheless I'm making up late for what I didn't have early. I cultivate my little benefit in my own little way. It amuses me more than anything that has happened to me in all my life. They may say what they like—it's my surrender, its my tribute to youth. One puts that in where one can—it has to come in somewhere, if only out of the lives, the conditions, the feelings of other persons. Chad gives me the sense of it, for all his grey hairs, which merely make it solid in him and safe and serene; and *she* does the same, for all her marriageable daughter, her separated husband, her agitated history. Though they're young enough, my pair, I don't say they're, in the freshest way, their *own* absolutely prime adolescence; for that has nothing to do with it. The point is that they're mine. Yes, they're my youth; since somehow at the right time nothing else ever was. (XXII:50–51)

But at this moment of reparation, the predicted future that promises *no* true recovery of a lost past erupts into the present. The eighth book, culminating in the wonderfully comic scene between Sarah

Pocock and Madame de Vionnet, provides a shocking prevision for Strether of his American potentiality and rereads his present in Woollett's terms. The great question, of course, is whether the Pococks will see how Chad has changed. As they give no evidence of seeing it, Strether is brought to wonder whether he has not been deluded—along with Maria, Madame de Vionnet, and Chad himself. "Did he live in a false world, a world that had grown simply to suit him, and was his present slight irritation . . . but the alarm of the vain thing menaced by the touch of the real? Was this contribution of the real possibly the mission of the Pococks?—had they come to make the work of observation, as *he* had practiced observation, crack and crumble, and to reduce Chad to the plain terms in which honest minds could deal with him?" (XXII:81). The relativity to which restricted subjective narration reduces ideas of the "real" is brought to the fore, and shakes our own as well as Strether's confidence in his personal vision.

His Woollett future—the plot he had once embraced—is exhibited in Jim Pocock, James's satiric type-portrait of the American Businessman who leaves a "whole side of life"—social relations, even "culture," presumably—to his women. Strether asks himself if *his* exclusion from this side, "had he married ten years before [would] have become now the same as Pocock's? Might it even become the same should he marry in a few months?" American society, Strether reflects on behalf of James, is "a society of women"—and Pocock knows this as he warns Strether, "Don't go home!" and thinks Chad ought to stay where he is. Strether then asks himself "if what Sally wanted her brother to go back for was to become like her husband" (XXII:82–84). Strether and Madame de Vionnet hope Jim will provide Chad with "a warning" of Woollett's idea of "redemption" from his present state (XXII:120). In fact, he is a more-than-likely anticipation of a plot outcome for Chad which is to be glimpsed beyond the last gateposts of the novel.

Sarah (Sally) Pocock may be seen as a belated restoration to the plot of its initial omission of Mrs. Newsome. When Maria suggests, a bit later, that Chad ought to go home for a visit to his mother, Strether observes "his mother has paid *him* a visit. Mrs. Newsome has been with him, this month, with an intensity that I'm sure he has thoroughly felt; he has lavishly entertained her, and she has let him have her thanks" (XXII:219). Despite some differentiation, Sarah is so much the same type as her mother as to forecast what

Strether's Woollett spouse would be. But her intrusion, now, is too late to modify the truncation from the past that Strether's European adventure has effected. At their meeting, Madame de Vionnet's intimations of intimacy with him can only be read in one way by Sally, in terms of the discarded trite plot of Paris. Stories depend upon their readers, and Strether is appalled to discover that "it would be exactly *like* the way things always turned out for him that he should affect Mrs. Pocock and Waymarsh as launched in a relation in which he had really never been launched at all" (XXII:94). Strether himself momentarily goes back to such an interpretation when he mentally says to the woman he has thought of as the goddess of love, "After all, what *is* between us when I've been so tremendously on my guard and have seen you but half a dozen times?" (XXII:94).

But, immediately, he dismisses his fear of Woollett's inferences and recaptures his own version of things. "He had quite the consciousness now that not to meet [Madame de Vionnet] at any point more than halfway would be odiously, basely to abandon her. Yes, he was *with* her, and opposed even in this covert, this semi-safe fashion to those who were not, he felt, strangely and confusedly, but excitedly, inspiringly, how much and how far. It was as if he had positively waited in suspense for something from her that would let him in deeper, so that he might show her how he could take it" (XXII:99). He goes willingly into Madame de Vionnet's "boat," we are told in an image that anticipates the literal later scene of Chad and the same woman on the river in the country, in book II; by this fusion of images he anticipates his replacement of Chad. "It rocked beneath him, but he settled himself in his place. He took up an oar and, since he was to have the credit of pulling, pulled" (XXII:94–95). The image, of passive submission to the flow of things, exactly fits his own version of his experience. Later, in their scene of final confrontation and rupture, Sarah will accuse him of "sacrific[ing] mothers and sisters to [Madame de Vionnet] without a blush, and . . . mak[ing] them cross the ocean on purpose to feel the more, and take from [him] the straighter how [he does] it"—but "purpose," the sense of narrative *telos*, is foreign to Strether's impressionistic receptivity. He can only respond to her, "Everything has come as a sort of indistinguishable part of everything else. Your coming out belonged closely to my having come before you, and my having come was a result of our general state of mind. Our general state of mind had proceeded, on its side, from our queer ignorance, our queer misconceptions and confusions—from which, since then, an inexorable tide of light seems to have floated us into our perhaps still queerer knowledge" (XXII:200–201).

The Pococks and Waymarsh comically demonstrate how their own plots reverse themselves, even as Strether's own is doing—and refute the very conception of design and consistency they have seemed to uphold. Mamie, who was destined to marry Chad, turns out to prefer Little Bilham. Intelligent Mamie has had the mission, like Strether's own, of saving Chad, and she has rejected it because, alone of her family, she has seen that he is already improved—and, besides, she doesn't even like Chad! Mamie provides one of those surprises for which Strether's own surrender of prejudice makes him ready when he finds her alone in the Pocock hotel suite and discovers her difference from his preconceptions, her possession of "something . . . that touched him to a point not to have been reckoned beforehand" (XXII:146).

Not only does Jim form a certain alliance with Madame de Vionnet—whom he continues to see as a wicked, fascinating woman—but Mrs. Pocock, the representative of Woollett propriety, has her Paris escapade with Waymarsh. And Waymarsh, who once hated Europe and urged Strether to abandon his embassy, is entrained in Woollett's service. At the same time, this same Waymarsh is having the time of his life, a Paris fling, a romantic "adventure." Strether envies him, and thinks himself, by comparison, still stuck after all, in that condition of "too late" he had bewailed to Little Bilham. And he feels this—with a backtracking swing of the story—despite the liberation he has felt with Maria Gostrey, despite his recent commitment to Madame de Vionnet: "It came to him in the current of thought, as things so oddly did come, that *he* had never risen with the lark to attend a brilliant woman to the Marché aux Fleurs; this could be fastened on him in connexion neither with Miss Gostrey nor with Madame de Vionnet; the practice of getting up early for adventures could indeed in no manner be fastened on him. It came to him in fact that just here was his usual case: he was for ever missing things through his general genius for missing them" (XXII:185).

But such mild ironies over the meaning of "adventure" give place, at the end of the tenth book, to the absolute clash of

Strether's and Woollett's reading of the story of Chad and Paris. The woman Strether calls "charming and beneficent" Sarah refuses to consider "even an apology for a decent woman" (XXII:200–202); she finds Chad's development under Madame de Vionnet's influence, not "fortunate," as Strether urges, but "hideous," their life together not "a thing one can even *speak* of." Strether's despairing exclamation, "Oh, if you think *that*—" is finished for him by Sarah with "Then all's at an end" and her own "I do think that," after which "resolute rupture" she charges off. It *is* an ending to the tale of ambassadorship and reward. "It probably all *was* at an end" (XXII:205–206).

There follow two chapters of postmortem—the first with Chad and the second with Maria.[8] Chad remonstrates that Strether is giving up so much—"dished," as far as his prospects with Mrs. Newsome; an "assured future" and "a good deal of money" gone (XXII:236, 238, 239). "What I don't for the life of me make out is what you *gain* by it" (XXII:244), the young man says—missing the sense of forward movement toward some discernible end in Strether's behavior. To Maria, Strether admits that he does "lose everything," but though he might still recover the Woollett story by releasing Chad from his promise not to return, he seems not to mind the loss of the "opulent future" represented by Mrs. Newsome, and even of Mrs. Newsome herself.

For she has shown no interest in surprises, while he has, from the first, been ready for the unexpected effect of new impressions; as Maria notes, he "came over more or less for surprises." And they have come—his surprise at his renewed view of Chad, his surprise in his discovery of Madame de Vionnet, most of all, but many others stimulated by new circumstance and by the very experience of Paris. For Mrs. Newsome there can be only one narrative.

> That's just her difficulty—that she doesn't admit surprises. It's a fact that, I think, describes and represents her; and it falls in with what I tell you—that's she's all, as I've called it, fine cold thought. She had, to her own mind, worked the whole thing out in advance, and worked it out for me as well as for herself. Whenever she has done that, you see, there's no room left; no margin, as it were, for any alteration. She's filled as full, packed as tight, as she'll hold, and if you wish to get anything more or different either out or in . . . what it comes to . . . is that you've got morally and intellectually to get rid of her.   (XXII:221–222)

Chad asks him what he stands to gain for his sacrifice—to which Strether responds that Chad has "no imagination," and Chad in turn declares that Strether has "rather too much." It is by imagination that Strether will "gain," while the future captain of industry has admitted, even in his concern for Strether, only his own definition of profit (XXII:244). In one sense, of course, Mrs. Newsome has had plenty of imagination for the conventional "horrors" she expected him to find. "I was booked, by her vision—extraordinarily intense, after all," he observes, "to find them; and that I didn't, that I couldn't, that, as she evidently felt, I wouldn't—this evidently didn't at all, as they say, 'suit' her book" (XXII:224). What he now does want he has "ceased to measure or even to understand," but his own "book" is like James's, full of impressionistic fertility.

As he gazes out into the Paris night from Chad's balcony, Strether hangs over that kind of impressionistic window view which appears in so many paintings—in Monet's "Boulevard des Capucines," for example—in which the street below becomes a vague, poetic implication of sight and sound, and the window frame suggests that the drama, the subject, is the perception of these things. From the same balcony Strether had seen, more than three months earlier, a multitude of signs that reminded him of the "youth he had long ago missed," but signs also that what he had missed, what Paris represents, is "an affair of the senses" (XXII:230). The senses—rather than the analytic mind, of course—are the gateways of "impressions"; this is the reason that visual experience seems so insistently to represent Strether's immediate reception, before intellection, of what stands outside him.[9]

But the reader, if not Strether, is also being prepared for the famous moment in the eleventh book when, out for a day in the country, Strether unexpectedly encounters his friends. He realizes, seeing them so obviously prepared for a clandestine night, that the idea of the "virtuous attachment" is a blind. Theirs has been "an affair of the senses." The episode is also a culmination of the meaning of the novel because it is concerned with the characters' relation to the plots that have obsessed them and us. The disclosure of their enacted sexual connection is a refutation, by Strether's beloved pair, of the plot which they have encouraged him to believe in—that they, like himself, have willingly maintained a gap of nondoing in *their* "affair of life." Their sexual "doing" refutes Strether's conception that mere being what they are has been enough for them. It refutes the idea that Chad's character has gained simply by association with a charming woman, excluding what is properly called the sexual "act." Strether has to concede that "intimacy at such a point, was *like* that—and what in the world else would one have wished it to be like?" (XXII:266).¹⁰

He has come to this moment in a mood of holiday and a return of that readiness, felt so thrillingly in Chester, to take things as they come. Appropriately, he receives his new understanding of his friends as though viewing an Impressionist painting. First, he sees the river, then a boat, then two persons in it, one a woman with a pink parasol; *then*, he identifies the human figures, *then* he understands the nature of their relation. It is the progression made by the viewer who, stepping back from the confusion of color and light on a canvas comes to the naming of persons, the analysis of situation not first but last. Identity, significance, literary plot, have followed as mental afterthought the impact of sensation. The remembering and anticipating mind corrects the eye. Not so much the visual similarity of the scene to a painting as the process of such viewing is impressionist and a correlative for the way we pass from the sensation of the moment to understanding.

Strether's excursion had begun with a preimpressionist idea of landscape, the viewpoint of the Barbizon school represented by a Lambinet he had admired long before in a Tremont Street gallery. The remembered painting causes him to expect a scene as it might be located within "the oblong window of the picture frame," a "land of fancy . . . the background of fiction, the medium of art, the nursery of letters, practically as distant as Greece"—romance rather than reality. The Lambinet is a symbol, too, of the life-that-might-have-been that Strether wished he had had; it is, after all, the picture he "would have bought" if he could have afforded it, in his youth. He walks into a space of poplars and willows, reeds and river, "a river of which he didn't know, and didn't want to know, the name," till what he sees falls "into a composition, full of felicity," like the Lambinet—"the sky was silver and turquoise and varnish; the village on the left was white and the church on the right was grey." Yet his impressionistic susceptibility already expresses itself in the way he takes a train and dismounts at a station selected "almost at random." Free of his Woollett mission—of any sense of "mission" or "end" at all—his "idleness" seems sweet as "he walked and walked as if to show how little he had now to do; he had nothing to do but turn off to some hillside where he might stretch himself and hear the poplars rustle." He has brought a book along, but it stays in his pocket, though the Seine region reminds him of Maupassant as once Notre-Dame had reminded him of Hugo—with different effect, his expectations now being as different from that earlier moment as Maupassant's mode of story-telling might be from Hugo's (XXII:245–247).

Nothing has been better proof of his freedom from former obsessions than his latest meetings with Madame de Vionnet. There had been no more "tiresome" talk between them, Chad's name had not even come up, it was as if he had been calling on her for the first time. He felt himself acting as if he told her aloud, "Don't like me, if it's a question of liking me, for anything obvious and clumsy that I've, as they call it, 'done' for you . . . don't be for me simply the person I've come to know through my awkward connexion with Chad." They had escaped the plot of Chad and begun another by simply doing nothing as time "slipped along so smoothly, mild but not slow, and melting, liquifying, into his happy illusion of idleness" (XXII:251). Maria has asked him, "Are you really in love with her?" and he has answered, "It's of no importance I should know" (XXII:211). He needs only to submit to his impressions without titling his feelings by an obvious term.

But the old story-making compulsion returns upon the encounter at the river. The narrative now insistently resorts to the language of literary forms. "It was as queer as fiction, as farce" (XXII:257) that their meeting should occur. The whole incident appears like a flagrant literary use of coincidence in "the general *invraisemblance* of the occasion" (XXII:259). But Madame de Vionnet makes the chance meeting a happy element in a tale contrived on the spot; her remark, *"comme cela se trouve!"* (XXII:260) is the complacent observation of the successful storyteller. "Fiction and fable *were* inevitably in the air," as everything fell with "a marked drop into innocent friendly Bohemia" (XXII:262), a light tale, that is, of *la vie bohème.*

Madame de Vionnet herself reverts to convention, no longer the incalculable beloved of his recent view. Her nervous chattering in her own French has the effect of "veiling her identity, shifting her back into a mere voluble class or race" (XXII:261)—she becomes a familiar "type," for which Winterbourne would have had a ready name. The tale of her relationship with Chad relapses almost to its earliest formulation before Strether had met her—it *is*, after all, "a typical tale of Paris," in which, perhaps, they were all "floating together on the silver stream of impunity" (XXII:271–272). When he sees her again in her apartment full of historic memorabilia she reminds him of Madame Roland, ready for execution, and he is not sure to which story, farcical or tragic, he should assign her. In the end he realizes that she is both type and unfathomable individuality, unexpressed in either conventional story: "the finest and subtlest creature, the happiest apparition, it had been given him in all his years, to meet"—"vulgarly troubled . . . as a maidservant crying for her young man" (XXII:286).

Chad is likewise again a "type" rather than the mysterious personality developed under her influence. Strether realizes that though Chad has been made "better," he has not been made "infinite" (XXII:284). Can he live up to the sublimity Strether had imagined for him? "You'll be a brute, you know—you'll be guilty of the last infamy—if you ever forsake her," Strether tells him, and Chad denies any intention of the sort. But what he says is, "I don't know what should make you think I'm tired of her." For us, as for Strether, there must be "in the allusion to satiety as a thinkable motive a slight breath of the ominous . . . he spoke of being 'tired' of her almost as he might have spoken of being tired of roast mutton for dinner" (XXII:308, 311–312). Here, surely, is the closure of the story of sexual adventure. Can we not say that we know the end without the further suspicion, admitted by Strether in his last conversation with Maria, that there is "some other woman in London" (XXII:325)?

It would almost seem, by this, that Strether's policy of impressionistic receptivity has been refuted, for, in the end, one does name and interpret; mere impressions must be corrected by knowledge. In interpreting the story of Chad and Marie de Vionnet, Strether has suspended judgment to the point of imbecility in the eyes of a great many readers, whose reaction seems anticipated in Maria Gostrey's mocking, "What on earth—that's what I want to know now—had you then supposed?" He recognizes that "he had really been trying all along to suppose nothing" (XXII:266). He has cultivated ignorance as he long before persuaded Maria to do concerning the domestic article manufactured in the Newsome factory, a "vulgar" actuality which he never got around to naming.

His cultivation of ignorance has also made him indifferent to the romantic momentum of the plot initiated in Chester with Maria Gostrey, and now he is unready for its closure. His obliging *ficelle* has waited and watched with him, helped him to interpret the story of others—and quite possibly loved him. But she has come to realize, after his commitment to Marie de Vionnet, that his relationship with her was "no longer quite the same. . . . The time seemed already far off when he had held out his small thirsty cup to the spout of her pail. Her pail was scarce touched now, and other fountains flowed for him; she fell into her place as but one of his tributaries, and there was a strange sweetness—a melancholy mildness that touched him—in her acceptance of the altered order" (XXII:48). Her final offer to him—an alternative to his unpromising return to Woollett—is refused, though she tells him "There's nothing, you know, I wouldn't do for you" (XXII:326). Though he is not as oblivious as Marcher is of May Bartram's offer, his rejection has something in it of the intransigent and fantastic, like Marcher's tenacious, egotistical expectation. In a sense, too, he has duplicated Chad's own casting off of the woman who has done so much for the man she has loved, educated, and refined—and he is no less a "brute."

He has, of course, never been so exaltedly in love with his good friend Maria as he has been with her namesake Marie de Vionnet; one can guess that he is too much in love with love to accept the consolation she offers. This is not, however, what James's hero himself says. What he says, rather, is that the only way he knows of being "right" is "not, out of the whole affair to have got anything for myself" (XXII:326)—rejecting all possibility of gain as a result of the mission that had begun with the expectation of gain—rejecting any "end." Maria's answer is profound: "But with your wonderful impressions you'll have got a good deal." The supreme impressionist has gained after all. He has mended the ellipsis of his lost youth by an adventure of the generous imagination. If so, James's story ends optimistically with the restoration of narrative deficiency. The past can be recovered; his bright illusions, though passing, have been his experience of what he had missed. Chad and Marie de Vionnet have been, for *him*, as he had told Maria earlier, his lost youth, whether or not they are their own best and brightest selves.

Yet this is not, despite such restoration, an ending that satisfies the appetite for final closure. The story of Chad and Madame de

Vionnet, once an enigma whose solution is withheld, is now told, in one sense—though we must reflect that we are never to know positively what each is and feels. More blatantly, Strether's own plot, the detective's own story, remains unconcluded. Many readers have felt that James makes his hero simply eccentric—or unnatural—when he refuses Maria, his breach with Mrs. Newsome being "past mending." But his future must remain open since he is the representative of the potentiality of character which cannot be exhausted by plot. It is completely appropriate to this novel that its structure, its very style—those sentences which delay exact significance till the end and even leave it problematic then, casting the reader upon his impressions like a boat surrendered to a stream—should reflect the hero's experience.

James observed in his preface to the novel, "One's bag of adventures, conceived or conceivable, has been only half-emptied by the mere telling of one's story. It depends so on what one means by that equivocal quantity. There is the story of one's hero, and then, thanks to the intimate connexion of things, the story of one's story itself" (2:1309). The telling of *The Ambassadors* "empties," as we have seen, only certain of Strether's possible adventures from out the bag of what might be imagined for him—yet our sense of his potentiality allows us to see what these alternatives might be, to see them latent in the narrative. Intimately connected with this is the story of James's story, its own advances and retreats of self-making, its very method of seeming to refrain from conclusion, of being blind to the obvious way to go on or to unravel its knot, and then of saving or solving itself after all, while, to the last, being ready to admit that other courses are possible. The hero's adventure and the novel's adventure are the same.

Notes

1. Henry James and Narrative Meaning

1. George Steiner's essay "On Difficulty" distinguishes between difficulties he calls "contingent," which are purely lexical or referential; "modal," due to the need to supply contexts of style and cultural consciousness; "tactical," due to the writer's deliberate abandonment of the connection between meaning and its accepted representation, caused by his desire to forge a new language; and "ontological," the consequence, visible particularly in modern writing, of deliberate hermeticism, of an "inspired movement towards darkness" (*On Difficulty and Other Essays,* New York, Oxford University Press, 1978, pp. 18–47; quotation from p. 41). But it is not only the last variety that presents the reader with unresolvable problems of interpretation; most literary works of any complexity contain irresolvable difficulties.

2. Erich Auerbach, *Mimesis: The Representation of Reality in Western Literature* (New York, Doubleday & Co., 1957), p. 10.

3. Frank Kermode, *The Genesis of Secrecy: On the Interpretation of Narrative* (Cambridge, Mass., Harvard University Press, 1979).

4. *The Novels and Tales of Henry James: New York Edition* (New York, Charles Scribner's Sons, 1907–1909), XV:231. Subsequent references to James's fiction, unless otherwise noted, will be to volume and page of this edition; volume numbers will be in roman numerals to distinguish works of fiction from James's critical writings (see chapter 1, note 17).

5. J. Hillis Miller has argued that the story dramatizes in its own resistance to interpretation—as well as taking for its theme—the condition of "unreadability" rather than that of multiple or ambiguous significance which other readers have found in it. See "The Figure in the Carpet," *Poetics Today* 1, no. 3 (1980), 107–118. Shilomith Rimmon-Kenan objects that Miller's discussion of the story as "allegorizing" its own unreadability "yields precisely that unified totality which unreadability is supposed to subvert," *Poetics Today* 2, no. 1b (1980–1981), 187. Wolfgang Iser has come closest to my own view when he declares . . . that the lesson of James's

354

story is the fact that the "division between subject and object no longer applies, and it therefore follows that meaning is no longer an object to be defined but is an effect to be experienced" (*The Act of Reading: A Theory of Aesthetic Response* (Baltimore, The Johns Hopkins University Press, 1978), p. 10). Though I think the story warns us against a totalizing reduction of meaning in literature, it does not urge the futility of the effort to interpret. My belief is that reading is not so much "indeterminate" as an encounter with successive rather than simultaneous interpretive conditions, and that this process, rather than some final state of meaning—or nonmeaning—is the experience of literature.

6. E.M. Forster, *Aspects of the Novel* (London, Edward Arnold & Co., 1927), p. 34.

7. Walter Benjamin, *Illuminations,* trans. Harry Zohn (New York, Harcourt, Brace & World, Inc., 1955), p. 87.

8. R. Barthes, L. Bersani, Ph. Hamon, M. Riffaterre, I. Watt, *Litterature et Réalité,* ed. Gerard Genette and Tzvetan Todorov (Paris, Editions du Seuil, 1971), pp. 81–90.

9. Jonathan Culler, *Flaubert: The Uses of Uncertainty* (Ithaca, N.Y., Cornell University Press), 1974.

10. François Fosca, *Degas* (Geneva, Switzerland, Editions d'Art Skira, 1954), p. 38.

11. Henry James, *Autobiography,* ed. Frederick W. Dupee (New York, Criterion Books, 1956), p. 4.

12. F. O. Matthiessen, "James and the Plastic Arts," *The Kenyon Review* 5, no. 4 (Autumn 1943), 535–550.

13. My use of "impressionism" is broadly cultural. How accurate the capitalized term has been in the specific definition of late-nineteenth-century painting is actively debated today by art historians from John Rewald, whose writings have dominated the subject since the first publication of his *History of Impressionism* (New York, Museum of Modern Art, 1946); to revisionists like Albert Boime who argues for the linkage of Impressionist painting with the salon tradition (*The Academy and French Painting in the Nineteenth Century;* New Haven, Conn., Yale University Press, 1971), and T. J. Clark (*The Painting of Modern Life: Paris in the Art of Monet and His Followers;* New York, Alfred A. Knopf, 1985), who has insisted on the importance of social reference in Impressionist canvases; to Richard Shiff (*Cézanne and the End of Impressionism: A Story of the Theory, Technique, and Critical Evaluation of Modern Art;* Chicago, University of Chicago Press, 1984), who, drawing chiefly on the theoretical statements of the artists, stresses the continuity between Impressionism and Symbolism. In a more general context, however, I wish to relate James's practice to late-nineteenth-century discussions of literature and the fine arts, in which attitudes toward the interpretation of

experience were already beginning to collect under the heading of "impressionism." In *The Phenomenology of Henry James* (Chapel Hill, University of North Carolina Press, 1983, pp. 37–98), Paul Armstrong describes James's view of the constructive role of the imagination, as well as his emphasis upon the experiential foundations of knowledge, by employing the language of Maurice Merleau-Ponty and Edmund Husserl among others. But such description, though analytically useful, invokes a school of formal philosophy still to make its appearance when James was writing, even though *William* James's empiricism offers some anticipation of it. In *The Challenge of Bewilderment: Understanding and Representation in James, Conrad, and Ford* (Ithaca, N.Y., Cornell University Press, 1987), Armstrong seems to have dropped his use of "phenomenological" for a modified conception of the "impressionistic," and argues, in a way I find supportive of my own views, not only for James's emphasis on immediate apprehensions, but for his interest in the "composing powers of consciousness."

14. Of the contributors to the 1876 Impressionist exhibit in Paris, James wrote, "they are partisans of unadorned reality and absolute foes to arrangement, embellishment, selection, to the artist's allowing himself, as he has hitherto, since art began, found his best account in doing, to be preoccupied with the idea of the beautiful." Soon after, he wrote that Whistler's "manner is very much that of the French 'Impressionists,' and like them, he suggests the rejoinder that a picture is not an impression but an expression just as a poem or a piece of music is." Henry James, *The painter's Eye: Notes and Essays on the Pictorial Arts*, ed. John L. Sweeney (London, Rupert Hart-Davis, 1956), p. 114.

15. Sweeney, ed., *The Painter's Eye*, p. 217.

16. Henry James, *The American Scene*, ed. Leon Edel (Bloomington, Ind., Indiana University Press, 1968), pp. 45–46.

17. Henry James, *Literary Criticism: Essays on Literature, American Writers, English Writers* (New York, The Library of America, 1984). Subsequent references to James's critical writing will be to volume and page of this book (as 1) and of its companion volume, *Literary Criticism: French Writers, Other European Writers, The Prefaces to the New York Edition* (as 2); volume numbers will be in arabic numerals, to distinguish the critical writings from James's fiction (see chapter 1, note 4). Maupassant's preface to *Pierre et Jean* praised the "objective" over all other forms of the novel: "Les partisans de l'objectivité (quel vilain mot!) prétendant . . . nous donner la représentation exacte de ce qui a lieu dans la va, évitent avec soin toute explication compliquée, toute dissertation sur les motifs, et se bornent à faire passer sous nos yeux les personnages et les événements." *Pierre et Jean* (Paris, Albin Michel, 1973), p. 18.

18. Walter Pater, *The Renaissance: Studies in Art and Poetry* (London, Macmillan and Co., Ltd, 1910), pp. 235–236.

19. Joseph Conrad, Preface, *The Nigger of the "Naracissus"*, ed. Robert Kimbrough (New York, W. W. Norton & Co., 1979), p. 145. In her recent article, "Proust, James, Conrad, and Impressionism," *Style* 22, no. 3 (Fall 1988), 368–381, Eloise Knapp Hay argues that James, very much like Conrad and Proust, never embraced an extreme dismissal of all but the fleeting and superficial "aspect," and believed in the powers of mind which enabled the artist, as James said in "The Art of Fiction," to guess at the unseen, though impressions "are the very air we breathe" (1:53). But these writers, despite their own occasional statements to the contrary, were not, I believe, confident of a persistent truth beneath the blur and contradiction of experience, and their fiction does not rest in such a certainty.

20. Ian Watt, "Impressionism and Symbolism in Heart of Darkness," in *Joseph Conrad: A Commemoration: Papers from the 1974 International Conference on Conrad* (New York, Barnes & Noble Books, 1974), pp. 39–40.

21. The idea of "spatial form" as a particular characteristic of the modern novel was first enunciated by Joseph Frank in "Spatial Form in Modern Literature," *Sewanee Review* (Spring, Summer, and Autumn 1945), reprinted in Frank, *The Widening Gyre: Crisis and Mastery in Modern Literature* (Bloomington, Ind., Indiana University Press, 1963), pp. 5–62. Frank and a group of commentators review his proposition in Jeffrey R. Smitten and Ann Daghistany, eds., *Spatial Form in Narrative* (Ithaca, N.Y., Cornell University Press, 1981).

22. See Geoffrey Hartman and Stanford Budick, *Midrash and Literature* (New Haven, Yale University Press, 1986).

23. Other familiar structuralist terms are "recuperation" or "naturalization." For a convenient summary of this and related concepts including "intertextuality," see Jonathan Culler, *Structuralist Poetics* (Ithaca, N.Y., Cornell University Press, 1975).

24. Martin Heidegger, *Being and Time*, trans. John Macquarrie and Edward Robinson (New York, Harper and Row, 1962), p. 191.

25. Roland Barthes, *S/Z: An Essay*, trans. Richard Miller (New York, Hill and Wang, 1974), pp. 15–16.

26. Some landmark titles are: Roman Ingarden, *The Cognition of the Literary Work* (Evanston, Ill., Northwestern University Press, 1973) and *The Literary Work of Art: An Investigation on the Borderlines of Ontology, Logic and the Theory of Literature* (Evanston, Ill., Northwestern University Press, 1973); Wolfgang Iser, *The Implied Reader: Patterns of Communication in Prose Fiction from Bunyan to Beckett* (Baltimore, Md., The Johns Hopkins University Press, 1974), and *The Art of Reading: A Theory of Aesthetic Response* (Baltimore, Md., The Johns Hopkins University Press, 1978); Stanley Fish, *Is There a Text in this Class? The Authority of Interpretive Communities* (Cambridge, Mass., Harvard University Press, 1980); Norman N. Holland, *The Dynamics of Literary Response* (New

York, Oxford University Press, 1968). My own approach comes closest to Iser's in recognizing that the reader's role in creating the work takes place in those "gaps" which seem to create indeterminacy. However, Iser emphasizes insufficiently the dialectics of this process, which does not simply program interpretation in a particular direction but continues to keep alternatives in play.

27. Barthes, *S/Z*, pp. 11–12. Although his method of analysis is quite different from mine, I admire the approach to reading fiction of D. A. Miller (*Narrative and its Discontents: Problems of Closure in the Traditional Novel*, Princeton, Princeton University Press, 1981). Denying that narrative ending—even in the traditional novel—"is an all-embracing cause in which the elements of a narrative find their ultimate justification" (xiii), Miller observes symptoms of narrative "unease" in works by Austen, Eliot and Stendhal.

28. H. G. Wells, *Boon* (1914), in *Henry James and H. G. Wells*, ed. Leon Edel and Gordon Ray (Urbana, Ill., University of Illinois Press, 1958), pp. 245–246. *Boon* was written partly in response to James's "The Younger Generation," *Times Literary Supplement*, 19 March and 2 April 1914, reprinted as "The New Novel" in James, *Notes on Novelists* (New York, Charles Scribner's Sons, 1914).

29. "I have been interested . . . to recognize my sense, sharp from far back, that clearness and concreteness constantly depend, for any pictorial whole, on some *concentrated* individual notation of them . . . I should even like to give myself the pleasure of retracing from one of my own productions to another the play of a(n) . . . instinctive disposition, of catching in the fact, at one point after another, from 'Roderick Hudson' to 'The Golden Bowl,' that provision for interest which consists in placing advantageously, placing right in the middle of the light, the most polished of possible mirrors of the subject," (2:1094–1095)

30. Georges Poulet, *The Metamorphoses of the Circle*, trans. Carley Dawson and Elliott Coleman (Baltimore, Md., The Johns Hopkins Press, 1966), p. 313.

31. James's "open" endings have been discussed by Mariann Torgovnick, *Closure in the Novel* (Princeton, Princeton University Press, 1981), pp. 121–156. "Closure" in general has been discussed by Barbara Herrenstein Smith (Poetic Closure, Chicago, University of Chicago Press, 1968); David Richter, *Fable's End* (Chicago, University of Chicago Press, 1978); Robert M. Adams, *Strains of Discord: Studies in Literary Openness* (Ithaca, N.Y., Cornell University Press, 1968); Frank Kermode, *The Sense of an Ending* (New York, Oxford University Press, 1966); and by D. A. Miller in *Narrative and its Discontents*.

32. Undated entry in *The Notebooks of Henry James*, ed. F. O. Matthiessen and Kenneth Murdock (New York, Oxford University Press, 1961), p. 18.

33. See Kermode, *The Sense of an Ending: Studies in the Theory of Fiction* (New York, Oxford University Press, 1966).

34. R. W. B. Lewis, *The American Adam* (Chicago, University of Chicago Press, 1955), p. 5. Carolyn Porter, on the other hand, argues that "classic" American writers from Emerson to Faulkner saw and gave expression to the social issues of their times, not always resisting the dictates of dominant social attitudes in doing so. She insists that James's "visionary seers" are both complicit with the world from which they seem to withdraw and impotent to affect it. Only in James's *The Golden Bowl*, she believes, does identification of the "transcendental seer" with the capitalist entrepreneur receive an anti-idealist expression in the triumph of Maggie Verver (Porter, *Seeing and Being: The Plight of the Participant Observer in Emerson, James, Adams, and Faulkner*, Middletown, Conn., Wesleyan University Press 1981). But the older view of the "Adamic" hero may not so much be invalidated as supplemented and given explanatory grounding by new historicist or "New Historicist" or Marxist criticism. The myth may have been a vulnerable illusion, but it was also, especially in James, a means of criticizing the limiting compulsions of society and even making the leap from idealism to skepticism. Porter's view, while persuasive, may go too far in ignoring the "oppositional" forces in James's novels. For another view see Jean Cristophe Agnew, "the Consuming Vision of Henry James," in Richard Wightman Fox and T. J. Jackson Lears, ed., *The Culture of Consumption: Essays in American History 1880–1890:* (New York, Pantheon Books, 1983). Agnew sees James's career as marked by "a deepening awareness of the commodity world, an awareness that becomes by the end of this life wholly critical *and* wholly complicit" (p. 84).

35. The passage is well known: "A skillful artist has constructed a tale. He has not fashioned his thoughts to accommodate his incidents, but having deliberately conceived a certain *single effect* to be wrought, he then invents such incidents, he then combines such events, and discusses them in such tone as may best serve him in establishing this preconceived effect. If his very first sentence tend not to the out-bringing of this effect, then in his very first step has he committed a blunder. In the whole composition there should be no word written of which the tendency, direct or indirect, is not to the one preestablished design . . . The idea of the tale, its thesis, has been presented unblemished, because undisturbed—an end absolutely demanded, yet, in the novel, altogether unobtainable." Edgar Allan Poe, "Tale-Writing: Nathaniel Hawthorne," *Godey's Lady Book*, November 1847; reprinted in *The Complete Works of Edgar Allan Poe*, ed. James A. Harrison (New York, AMS Press, Inc., 1965, reprinted from 1902 edition), 13:153. The idea of such "organic" form is, of course, very old, going back to Plato's description in the *Phaedrus* of ideal discourse and to Longinus' dec-

laration that the removal of any syllable from the rhythms of Demosthenes' speeches mutilated its effect.

36. Vladimir Propp, *The Morphology of the Folktale*, trans. Laurence Scott (Bloomington, Ind., Indiana University, 1958).

37. See William Veeder's valuable pioneer study of the influence of popular formulas of fiction on James, *Henry James: The Lessons of the Master: Popular Fiction and Personal Style in the Nineteenth Century* (Chicago, University of Chicago Press, 1975).

38. Carol Ohmann, " 'Daisy Miller': A Study in Changing Intentions," *American Literature* 46 (March 1964), 1-11.

39. See Judith Fetterley, *The Resisting Reader: A Feminist Approach to American Fiction* (Bloomington, Ind., Indiana University Press, 1978), pp. 101-55, which summarizes the anti-Olive, pro-Ransom views of previous critics and argues the opposite.

40. Alfred Habegger, "The Disunity of *The Bostonians,*" *Nineteenth Century Fiction* 24 (1969), 193/209.

41. See letter to Edmund Gosse, August 25, 1915, in *Henry James: Letters,* ed. Leon Edel (Cambridge, Mass., Harvard University Press, 4 volumes, 1974-1984), 4:777.

42. See introduction by Derek Brewer, Henry James, *The Princess Casamassima* (London, Penguin Books, 1977), p. 11.

43. Entry of February 15, 1895, in Matthiessen and Murdock, eds., *Notebooks,* pp. 182-183.

44. Barthes, *S/Z*, p. 12.

45. While older views of Jamesian renunciation have tended to stress the implied religious value of self-sacrifice in James's self-denying protagonists (e.g., Dorothea Krook, *The Ordeal of Consciousness*, Cambridge, Eng., Cambridge University Press, 1967), the most interesting *negative* moral evaluation of Jamesian renunciation in recent years has been that of Carren Kaston (*Imagination and Desire in the Novels of Henry James*, New Brunswick, N.J., Rutgers University Press, 1984). Kaston believes that such protagonists as Christopher Newman, Catherine Sloper, Isabel Archer, Milly Theale, and Lambert Strether fail to achieve full imaginative expression of themselves; they exhibit, in renunciation, "an evacuated self, which has abandoned its 'center' to the fictions and versions of life created in it by the other feelings and points of view that it contains" (p. 2). Only in such rare instances as the heroine of *What Maisie Knew* or Maggie Verver in *The Golden Bowl,* she believes, does James allow for the possibility of a self which can "reconcile vision with desiring presence in the world of matter" (p. 136). From a quite different starting point, a Marxist view of James's renunciatory or contemplative characters as victims of a process of "reification" is offered by Carolyn Porter in *Seeing and Being.* Finally, moreover, the argument that James saw renunciation of possession

as yielding the harvest of the imagination—so connecting it with the artistic act itself—has been developed in such persistently important critiques as those of Lawrence B. Holland, *The Expense of Vision: Essays in the Craft of Henry James* (Princeton, Princeton University Press, 1964) and Leo Bersani, "The Jamesian Lie," *Partisan Review* 36:1 (1969), 53–79. My own argument builds upon this identity in seeing James's own formal openness as a duplication of his characters' positive attachment to potentiality, but I am also convinced that historic circumstances promoted in James, as in much modern literature, a reluctance to accept the conventional containments of life, even its "rewards."

46. Forster, *Aspects of the Novel,* p. 54.

47. Joseph Conrad, "Henry James," in *Notes on Life and Letters* (New York, Doubleday, Page & Co., 1924), pp. 18–19.

48. Charles-Pierre Baudelaire, "La peintre de la vie moderne," in *Oeuvres complètes,* ed. Claude Pichois, Bibliothèque de la Pléiade (Paris, Gallimard, 1976, 2 vols.), 1:698–699. Baudelaire's Constantin Guys is a convalescent who lives apart, just as ill health restrains Ralph Touchett from active life and from love, his inertia and remove also standing for a quality that others of James's witnessing characters feel without medical cause. Guys was not, actually, an Impressionist artist, but Baudelaire's description of him, assailed by "une émeute" of details all and equally demanding representation, like a crowd of democratic revolutionaries—makes him one, and fits the very conditions often expressed by James who felt the threat of a crowded reality too unruly and undifferentiated to be successfully "kept down."

49. Nathaniel Hawthorne, *The Blithedale Romance* (New York, W. W. Norton & Co., 1978), p. 157.

50. Henry James, *The Complete Tales of Henry James,* 12 vols., ed. Leon Edel (New York, Vintage Books) 8 (1963):202.

51. Henry James, "The Art of Fiction," *Longman's Magazine* (September 1884), 502–521.

52. Walter Besant's lecture, given at the Royal Institution, London, April 25, 1884, was published as *The Art of Fiction* (Boston, Cupples, Upshaw and Co., 1884).

53. W. D. Howells "Henry James Junior," *Century Magazine* 25 (November 1884), 24–29, reprinted in *William Dean Howells as Critic,* ed. Edwin H. Cady (London, Routledge & Kegan Paul, 1973), pp. 58–72.

54. Jean-Paul Sartre, *Huis Clos* (New York, Appleton-Century-Crofts, 1962), p. 87.

55. "You think me a child of my circumstances: I make my circumstances . . . I—this thought which is called I—is the mould into which the world is poured like melted wax. The mould is invisible, but the world betrays the shape of the mould . . . You call it the power of circumstances,

but it is the power of me." Ralph Waldo Emerson, "The Transcendentalist," in *Ralph Waldo Emerson: Essays and Lectures,* ed. Joel Porte (New York, The Library of America, 1983), p. 96. "The Soul . . . is a watcher more than a doer, and a doer, only that it may the better watch." Emerson, *Nature,* in ibid., p. 39.

56. Walter Pater, "Wordsworth," in *Appreciations, with an Essay on Style* (London, Macmillan and Co., Ltd, 1910), p. 62.

57. Pater, *The Renaissance,* p. 236; Walter Pater, *Marius the Epicurean: His Sensations and Ideas* (New York, The Macmillan Company, 1907), p. 346.

58. James, *Autobiography,* pp. 268, 278.

59. D. H. Lawrence, *Women in Love,* ed. David Farmer, Lindeth Vasey, and John Worthen (Cambridge, Cambridge University Press, 1987), p. 7.

60. See letters to Elizabeth Boott, December 11, 1883, and to Grace Norton, November 3, 1884, in Edel, ed., *Letters,* 3:17, 54.

61. Letter to H. G. Wells, July 20, 1915, in Edel, ed., *Letters,* 4:770.

2. *"Daisy Miller" and Washington Square*

1. James's depiction of the American Girl was not altogether his own typological discovery, though he is sometimes assumed to have fastened this conception upon the cultural consciousness. In 1874, he had reviewed Howells's *A Foregone Conclusion* and praised the depiction of Florida Vervain in that novel, as well as that of Kitty in *A Chance Acquaintance*— "delicate, nervous, emancipated young women, begotten of our institutions and our climate, and equipped with an irritable moral consciousness" (1:494)—a description that fits Isabel Archer better than it does Daisy Miller, but Daisy's cruder variant is implied.

2. James, *The American Scene,* p. 347.

3. The English Friend was the actress Fanny Kemble; cf. James's entry of February 21, 1879, in Matthiessen and Murdock, eds., *Notebooks* pp. 12–13.

4. Henry James, review of *Azarian: An Episode* by Harriet Elizabeth (Prescott) Spofford (1:607).

5. Henry James, *Novels, 1881–1886* (New York, Library of America, 1985), p. 15. All quotations from *Washington Square* will be taken from the 1881 Macmillan and Co. text reprinted in this edition.

6. Letter to W. D. Howells, January 31, 1880, in Edel, ed., *Letters,* 2:267.

7. "The drama is the very drama of that consciousness," James admitted (1:1750).

8. James used this expression to designate first-person narrative in the preface to *The Ambassadors* (2:1316).

9. The case of Daisy Miller is the first among several of James's female portraits to be considered in this book which seem to invite criticism of his

own categorical thinking. One school of feminist criticism has accused James of creating sexist stereotypes. Judith Fryer argues that James's women "are not women at all, but reflections of the prevailing images of women in the 19th century" (*The Faces of Eve: Women in the Nineteenth Century American Novel,* Oxford, Oxford University Press, 1976, p. 23). Nan Bauer Maglin believes that James's attitude "toward independent women, the women's movement, and women in general" is one of "disgust and mockery (perhaps with the exception of women in their 'proper place')"; "Fictional Feminists in *The Bostonians* and *The Odd Women,*" in *Images of Women in Fiction: Feminist Perspectives,* ed. Susan Koppelman Cormillion, (Bowling Green, Ohio, Bowling Green University Popular Press, 1972). See also Wendy Martin, "Seduced and Abandoned in the New World: The Image of Woman in American Fiction," in *Women in Sexist Society: Studies in Power and Powerlessness,* ed. Vivian Gornick and Barbara K. Moran (New York, Basic Books New American Library, 1971), pp. 329–346. But James gives us in Winterbourne a detached, ultimately critical image of the masculine representative of such views, and he may be assumed to have had some sympathy with Daisy's unideological and primitive will to independent being. I shall argue that his own critical detachment from masculine stereotypes is even alive in *The Bostonians* as the narrator separates himself from Ransom. James is by no means to be identified with this later girl-watcher, either, as Judith Fetterley insists correctly in *The Resisting Reader: A Feminist Approach to American Fiction* (Bloomington, Ind., Indiana University Press, 1978).

10. Letter to Thomas S. Perry, May 13, 1860, in Edel, ed., *Letters,* 1:19.

11. "Daisy Miller: A Study," *Cornhill Magazine* 37 (June 1878), reprinted in *James's Daisy Miller: The Story, the Play, the Critics,* ed. William T. Stafford (New York, Charles Scribner's Sons, 1963), p. 8. James's revisions for the first book edition of his story (New York, Harper & Brothers, 1878), do not appreciably alter the text in the direction I am observing. Further references to the 1878 text will be to the Stafford reprint.

12. Henry James, *Transatlantic Sketches* (Boston, James R. Osgood and Co., 1875), p. 58.

13. Ibid., p. 58.

14. That this more obscure intention may have lingered in James's mind may be indicated by his casual insertion in *Daisy Miller* of a reference to *Paule Méré,* when Winterbourne, in Geneva, receives his aunt's report of the arrival of the Millers in Rome. She concludes her letter, seemingly without point: "Bring me that pretty novel of Cherbuliez's—Paule Méré" (XVIII:45).

15. Letter to Mrs. F. H. Hill, March 21, 1879, in Edel, ed., *Letters,* 2:221.

16. Henry James, *The Europeans* (Harmondsworth, Eng., Penguin Books, 1964), p. 114.

17. James recalled a Miss Rogers "who beat time with a long black ferule, at the Chelsea Female Institute on Waverley Place, though he had attended an earlier "dame's school" in Albany where his only grandmother, Catherine Barber, lived (James, *Autobiography*, p. 12). He wrote of these same memories to his New York friend, Mary Cadwalader Jones, "I kind of make you out, 'down there,' I mean in the pretty, very pretty as it *used* to be, New York autumn, and in the Washington Square region trodden by the steps of my childhood, and I wonder if you ever kick the October leaves as you walk in Fifth Avenue, as I can to this hour feel myself, hear myself positively *smell* myself doing" (October 23, 1902, in Edel, ed., *Letters,* 4:245-246).

18. See Chapter 2, note 3.

19. Darshan Singh Maini has argued that the story describes the oedipal bondage to her father, which encloses her to the end. "*Washington Square:* A Centennial Essay," *Henry James Review* 1 (1979-1980), 96.

3. Isabel Archer and the Affronting of Plot

1. The only statement that is, if we except "the Future of the Novel" (1899, 1:100-110), which discusses less technical contemporary questions such as the place of sex in the novel, women writers, etc.

2. Peter Brooks, *The Melodramatic Imagination: Balzac, Henry James, Melodrama, and the Mode of Excess* (New Haven, Yale University Press, 1976), pp. 158-159.

3. See the New York Edition, preface to "Daisy Miller," 2:1273.

4. Richard Poirier, *The Comic Sense of Henry James: A Study of the Early Novels,* (New York, Oxford University Press, 1960).

5. In addition to Manfred MacKenzie (see note 10 below), William Bysshe Stein sees Isabel as vulnerable to the reader's—and by implication the author's—criticism. Stein finds her to be a victim of sexual inertia, "perversely enjoying her role of a Victorian Griselda," who is treated sardonically by James; "*The Portrait of a Lady:* Vis Inertiae," *Western Humanities Review* 13 (Spring 1959), 177-90; see also Oscar Cargill, *The Novels of Henry James* (New York, Macmillan, 1961). pp. 78-119. Juliet McMaster argues that Isabel has a "perverse" desire for unhappiness, and that James wishes us to see her that way; "The Portrait of Isabel Archer," *American Literature* 45 (1973-1974), 50-66. Mary S. Schriber insists that Isabel is from the first a Victorian "lady" who understands the subtle use of power and manipulation; "Isabel Archer and Victorian Manners," *Studies in the Novel* 8 (1976), 441-57.

6. See Chapter 1.

7. *Henry James's "The Portrait of a Lady"*, ed. Harold Bloom (New York, Chelsea House Publishers, 1987), p. 6.

8. Arnold Kettle, *An Introduction to the English Novel* (New York, Harper & Brothers, 1960), pp. 31–32.

9. A. N. Kaul, *The Action of English Comedy: Studies in the Encounter of Abstraction and Experience from Shakespeare to Shaw* (New Haven, Conn., Yale University Press, 1970), p. 252.

10. Manfred Mackenzie, "Ironic Melodrama in *The Portrait of a Lady*," *Modern Fiction Studies* 12, no. 1 (Spring 1966), 7–23.

11. F. R. Leavis, "*The Portrait of a Lady* Reprinted," *Scrutiny* 15 (Summer 1948), 235–241.

12. Richard Chase, *The American Novel and its Tradition* (New York, Doubleday & Co., 1957), p. 134.

13. F. R. Leavis, *The Great Tradition* (New York, Doubleday & Co., 1954), p. 139.

14. In an interesting application of the idea of portraiture to the problem of *The Portrait of a Lady*, David M. Lubin has observed that the portrait painter's antithetical impulses toward inclusive realism and selective formalism are themselves represented in Isabel's own contradictions—including her tendency to "type" others while resisting such a process for herself. *Act of Portrayal: Eakins, Sargent, James* (New Haven, Conn., Yale University Press, 1985).

15. Nina Baym, "Revision and Thematic Change in *The Portrait of a Lady*," *Modern Fiction Studies* 22, no. 2 (Summer 1976), 183–200.

16. James, *Autobiography*, pp. 4–5.

17. Many years later Alice recalled her feelings at fourteen in Newport: "In that winter of 62–63 . . . I used to peg away pretty hard, 'killing myself,' as someone calls it—absorbing into the bone that the better part is to clothe oneself in neutral hints, walk by still waters and possess one's soul in silence." *The Diary of Alice James,* ed. Leon Edel (New York, Dodd, Mead and Co., 1964), p. 95.

18. James's employment of the metaphor of the book for the person or the personal history is more than a passing ingenuity. That he conceived of literary story-making as allied to the living process of personal enactment is made evident by his use of the metaphor. The life that cannot be fitted to narrative expectation is a text that cannot be *read*. Almost a decade later, in "The Pupil," he writes that the tutor, Pemberton, finds little Morgan to be "as puzzling as a page in an unknown language . . . Indeed the whole mystic volume in which the boy had been amateurishly bound demanded some practice in translation. To-day, after a considerable interval, there is something phantasmagoric, like a prismatic reflexion or a serial novel, in Pemberton's memory of the queerness of the Moreens" (XI:518). Finally, in *The Ambassadors*, Little Bilham describes the Chad who has altered so much since coming to Paris as a "new edition of an old book that one has been fond of—revised and amended, brought up to date, but not quite the

thing one knew and loved," and confessed a preference for the previous "pleasant well-rubbed old-fashioned volume" (XXI:177–178).

19. Henry David Thoreau, "Walden," *The Writings of Henry David Thoreau* (Boston and New York, Houghton Mifflin Company, 1893, 20 vols.) 2:350.

20. Stein, "Vis Inertiae" See also, David Galloway, *Henry James: The Portrait of a Lady* (London, Edward Arnold, 1967) and Tony Tanner, "The Fearful Self: Henry James's *The Portrait of a Lady*," *Critical Quarterly* 7 (1965), 205–219.

21. "James has to recuperate Madame Merle morally by incorporating her into Isabel—that is by creating a character whose intentions coincide exactly with his or her fictions." Leo Bersani, "The Jamesian Lie," *Partisan Review* 36, no. 1 (Winter 1969), 62.

22. Chase, *The American Novel and its Tradition*, p. 130.

23. Veeder, *Henry James*, p. 132.

24. Ralph speaks to his father of sixty thousand pounds (III:264), but after the latter's death, the larger sum is mentioned (III:298, 348, 392).

25. Undated entry in Matthiessen and Murdock, eds., *Notebooks*, p. 15.

26. E.g., her feeling his "disagreeably strong push, a kind of hardness of presence, in his way of rising before her" and the two major scenes of rejection in volume 2—in Rome, before his departure with Ralph, and in the garden at Gardencourt when, as his kiss flashes through her "like white lightning," she feels "each thing in his hard manhood that had least pleased her, each aggressive fact of his face, his figure, his presence, justified of its intense identity and made one with his act of possession" (IV, 436), and feels herself to be drowning.

27. Undated entry in Matthiessen and Murdock, eds., *Notebooks*, p. 18.

4. The Determinate Plot: The Bostonians

1. Erving Goffman, *The Presentation of Self in Everyday Life* (Anchor Books, New York, 1959). George Santayana's statement occurs in his *Soliloquies in England and Later Soliloguies* (New York, Charles Scribner's Sons, 1922), pp. 131–132.

2. Dorothy Van Ghent, *The English Novel: Form and Function* (New York, Holt, Rinehart and Winston, Inc., 1953), pp. 215–216.

3. George Eliot, *Adam Bede* (New York, New American Library, 1961), p. 138.

4. The view that James was, at least temporarily, a subscriber to the views of the French naturalists has been put forth by Sergio Perosa and Lyall Powers, who regard these novels as James's attempts to fulfill the prescriptions of Zola's *Le roman experimental*. Perosa writes, "James . . . for some time at least, felt at heart, and was in his fictional practice, a full-

fledged, *scientific* naturalist in the sense that Zola had given to those terms"; *Henry James and the Experimental Novel,* (Charlottesville, Virginia, University of Virginia Press, 1978), p. 18. Lyall Powers calls *The Bostonians* James's first *roman experimental* and attempts to demonstrate that it illustrates that "heredity and environment are "determining agents in the lives of the principal characters (especially Verena)." He calls *The Princess Casamassima* "the clearest example of the Jamesian experimental novel," and asserts, "nowhere else in James's work does the determining effect of heredity and environment play so large a role. It is a complex little case for experimental examination"; *Henry James and the Naturalist Movement* (East Lansing, Mich., Michigan State University Press, 1971), pp. 58, 72, 110. Peter Buitenhuis argues that *The Bostonians* "derives directly from French naturalism and signifies a radical if temporary shift in [James's] method and style" in *The Grasping Imagination: The American Writings of Henry James* (Toronto, University of Toronto Press, 1970), p. 141. That I differ from these interpretations will be evident.

5. Entry of April 8, 1883, in Matthiessen and Murdock, *Notebooks,* p. 47.

6. This subject was first discussed at length by Marius Bewley in *Scrutiny* in 1950 (reprinted in his *Complex Fate* (London, Chatto and Windus, 1952), pp. 11–30). Bewley's view of this primary relation was disputed by Leon Edel ("Correspondence," *Scrutiny* 17[1950], 53–60, who argued for the primary importance of *l'Evangeliste.* Buitenhuis also argues, in *The Grasping Imagination,* that Daudet's novel is the more significant influence, and that to this model James owed not only his characters and plot but his realist style and tone (p. 145). Others have deprecated the importance of Daudet, insisting that *l'Evangeliste* could only have provided an initial suggestion (see Matthiessen and Murdock, eds., *Notebooks,* p. 48, and Cargill, *The Novels of Henry James,* p. 128). But, as I am observing, James's expressed resolution to improve upon Daudet is balanced by his critical correction of *The Blithedale Romance* in his *Hawthorne* (London, Macmillan and Co., Ltd, 1879), and both must be considered intertexts to his own novel. The parallels with Hawthorne are also reviewed by Robert Emmet Long in *The Great Succession: Henry James and the Legacy of Hawthorne* (Pittsburgh, University of Pittsburgh Press, 1979), pp. 139–154 and Richard Brodhead in *The School of Hawthorne* (New York, Oxford University Press, 1986), pp. 147–157. Most recently, Sandra M. Gilbert and Susan Gubar have commented on the relation of *The Bostonians* and *The Blithedale Romance* from a feminist point of view in their *No Man's Land: The Place of the Woman Writer in the Twentieth Century,* vol. 1: *The War of the Words* (New Haven, Conn., Yale University Press, 1988), pp. 23–27.

7. Gilbert and Gubar, *No Man's Land,* 1:26–27.

8. Lionel Trilling, *"The Bostonians,"* in *The Opposing Self* (New York, The Viking Press, 1955), p. 104.

368 NOTES TO PAGES 131-139

9. Buitenhuis, *The Grasping Imagination*, p. 145.

10. Henry James, *The Bostonians,* ed. Alfred Habegger (The Bobbs-Merrill Co., Inc., Indianapolis, Ind. 1976), p. 140. Subsequent references to the novel will be this edition.

11. James wrote Grace Norton on November 3, 1884, shortly after he began *The Bostonians,* "Singleness consorts much better with my whole view of existence (of my own and of that of the human race), my habits, occupations, prospects, tastes, means, situation 'in Europe,' and the absence of desire to have children." Edel, ed., *Letters,* 3:54.

12. James wrote to Elizabeth Boott, "What strikes me most in the affaire is the want of application on the part of society of the useful, benefecent and civilizing part played in it by the occasional unmarried man of a certain age." December 11, 1883, in Edel, ed., *Letters,* 3:17.

13. Elaine Showalter, *A Literature of Their Own: British Women Novelists from Brontë to Lessing* (Princeton, N.J., Princeton University Press, 1977), p. 219.

14. Ann Douglas in *The Feminization of American Culture* (New York, Alfred A. Knopf, 1977) seems to argue for Ransom's view but, of course, what she is saying is that religion, the home, and the arts became feminized, not that authority and force slipped from the hands of men; masculinity, in the halls of real power, only became more grossly its unmodified self, though Olive, taking an opposite view of the effect of masculine dominance, feels that the age has become "relaxed and demoralized, and . . . she looked to the influx of the great feminine element to make it feel and speak more sharply" (119).

15. Barbara Berg suggests that the polarization of female and male typologies in the nineteenth century was a consequence of the uncertainties of a developing democracy. "As it became increasingly difficult to claim *natural* differences among men, the male sense of personal identity crumbled." *The Remembered Gate: Origins of American Feminism; The Woman and the City, 1800–1860* (New York, Oxford University Press, 1978), p. 73. In the absence of a *class* standard by which men established their relation to one another, women were placed on a level which at least illustrated the superiority of all men to all women, Berg explains. But the substitution of woman for the lower classes, who now challenged their subject status, is a general shift made historically most dramatic by the abrupt cessation of slavery, despite the fact that the social and economic subjection of American blacks has continued into modern times, still serving the function of ego-enhancement for white American males.

16. "There were two or three moments during which he felt as he could imagine a young man to feel who, waiting in a public place, has made up his mind, for reasons of his own, to discharge a pistol at the king or the president" (407–408).

17. Nina Auerbach writes: "For Olive, letting herself go and letting Verena go may be equally therapeutic means of realizing her vision of woman standing alone and 'clinging to a great vivifying redemptory idea.'" *Communities of Women: An Idea in Fiction* (Cambridge, Mass., Harvard University Press, 1978), pp. 134–135.

18. Habegger, "The Disunity of *The Bostonians.*"

19. Entry of April 8, 1883, in Matthiessen and Murdock, eds., *Notebooks,* p. 47.

20. Even Ransom, who discounts completely the sense of what she says, is overcome so that he loses count of the time by "her strange, sweet, crude, absurd, enchanting improvisation" (58) when he sees her for the first time at Miss Birdseye's. The portion of her speech we are given directly (59–60) is not without a simple eloquence, moreover, and hardly the "harangue" Ransom calls it, though most critics have tended to accept Ransom's dismissive judgment. The same positive qualities are apparent in the speech she offers at Mrs. Burrage's in New York (of which, again, we have a quoted sample, 254–255)—despite Ransom's scorn for its message.

21. James defies while seeming to subscribe to the naturalist explanation of his exceptional character in a similar way when in "The Pupil," he describes Morgan Moreen, so inexplicably a member of the deplorable Moreen family, as a demonstration of "the mysteries of transmission, the far jumps of heredity. Where his detachment from most of the things they represented had come from was more than an observer could say—it certainly had burrowed under two or three generations" (XI:522).

22. Lee Ann Johnson has charged that James reduces the status of Verena "from person to nonentity" by failing to properly reveal her thoughts and feelings, making her *seem,* at an rate, to have no personality of her own. "The Psychology of Characterization: James's Portraits of Verena Tarrant and Olive Chancellor," *Studies in the Novel* 6 (Fall 1974), 298.

23. This view is strongly argued by Alfred Habegger in his recent *Henry James and the "Woman Business"* (Cambridge, Eng., Cambridge University Press, 1989). Habegger believes that Verena's stereotypical femininity "determines her behavior, and this femininity has two related components, a weak capacity for thought and an emotional disposition to yield to others—'give herself away, turn herself inside out' " (p. 217).

5. The Determinate Plot: The Princess Casamassima

1. Letter to Thomas Sargent Perry, December 12, 1884, in Edel, ed., *Letters,* 3:61.

2. Georg Lukacs, *Realism in Our Time: Literature and the Class Struggle,*

trans. John and Necke Mander (New York, Harper Torchbooks, 1971), p. 34.

3. Peter Brooks, *The Melodramatic Imagination: Balzac, Henry James, Melodrama, and the Mode of Excess* (New Haven, Yale University Press, 1976), p. 155.

4. Henry James, *Essays in London and Elsewhere* (New York, Harper & Brothers, 1893), p. 41.

5. F. W. Dupee, *Henry James* (New York, William Sloane Associates, 1951), p. 153.

6. Baudelaire, *Oeuvres complètes,* 1:691–692.

7. Gerald Needham, *Nineteenth Century Realist Art* (New York, Harper & Row, 1988), p. 249.

8. Zola himself wrote, "I not only supported the Impressionists, I translated them into literature, by the touches, notes, coloration, by the palette of many of my descriptions.' R. J. Niess, *Zola, Cézanne, and Manet: A Study of "l'Oeuvre"* (Ann Arbor, Mich., University of Michigan Press, 1968), p. 285.

9. James J. Kirschke, for example, insists that Zola's descriptions, especially of cityscapes, "bring to mind many of Monet's best canvases." *Henry James and Impressionism* (New York, Whitston Publishing Co., 1981), p. 69.

10. Letter to Charles Eliot Norton, December 6, 1886, in Edel, ed., *Letters,* 3:146.

11. The evidence that James knew about anarchism through Turgenev is summarized by Oscar Cargill, *The Novels of Henry James* (New York, Macmillan, 1961), pp. 151–152.

12. Lionel Trilling, *The Liberal Imagination: Essays on Literature and Society* (New York, Doubleday & Co., 1953), p.73.

13. Irving Howe, *Politics and the Novel* (New York, Avon Books, 1970), pp. 144, 150.

14. See also V:355–356, "He seemed to see, immensely magnified, the monstrosity of the great ulcers and sores of London . . . "; V:358, "the huge, tragic city where unmeasured misery lurked beneath the dirty night . . . " Such a winter of discontent in London was, in fact, the very state of the great city while James's novel was appearing in installments (September 1885–October 1886) in the *Atlantic;* the "Pall Mall riots" of unemployed workers occurred on February 8, 1886, and their mood may be reflected in the discussions Hyacinth hears in the "Sun and Moon."

15. See passage beginning, "A moment later they found themselves in a vast interior dimness . . . " (V:46–48).

16. Mark Seltzer, *Henry James and the Art of Power* (Ithaca, N.Y., Cornell University Press, 1984), pp. 25–58.

17. Leon Edel, *Henry James* Philadelphia, Penn., J. B. Lippincott Company, 1953–1972, 5 vols.), 2:329.

18. In George Eliot's *Felix Holt,* Esther Lyon is expected to learn French readily because of her French ancestry. Daniel Deronda becomes interested in Hebraic tradition and falls in love with a Jewish girl before it is discovered that his mother was Jewish.

19. Howe, *Politics and the Novel,* p. 142.

20. *The Complete Tales of Henry James,* ed. Leon Edel (Philadelphia, Penn., J. B. Lippincott, 1961–64, 12 vol.), 3:89–90.

6. *"The Aspern Papers"*

1. "No author, without a trial, can conceive the difficulty of writing a romance about a country where there is no shadow, no antiquity, no mystery, no picturesque and gloomy wrong, nor anything but a common-place prosperity, in broad and simple daylight, as is happily the case with my dear native land," Nathaniel Hawthorne, *Novels,* ed. Millicent Bell (New York, The Library of America, 1983), p. 854.

2. James, *Autobiography,* p. 480.

3. Jacob Korg, "What Aspern Papers? A Hypothesis," *College English* 23, no. 5 (February 1962), 378–381.

4. The exact nature of Hyacinth's final instructions from Hoffendahl, which we never learn, is contained in a letter. Other letters that announce narrative gaps include, in "The Turn of the Screw" the letter from Miles's school, whose text is never given to the reader, and the letter the governess writes to the children's uncle, which is destroyed by Miles; in *The Wings of the Dove,* the letter from Milly which Kate throws into the fire and that from Milly's lawyers, which Densher gives her unread at the end of the novel.

5. Some though not all of the resemblances I am noting between *The House of the Seven Gables* and "The Aspern Papers" are observed by Richard Brodhead in *The School of Hawthorne,* p. 106.

6. Henry James, *"The Aspern Papers" and Other Stories,* ed. Adrian Poole (New York, Oxford University Press, 1983), p. ix.

7. A number of critics have overlooked the purely speculative nature of these suggestions along with other hints gathered by the narrator and his colleague, and even extrapolated from them with confidence. John Carlos Rowe, in a stimulating discussion which explores the feminist implications of the story, makes use of the guess that Tina Bordereau is the illegitimate child of Aspern and Juliana. As Rowe himself warns, however, "the critical choices we make between such 'undecidables' tell ourselves and our readers precisely what uses to which we are putting our literary subjects"; *The Theoretical Dimensions of Henry James* (Madison, Wis., The University of Wisconsin Press, 1984), p. 106. That the true history of Juliana is an irretrievable piece of lost history is very much the point, though as Rowe

detects, James has allowed some of the darker implications of the romantic poet myth to cling to the Aspern legend.

8. Henry James, *"The Aspern Papers" and Other Stories* (New York, Penguin Books, 1976), p. 106. References to the 1888 text will be to this edition.

9. Wayne C. Booth, *The Rhetoric of Fiction* (Chicago, University of Chicago Press, 1961), pp. 354–364.

7. The Disengagement from "Things"

1. Edith Wharton, *A Backward Glance* (New York, Charles Scribner's Sons, 1934), pp. 190–191.

2. Bernard Richards, "James and His Sources: The Spoils of Poynton," *Essays in Criticism* 19 (October 1979), 302–322.

3. Entry of December 24, 1893, in Matthiessen and Murdock, eds., *Notebooks*, p. 137

4. His friend Henri De Latouche wrote Balzac in 1828, "Your heart clings to carpets, mahogany chests, sumptuously bound books, superfluous clothes and copper engravings. You chase through the whole of Paris in search of candelabra that will never shed their light on you, and you haven't even got a few sous in your pockets that would enable you to visit a sick friend. Selling yourself to a carpet-maker for two years! You deserve to be put in Charenton lunatic asylum" Quoted in V. S. Pritchett, *Balzac* (New York, Alfred A. Knopf, 1973), p. 82.

5. Willa Cather, "The Novel Démeublé," in *Not Under Forty* (New York, Alfred A. Knopf, 1936), pp. 43–51.

6. James's "though technically incorrect" should warn the critic against overreading the symbolic significance of the cross, as does John Carlos Rowe when he writes, "The Maltese cross is, of course, the heraldic insignia of the Knights of St. John of Jerusalem, and as such represents their charity to pilgrims, the militarism of the Crusades, and those Catholic traditions that secretly draw the most conservative strain of English aristocracy. It also has the ecclesiastical significance of its association with St. John the Baptist, and thus represents typologically the spiritual regeneration that he brings. I need hardly explain how Fleda's surrender has made such as transfer of power to the unlikely figure of Owen possible, permitting him not just to assume the fetishized 'objets d'art' of some country gentleman's private collection, but to invest such objects with this wide range of political, economic, philosophical, literary and religious significances"; *Theoretical Dimensions*, pp. 103–104. That Owen's inheritance *is* a "country gentleman's collection" of "objets d'art" which have lost their connection with such significances and become only "things" is precisely the point. There is only irony in the religious association that the cross—

like *any* cross—brings to bear. Fleda expressly refers to the cross as "a bibelot," which, when it reappears at Ricks, only reminds her how its presence or absence makes little difference in Mrs. Gereth's achievement as "the greatest of all conjurers."

7. Lawrence B. Holland, *The Expense of Vision: Essays on the Craft of Henry James* (Baltimore, Md., The Johns Hopkins University Press, 1982), p. 102.

8. *"The Turn of the Screw"*

1. Letter to H. G. Wells, December 9, 1898, in Edel, ed., *Letters,* 4:86.

2. The subject of the Victorian governess has been treated in a number of recent studies based on nineteenth-century sources—e.g., M. Jeanne Peterson, "The Victorian Governess: Status Incongruence in the Family and Society," in *Suffer and Be Still: Women in the Victorian Age,* ed. Martha Vicinus (Bloomington, Ind., Indiana University Press, 1972); and Mary Poovey, *Uneven Developments: The Ideological Work of Gender in Mid-Victorian England* (Chicago, Ill., The University of Chicago Press, 1988), pp. 126–163.

3. Poovey, *Uneven Developments,* pp. 129–130.

4. Edmund Wilson's Freudian speculation about the governess's psychic disorder in "The Ambiguity of Henry James," in *The Triple Thinkers* (New York, Oxford University Press, 1963), pp. 88-132, initiated a flood of critical controversy that seems now to have come to an end in Shoshana Felman's definitive burial in "Turning the Screw of Interpretation," *Literature and Psychoanalysis: the Question of Reading: Otherwise* (Baltimore, Md., The Johns Hopkins University Press, 1982), pp. 94–207.

5. Bruce Robbins, "Shooting Off James's Blanks: Theory, Politics, and *The Turn of the Screw,*" *The Henry James Review* 5, no. 3 (Spring 1984), 193–199.

6. Richard Ellmann, "A Late Victorian Love Affair," *The New York Review,* August 4, 1977, pp. 6–7.

7. Leo Bersani, "The Jamesian Lie," *Partisan Review* 36, no. 1 (Winter, 1969), 65.

8. John Clair, *The Ironic Dimension in the Fiction of Henry James* (Pittsburgh, Penn., Duquesne University Press, 1965), pp. 37–58.

9. Tzvetan Todorov, *The Fantastic: A Structural Approach to a Literary Genre,* trans. Richard Howard (Ithaca, N.Y., Cornell University Press, 1973).

10. Ernest Gombrich, *Art and Illusion: A Study in the Psychology of Pictorial Representation,* 2nd edition (New York, Pantheon Books, 1961), p. 5.

11. See John Silver, "A Note on the Freudian Reading of 'The Turn of the Screw,'" in *A Casebook on Henry James's "The Turn of the Screw,"* ed. *Gerald Willen (New York, Thomas Y. Crowell Company, 1960), pp. 239–243.*

12. The resemblance holds despite the fact that Bly seems to have been more precisely modeled on Ford Castle in Northumberland, with its two crenellated towers, where James was a guest while he was writing "The Turn of the Screw" in 1897. See E. A. Sheppard, *Henry James and "The Turn of the Screw"* (Auckland, Australia, Auckland University Press, 1974), p. 91.

13. See remarks of Katherine Anne Porter and Allen Tate in "James's 'The Turn of the Screw': A Radio Symposium," reprinted in Willen, ed. *Casebook*, p. 163.

14. One of the earliest statements of this view, anticipating the Freudian analysis of Edmund Wilson, was that of Edna Kenton, who said, in language that responds better than her famous successor's to the idea of the story as literary design, that James "permitted his innocent governess to write herself his novel of evil," and that the ghosts and the children themselves are "only exquisite dramatizations of her little personal mystery, figures for the ebb and flow of troubled thought within her mind, acting out her story." Edna Kenton, "James to the Ruminant Reader: *The Turn of the Screw*," *The Arts* 6 (November 1924), reprinted in Willen, ed., *Casebook*, pp. 113-114. That these figures are *literary dramatizations* is quite another thing than saying, indeed, that they are the fantasies of a hysterical imagination.

15. That she *cannot* make a story that will hold fast for either of her absolutist alternatives has, also, an explanation supplied by history. As I suggested at the beginning of this discussion, one must think of the governess as one whom class categories fail to securely contain; she is not of her employer's class nor yet a servant. In her aspiration to leave the lower classes altogether and join the upper ranks of society through marriage to a gentleman, she is someone tossed between social alternatives, unable to rest securely in either. The "good" master to whom she would be affiliated is inaccessible, while her identity with Miss Jessell enforces the realization that she can be the class victim of the fine gentleman in Harley Street, or the victim of the master as Peter Quint. In the bipolarism of these alternatives we may suspect the source of her tortured alterity.

9. The Language of Silence

1. Sallie Sears, *The Negative Imagination: Form and Perspective in the Novels of Henry James* (Ithaca, N.Y., Cornell University Press, 1968), pp. 27.

10. The Inaccessible Future

1. Allen Tate, "Three Commentaries," *The Sewanee Review* 58 (1950), 5. More recently, Richard Brodhead has enlarged on this perception, and attributes the story's abstractness, its parabolic form, which I discuss

below, to an intensified return to the example of Hawthorne. *The School of Hawthorne,* pp. 179–187.

2. Eve Kosovsky Sedgwick, "The Beast in the Closet: James and the Writing of Homosexual Panic," in *Sex, Politics, and Science in the Nineteenth Century Novel,* Selected Papers from the English Insititute, 1983–84, New Series, no. 10, ed. Ruth Bernard Yeazell (Baltimore, Md., The Johns Hopkins University Press, 1986), pp. 169, 170–171.

3. Nathaniel Hawthorne, *The American Notebooks,* Centenary Edition, ed. Claude M. Simpson (Columbus, Ohio, Ohio State University Press, 1960), p. 251.

4. Tate, "Three Commentaries," p. 7.

II. The Presence of Potentiality

1. In *The English Review,* just months before its volume of the New York Edition.

2. *The Letters of William James,* ed. by Henry James (Boston, Atlantic Monthly Press, 1969, 2 vols), 1:310–311.

3. Undated entries in Matthiessen and Murdock, eds., *Notebooks,* pp. 315, 323. The portrait, which Higginson gave to Harvard to be hung in the Union in 1901, can still be seen there today.

4. James, *The American Scene,* p. 60.

5. Bliss Perry, *Life and Letters of Henry Lee Higginson* (Boston, Atlantic Monthly Press, 1921), p. 267.

6. "Preliminary sketch for "The Sense of the Past" (1914), in Matthiessen and Murdock, eds., *Notebooks,* pp. 367–368.

7. James, *Autobiography,* p. 196.

12. The Wings of the Dove

1. The novel, James writes in the New York Edition preface, "represents to my memory a very old—if I shouldn't perhaps rather say a very young—motive . . . that of a young person conscious of a great capacity for life, but early stricken and doomed, condemned to die under short respite, while also enamored of the world; aware moreover of the condemnation and passionately desiring to 'put in' before extinction as many of the finer vibrations as possible, and so achieve, however briefly and brokenly, the sense of having lived" (2:1287). That the source of this "motive" was his memory of his cousin is made fairly certain in *Notes of a Son and Brother,* published in 1914. There, he describes Minnie's character in terms that match this description, calls her death, which affected him deeply, the "end of [his] youth," and seems to point back to his novel: "I was in the far-off aftertime to seek to lay the ghost by wrapping

it, a particular occasion aiding, in the beauty and dignity of art" (James, *Autobiography,* p. 544).

2. Letter to Ford Madox Ford, September 9, 1902, in Edel, ed., *Letters,* 4:239.

3. Entries of November 3, 7, in Matthiessen and Murdock, eds., *Notebooks,* pp. 169–174.

4. F. O. Matthiessen, *The James Family, Including Selections from the Writings of Henry James, Senior, William, Henry, & Alice James* (New York, Alfred A. Knopf, 1947), p. 200.

5. Leo Bersani has brilliantly argued that James, yielding to the appeal Milly makes to his imagination, has allowed himself to "underplay Densher's failure to respond to a sense of the great danger of continuing to deceive" Milly, and that there is a "curious sort of discontinuity" between Densher's concern over how he can justify his staying in Venice, and his recognition of Milly's personal poetry." The comfort Densher takes from the fact that it is Lord Mark and not he who deals Milly her death blow seems immoral, and the excuse that he "had meant awfully well" is, says Bersani, "shockingly inadequate." This is undeniable, unless one accepts the idea that, as Bersani also says, "the subject of the novel is so entirely the growth of a certain point of view (which belongs to none of the characters individually) . . . that the plot seems to be created step by step by the inner recognition and choice to which James wants his center to proceed." Bersani feels that this point of view is condemnable, "that of a single isolated individual justifying and consecrating his alienation from everything except his inner vision of an ideal above and beyond the unacceptable real possibilities of life." I think one can assess the paradoxes of Densher's story differently, however, by seeing them as the consequences of successive states of mind which represent conditions that resist a totalizing judgment. Martin Price has rightly, I think, seen Densher's "merciful muddle" of mind as a device by which James give his novel an exploratory structure. See Leo Bersani, "The Narrator as Center in *The Wings of the Dove,*" *Modern Fiction Studies* 6 (Summer 1960), 131–144, and Martin Price, *Forms of Life: Character and Moral Imagination in the Novel* (New Haven, Yale University Press, 1983), pp. 204–207.

6. Letter to Ford Madox Ford, September 9, 1902, in Edel, ed., *Letters,* 4:239. F. R. Leavis, in more recent times, praised the presentation of Kate for just the naturalist particularity and explanatory strength I have been noting ("The pressures driving her—her hateful outlawed father, the threatening fate represented by her married sister's overwhelming domestic squalors, the inflexible ambition of her magnificently vulgar aunt, Mrs. Lowder—are conveyed with such force as to make them seem for a person of such proud and admirable vitality, irresistible"), while the portrait of Milly struck him as "the great, the disabling failure" of the novel.

"A vivid, particularly realized Milly might for him stand in the midst of his indirections, but what for his reader these skirt round is too much like emptiness; she isn't there, and the fuss the other characters make about her as the 'Dove' has the effect of an irritating sentimentality." F. R. Leavis, *The Great Tradition* (New York, Doubleday & Co., 1954), pp. 192–193.

13. The Ambassadors

1. Entry of October 31, 1815, in Matthiessen and Murdock, eds., *Notebooks*, pp. 225–226.

2. Letter to W. Morton Fullerton, October 2, 1900, in Edel, ed., *Letters*, 4:170.

3. Letter to Jocelyn Persse, October 26, 1903, in Edel, ed., *Letters*, 4:286.

4. "Project for *The Ambassadors*," in Matthiessen and Murdock, eds., *Notebooks*, p. 397.

5. Letter to Millicent, Duchess of Sutherland, December 23, 1903, in Edel, ed., *Letters*, 4:302–303.

6. Charles R. Anderson, *Person, Place and Thing in the Novels of Henry James* (Durham, N.C., Duke University Press, 1977), pp. 239, 273–284.

7. See note 18, chapter 3.

8. Chapters 1 and 2 of book 11 were, in the New York Edition, printed in reverse order, an error perpetuated in many reprints until 1960. My discussion considers the chapters in their correct order but page references are to the original printing of the two volumes of the Edition in 1909.

9. More negatively, Tony Tanner has noted these balcony scenes and interpreted them to signify Strether's preference for a "perched privacy" by which he takes "visual possession from above" and contemplates life without being reached by it. "The Watcher from the Balcony: *The Ambassadors*," *Critical Quarterly* 8, no. 1 (Spring 1966), pp. 35–52. If, on the other hand, they suggest Strether's impressionistic receptivity, they signify his openness to life, his refusal to exercise discriminatory judgments that would reduce perception to preconception.

10. Negatively, also, Philip Sicker has found Strether's blindness and his behavior with women throughout the book a symptom of "the perfect condition of psychosexual androgyny." *Love and the Quest for Identity in the Fiction of Henry James* (Princeton, N.J., Princeton University Press, 1980). And Maxwell Geismer has diagnosed Strether's as a case of suppressed homosexuality. *Henry James and the Jacobites* (Boston, Mass., Houghton Mifflin Co., 1963), p. 277. James's text does not forbid such filling in of psychological gaps in his portraits, but such gaps also encourage us to read Strether's adventure of perception more philosophically, as a willed suspension of judgment, a willingness to entertain even improbabilities, a reluctance to "conclude."

Index